EX-CENTRIC MIGRATIONS

EX-CENTRIC MIGRATIONS

Europe and the Maghreb

in Mediterranean Cinema,

Literature, and Music

Hakim Abderrezak

Indiana University Press

Bloomington and Indianapolis

This book is a publication of

Indiana University Press
Office of Scholarly Publishing
Herman B. Wells Library 350
1320 East 10th Street
Bloomington, Indiana 47405 USA

iupress.indiana.edu

Manufactured in the United States of America

Cataloging information is available from the Library of Congress

ISBN 978-0-253-02065-9 (cloth)
ISBN 978-0-253-02075-8 (paperback)
ISBN 978-0-253-02078-9 (ebook)

1 2 3 4 5 21 20 19 18 17 16

For my parents, sisters, brother, nephews, and nieces

Contents

Preface

THE TOPIC OF clandestine migration was a personal concern of mine before it became an academic avenue of research that led me to write *Ex-Centric Migrations* and several articles and book chapters. The theme of clandestine migration has been a crucial part of my scholarship and inspired my work in the fine arts. One of my paintings, *Burning the Sea,* appears on the cover of this volume. The work illustrates the major topic of the book, namely, the concept of "burning," a Maghrebi term for clandestine migration, which the painting presents in a literal as well as a figurative fashion.

When *Ex-Centric Migrations* was in its last stage of production, the maritime tragedies of 2015 occurred, in which thousands of individuals attempted to cross the Mediterranean to Europe. Some of the journeys were successful, but many overloaded boats capsized and individuals drowned. These events were named "the refugee crisis" and designated as "Europe's biggest humanitarian crisis since WWII." Although this book examines the Western Mediterranean (migrations from Tunisia, Algeria, and Morocco, mostly to France, Spain, and Italy), many of its ideas and conclusions apply to the refugee crisis in the Eastern Mediterranean and the Middle East. The attention and reactions the phenomenon has garnered is similar to the ways in which the Western Mediterranean migrations have been internationally received, with the same broad themes at work: identity politics, nativism, globalism, Islamophobia, and "clash of civilizations" mind-set. There are major similarities in the coverage of clandestine crossings by mass media and the many political reactions and discourses that have ensued. Although to date—with the exception of Turkish writer Hakan Günday's novel *Encore* about human trafficking, which won the prestigious Le Prix Médicis du roman étranger in 2015—there are not yet cinematic, literary, and musical accounts of the recent Middle Eastern refugee tragedies, *Ex-Centric Migrations* may serve as a valuable resource for future comparative studies. Indeed, both Syria and Tunisia have experienced an unprecedented exodus of individuals ensuing the Arab Spring and the resultant regional chaos. Furthermore, because of shared languages (mostly Arabic) among the Western and Eastern Mediterranean migrants and refugees, common exclusionary, anti-immigration politics from the West, and a war that has caused a strong enough sense of despair to lead individuals to flee regardless of the risks of drowning, this book provides a study that helps understand the refugee crisis—its causes, its consequences, how the crossing of the Mediterranean Sea is translated into mass media, and the political ramifications when it comes to depicting the Arab making his or her way toward the West. An in-depth linguistic analysis allows for a more informed vision than that of many media accounts. For instance, the latter have often used the terms *migrants* and *refugees* interchangeably, while these terms in fact denote statuses that are differentiated clearly by international law. Whereas a potential host country facing an economic crisis or not needing labor could decide to refuse to welcome a migrant on the grounds that a migrant is an individual who attempts to settle abroad primarily to improve his standard of life, a refugee is an individual whose life back home is threatened. On its website's landing page in late 2015, the United Nations High Commissioner for Refugees warned, "Refugee or Migrant? Word Choice Matters." Indeed, the distinction is crucial in order to avoid misconceptions that could potentially contribute to nationalist, populist, and xenophobic discourse, that in turn, impact upon foreigners arriving in Europe. Additionally, this sort of imprecision can obfuscate the dangers humans face when their right to asylum is not respected. This common error in naming is menacing in that it masks Europe's moral responsibility to refugees, who are protected by international law.

The link between this book and the global refugee crisis is the 2013 and 2015 tragedies of capsized ships of migrants departing from Libya and Syria. With these events, the phenomenon of clandestine migration, which had been occurring for decades, finally reached an international audience and shocked the world. But as this book exemplifies, contrary to portrayals in popular news reports, these crossings are not a new phenomenon; furthermore, they are not always the consequence of violent political instability. Before Tunisia, clandestine migrants from Algeria and Morocco had been on the Western media's radar. The global refugee crisis makes the examination of Mediterranean clandestine crossings a timely one, but most importantly represents a call for attention to the dangerous nature of migrating when migration is in fact a right also granted by international law. I hope that *Ex-Centric Migrations* will make its own modest contribution to shedding light on these dynamics, their causes, and consequences, as well as the media reportage and the political rhetoric—both of which are complex machines that shape opinion and policy. In the meantime, cinematic, literary, and musical productions propose their own visions of the events, offering alternative and highly informative views on how the objects of hegemonic discourse see themselves and what narratives they propose as subjects in their own accounts.

Acknowledgments

Ex-centric migrations started as a new project when I was an assistant professor at the University of Minnesota. I am indebted to my colleagues who read early versions of chapters: Daniel Brewer, Mária Minich Brewer, Susan Noakes, Judith E. Preckshot, Eileen Sivert, and Christophe Wall-Romana. Dominic Thomas read the manuscript and gave excellent advice, for which I am deeply appreciative.

Throughout the writing of *Ex-Centric Migrations,* I was able to share my work in the United States and overseas in many professional conferences, symposia, and colloquia. I thank the scholars, their departments, and institutions for inviting me to speak: Silvia Bermúdez (Spanish and Portuguese) and Roberto Strongman (Black Studies), University of California, Santa Barbara; Sylvie Durmelat and Miléna Santoro (French and Francophone Studies), Georgetown University; Nouri Gana (Comparative Literature and Near Eastern Languages and Cultures), University of California, Los Angeles; Ralph Heyndels and Gema Pérez-Sánchez (Modern Languages and Literatures), University of Miami; and Christopher L. Miller and Edwige Tamalet-Talbayev (French), Yale University. Other venues where I presented parts of this book include the Twentieth- and Twenty-First-Century French and Francophone Studies International Colloquium, the Middle East Studies Association, and the Modern Language Association. I thank my interlocutors on panels and in audiences for their questions.

Several grants at the University of Minnesota were instrumental in bringing the manuscript to completion. A College of Liberal Arts course release allowed me to craft one of the chapters and two Imagine Fund Faculty Research Awards helped to fund the research I did in Paris, France. The Institute of Global Studies, the Imagine Fund Special Events, and cosponsoring institutes, centers, departments, and programs provided substantial financial aid that allowed me to organize a symposium titled "Burning the Sea: Clandestine Migrations in the Global Age" in April 2013. This was the first U.S.-based interdisciplinary symposium on clandestine migration and its literary and artistic representations bringing together a wide array of distinguished scholars working across national languages in the humanities and social sciences.

At Indiana University Press, I wish to thank Raina Polivka for her enthusiasm for the book. My thanks also go to Jenna Lynn Whittaker, Janice Elizabeth Frisch, and Nazareth Pantaloni III for answering technical and formatting questions. In addition, I express my gratitude to Debbie Masi and the copyeditor, Karen Hallman, for their detailed screening of the manuscript.

Furthermore, I appreciatively acknowledge the editors of the journal *Contemporary French & Francophone Studies: Sites* for giving me permission to use and expand upon my article "'Burning the Sea': Clandestine Migration across the Strait of Gibraltar in Francophone Moroccan 'Illiterature,'" which was published in their September 2009 issue and guest co-edited by Andrew Sobanet. I would also like to acknowledge with appreciation the University of Nebraska Press for allowing me to reproduce a slightly different version of "Turning Integration Inside Out: How Johnny the Frenchman Became Abdel Bachir the Arab Grocer in *Il était une fois dans l'oued* (2005)," which appeared in 2012 in *Screening Integration: Recasting Maghrebi Immigration in Contemporary France*, edited by Sylvie Durmelat and Vinay Swamy.

The collegiality and camaraderie of my peers has been such a gift. I am thankful to Ragui Assaad, Carla Calargé, Giancarlo and Sinem Casale, Evelyn Davidheiser, Sylvie Durmelat, Claudia Esposito, Roderick A. Ferguson, Ofelia Ferrán, Barbara Frey, Donna R. Gabaccia, Priscilla Gibson, Njeri Githire, Michael Goldman, Jaime Hanneken, Lisa Hilbink, Trica Danielle Keaton, Rachmi Diyah Larasati, Patricia M. E. Lorcin, Anouar Majid, Nabil Matar, Brinda J. Mehta, Valérie K. Orlando, Gema Pérez-Sánchez, Sadik Rddad, Kathryn L. Reyerson, Ajay Skaria, Liliana Suárez-Navaz, Shaden M. Tageldin, Edwige Tamalet-Talbayev, William Viestenz, and John Watkins. Within and beyond academe, friends have been stimulating interlocutors: Robyn Anderson, Ali Hasmut, Dominique Licops, Samara Reigh, Nathan Syverson, and Christopher Wagner. I owe more than I can say to Mireille Rosello, Brian T. Edwards, Doris L. Garraway, Jean Mainil, Nasrin Qader, and Alessia Ricciardi for continuing to be an invaluable presence. Paula Durbin-Westby and Samara Reigh compiled the index.

My greatest personal debt is to my friends Rocky Shilhanek, Heather Walters, and the Mead and Shilhanek families for their priceless encouragement over the years. My scholarship would not have been possible without the love and support of my family back in France, Morocco, and Algeria. I express my profound love for my father Mustapha, who sadly passed away before seeing the book in print, and for my mother Zahra—their lives stand as paragons of humility, kindness, and open-mindedness. My most heartfelt love also goes to Faïza; Hayate and Ali; Kamel and Khadija; Inès, Ilyess, Ib Tissem, Yanis, Ryan, Farès, Hind, Sabri, and Jade for showering me with a sea of love both while I am with them and when I am across the ocean.

To all of you in five countries and on three continents, whose conversations and friendship accompanied me over the years, I am most grateful. If I forgot to mention your name, memories cannot be forgotten, and your contributions will forever be inscribed in this book.

Note on Translation
and Transliteration

Whenever a novel was available in translation, I quoted passages from the English version. The translations of excerpts from critical, theoretical, and journalistic works not available in English are mine. For films, I used subtitles when appropriate. However, if a translation or subtitle was inadequate, missing, or misleading, I proposed my own translation. As for music, the translated lyrics from Arabic, French, and Spanish are mine.

Transliterations from the Arabic do not necessarily follow the *International Journal of Middle East Studies* (*ijmes*) system. I privileged a nonsystematic method instead. One of the reasons for such a decision is my juggling of a wide variety of forms of Arabic in this book (Modern Standard, Moroccan, Algerian), along with Arabized French, which contains a notable quantity of Arabic loanwords. While it is expected to use a codified form of transliteration for classical and Modern Standard Arabic, it is not common to do so for variants of Arabic often referred to as "dialects." Therefore, I favored a looser, more phonetic approach, which does not always include diacritical points or attempt to reproduce certain linguistic rules by means of markers. For example, in chapter 4 where I transcribed fragments of lyrics in spoken colloquial Arabic, I made no indication of the difference between either regular and emphatic sounds or short and long vowels. In addition, in various places I used the Roman letter *h* (sometimes capitalized, sometimes not) for two close and yet different sounds. Furthermore, I followed the Maghrebi practice of typing *gh* for the sound [ʁ] (known to be close to the French *r*), *kh* for the guttural sound [x] existent in German and Castilian, and *r* for the rolled r [ɾ] common in Spanish and Italian, as well as many other languages spoken around the Mediterranean basin.

EX-CENTRIC MIGRATIONS

Introduction

Mediterraneans and Migrations in the Global Era

I am neither French nor Moroccan, I am in between. I am Spanish!
—Mustapha Al Atrassi

The (Dead) End of Francophilic Migrations?

The end of summer at the port of Melilla, a Spanish enclave in northern Morocco. Arabic music played loudly, drowning out the conversations of families in cars and vans. It was late at night in this remnant of Spain's protectorate. About an hour earlier, the drivers were directed to form lines near the ferryboat so that Spanish customs security employees could check vehicles and identification papers. I was seventeen years old when, at this same port, I watched a dog sniff out a teenager hidden in a bag tucked under the feet of the rear seat passengers in the car parked in front of us. As my family waited to be searched, we observed the entire episode. From inside our car, we saw the frightened teenager being taken away, gasping for air and sweating heavily. We never knew what became of him or the other people in that vehicle. Every September on our way back to France, we would see young men walking back and forth on the rampart that overlooked the docks. They would get as close as possible to vehicles waiting to board the ferry in hopes of catching a ride. The vigilant agents of the Guardia Civil relentlessly chased the migrant hopefuls away. On one particular trip, I saw a young man try to board our ship by climbing up an anchor rope. Alerted by the cheering of travelers, agents ran to the ferry and attempted to shake the man off his precarious perch on the rope. The crowd grew anxious when he seemed likely to fall to the ground. Moroccan strangers were imploring God's help. Some women covered their eyes, anticipating a tragic end. A few passengers were screaming. Two couples, however, who happened to be taking an evening walk took in the scene with seeming amusement, probably because they were accustomed to witnessing such events. The man was finally captured upon reaching the deck and then escorted into the rear of the patrol van and driven away in the night. This was one of several encounters I had with this type of chase on both sides of the Strait of Gibraltar.

Although those disturbing events had receded in my memory, in my scholarly work I began to research clandestine border crossings. Only recently have I made the connection that those firsthand experiences likely played a role in leading me to this line of research. When I started investigating the topic, I was not sure how much work had been done on it. I first gave a talk in 2008 on the depiction of clandestine migration in three Moroccan literary works, namely Ben Jelloun's *Partir,* Mahi Binebine's *Cannibales,* and Youssouf Amine Elalamy's *Les Clandestins.* I then decided to deepen my research and extend it to other media. I found that numerous works of literature, film, and music on the topic of clandestine North African migration had been generated over the last two decades. However, I soon realized there had hardly been any academic criticism on the various issues explored. I felt encouraged to investigate this phenomenon—which many a Maghrebi (North African) and *Beur* (French national of North African descent) is keenly aware of, having experienced it.[1]

The predominance of North African migration to France in the twentieth century has much to do with France's colonial past.[2] Though I do not have the space here to trace the genesis of the French Empire's colonization, I would like to lay out a succinct history of France's colonial presence in the region, as well as postcolonial alignments in order to better understand later developments of Maghrebi migratory patterns.[3] European empires including France, Spain, Italy, Belgium, Great Britain, Germany, and the Netherlands conquered the African continent, and France settled mostly in North and West Africa. In 1830, France began its conquest of the northern regions of Africa, starting with Algeria, first using a pretext for its presence (a punitive expedition against the dey of Algiers who had hit the French consul-general with a flyswatter) before turning the retaliation into warfare against the Arabs and Berbers.[4] The French government extended its African intrusion to Morocco in 1912 and Tunisia in 1916, justifying its lingering presence on the continent as a "civilizing mission." While Morocco and Tunisia were called protectorates and earned their emancipation in 1952 and 1956, respectively, Algeria—made into a *département* of France—gained its independence only after a lengthy war of liberation (1954–1962). During its rule in North Africa, France encouraged the immigration of young and fit local men, who were recruited to help in the development of the *métropole* and its reconstruction after World War II. Following the 1973 oil crisis, the French government decided to make its immigration laws more stringent—a change of direction that underwent subsequent iterations in future years, especially under conservative governments. Map 0.1 indicates the movement of human labor in 1973. The decision to limit the number of "legal" immigrants from North Africa and to fight "illegal" immigration from this region has had a significant impact on the nature of migratory patterns out of the Maghreb.

Ex-Centric Migrations contests the common notion that emigrants from former European colonies migrate predominantly to the land of the ex-colonizer.[5] It

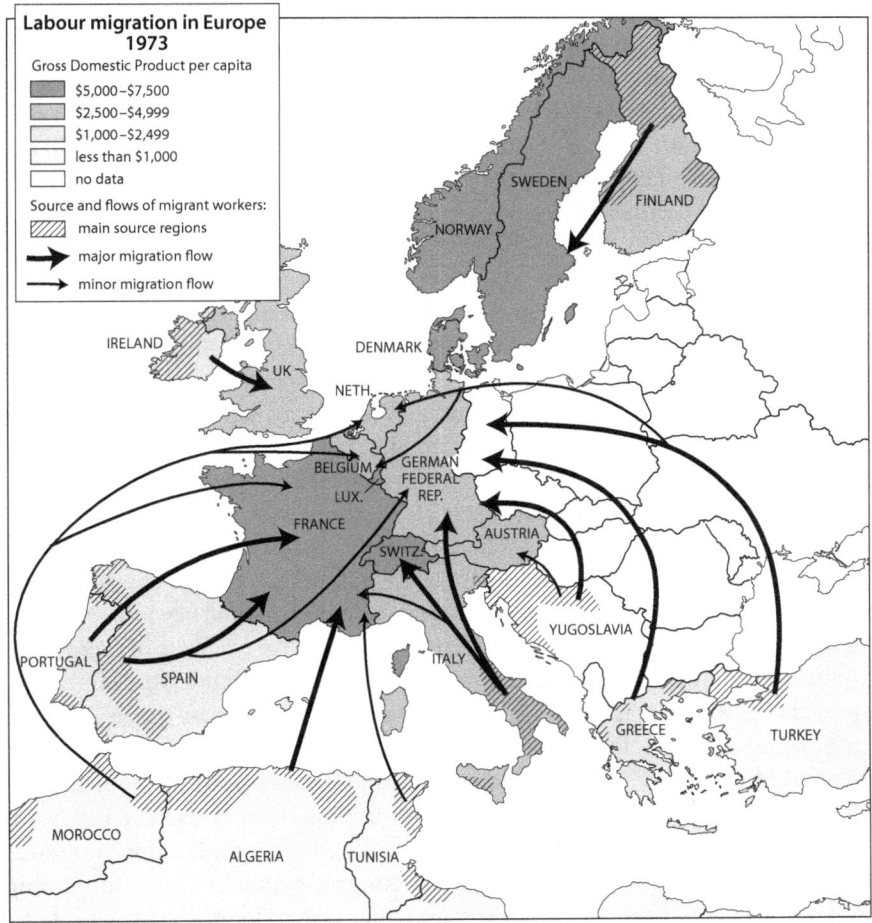

Map 0.1 "Labor Migration in Europe 1973" from Russell King's *People on the Move: An Atlas of Migration.* Used with permission.

shows that despite a linguistic affinity with the colonizer, a tradition of laboring for that nation, and additional historical ties, migrants from the Maghreb (Morocco, Algeria, and Tunisia) accomplish *ex-centric* migrations more and more. In this term is a dual designation that entails, first, an ex-centeredness or movement away from France as a privileged destination for migrants and toward places such as Spain, Italy, Great Britain, Germany, and the Netherlands. In other words, journeys that deviate from the historical norm for this region. Second, these migrations exhibit an eccentricity not only in the direction of travel—that is, from north to south or north to east—but also in the methods migrants use to travel:

by fishing boat, as stowaways in ferries, hidden in trucks, or even posthumously. These unauthorized passengers come from North and sub-Saharan Africa, from countries at war, places in peace, close shores such as those of Morocco and Tunisia, and faraway lands such as Libya, Senegal, Syria, Nigeria, and Asia.

This book aims to draw the reader's attention to the double-edged nature of some of the latest movements of people between the global North and the global South and the literary and cultural representations of those journeys. It focuses on the northern and southern shores of the Western Mediterranean. I contend that since the 1990s, Maghrebi migrations have become progressively ex-centric. This study examines literary, cinematic, and musical representations of atypical migrational trends in Francophone, Arabic, and Spanish high and popular cultural works produced since the 1990s. Such works challenge mass media coverage and mainstream political discourses, and they reveal the motives behind emerging migration movements and reshaped diasporic patterns. I posit that in contemporary Western Mediterranean cultural productions, we encounter new scenarios with, first, northward maritime clandestine crossings in the Mediterranean Sea; second, a reversal of traffic (originating instead from France to North Africa); and finally, the proliferation of tentacular human movements to peripheral lateral countries (from France to other parts of Europe and beyond, especially to the Middle East). Indeed, the book provides extensive evidence of these three trends emerging in the last three decades. In the case of clandestine migration, individuals emigrate "illegally" in (often unsound) vessels across the sea. Reverse migration, which so far has received minimal academic attention, concerns the children of immigrants in France driving to their ancestors' homeland in the Maghreb to lay their parents to rest, thus finding themselves in an unknown country and culture.[6] I argue that in what I call "diverging migration" migrants strive to strip themselves of the status of émigrés paradoxically by migrating again, elsewhere. It represents current individuals abandoning France for destinations as far away as Saudi Arabia. In this instance, even French nationals of foreign ancestry, who feel excluded, shun France for a remote and unusual destination, which provides an option more appealing than their experience of second-class citizenship in Europe. The book's corpus covers a wide spectrum of works in literature and cinema. And, for the first time, it explores the production of music hitherto neglected by scholars of Maghrebi migration.

By looking at North African cultural works that give attention to underexplored patterns of migration, this study sets out to fill a void in current scholarship, which has historically conceptualized migrations in terms of center (France) and periphery (the former colonies to the south). Map 0.2 shows the number of migrants in 2007 to Spain and Italy from various countries including Morocco. One of the book's theses that France has been portrayed as an ex-center, or phrased differently, that it has lost its magnetic pull for incoming migrants and in turn has

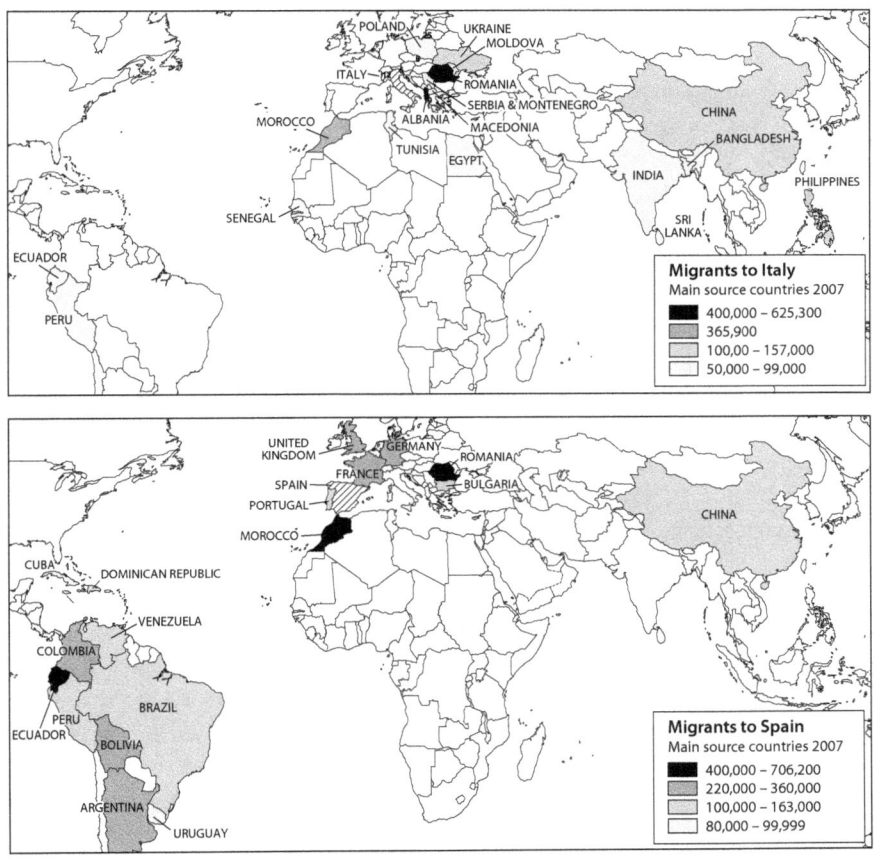

Map 0.2 "Migrants to Italy/Migrants to Spain" from Russell King's *People on the Move: An Atlas of Migration*. Used with permission.

become increasingly marginal in Francophone cultural works, constitutes a major paradigm shift in studies of *Beur* literature and the literature of immigration in general. Whether this trend is irreversible, will last, or not, is not a question this study seeks to answer or to even pose, for the answer could only be a risky prognostication. What this book does is examine recent works that have reflected (on) a reality that has prompted artists to consider France in a different position in light of new developments in Maghrebi migration trends. *Ex-Centric Migrations* therefore takes up where previous research stops, with conventional migration to France. The book offers an alternative for Francophone, Spanish, North African, and migration studies in general. Indeed, it challenges a fundamental assumption of the postcolonial field, as it reconfigures parameters that have traditionally put the ex-colonizer's country and culture in the position of privileged destination. At the end of the past millennium, alongside an established body of migrant literature and visual works about "classic" migration to France, a growing number of novels, films, and songs concerned with eccentric/ex-centric types of journeys emerged.

Eccentric Claims?

Mehdi Sekkouri Alaoui's article "Petit Mustapha devenu grand" published in the Francophone Moroccan weekly magazine *TelQuel* in January 2010 exemplifies a type of ex-centricity. Indeed, in it one finds a startling and thought-provoking claim made by the French-born Mustapha Al Atrassi, a humorist of Moroccan ancestry. Al Atrassi, a celebrity on both sides of the Mediterranean, asserts, "I am neither French nor Moroccan, I am in between. I am Spanish!" This statement recalls the "cul entre deux chaises" (ass between two chairs) position discussed by Mireille Rosello.[7] In this quote from Al Atrassi, the difficult cultural in-betweenness felt by the children of Maghrebi immigrants in France goes beyond "neither . . . nor . . ." and becomes something other altogether. The originality of Al Atrassi's self-identification is that instead of claiming an attachment to one country or the other, or to one country more than the other, or even to both, it resides somewhere else—in Spain. His positionality in a third space proposes that his identity evades binarism in search for a third element that is elsewhere. His claim speaks to various recent changes. First, it resonates as a message of hope for those feeling culturally torn between two countries and for whom a third entity might constitute a better space of belonging. It also calls into question the controversial debate on national identity. The debate focused on the idea that individuals who cannot integrate into French society belong to their families' countries of origin. This premise is oblivious to the fact that *Beurs* may feel a different affiliation than to the two proposed options, French and Maghrebi, and that within the European Union (EU) they are free to migrate to alternative places. What Al Atrassi frames as a joke in fact points implicitly to the late migratory patterns involving the Maghreb. In a nutshell, what Al Atrassi is telling us is that Spain is now on the Maghrebis' radar. The humorist presents a new vision to replace a now passé binary. Specifically, Spain, a third element, constitutes a novel factor in contemporary Maghrebi migration trends. Instead of an exclusive affair between the Maghreb and France, the relationship is between the Maghreb and Europe more generally. For a long time, Spain was a country of transit for those who had chosen to settle in more northern countries that were perceived as richer. The Iberian Peninsula was often considered no better off socioeconomically than the countries of the Maghreb were. To the question "Why not Spain?," a common answer among prospective migrants was, "I might as well stay in Morocco!" This mindset has shifted in the past several years, making Spain a coveted destination. The other implication of Al Atrassi's statement is that when Spain experienced an economic boost, it presented life-improving opportunities for Maghrebis.[8]

Other countries have witnessed rising numbers of newcomers on their soil, but given the proximity of the Iberian Peninsula and that some nations have been closing borders, Spain has not only become a port of entry into Fortress Europe, but also a country of settlement. The same statement holds true for Italy, the other peninsula in the Western Mediterranean. Literary and cultural depictions of this trend have emerged in Francophone works published in the Maghreb region and France, as well as in Spain and Italy themselves. As Graziella Parati writes, "migration to Italy, whether motivated by a rejection of the 'natural' migration to France, the ex-motherland, or facilitated by the initially more elusive Italian immigration laws, has changed the structure of Italian society and is gradually influencing its culture and language."[9] Indeed, the versatility of human migratory fluxes not only has revealed a notable detour from France, but it has also had important impacts on the cultural, linguistic, economical, and political landscapes of the surrounding European countries.

Since 1974, the year the Family Reunion Law passed in France, the wives and children of the misnamed *travailleurs célibataires* (single guest workers) have been allowed to join fathers and husbands on French soil. This type of state-sanctioned migration engendered creative output by Maghrebi immigrants and *Beurs*. But the majority of these cultural productions, from the 1980s and early 1990s, provided highly predictable literary and cinematic art of families who left the Maghreb to work and settle in France legally, as well as narratives documenting their children's experiences in France (e.g., *Beur* literature) and their lives in inner cities (e.g., *Banlieue* cinema). Most of those storylines are set along a bipolar, south-north axis with the Maghreb as the point of departure and France as the point of arrival. Laws restricting human migratory movement such as Immigration Zero, which the French government instituted following the 1973 oil crisis, highly contributed to influxes of immigrants redirecting successively to neighboring countries, such as French-speaking Belgium and Spain, where Moroccans already held a strong minority presence. Once a country of high emigration rates, Spain has received, since the mid-1970s, a significant number of immigrants, many of them "illegal." The number of clandestine migrants rose especially after Spain's accession to the EU in 1986 and its implementation of a series of stringent immigration laws since 1988. Table 0.1, included in Frontex's 2013 *Annual Risk Analysis* pamphlet, provides some indication of the breadth and intensity of this northerly migratory pull.[10]

Maghrebi clandestine migration has come to be known in the Maghreb as *hrig* and *harga*, or "burning," in Arabic.[11] These terms come from the Arabic trilateral root (*ha-ra-qaf*) [ح ر ق], which refers to the act of burning. Transcriptions include *lahrig, l'hrig, el hrig, h'rig, harq,* and *hrague*. Hrig covers the clandestine migrant's (1) burning desire to leave, (2) burning of kilometers to the final destination, and (3) burning identification papers in hopes to make repatriation more

Table 0.1 Indicator 1A—Detections of illegal border-crossing between border-crossing points.

Routes	2010	2011	2012	Share of Total	Percentage Change from Previous Year
Eastern Mediterranean Route (Greece, Bulgaria, and Cyprus)	55,688	57,025	37,224	51	−35
Land	49,513	55,558	32,854		−41
Afghanistan	21,389	19,308	7,973		−59
Syria	495	1,216	6,216		411
Bangladesh	1,496	3,541	4,598		30
Sea	6,175	1,467	4,370		198
Afghanistan	1,373	310	1,593		414
Syria	139	76	906		1,092
Palestine	1,500	128	408		219
Central Mediterranean Route (Italy and Malta)	1,662	59,002	10,379	14	−82
Somalia	82	1,400	3,394		142
Tunisia	650	27,964	2,244		−92
Eritrea	55	641	1,889		195
Western Mediterranean Route	5,003	8,448	6,397	8.8	−24
Sea	3,436	5,103	3,558		−30
Algeria	1,242	1,037	1,048		1.1
Morocco	300	775	364		−53
Chad	46	230	262		14
Land	1,567	3,345	2,839		−15
Not Specified	1,108	2,610	1,410		−46
Algeria	459	735	967		32
Morocco	0	0	144		NA
Western Balkan Route	2,371	4,658	6,391	8.8	37
Afghanistan	469	983	1,665		69
Kosovo*	372	498	942		89
Pakistan	39	604	861		43
Circular Route from Albania to Greece	35,297	5,269	5,502	7.6	4.4
Albania	32,451	5,022	5,398		7.5
Macedonia (fYROM)	49	23	36		57
Kosovo*	21	37	34		−8.1
Apulia and Calabria (Italy)	2,788	5,259	4,772	6.6	−9.3

Table 0.1 (*continued*)

Routes	2010	2011	2012	Share of Total	Percentage Change from Previous Year
Afghanistan	1,664	2,274	1,705		−25
Pakistan	53	992	1,156		17
Bangladesh	12	209	497		138
Eastern Borders Route	1,052	1,049	1,597	2.2	52
Georgia	144	209	328		57
Somalia	48	120	263		119
Afghanistan	132	105	200		90
Western African Route	196	340	174	0.2	−49
Morocco	179	321	104		−68
Gambia	1	2	39		1,850
Senegal	2	4	15		275
Other	3	1	1	0	0
Iran	0	0	1		NA
Russian Federation	2	0	0		NA
Somalia	0	1	0		−100
Total	104,060	141,051	72,437		−49

Notes: These are the numbers of third-country nationals detected by member state authorities when illegally entering or attempting to enter the territory between border-crossing points at external borders only. Detections during hot pursuits at the immediate vicinity of the border are included. This indicator should not include EU or Schengen Associated Country nationals.
*This designation is without prejudice to positions on status, and is in line with UNSCR 1244 and the ICJ Opinion on the Kosovo declaration of independence.
Source: Frontex, *Annual Risk Analysis,* 2013, p. 65. Used with permission.

difficult for authorities. In the Maghrebi vernaculars, both the act of leaving one's country clandestinely and the desire to do so are often designated by the terms *hrig* and *harga*. Nevertheless, it is necessary to differentiate between the prospect of emigrating on one hand and the actual act on the other, as the expectation of migrant hopefuls does not necessarily imply an ultimate departure. To this end, I call *leavism* the insatiable desire to cross the sea, which precedes an actual instance of clandestine migration. Both leavism and hrig are tackled in various literary, filmic, and musical materials discussed in this book.

Accounts of hrig are broadcast profusely via televised programs, radio, internet, and print media. I examine leavism and the fates of those who choose to undertake this often dangerous journey. In response to this shift in migratory trends, there has been a sharp increase in fictionalized accounts on the subject including works by prominent Francophone Maghrebi writers. Interestingly, scholarship on unauthorized border crossings in the Mediterranean region remains scarce, just as artistic representations of hrig in the Western Mediterranean have only been critiqued in a handful of articles. The trenchant analyses that compose Najib Redouane's edited volume *Clandestins dans le texte maghrébin de langue française* explores Francophone novels from the renowned Algerian writer Boualem Sansal to the up-and-coming Moroccan Mohamed Teriah. The essays, however, have not addressed the augmenting production in other media inspired by migration tragedies. Furthermore, Redouane's collection is in French. Catherine Mazauric's *Mobilités d'Afrique en Europe* is another scholarly volume on the topic written in French. It deals primarily with Maghrebi, sub-Saharan, and European literary accounts. *Ex-Centric Migrations* builds on the scant literature available to lay the groundwork for this new field and to address the problem of the invisibility in humanistic disciplines of Mediterranean untraditional exilic modes. Moreover, this book offers the first academic, book-length study in English accounting for the intervention of literature, music, and cinema in expressing the realities of nonstandard migrational patterns in the Mediterranean.

Of Clandestine Migration in Particular

The central chapters of this book consider the daring and original ways in which Mediterranean writers and artists have reflected upon the issue of clandestine migration among Morocco, Algeria, Tunisia, Spain, and France that are usually either sensationalized for general consumption or are markedly absent in mainstream media and politics. These artistic works produce counternarratives that strive to decriminalize and rehumanize the figure of the clandestine in the global era. Conservative political parties have presented immigration in Europe as a threat, despite official statistics disproving conceptions of "invasion" from the global South. As French historian Gérard Noiriel explains, the most efficient way to eternalize the "problem" of immigration—as it is widely referred to— was to make it become an affair of the state. Thus, the officials of the ministère de l'Immigration et de l'Identité nationale (Ministry of Immigration and National Identity) were forced to repeat almost daily that "'foreigners' (namely, 'clandestines' and 'communitarists') allegedly represent a 'fundamental problem for the future of France,'" regardless of the fact that "today immigration has reached its lowest numbers for over a century. This renders less and less credible the catastrophic discourses . . . on the topic."[12] Noiriel indicates that the newly formed ministry is based on national identity, of which "no definition [was] agreed upon among the body of scholars and experts."[13] He remarks that "the association 'immigration and national identity,' now inscribed in the law, has become a category of thought and action that imposes itself on everyone regardless of the ongoing daily news."[14] The historian writes that "the foreign threat" is "an age old nationalist discourse."[15] He adds that mass media tends to be complicit with dominant political discourses, rather than challenging them—"truth belongs to the one who speaks the loudest, namely, the one who controls the media."[16] My decision to place Europe first and the Maghreb second in the subtitle of this book is to restitute the hegemonic discourse of Western media and politics about immigration. The artists and writers of the southern rim of the Mediterranean have created a vibrant response of a diverse nature, responding to and re-envisioning the essentializing, reductive, and deprecating narrative generated in Europe.

Sociologist Franck Düvell points out that "the concept of 'clandestine migration' dates back to the 1930s" and "only when states issued legislation that declared unwanted immigration illegal and made it punishable *and* introduced technologies (photographs, passports, visas), administrations (immigration authorities) and enforcement procedures (deportation), did migration finally become clandestine."[17] Mass media and political discourses in the West have largely embraced the notion that to emigrate clandestinely is an "illegal" act. By contrast, the novels, films, and songs that form the basis of my study present the topic from the position of clandestines and clandestinity. In other words, they remind us that characters must go into hiding and that their identity is being obscured by data and discourse. In accordance with the Arabic terminology for this phenomenon, *hijra sirriya* ("hidden" or "secret" emigration), these artists compel us to think of "illegal" emigration in human terms, rather than from the point of view of the nation-state and also from the perspective of individuals caught in a sickening situation that undercuts the paradisiacal Eldorado they had sought.[18] In line with these artistic interventions, in chapter 2, I make a plea for the use of the appellation *clandestine migration* instead of *illegal migration*. Table 0.2 and table 0.1 are both from the Frontex agency, but the reader notices that while "illegal" is shown in table 0.1 (and in most of the brochure), "illegal" and "clandestine" coexist on the same page where table 0.2 appears. The question is whether the usage of the two terms is meant to help Frontex be regarded as both a police and a humanitarian body fulfilling its dual function of safeguarding Europe's borders and saving the lives of endangered migrants on their way to the border-crossing points, or if it is meant to indicate the agency's refusal to recognize the importance of distinguishing the two appellations.[19]

Ex-Centric Migrations also proposes that disparate movements toward regional unification across the Mediterranean are underway. Indeed, this book shows that contemporary Mediterranean artists have for the last three decades released works inspired by the urgent and deadly nature of clandestine migration, which Spaniards have come to call "the tragedy of the Straits (of Gibraltar)," in order to plead for a unification of the region. I argue they have done so in various unprecedented ways: First, they have proceeded conceptually thanks to

Table 0.2 Indicator 1B—Detections of illegal border-crossing at border-crossing points.

Border Type	2009	2010	2011	2012	Share of Total	Percentage Change from Previous Year
Land	137	168	159	486	81	208
Sea	159	74	123	115	19	−6.5
Top Ten Nationalities						
Afghanistan	18	8	58	190	31	228
Algeria	30	35	55	61	10	11
Syria	2	3	6	36	6.0	500
Morocco	20	14	15	24	4.0	60
Palestine	14	4	17	24	4.0	41
Philippines	0	8	1	17	2.8	1600
Others	130	56	83	126	21	62
Total	296	242	282	601		115

Note: These are the numbers of third-country nationals detected by member state authorities when entering clandestinely or attempting to enter illegally (such as hiding in transport means or in another physical way to avoid border checks at border-crossing points) the territory at border-crossing points at external borders only, whether they result in a refusal of entry or not. This indicator should not include EU or Schengen Associated Country nationals.
Source: Frontex, *Annual Risk Analysis,* 2013, p. 67. Used with permission.

a symbolic corpus around the Arabic word *harragas* (clandestine migrants), as well as the Spanish word *patera* (a fishing boat that transports harragas clandestinely to Europe).[20] Both words have been used in the titles of books in Arabic, French, and Spanish, and *patera* has become a "key metaphor for immigration."[21] Second, the corpus invites Spanish landscapes into the storytelling of contemporary Maghrebi displacements, which constitutes a new enterprise. Third, the unification of the Mediterranean operates linguistically with the systematic hybridization of Maghrebi texts—not only because the inclusion of Arabic and Arabized French is still commonplace, but also due to the insertion of Spanish idioms into Francophone Maghrebi fiction for the first time. This linguistic subversion, I argue, is yet another means of ex-centrization of France and French in Maghrebi cultural productions. It is also in line with my main contention that Maghrebi Francophone studies have crossed linguistic and national boundaries. Indeed, my "Francophone" corpus is not exclusively Francophone in that it contains texts reflecting the web of languages spoken on both sides of the Mediterranean.

By analyzing Western Mediterranean migrations in a transnational dimension, this book puts French, Francophone, and Arabophone scholars into dialogue with their Spanish counterparts, whose work has heretofore been confined to each scholar's respective language(s) and region(s). The fact that artists, authors, filmmakers, and singers have felt the need to unify the Mediterranean in their works is a sign that they have identified, and seek to counteract, the effects of divisive political discourses and media depictions, which concentrate a certain vision of the world in general and of the Mediterranean in particular. As sociologist Nancy L. Green writes, "language reflects as much as it produces different perceptions of the migratory phenomenon."[22] This is precisely why one should exercise caution when using words listed by Green such as *vagues* (waves), *flux* (flows), *courants* (streams), *marée humaine* (human tide), and *débordements* (spilling over) in connection with shifts in migration patterns and human migratory trends. Words referring to migration that evoke images of water or fluidity can carry negative connotations. For this purpose, I will avoid these controversial terms, except in contexts where no other phrase will suffice. Considering the operative role of language and taking as a premise that discourse on the Mediterranean Other will not necessarily be the same on both sides of the sea, I base a major part of my argument on a philological analysis of important subtleties imbedded in the language of selected films, songs, and novels by Maghrebi authors. I also look at terms in common parlance, political discourse, and media representations, the scrutiny of which permits a fuller and more precise understanding of concepts employed, often vaguely or loosely, in literary and cultural criticism. For instance, the use of *ilegales* ("illegal immigrants") in Spain reveals an unnuanced criminalization of the southern Other in current debates on migration, so I consider *clandestinos* (clandestine immigrants) in lieu of that term. A linguistic lens also reveals phonetic and/or transliteration promixity between the Arabic words *hrig* or *harga* (burning), *harragas* (clandestine migrants), *hogra* (humiliation), and *Hijra* (the emigration of the Prophet Muhammad and the original sacred Muslim community or *Ummah*), which in turn feeds into a historical, social, and religious legitimization of human migration in Islam-based cultures.

Language being central to our understanding of migration—ex-centric migration in particular because of the many languages in play, along with the political, cultural, and religious discourses applied to the phenomenon—my study will take a close look at the paratextual components of the discussed artistic works, in which various languages (French, Arabic, Berber, and Spanish) of various types (spoken, written—with the exception of Berber—subliminal, and promotional) are treated and pass unnoticed. Yet these elements contain crucial information to help us understand common conceptions in addition to unconventional notions and tropes. I will therefore linger on the design of subtitles,

titles, DVD jackets, and film posters, noting such important choices as inaccurate subtitles and multilingual titles on DVD covers.[23] Additionally, I will scrutinize the marketing language and commercial art on CD covers. The juxtaposition of multiple language scripts and imagery on a piece of visual media is not an innocent mechanical choice. The nature of paratextual elements should not be disregarded, as they are often rich with cultural and political meaning.

The Mediterranean through the Experiences of Harraga

In the modern era, there have been efforts to make North Africa a more active player in the Mediterranean. After the disillusionment with pan-Arabism, countries such as Morocco insisted on their Mediterraneanness—seeking another doorway to additional political and economic participation beyond the confines of national borders. Paul Silverstein writes, "King Hassan II made claims to Morocco's *méditerranité,* and not to its *arabité,* in his petitions for admission to the EEC and, later, the EU."[24] Silverstein shows that this constituted a move away from the Middle East, as well as a determined step toward modernity and Europe. Indeed, King Hassan II made clear his determination to advocate Morocco's inclusion in the EU. In 1989, the kingdom, along with Algeria, Tunisia, Mauritania, and Libya formed the Maghreb Arab Union in order to try to establish a unified North African group of signatories as a major partner of the EU. The Maghreb Arab Union was short lived and the hopes of many to see the space of exchange extend to the south came to a halt. While it is true that political turmoil and wars in countries such as Syria and Afghanistan account for a substantial portion of migratory movements across the planet, one can hypothesize that the failure of the Maghreb Arab Union imposed additional migratory pressure on the EU, partly because destination countries within the collapsed union were no longer options for those who may have considered emigrating to other Arab countries. In addition to that, the dream of creating a Euro-Maghreb "Super-Union" vanished right along with the Maghreb initiative.

By revisiting the notion of transgression, the discussed artistic productions invite the reader, spectator, and listener to rethink the concept of Mediterraneanness. The space dedicated to clandestinity in the discussed works put the contemporary Mediterranean in the foreground. Indeed, the geographical and cultural locus of *Ex-Centric Migrations* is in, under, across, and around the Mediterranean Sea. My study of this entity through contemporary literary and cultural works produced in this region—with a peculiar thematic unity and a unique engagement with societal matters—will allow me to highlight the geopolitical dynamics of migrations in the Mediterranean. In this sense, I would like to suggest that the works discussed in this book, all of which entail a crossing of the

Mediterranean Sea, convey a vision of the *Maghrobal* (see chapter 3), a term I would like to propose in order to better understand Roland Robertson's "glocal" in its deployment in the Maghreb.[25] In other words, aspects of daily life closely associated with globalization (such as modes of transportation) offer a specific engagement with local realities. As globalization scholar Arjun Appadurai explains: "The path or vectors taken by these kinds of things . . . in motion including objects, persons, images and discourses . . . have different speeds, axes, points of origin and termination, and varied relationships to institutional structures in different regions, nations, or societies. Further, these disjunctures themselves precipitate various kinds of problems and frictions in different local situations. Indeed, it is the disjunctures between the various vectors characterizing this world-in-motion that produce fundamental problems of livelihood, equity, suffering, justice, and governance."[26] As the various literary, filmic, and musical narratives reveal, the Maghrobal has its own "points of origin and termination," "disjunctures," and "speeds." Like for all geopolitical entities, it has specificities even when what is being considered is a universal phenomenon such as migration. A theme connecting the six chapters of this book is the disparity in the degrees of globalization between the northern and southern shores of the Mediterranean, which has created a sense of unbalanced globalization. Many individuals who hail from the South are determined to get their share of opportunity, but when they try to make their way to a better life, they are portrayed as unwelcome suspects. Thus, the disproportionate globalization of the Mediterranean has altered the nature of migrations and shifted the image of the Maghrebi migrant from guest worker to suspect alien.

The Mediterranean Basin has been transformed into a space of rupture. The Integrated System of External Surveillance is the most sophisticated electronic surveillance system in Europe and was implemented in 1998 (the same year the wall in the Spanish enclave of Ceuta in Morocco was erected), precisely when signed agreements on free association between Europe and Morocco were about to come into effect, thus turning the sea into an impassable body of water.[27] Sociologist Saskia Sassen writes, "the European Union has actually accumulated a series of innovations that move it towards governing, rather than controlling, immigration inside the EU. . . . Its first effort was to construct the equivalent of the Maginot line on its southern and eastern perimeter. . . . Now it is moving toward the construction of a sort of Berlin wall across the Mediterranean into the Atlantic."[28] Writers, filmmakers, and songsters working on clandestineness in their function as *citoyens engagés* advocate for a revision of a cohesive Mediterranean.[29] In the corpus examined in this study, the contemporary Mediterranean becomes the locus par excellence for interrogating clandestine migration. I hope through my analysis to answer questions such as those posed by Kären Wigen and Jessica

Harland-Jacobs: "What if seas were shifted from the margins to the center of academic vision? What new processes and relationships would become apparent if littorals on opposite sides of a given ocean or sea were grouped under a single rubric?"[30]

Peregrine Horden and Nicholas Purcell, the authors of *The Corrupting Sea: A Study of Mediterranean History*, remark that "by the beginning of the first millennium B.C., in the Semitic languages of the Levant, the term 'Great Sea' is quite widely diffused, and it is probably from this tradition that it reached the Greeks."[31] They note, further, that "from the time of Plato and Aristotle, the Greeks referred to the Mediterranean as the 'Sea over by Us'; the Romans more simply came to regard it as *Mare Nostrum*, 'Our Sea.'"[32] This investigation into the history of the linguistic appropriation of part or the totality of the sea tells us much about the ideological and political biases imbedded in the discourses of once powerful empires and brings to light the fact that the appropriation of the sea by dominant northern discourses is not a recent phenomenon in the Mediterranean region.[33] Horden and Purcell argue that in Western discourses, the Mediterranean continues to be configured as a continental divide between Europe and Africa. However, the division between an "advanced" Europe and a "backward" Africa is in itself problematic. As the authors write, it is even more so in that it allegedly starts in the hot regions of southern Europe, likened to its southern neighbors in the words of W. H. Auden, whose poem, "Spain 1937" claims that Spain was "nipped off from hot Africa, soldered so crudely to inventive Europe," and in "the popular Torinese saying that Garibaldi did not unite Italy, he divided Africa."[34]

Europe's divisive and protectionist agenda is not of recent vintage—"from a historical point of view, the Mediterranean region has never been unified since the fall of the Roman Empire; it has in fact frequently been at war with itself."[35] The vocabulary used in Europe's protectionist discourse is akin to medical language, for as Chambers indicates, "Europe . . . frequently feels secure only when purged of 'foreign' bodies."[36] To bring a diseased body back to health, living organisms mobilize antibodies to fight against "foreign bodies." However, in certain autoimmune disorders, an overproduction of antibodies can actually damage the body as it tries to protect itself. Advocates of this war against "foreign" bodies seem to forget this physiological consequence when they focus on eradicating or containing a spreading disease: "It is the same nebulous psychosis of the fear of being 'overrun,' 'invaded,' 'contaminated,' and ultimately 'destroyed' that also leads to . . . a pathology."[37] Like cancer—a common trope used to vilify the unwelcome Other in racist discourse—the disease does not attack one body or limb (one remote European location) but metastasizes to the entire entity ("our" part of Europe). As it spreads, the cancer mutates: temporary visitors overstay their welcome for instance, and legal immigration becomes "illegal." As

Chambers shows, while the presence of the foreign body is acknowledged, it is also silenced: "There is, most obviously, the almost complete absence of the Muslim Mediterranean from the Occidental narrative of the sea—the deliberate ignoring of the complex historical and cultural networks that Islam provided from the Atlantic to central Asia, and then southward to India and Africa and the portals of the Pacific."[38] This Western view contrasts with the Arab cognitive conception, which, according to Horden and Purcell, has been inclusive of other peoples: "The Arab tradition portrayed the sea as poor, alien and uninviting, but by and large as a unity—a single sea, full of islands, whose integrity was maintained by its geographers despite obvious pressures to divide it conceptually between Islam and the rest of the world."[39]

Common appellations of the Mediterranean Sea include *Mare Liberum* (Free Sea); North African cultural works on clandestineness have portrayed this watery border instead as a dystopia, that is, as *Mare Clausum* (Closed Sea) or what I call *Mare Vostrum* (Your Sea) in reference to European domination of those waters. At the same time, by deconstructing the political and media constructions of the Mediterranean frozen into regional blocs within global North and global South, ex-centric writings set out to unfracture the sea. Ex-centric texts advocate a political, discursive, and economic sedimentation of Mediterraneans in order to restore the traditional Arabic collective imagination of a single Mediterranean and its idealized centrality, that is, the "White Sea of the Middle" as it is called in Arabic. Unlike the Greek and Roman empires, which claimed the sea as their own, Arabs from their Golden Age until today have given the Mediterranean a name devoid of exclusive appropriation. That poetic name inscribes the sea as a space for everyone to share.

Europe's exclusionary principle is continued and complicated in the contemporary era. Countries such as Spain and Italy are called on to deal with EU regulations and restrictions involving the Maghreb. The issue of clandestine migration into Spain and Italy has become a federal concern because European incentives such as funds, partnerships, and sponsorships are being granted to the Maghreb on the condition that the southern Mediterranean countries make the fight against clandestine migration a priority. I argue that the two blocs, Europe and Africa, are further divided into multiple regional blocs, such as southwestern Europe and the Maghreb. Indeed, though immigration policies are decided at the federal level, as are all matters European, special attention and pressures are put on border countries such as Spain and Italy to preserve the stability of EU borders.

To posit that today the Mediterranean is a bloc of blocs is no provocative statement. Horden and Purcell note that the appellation "Mediterranean Sea" emerged during the Roman Empire and that from Homer to the Hellenistic age, the Western Mediterranean was conceived of as a sort of Near West and Far

West.[40] Chambers insists that the Mediterranean narrative has always excluded non-Western subplots, and that the "Mediterranean" as a concept entered the European lexicon only in the early nineteenth century.[41] According to Horden and Purcell, the vision of a whole Mediterranean has not yet been a popular one in disciplines such as anthropology, political science, and economy, and in fact, "within the whole field of current academic thinking and social policy the only context in which the Mediterranean has been treated as a single entity appears to be that of environmental concern."[42] They add that the official narrative surrounding this area was possessively kept as a historical object for fear that other disciplines might alter the discourse: "it is clear that historians of Europe would not lightly delegate the writing of 'southern' history to some neighbouring discipline such as 'Mediterranean Studies' whose practitioners might also—impartially—embrace North Africa and the rest of the Middle East."[43] In the recent fictional works I will be examining, the sea is portrayed ironically as a body of interrupted flow. The works reveal the impact of the European notion of "Our Sea," and how European ideologies have impacted the various peoples around the rim of her waters. Those who seek to leave its southern shore, thus honoring the sea's function as a means of transportation, communication, and connection, are stopped on their way.

Ex-Centric Migrations also covers eccentric modes of transportation, and close analyses of these will be undertaken throughout this book. In the past century, filmic portrayals of state-sponsored migration to France were often of a ferryboat leaving a Maghrebi port. In films released prior to 2000, characters tended to embark on large ferries to northward destinations and for the most part were determined to remain in the North. But in the contemporary era, a time when family reunions are not promoted and immigration laws are reinforced, the means of travel depicted in more recent films do not conform to mainstream expectations. Scenes no longer show imposing ferries full of migrants awaited by employers and family members, but rather they depict fishing boats packed with desperate migrant hopefuls. Today, even when films show a monstruous ferry, it is already on the southern shores, rusting in the background (see chapter 5). Demoted, that ship has lost its function as metaphor. Or the ferry is moving southward. The changed itinerary is a sign of a new paradigmatic journey, perhaps multidirectional and of an uncertain outcome (see chapters 3 and 5).

Death, Burial Sites, and Corpus of Corpses

While clandestine migration constitutes this book's most discussed theme—one that I tackle in chapter 6, which deals primarily with return migration—all the chapters of *Ex-Centric Migrations* are also linked to the notion of death. Indeed, as map 0.3 demonstrates, the migrant is often met with death at the borders of

Europe. But even when safely at the destination, death and the notion of trespassing remain important issues for immigrants. The question of where to bury migrants is becoming a pressing issue, as certain demographic groups age. It also becomes an important question for the children of the deceased for whom a binational identity multiplies the possibilities of sites of burial while it complicates the "choice." The older generation of Maghrebi immigrants is currently dying (see chapters 1 and 6), and impending death has led various artists to reflect on burial sites (see chapter 6). In addition, as conventional migration trends give way to more desperate and ex-centric attempts to move, many migrants are drowning on a daily basis. This reality has forced artists and scholars, such as myself, to reckon with the tragedies of displacement.

This book draws on theories concerned with questions of identity, borders, exile, language, community, and multiculturalism in addition to new scholarship from disciplines such as anthropology, history, ethnomusicology, sociology, and Maghrebi, Mediterranean, Spanish, and cultural studies. It uses the extensive research done in the social sciences to help understand the complex contexts of ex-centric texts that are of growing interest for the humanities, where research has just started to emerge. Making use of an interdisciplinary approach at the interface of the humanities and social sciences, the book challenges readers to reframe concepts of migration, emigration, and immigration in the context of recent socioeconomic shifts and the artistic output they have engendered. Most established Mediterranean writers (Tahar Ben Jelloun and Boualem Sansal), filmmakers (Merzak Allouache and Tony Gatlif), and singers and bands (Manu Chao and Chambao) have begun or continued to address ex-centric migrations. In the years to come, Spanish migration scholarship will need to engage with the cultural phenomenon of eccentric ex-centeredness in the works of these and other Maghrebi/Mediterranean artists.

Since my analysis lays out the foundations of a new field, I am compelled to name my object of study. *Ex-Centric Migrations* carries out the task of identifying and defining idiosyncrasies in the latest migratory experiences in the Western Mediterranean as an effort to take ongoing scholarship further. I propose to reorient scholarly vocabulary with neologisms because Maghrebi migration to and from Europe is better understood if the language of the region, individuals' experiences, their view of the world that is being refused to them, and their (dreams of) leaving are brought into scholarly criticism. I also choose to utilize new terms to reflect the shifting realities expressed by the artists whose creative works I examine. A few of my chapters either take a neologism as a point of departure or guide the reader through original concepts, which offer new perspectives. Therefore, my approach aims at combining Western scholarship with Arab and Muslim social, linguistic, and religious specificities in order to provide a comprehensive assessment of a multiform cultural landscape, informed

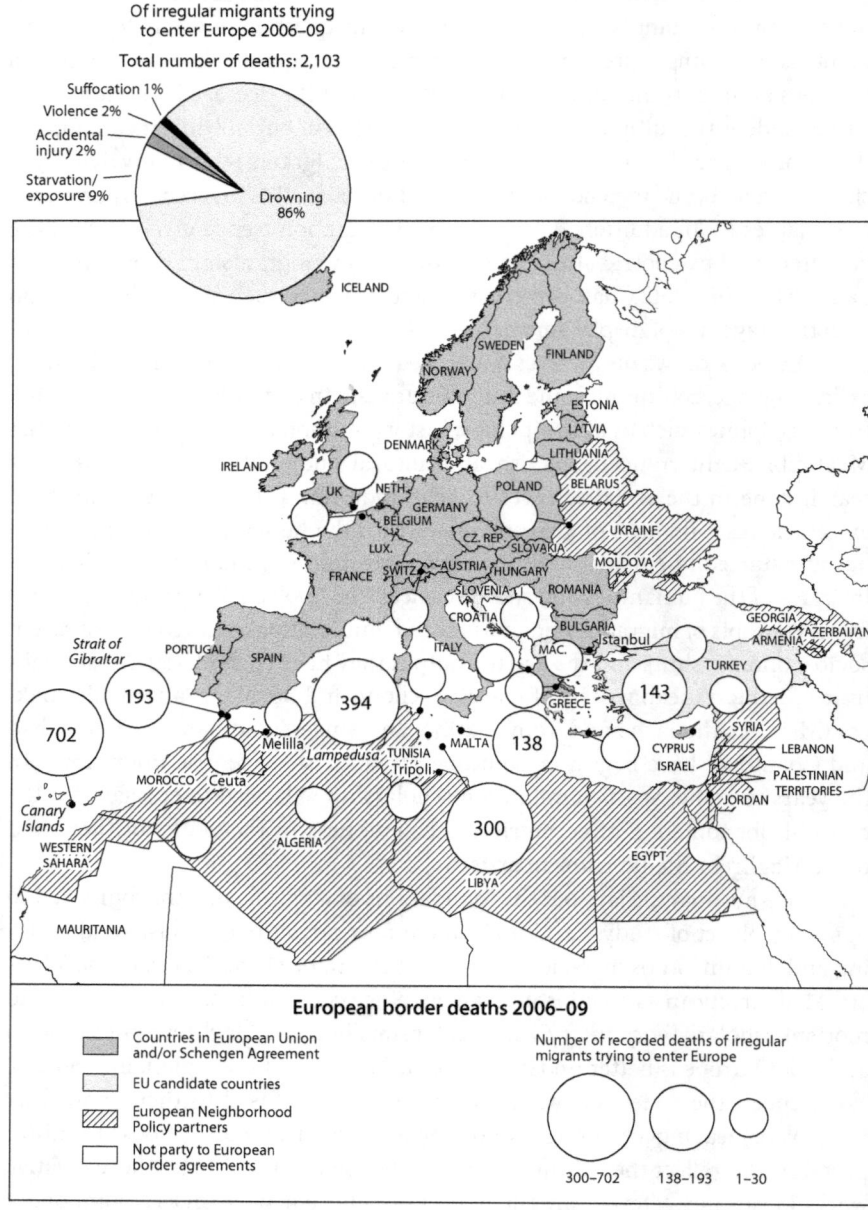

CAUSE OF DEATH
Of irregular migrants trying
to enter Europe 2006–09

Total number of deaths: 2,103

Suffocation 1%
Violence 2%
Accidental injury 2%
Starvation/exposure 9%
Drowning 86%

European border deaths 2006–09

Countries in European Union and/or Schengen Agreement

EU candidate countries

European Neighborhood Policy partners

Not party to European border agreements

Number of recorded deaths of irregular migrants trying to enter Europe

300–702   138–193   1–30

Map 0.3 "European Border Deaths 2006–09" from Russell King's *People on the Move: An Atlas of Migration.* Used with permission.

by literature, film, and music produced in various languages. I aim to show the impacts of such migrations on today's culture in addition to artists' critical interventions into political and mass media debates.

One of the contributions I hope this book will make is to reveal the ways in which drastic changes in immigration laws have inspired fictional texts that portray new immigrants, "legal" and "illegal," attempting nearly impossible border passages. A plethora of mass media depictions and isolationist discourses from both shores of the Mediterranean have helped shape the public opinion that clandestines are economic opportunists or traitors. Public opinion thus fails to recognize clandestines' wish to partake in the right to move freely across the White Sea of the Middle granted to them by the Universal Declaration of Human Rights. Representational essentializing faced by Maghrebis has impelled them to take life-threatening journeys northward as a last resort. Meanwhile, children of immigrants face taxing administrative procedures in their travels out of France, and their journeys—even those for leisure—can be read as politically or ideologically motivated.

The works I will analyze embrace a great variety of literary, cinematographic, and musical productions that have attracted considerable attention in North Africa, Europe, and the United States due to their academic value, artistic qualities, commercial successes, and international impact. Indeed, *Ex-Centric Migrations* scrutinizes novels and films that have become bestsellers and blockbusters in Europe and the U.S., along with others that have triggered new lines of study (e.g., *Cannibales* and *Les clandestins*). A number of the book's primary works have garnered the praise of critics and audiences worldwide, receiving domestic and international honors and awards (e.g., *Le Grand voyage, L'Enfant endormi, Partir,* and *Il était une fois dans l'oued*). Singer Manu Chao's fame has spread notably from the European continent to the Americas, and Chambao is recognized as one of the leading pop bands in Spain. As for the discussed Raï n'b compilations, they are among the bestselling CDs in France.

It is customary for historical studies to unfold in a chronological perspective. This methodology also applies to studies covering immigration to France or Europe in general. In such scholarly works, clandestine migration would appear at the end for being the most recent or "newer" pattern. In *Ex-Centric Migrations,* the chapters devoted to clandestiny are in the center to highlight the central position they have in this book, in recent political debates, in the realm of contemporary regional migratory trends, as well as in fictional representations of trans-Mediterranean migrations. The first and last chapters cover diverging and reverse migrations, respectively. I deliberately chose to use fiction among other tools as a base to claim that the discussed migrations have become ex-centric. I do so partly because the selected novels, films, and songs are based on real events, inspired by media accounts, influenced by data, etc. All the chapters are interrelated, but each one treats a discrete subject, so the reader may decide to read the book in its entirety or in parts.

Chapter 1 shows that the children of immigrants, such as French-Moroccan filmmaker Ismaël Ferroukhi, are imagining a form of diverging migration, which I call *disimmigration*. Disimmigration, I propose, consists in the redefinition of the concept of *émigré* and its false attribution to the children and grandchildren of immigrants, by way of a physical or symbolical journey outside the traditional Maghrebi migratory pole (North Africa → France). In Ferroukhi's road movie, *Le Grand voyage* (2004), this journey takes the form of a trip to Mecca. The father insists that his son drive him to the holy site. I contend that this unexpected pilgrimage is the old man's tactic to steal his son away from secular France to teach him about his roots, from which he is totally severed.

Chapter 2 studies a new subfield, which I have dubbed *illiterature,* a term that compresses *illegal* and *literature* in order to reflect the current ideological undertones of sociopolitical alarmism surrounding North African migration to Spain. Here I undertake a close analysis of three Moroccan novels: *Partir* (2006) by Tahar Ben Jelloun, *Cannibales* (1999) by Mahi Binebine, and *Les Clandestins* (2000) by Youssouf Amine Elalamy. In addition, this chapter explores the links between illiterature and *littérature-monde,* a concept delineated in a 2007 manifesto by major writers to question the partitioning of writings in the French language into "French" and "Francophone." I tackle the idea that the sea has become a materialization of the neocolonial European Empire and therefore an additional border to cross, another system to elude, as well as a military barrier to evade for people from the global South. I then consider the likely future visibility of Spanish writers and artists of North African descent and their much-awaited literary and cultural contributions to illiterature in addition to the interdisciplinary academic research that invariably will result in response.

Chapter 3 explores two films. The first, *Il était une fois dans l'oued* (2005), reveals a French-Algerian filmmaker's novel notion of a Frenchman who travels to Algeria as a stowaway. This unprecedented vision, I suggest, questions the rhetoric of the stereotypical perception of the northward "flow" of clandestine migrants institutionalized by mainstream mass media and presents North Africa as a recently established hideaway or getaway. This approach brings to light one of the many blind spots in current scholarship, that of the portrait in reverse of the clandestine: "illegal" French migration to Algeria. The second film, *Exils* (2004), by French Roma Tony Gatlif, depicts the trip to Algiers taken by a young couple who mistakenly embark on a ferry to Morocco. My study scutinizes the importance of terrestrial means of travel in the characters' identitarian touristic tour across the Mediterranean. The clandestineness of the protagonists is portrayed in a double fashion due to their failing to pay their fares and by their crossing of the closed Moroccan-Algeria border "illegally," even though they come from the north. The uninterruption of their voyage facilitated by their Frenchness serves as a backdrop against which to examine the fates of Maghrebi clandestine migrants.

In chapter 4, "The New Eldorado in Mediterranean Music," I dissect the lyrics of songs of the French songster Manu Chao, the Spanish band Chambao, and binational duets and trios featured on a series of Raï n'b albums, which is a hodgepodge of French raï, rap, and rhythm and blues. In my view, these artists express strong ideological positions on hrig (or harga). They condone and/or condemn popular conceptions of clandestine crossings. This chapter argues that the discussed Raï n'b songs portray the Maghreb as a new Eldorado for French citizens of North African descent who do not feel at home in their countries of birth. A close look at Chambao's song "Papeles Mojados" reveals a call for empathy and the rehumanization of *ilegales,* depicting them as *buena gente* (good people) in response to the widespread fear of the stigmatized postcolonial migrant. As for Manu Chao's song "Clandestino," I make the assertion that it plays on the Spanish ambivalence about clandestinity and "illegality" and questions common beliefs and biases.

Chapter 5 looks at four films, namely *Harragas* (2009) by Algerian-born filmmaker Merzak Allouache, *Bled number one* (2006) by Frenchman of Berber origin Rabah Ameur-Zaïmeche, *L'Enfant endormi* (2004) by the Moroccan-Belgian director Yasmine Kassari, and the short film *Visa* (2005) by the Tunisian-born Ibrahim Letaief. My analysis of *Harragas* focuses on a few key concepts such as deportation and legalization besides the underlying implications of the paratextual elements contained in the film's poster and DVD cover. In *Bled number one,* I tackle the dead-end situation in which an individual is sent to Algeria, his country of origin, after committing a crime in France. The latter two films provide an avenue for a discussion of maritime modes of transportation in the context of contemporary Algeria. The sea never appears in *L'Enfant endormi,* yet the Mediterranean divides the lives of men and women who cannot meet physically across the straits and resort to meet virtually instead. This impasse teases out a sociopolitical reality denounced in the films discussed here: the problematic disconnect between the demand for visits overseas and the scarcity of visas, which constitutes one of the major themes of Letaief's short film.

Chapter 6 scrutinizes reverse migration through the genres of the road movie and the travelogue. As various critics have shown, Maghrebi immigrants' dreams of returning home have been impeded by the process of raising and educating their children in France. Literary criticism, among other fields, has called the failed project "the myth of return." I claim in this chapter that, whether or not due to a debt they feel they must pay off, French children endeavor to make their parents' dream come true by laying their bodies to rest in their countries of origin. I call this notion of the return that is felt as the *ethical* thing to do for familial expectations, religious reasons, or personal will *methical return* in order to express that it is undertaken by the same children who had turned their parents' dream of returning to their country of origin into a *myth* by refusing to leave their own country of birth. The corpus is composed of two first works, namely, Houda Rouane's novel *Pieds-blancs* (2006) and the film *Ten'ja* (2004) by the Moroccan director Hassan Legzouli. The film deals with burial; the main character transports the corpse of his father to his native village for interment. The novel investigates issues of identity and citizenship via the crossing of national borders along with issues of memory and guilt through the topic of burial.

1 *Disimmigration* as a Remedy for the Illness of Immigration in Ismaël Ferroukhi's *Le Grand voyage*

The Monolingualism of the Host(age)

On November 2, 2009, a *grand débat* (great debate) was initiated by Eric Besson, Nicolas Sarkozy's minister of the lengthy and ambitious Ministère de l'immigration, de l'intégration, de l'identité nationale et du développement solidaire (Ministry of immigration, integration, national identity, and solidarity development). The debate on national identity soon turned into a reflection on how to assert one's Frenchness, and the consequent stigmatization of the supposedly "non-integrate-able" Other, embodied by the North African, the Arab, and in the post-9/11 era, the "out of place" Muslim in "secular" France. The goal was to win the votes of the most conservative fringe, but confusion and controversy caused the debate to be dropped within a few months. Racist comments were made by average French citizens and governmental officials alike, as was evidenced by many unfortunate statements that circulated on television and the internet. The debate was an avenue for what some may deem slippages of speech, and for others, a willful decision to say aloud what many were thinking softly. Such a discourse evolves in a Foucauldian sense as a discursive practice and is thus subject to power structures. It is a production that becomes a grid, reading the Other and confining him behind it. The national debate showed its limits and its sinister nature. Aware of its stigmatizing effect, many politicians warned the government against the second debate that Sarkozy asked his government to initiate, *le débat sur l'Islam* (the debate on Islam), right before the *cantonnales* (local elections, which took place in spring 2011), and a few months before the French presidential elections of May 2012.

The underlying questions that the film *Le Grand voyage* poses are relevant in the context of the major nationwide debate on French identity and the ongoing questioning of the compatibility of Islamic values with secularism. It is also pertinent within a revival of nationalism and Islamophobia in Europe, which have not spared France. Finally, it is a response to a pervasive racist environment that continues to affect the social fabric of various nations. One of the questions the film asks is: do we need to revisit the idea of immigration to, and integration in,

France? *Le Grand voyage* was released by Moroccan-French filmmaker Ismaël Ferroukhi in 2004.[1] Michel Cadé observed, "If *Le grand voyage* won the Luigi de Laurentis prize at the 2004 Venice Film Festival, and had a certain success in North America and Britain, it found only a small audience in France (76,501 entries since 2004)."[2] In this production, Réda (Nicolas Cazalé), a young Frenchman who grew up in southeastern France, learns that his father (Mohamed Majd) wishes to go on a pilgrimage to Mecca and has decided to travel by car. For practical reasons, Muslims usually fly from Europe to Saudi Arabia. The son is therefore taken aback by such an eccentric proposition. He is even more surprised to hear that his father has chosen him to drive to the Arabian Peninsula. The three thousand–kilometer trip will lead them through Italy, Slovenia, Serbia, Bulgaria, Turkey, Syria, and Jordan before they reach Saudi Arabia. Flabbergasted, Réda claims in vain that the timing is not right, for he is about to take his baccalaureate exam again, which he failed the previous year. "Sullen and angry at being torn from his student lifestyle to this elongated journey," the young man obliges in spite of the fact that he is also not happy at the prospect of being separated from his girlfriend.[3]

Contrary to the potentially misleading title of the film, *Le Grand voyage* (The Grand Journey) is not a leisurely enterprise. It refers to the long-awaited trip that a man is eager to undertake in order to fulfill one of his religious duties as a Muslim.[4] One may argue that *Le Grand voyage* is only that. After all, the religious aspect of the journey is made clear from the very beginning of the film and it remains present until the very last scene. Yet the "voyage" is not "grand" exclusively for its spiritual component. It also owes its grandeur to its ability to intertwine many themes. The journey, I contend, is also a migratory endeavor. But how could a film that is incontestably about the theme of hajj ("pilgrimage" in Arabic) be a representation of emigration? How can one claim that *Le Grand voyage* welcomes such a reading when the two men did not go through any administrative procedure to seek asylum or migrant status outside of France?[5]

Here are a few elements of response, which I will supplement in the course of the chapter. As in many cases of emigration, such as those of Maghrebis to France in the second half of the past century, many sojourns intended to be temporary ended up being permanent. This historical reality is illustrated in *Le Grand voyage* where a Maghrebi community has settled in a *banlieue* (inner city) near Marseilles and will most likely continue to be embedded in it unless it decides to leave, and thus follow the steps of the spiritual archetypal character of the film, the hājj-to-be.[6] And besides being a model for showing his relatives and neighbors how to carry on the tradition and fulfill the religious obligation of visiting the holy sites of Islam, Réda's father, who remains nameless throughout the film, is also a migratory leader. Indeed, the patriarch dies in his place of destination. He will not be able to return home alive or even dead.[7] Saudi Arabia welcomes and keeps the old man *ad eternam*. It thus becomes his new host country. As a matter of fact, it is customary for pilgrims who pass away during their pilgrimage to be buried in the holy cities in order to facilitate their access to Paradise. As for Réda, though we logically expect him to be off to the airport to catch a flight to France after his father's death, the film closes on an open-ended shot of the young man in a Saudi cab on his way to an unrevealed destination. The last sequence purposefully stops the trip short thousands of miles away from Réda's homeland. This ending instills in the viewer a feeling of uncertainty as to Réda's future plans. However, regardless of whether the young man intends to go back to France or not, *emigration* after all is derived from the Latin word *migratio,* which simply means to move from one place to another.

I propose to read *Le Grand voyage* as a film that uses religion to tell us about the protagonists' positions vis-à-vis issues of migration. The film reaches its climax in a beautiful shot of the Ka'aba surrounded by millions of pilgrims, yet in the form of an oblique sociological commentary it delivers an additional message—not religious—that the father had been carrying throughout the film ever since he and his son left their family back in France. This message concerns the old man's feeling that migration has had a heavy toll on the relations between the Maghrebi community in France and its French-born offspring. The father is adamant about getting this message across through a trip in which the son is trapped. The scene at the Ka'aba is a focal point of the film. It is also the point of departure for my argument, for it raises various questions. One of them is "what happens next?" Indeed, the father dies and leaves his *Beur* son stranded miles away from his land, language, and culture, just as in an act of treason or abandonment, or perhaps instead as a way of cutting the son's moorings to France and giving him independence from his past.

But before I discuss in depth my claim that *Le Grand voyage* reflects on the theme of *Beur* and Maghrebi ex-centric migration, I would like to touch briefly on the most common interpretation of this film, namely that it is about two protagonists who learn about one another. There is no doubt that the film lends itself to this analysis as well. In fact, from the very first shots, the spectator witnesses stark differences in the portrayal of the two characters. In the beginning, a polarization between the son's Frenchness and the father's Arabness is established. The son seems to ignore the Arab aspects of himself, from his family history to the motive of the trip he has been made obligated to take. The sharp dichotomy between the father and the son's personalities and ways of life is conveyed throughout in various ways, especially in the minimalistic conversations between the two men. Furthermore, the verbal exchanges take place in different languages, since the father addresses his son in Arabic and Réda responds in French. The limited verbal interactions and the sparse use of paradialogic additions symbolize the difficult cohabitation of two generations divided by linguistic differences. The following quotation I borrow from Derrida is easily applicable to monolingual Réda, who:

> speaks a language of which he is *deprived*. The French language is not his. Because he is therefore deprived of *all* language, and no longer has any other recourse—neither Arabic, nor Berber, nor Hebrew, nor any languages his ancestors would have spoken—because this monolingual is in a way aphasic (perhaps he writes because he is an aphasic), he is thrown into absolute translation, a translation without a pole of reference, without an originary language, and without a source language [*langue de départ*]. For him, there are only target languages [*langues d'arrivée*], if you will, the remarkable experience being, however, that these languages just cannot manage to reach themselves because they no longer know where they are coming from, what they are speaking *from* and what the sense of their journey is. Languages without an itinerary and, above all, without any superhighway of goodness knows what information.[8]

The French language is not eligible as one of *Le Grand voyage*'s "target languages," since French is reduced to a preposterous mode of communication in Eastern Europe and the Middle East where the two men are headed. Were they traveling through France's Maghrebi ex-colonies, Réda might be able to make himself understood in French. This option is not available to him in Saudi Arabia where the monolingualism of the other (*autre*)—to quote a Derridean expression—or the monolingualism of the host (*l'hôte*) is in effect. Instead, Réda is invited to engage in a process of arrival to languages, such as his father's Arabic and the various foreign languages of strangers met along the way. In this context, Réda's French is "without an itinerary" on the map of European languages. Neither does his survival English help Réda get anywhere. On the other hand, colloquial versions of Arabic cohabit successfully, as is demonstrated in the scene where the father communicates in Moroccan Arabic with a fellow pilgrim from Egypt, without Réda's being able to take part in the conversation. Indeed, the Egyptian man asks him what his name is, but Réda's monolingualism, which reinforces his status of stranger in the community of Arab speakers, needs his father's intervention. The latter answers the Egyptian's questions about his son. The helpless young man, a dependent of his father on many levels, is unable to be a resource and resorts to silence, irremediably turned into an object of discourse.

In the eyes of the father, the son's not being conversant in Arabic is unacceptable. Despite Réda's apparent absence of an identity crisis, he is disconnected from what linguists would call his "speech community." In the words of the director: "[Réda] lives in France, he has grown up in France, his friends are high-school students who speak French. So he has lost touch with everything that binds him to his language and culture. He is disconnected. . . . So we are watching a real discovery of a part of himself that he has lost touch with. The voyage is, in part, just that: Réda's rediscovery of himself."[9] The father's desperation prompts his surprising decision to initiate a return to the "originary" or source language, to show Réda "where [his language is] coming from, what [it is] speaking *from* and what the sense of [his] journey is" or as one could also put it, "where it speaks from, where it departs from." While driving along highways with his son, the father traces a trajectory, creating an "itinerary" for his son's monolingualism to arrive at the realization that his "mother tongue" (French) is not his mother's tongue (Arabic).

Though Islam and Arabness are not interchangeable, they are conflated here, for the trip to Saudi Arabia is presented as a voyage justified for religious, cultural, and linguistic reasons. Thus, the trip is a multipurpose endeavor designated to acquaint Réda with many things that he deems quaint, for example, his father's value system in addition to everything that the patriarch represents. I will therefore use *Arabness* to mean the Arabic language, the Muslim religious tradition, and the Maghrebi cultural background. The young man's lacunae are of various types. They are surely linguistic, but as many critics have noted, they are also religious. The father is a devoutly religious man; he reads the Qur'an and focuses all of his energy on completing the trip to Mecca. As for the son, he dresses like any young French man of his age, has a girlfriend, and does not show signs of religious belonging. More importantly, the film showcases his initial resistance to what his father incarnates, namely, all that is Arabic and Muslim. As a matter of fact, Réda asks his father questions on Islamic tenets, refers to his religion as "your religion," and partakes in *haram* (sinful) practices, such as an extramarital relationship and the consumption of alcohol. "[Réda] does not understand his father or his faith, and he certainly doesn't understand why they can't just take a plane."[10] Therefore, in the manner of a disciple asking a master, Réda, inquires about the apparent reason behind the old man's decision not to fly to Saudi Arabia. The father's reasoning is delivered in the form of a mystical parable in Modern Standard Arabic. This choice of register suits the formal nature of the parable, and the scene is accompanied by a lyrical piece of string music, which heightens the ceremonial quality of the topic:

RÉDA: Why didn't you fly to Mecca? It's a lot simpler.

FATHER: When the waters of the ocean rise to the heavens they lose their bitterness to become pure again.

RÉDA: What? [in Arabic]

FATHER: The ocean waters evaporate as they rise to the clouds. And as they evaporate, they become fresh. That's why it's better to go on your pilgrimage on foot than on horseback; and better on horseback than by car; and better by car than by boat; and better by boat than by plane.

In this dialogue, the son utters "Shnou?" ("What?" in Moroccan Arabic). This is one of the two instances in the entire film in which Réda speaks to his father in

Arabic. On both occasions, the young man produces only a single word, thus showing his monolingualism. However, it is important to note that once again the two protagonists do not speak the same language. Réda is asking the father to explain himself. The viewer wonders whether Réda is aware that his father is speaking in Modern Standard Arabic, as opposed to Moroccan Arabic, or whether he is asking that his father paraphrase, wrongly assuming that his inability to grasp the message is due to his not yet mastered vocabulary, the speed of his father's elocution, or the complexity of syntax. At any rate, should the father repeat or explain in this high variety of Arabic, the son would still not be able to understand. Réda asks "What?" in Moroccan and the father reformulates in Modern Standard Arabic. Réda remains perplexed. Ironically, the two men have agreed briefly to speak the same language, and yet they do not. This undetected shift of register highlights not only Réda's uneasiness with linguistic otherness, but also a gap to fill between himself and his father that he, in this moment, desires to fill. Réda fails to grasp his father's *disimmigrational* plan—that is, the old man's strategy of using dissimulation to express his views on immigration—for the son is too focused on comprehending the letter of his father's tale instead of its spirit. As a result, Réda cannot make heads or tails of it. This moment of reflection on religion and eccentric modes of displacement ultimately brings up underlying issues with regard to ex-centric migrations.

As for the parable's purpose, it is to convey a simple image to the trainee, who is not yet ready to access the full scope of the teaching. But his hermeneutic strategy is a maieutic approach, which leaves Réda even more perplexed. What the old man does is blur his explanation by providing a hermetic truism, whereby in various traditions, self-inflicted suffering at or en route to sites of pilgrimage is believed to have a more powerful redeeming potential. Not only does the father manage to render a simple image opaque, but he also chooses to express himself in a linguistic register that escapes his son. Indeed, the moral of the parable remains a mystery for Réda. But because the old man has the answer to Réda's questions, it is precisely a sense of dependency that the father tries to attain in order to keep his son's interest alive for the remainder of the trip. The old man's methodology is simple: the learner should feel the constant need for his elder to eliminate blind spots in his conceptualization of the nature of the journey.

The two men discussing philosophical matters, wearing heavy blankets as they sit together on a bench in a snow-capped landscape, recalls Sufi tradition, for the name *Sufi* is thought to be derived from the woolen cloaks the mystics used to wear. This visual parallel with Muslim mysticism signals the availability of multithematic readings of the film, among which one might include a commentary on migration, which is unpacked in the discussion of recommended modes of transportation. As a matter of fact, the father's enumeration happens to be the major element of his tirade. It is as if he insisted that religion and migration go hand in hand. The framing of the film as a parable also contains an indirect message. The director alerts us to the presence of alternative directions, unconventional interpretations, and hidden purports within this fable-like story. These various aspects of the film confirm that it is not only about a religious trip, and that it contains a number of embedded symbolical meanings, on which it falls to Réda and to the viewer to meditate.[11] Ferroukhi departs from the religious to lead us to other levels of interpretation.

An example of the combination of the religious with the sociopolitical is the scene in which Réda dances in a cabaret in Istanbul with a belly dancer. Religious chants and incantations are replaced by live singing and dancing on stage. However, like a master Sufi leading his disciples to a state of trance, the singer sings faster and faster as the music's tempo reaches a crescendo. Depressed Réda drinks beer and cheers up as he dances with the sensual female dancer. The dimly-lit lively atmosphere, his inebriated condition—Sufi terminology equates the bliss-like state of divine union as a state of drunkenness—and the fast-beating instruments help to make Réda appear as a trance-seeker. The camera focuses on Réda's body and face as he performs, while the singer and the cabaret dancer become marginal characters, almost extras now that the young man has been brought into the light. Réda extends his arms and forms arabesques above his head with his hands while pivoting around, his gestures mimicking the posture of whirling dervishes. They symbolize his flight, or his uprooting, from the local to the migrational. Indeed, Réda's dance shifts the religious/mystical signifier to lay bare the unfolding migrational project he has embarked upon.

As a road movie, *Le Grand voyage* belongs to what is now a booming genre in *Beur* and North African cinema, including documentaries such as *Garagouz* by the Algerian Abdenour Zahzah. This twenty-four–minute 2010 short shows similarities with *Le Grand voyage* in that the road trip is taken by a father and his son in a rundown vehicle. The road movie is not a new genre in *Beur* cinema. By the early 1980s, there were already two road movies made by *Beur* filmmakers (Tarr). *Le Grand voyage* is a *bildungsfilm,* a place imagined by Ferroukhi in which an excentric means of transportation is put to the test in order to try out imaginary scenarios. To go on pilgrimage by car from France, however, is an original scenario. It is even unfathomable, since Saudis do not allow foreigners to circulate throughout their territory as freely as Réda and his father do, for, in spite of the presence of guest workers in their country, they are known to be closed to immigration.[12] Therefore, the question Réda had asked his father, namely, "Why didn't you fly to Mecca?" makes sense. His eccentric way of performing the hajj is acceptable within the confines of a fictional narrative.

According to Réda, his father's sudden decision to have him drive to Mecca with no option of disobeying is experienced as a kidnapping. Indeed, soon after the announcement, the young man is separated from his girlfriend Lisa, going wherever his father desires and for however long it will take him to achieve his goal. The hospitality or gift that the father offers his son easily becomes, as Derrida shows, a forced hospitality, a poisoned gift: "the '*pse*' of *ipse* no longer allows itself to be dissociated from power, from the mastery and sovereignty of the *hospes* (here, I am referring to the semantic chain that works on the body of hospitality as well as hostility—*hostis, hospes, hosti-pet, posis, despotes, potere, potis sum, possum, pote est, potest, pot sedere, possidere, compos*, etc.—)."[13] Réda is a guest in spite of himself. The particular dynamics of the ethics of hospitality that such a framework has engendered would best be expressed in French—Réda is *l'hôté* ("hosted"— the victim of a regulated confinement). This neologism is inspired by Sufi terminology whereby "the raptured" attains a union with the object of love through an ambivalent experience, which has been reported by Muslim mystics commonly to start with pain and to end in bliss. The other neologism (*l'hôteur*) combines *hôte* (host) and *l'auteur qui ôte* (the one who takes away). In this configuration, the father would be the host—the "author" of the hostage and Réda *l'ôté* "the one snatched" (in this case, from his homeland). This ambiguous position is reflected in the ambivalence of the word *host* in French, which designates both the host and the guest.

There is also a political dimension to this "hosting," as the word *hostage* suggests. The situation of the hostage is a perversion of the terms of traditional hospitality. In the 1999 novel, *Méfiez-vous des parachutistes* by the Moroccan author Fouad Laroui, a guest overstays his welcome and thus becomes his host's *hôteur*. In a way, in *Le Grand voyage* the father's enterprise is of a hostile political nature, since he is withdrawing his son from all things French, including *L'École de la République*, one of France's secular institutions. The father's possessive act betrays a questioning of France's status as host country by the very act of becoming a temporary host himself, albeit a despotic one, until the old man provides his son with another potential host—Arabia.[14]

Disimmigration

I base my neologism *disimmigration* on the word *immigrances*, which inspired the title of a collection of essays edited in 2007 by Benjamin Stora and Émile Temime.[15] Disimmigration or *désimmigrance*, I suggest, can refer to an entire set of projects. In this chapter, I use disimmigration/*désimmigrance* as an umbrella term that designates first and foremost the revisiting of classic conceptions and patterns of emigration in fictional narratives.[16] In *Le Grand voyage*, disimmigration applies essentially to the old man's project to carry his son away from a French *cité* (inner city) and from *francité* (Frenchness), as well as to establish for Réda a symbolic link with Arabness, by way of a trip to the Arabian Peninsula.

The father's trip with his son aims at unraveling a curse. Indeed, the father's bitter realization that his culture and he himself are strangers to his son causes him to view his migration to France as a fault and his settling in France as a malediction. The father takes it upon himself to counteract the effects of integration into the French culture, which in his mind translate into an impoverishment of his son's Arabness, for which he feels responsible. Very likely, the patriarch views the fatalistic equation as a consequence of unfulfilled fatherly obligations, a failure to perform his function as a transmitter of Arabness. Given the religious undertones of the film and the fact that many of his son's practices would traditionally be labeled as "sinful" within Islam, the father sets off to remedy what he feels is illicit. The old man's decision to have Réda accompany him to Saudi Arabia may indeed indicate that the father views his son's lack of rootedness into the Arabic and Islamic cultures as a deep flaw. But Réda's mistakes were made by his father's mistake as defined by the Algerian sociologist Abdelmalek Sayad, that is, "the atypical mistake of absence" from his place of origin.[17] With regard to Maghrebi parents, Mehdi Charef, a well-known writer and filmmaker, claims the following:

> I think that they are not very proud of themselves, of the way they tackled the problems. They live a triple failure. First, they told themselves: we are going to France, we are going to become rich. They lost. This is their first failure. The second failure consisted in them believing they have not lost it all, since they made children who will be able to return to the country of origin. But it didn't take them long to realize that they couldn't. Finally, the third failure was when they saw that they too wouldn't make a final return home.[18]

The implication is that the old man's pilgrimage may not be successful until Réda's Arabness has been restored. Thus, the hajj is intended to redeem both himself and his son. He hopes to rid his son's sins by making a redeeming hajj on behalf of Réda. In some circumstances, individuals may perform hajj for others. Thus, the father plans to do so by proxy, through physical proximity. Réda's questionable faith and his inability to act out rituals in the Arabic language are, for the old man, suitable reasons for him to do this charitable deed on his son's behalf. The son's participation in the trip and his presence in the holy sites, albeit without him actually performing the prayers and partaking in the mandatory rituals of the pilgrimage, facilitate the father's intentions.

The father is seeking a remedy of another nature as well. Apart from the religious redemption he hopes to achieve for his son, he has a further goal of "detoxifying" Réda. In French, one would say that he is *désoxidant* his son, and by the same token *dés-occident* (de-Westernizing) Réda, for according to the French dictionary *Littré,* in alchemy *occident* is not only "darkness, which is the first hue of the masterpiece," but also, in the same dictionary, the word signifies "fall, ruin." Moreover, the patriarch deoccidizes his son by taking him eastward, thus symbolically de-Westernizing the young man.

As we have seen, the old man's program to disimmigrate his son is due to a combination of differences and lacunae (linguistic, religious, and cultural). It is also due to the fact that ironically it is the image of an émigré that French Réda keeps representing in his father's mind. Indeed, Réda never migrated to France but was born there and consequently he is a *Beur,* literally a reverse Arab, for *Beur* is the accepted reverse form of *Arab* in *verlan,* a variety of French slang in which syllables are spoken backward. The father's dissimmigratory project speaks to this reversal as being an affront. Réda is an Arab in reverse, one who de-Arabicizes himself, and is thus everything but his father's double, and given the son's initial hostile acceptance of his heritage, he also appears as an adverse Arab. And yet, the young man is not a Franco-French either. The character of the father disimmigrates Réda in order to deconstruct, or rather to discontinue, the contested appellation of his son as *"Beur."* Indeed, the father's agenda also helps tease out the incongruity of such misnamings as " 'young Maghrebi immigrants' or 'second generation Maghrebis' or 'offspring of Maghrebi immigration,' " which, according to Tunisian sociolinguist and postcolonial studies expert Nabiha Jerad, are applied to "those born on French soil" to the point that "in France, 'immigrant' and 'Maghrebi' had become synonymous by [1974]."[19] The critic adds: "The designation of all North Africans as 'Maghrébin' has become so normalized that it is used not only in the media and sociological discourse but even in institutional documents as a category of nationality."[20] In the midst of highly marginalizing national discourses that designate *Beurs* as second-class citizens, as well as conflate them with migrants—which they are not—the father feels compelled to come to his son's rescue by reidentifying him.

Though the old man hails from Morocco, *Le Grand voyage* presents us with an instance of reverse migration (as in backward migration, one that erases it by enacting it in reverse). Taking his *Beur* son to Arabia is a way for the father to show the *Beur*'s Arabness. Differently put, the tactic consists in reversing the French moniker *Beur* by reversing the migratory flow.[21] *Le Grand voyage* is a reversal of migration insofar as the émigrés "return home."[22] Theoretically speaking, the protagonists are Arabs, and the Arabian Peninsula is the historical and symbolic home. *Le Grand voyage* attempts to erase what it is to be an émigré, which in the words of Sayad is "a social condition."[23] The father emigrated from Morocco at some point in his life, and we assume that he is a migrant worker. While in Réda's view the old man is an émigré, in the father's relation with his son, Réda is construed as French, in other words, altogether Other. In the case of *Le Grand voyage,* disimmigration consists of a return to origins of various types. Disimmigration thus becomes a divergent movement made in an unexpected way and to a novel place in order to bury the burdensome notion of *émigré* where it all started. The father's endeavor succeeds because the pilgrim passes away in Saudi Arabia.

In place of degrading misnomers and falsified statuses, the old man offers his own fix to the hazardous narrative of identity and immigration. A symbolic illustration of this response is the scene where the father dumps his son's cell phone in a garbage bin in a rest area by the highway at night while his son is asleep in the car. This gesture signifies the father's refusal of a status quo institutionalized by social, political, and ideological circumstances that have affected the identity formation of his family nexus and the resulting nature of the father's relationship with his son. The director's tactical and revealing choice not to show us Réda's girlfriend, Lisa, is a way to frame her as a national allegory (of France). She is a phantasmagorical figure for both the son and the father. Réda connects with allegorical Lisa through the device of the telephone. We do not hear her voice, but we do see her name on the screen. Meanwhile, Réda is neglecting to make a connection with his father (signifier of the Maghrebi lineage). Ironically, absent Lisa is omnipresent all the way from Réda's thoughts to her inscription in the Arab land where the young man writes her name in the sand with his foot. The combined act of naming and writing is a profession of faith in the one whose identity is in flux in the symbolical motherland. To the old man, the inscription of Lisa's name is an allegory of how France haunts the son and hurts the father. If one were to read Lisa's name from right to left, ASIL (a homonym of *asile*, "asylum") would be revealed. But then, the question one may ask is: why read a name written in the Latin alphabet from right to left as if it were in Arabic script? It so happens that the messages of the film reveal concealed meanings when they are reversed, and this applies to names as well.

This chapter indeed is about reversing everything from migratory patterns to the word *Beur* itself in order to highlight what has been effaced in the first place. Thus, Réda writes Lisa's name in capitals and it remains visible, as if it were set in stone despite being fleeting letters drawn in the sand. He seems lonely, disillusioned, and is trying desperately to find something to grasp onto. He writes LISA rather halfheartedly. As he composes her name, we understand that he is moving away from her and his past. By making the gesture of missing Lisa/France, he realizes how empty it is. In this attempt to make Lisa materialize before his eyes and find *asile,* he fails. This outcome is symbolized by his night dream of being engulfed in shifting sands, while his father, dressed as a goatherd in the dream, walks by without lending a helping hand. In this eerie and highly symbolical scene situated in an Arab land without his French way of life, without his Lisa, without any means of orientation, the young man goes insane as if he were being locked in a different kind of *asile,* namely, a mental asylum. In turn, the father's fear is that France might be for Réda a *mère-patrie* (literally a "mother-father-land"). Still, the patriarch remains hopeful that this will not be so, because even in his son's French language Lisa's asylum (ASIL) is not satisfactory. Technically, it is both inaccurate and incomplete, for it misses the "e" of *asile*. Consequently, the father bets that Lisa will not fit in, that she will be kept at bay, that she will be left out, in short that she will altogether keep missing. This explains why the father takes Réda to Mecca, the original motherland of the Ummah; literally, the "mother" of the community. In the view of the old man, Lisa, Ferroukhi's "Marianne" (and allegory for France), represents a kind of utopian surrogate motherland for his son. She has an enigmatical power over the father as well, who runs away from her while making sure that he escapes with seduced Réda.

The old man's agenda to sever his son from Lisa's grip is accompanied by another ambitious endeavor. In the image of the sinuous route that the car takes across Europe and the Middle East, the journey presents itself as a daring attempt to tie Réda to something, somewhere, somehow. But what? In order to connect with his son, the father feels the need to disconnect him from a monolithic identity. He has to untie him (*détacher*) in order to turn him into a clean slate (*détâcher*), and vice versa. The father throwing away his son's cell phone as soon as they have left the French territory is proof of his political project to disintegrate, both literally and figuratively, the established link between his son and Lisa, the emblem of France.[24] As the father disposes of Réda's cell phone, he deposes the French allegorical figure, as in a *coup*. Put differently, the old man authorizes himself to go beyond limits, territorial and otherwise. The old man cannot be unaware that his son's present and future might take him away from the project he has for him should a French connection materialize, that is, a serious union with Lisa, which would seal the son's future and family line in the French land and culture. The father's objective is to prevent his son's Frenchness from being accessible and "portable" beyond the French national space, hence his willingness to deport his son. The throwing away of the phone—a portable device indeed—is a sign that the father is wishing to do away with his son's portability. He does so in an unexpected fashion, *d'un coup* (which conveniently means "in a coup," and "out of the blue"). The rebellious act occurs right after he crosses the French border. By situating himself outside of Lisa's national territory, the father is able to *déborder* (go over the edge). When Réda finds out about his father's act, he nearly bursts into a fit of rage but manages to contain himself. The father seems to have crossed the borderline by throwing the cell phone in a garbage bin, thus making the implicit statement that contacts with Lisa are refused and refuse, and thus should be disregarded and discarded.

In this unique instance of disimmigration, the father also deviates from several decades of Maghrebis' economic migration to France, in hopes of dismantling its insistent and insidious pattern. With his return to dust in the land of Arabs, the old man closes the circle of physical South-to-North migration. In turn, his peculiar trip opens the path and leads the way to a unique model of Maghrebi and *Beur* disimmigration. By reaffirming the link with the original land, the disimmigrator aims at boycotting a bond—the French connection. The prefix *dis* in disimmigration implies that the old man's enterprise aims to eliminate his status as émigré perpetuated by French mass media, as well as to reverse "the devalorisation of which [youth of immigrant background] are victims in the media-political discourse."[25] The father seeks to rescue both men from false attributes assigned to them by this powerful stigmatizing discourse.

Therefore, in order to be eliminated, the act of migrating as it is commonly undertaken or conceived, namely, as a South-to-North migratory flow into France, needs to be undermined. Oddly enough, disimmigration becomes valid in the act of emigrating again. But this enterprise requires that the destination be displaced from the common trans-Mediterranean vertical axis whose endpoints invariably have been the Maghreb and France. The father remaps the notion of migration by proposing an alternative migratory form and itinerary. This remapping simultaneously opens up a new chapter of immigration, through a type of disimmigration. The father's voyage to the Arabian Peninsula on what could be seen as a whim is in actuality a planned enterprise. Going to Saudi Arabia instead of the Maghreb tells us that the father is aware of the difficulty of disimmigrating his son when the migratory flux follows the expected vertical axis between France and the Maghreb. Historically speaking, as well as in classic fictional representations of Maghrebi migration, *Beurs* are here (in France) to stay. Réda's reluctance to leave France recalls the refusal of second- and third-generation children of immigrants to "return home" to a country they hardly know, if at all. Indeed, as many *Beur* and Maghrebi literary and cinematic narratives have shown, "to return" the children of immigration to the Maghreb has, for the most part, proven unsuccessful.[26]

In order to find a way around this problem, the father decides that his son will be his driver without consulting him first. As a preventive measure, the pilgrim-to-be makes his son become a migrant by taking him to another potential host country. Therefore, he is about to sponsor a candidate who is not one. Indeed, Réda is angered because he is forced to emigrate, that is, to move outside of his own quotidian spatial, linguistic, and cultural comfort zone. Whereas Réda speaks the language of integration, his father's behavior is an expression of disintegration. Contrary to common scenarios concerning the theme of Maghrebi emigration, Réda has been volunteered to leave. He is being deported (taken elsewhere) not by national authorities (for he is not a clandestine migrant but a French national) but by his father. The extreme gesture is a response to the presence of a social and historical situation, which may be too difficult to alter.

Dubious discourses and depictions of *Beurs* have aimed at denaturalizing the people labeled as such by questioning the nature of their Frenchness. The father strives to prescribe his son a remedy for this malady of constant societal incrimination. He offers an alternative by assigning to Réda another destiny: to abscond to a new and faraway destination. He avoids the Maghreb where his son would be a mere *l'facance* (i.e., a French holiday-maker of Moroccan descent).[27] The idea is to leave for a place that is a blank canvas where there is no predrawn picture that must be erased before new sketches can be begun. The father heads off with his son in hopes that one day they will be able to shed their obsolete category of émigrés (again, Réda is not one). Is his father one? Most likely he is retired by now. Therefore, since in the context of migratory policies an émigré is technically defined by his status as a foreign worker, logically he does not fit the category either.

This journey is initiated as a symbolic remedy for the "illness" of immigration. *Le Grand voyage* is timely. In the director's opinion, the timeliness of the film is justified by the fact that *Le Grand voyage* offers the viewer a counterpoint to misconceptions about Islam deepened by 9/11.[28] The film is opportune for other reasons as well. The aging of the "first generation" of Maghrebi immigrants in France is a crucial element. It reflects a sociological fact that has rarely been confronted in cinema, if at all. Emigrés who have spent most of their lives in France are now passing away. *Le Grand voyage* introduces the pressing question of the place of burial for the eldest among the Maghrebi émigrés. The film's engagement with the theme of burial is worthy of note and avant-garde in the sense that this topic has not yet become part of the commonly represented experiences of the migrant community in *Beur* and Maghrebi cinema.

In a concert of jarring expressions of discordances between the father and son's personalities, and their different linguistic and religious practices, Réda's cultural alienation is another crucial element of estrangement. This fact could be viewed by his kin as a manifestation of disintegration from the Ummah (community of believers). The father interprets his son's identitarian shame, ignorance, or indifference as a result of a too-successful integration into French society, which, in the French tradition, requires the renunciation of communitarian differences.[29] The father is adamant about disintegrating Réda's national status by disimmigrating him. His decision is based on a silenced feeling of rage and remorse. The father never expresses his anger at his son's evident signs of un-Arabness. However, this does not mean that the old man is not frustrated. His composure may well be conventional—it is required of pilgrims-to-be that they do not express feelings of anger on their trip in order for the pilgrimage to have its redeeming effect and for the individual to attain the status of hājj or hājja.

Host(ile) Hospitality

The director's choice not to name the father is a sign that the old man is another allegory in the film. He represents the first generation of Maghrebi immigrants. The communitarian nature of his disimmigratory project—tainted with regret— is contained in his persona. It carries the implication that the first generation of migrants has misbehaved in some way, that they missed the opportunity to be or to have, for the children they made in their country of emigration did not grow up to be the people that they thought they would be. Along the way, both generations missed each other, as is illustrated in the portrayal of Réda and his father as near-strangers to each other throughout their trip. Emigrés therefore failed to keep their offspring for themselves. In turn, France has had a strong seductive effect on the children of immigrants.[30] This effect is symbolized by the girlfriend we never see in person. We hear of her in absentia on various occasions: via Réda's conversation with a Turkish acquaintance, through Réda's anxiety to hear from her on his cell phone, in a picture Réda brought along with him, and in his attempt to reach her from a hotel room, cut short when his father emerged from the bathroom where he was performing his ablutions.

In the scene where the two characters are forced to huddle together under blankets in an open-air shelter, an improvised lesson takes place in the form of a short series of questions and answers. This lesson aims to preserve the sense of mystery necessary to inspire the son's curiosity until the end of the voyage. All along the journey, Réda is being held captive due to a sense of emergency and apparent desperation on the part of the father, whose ambitious disimmigrating project requires that the two men be close, or rather enclosed, side-by-side for a very long time. Indeed, Réda never goes far from his father, nor does he run away. The only times he does run, it is to get back into the car where his father is awaiting him, and to sit on a mountaintop where he waits for his father to retrieve him. Traveling in an automobile instead of by plane obviously lengthens the duration of the trip, and this is another reason why the father opted for that route. The old man is running a race against time, and his chances for a successful act of disimmigration are increased by keeping his son within reach at all times. The father also insists that they spend extensive time together because of his fear of his own approaching death. Should the old man pass away before the voyage has been completed, his teachings would be buried with him. This inauspicious scenario would thus force him to accept his son's condition of being a *Beur*—a name (in addition to a condition) the father wishes he could turn back into *Arabe*, in order to restore Réda's Arabness.

The spectator soon realizes that the old man kidnaps his son on this journey because it is his last chance to realize his pedagogical agenda. Since the father failed to pass on his ideals to his son in France, he decides that a different method might be needed, hence the lesson taught *in actu* and in situ, as fieldwork—a necessary work-in-progress along the way to the holy sites. From that moment on, the old man has his son all to himself. Réda is being trained while he sits next to his father, who evaluates his progress in his position as a student driver on the road of disimmigration. Like a guide, the father teaches his son. In other words, he molds him by prolonging the trip and showing him the right way, that is, by helping to rid him of old patterns of thinking.

An anthroponymic study can be helpful in the interpretation of a film or a novel, as filmmakers and writers also happen to choose the names of their characters to convey etymological or phonetic implications. Réda's name resonates for a speaker of French with the adjectives *raidi* (stiffened) and *raide* (stiff). These words convey the feeling of an awkward position—that of being a *Beur* and of a painful and lengthy cohabitation that takes place in the closed location of an old and unreliable automobile. Just like the two-fold experiences related by Sufis, Réda's own experience of transformation is initiated in pain, the uncomfortable identity he has been forced to inhabit. The same comment applies to Réda's father, who looks uncomfortable and stiff in the dark coarse suit he wears in France, until he dons the thin and plain pilgrim's attire—clothes in which he feels at ease. It is worth noting that while Réda's name conveys the idea of stiffness in French, it means "blessing" in Arabic. In the French language, Réda fits uneasily, whereas in his ancestral culture where parents' benedictions are an open door to eternal bliss, he is a natural blessing. Just as we read Lisa's name right to left, we can do the same with Réda's. A reversed reading of Réda's name gives us a homonym of *adhère*, one who adheres to someone else's views. We saw earlier that even though the two male protagonists do not seem to stick (another meaning of *adhère*) to the other's opinions in the beginning of the film, they learn to open up to accept each other's views along the way. Indeed, in the second part of the film, when the two men look more appeased, they express less resistance to each other's personal, cultural, and religious differences. In addition, they stick to each other until death do them part. Another possible reason for the choice of Réda's name is its closeness with *raid,* a proximity that highlights further "the act of riding with a hostile intent," as contained in the meaning of the word in Old English. In French, according to the Larousse, *raid* indicates a "long-distance course destined to show the endurance of the contestants." Réda views his father's "hostile" endeavor to cut him off from his French girlfriend and habits as part of a larger effort to test his endurance, which also is manifested in the father's refusal to stop along the way for food or sight-seeing.[31]

The two men have to "stick" and "ride" together partly because the ailing father cannot drive. He depends on his son's help. In the scene where the hājj-to-be donates the rest of their savings to a female beggar, who solicits the old man as he is performing his ablutions alongside a deserted road, exasperated Réda informs his father that he will not continue on the trip. The young man yanks his bag out of the car and walks away. Conscious that he needs his son to drive, the old man goes to fetch Réda, whom he finds in the unexpected posture of a mystic. Réda is sitting, looking ahead at the immensity of the desert, maybe meditating. His being portrayed alone and introspective on a mountain in a Muslim country recalls the image of the Prophet meditating in ġār ḥirāʾ, a cave located on Mount Jabal al-Nūr when he had his first revelation. Of course, religious figures cannot be compared lightly to these two fictional characters. My intention is certainly not to do so but rather to show that, working from a religious background, the director may be suggesting a hermetic reading of disimmigration. It relies on the very choice of the place of destination, intrinsically associated with an essential and existential origin, Arabia, which is historically the place of religiously mandated emigration for the Muslim community. Ferroukhi's camera draws a parallel with Archangel Gabriel leading the Prophet Muhammad and his community to instigate an endless emigration. This analogy indicates that the voyage is the advent of a new type of migration. The fact that these contemporary travelers are tracing their way to the original point of historical Muslim migration can be read as a sign that they are messengers of disimmigration. This similarity allows Ferroukhi to remind us that Réda is being trained by his father, who, like Archangel Gabriel, towers over Réda—the reluctant receiver—and talks him into embarking on a mission whose spirit Réda (as well as the Prophet) resisted in the beginning.

When the protagonists get lost on a side road, Réda attempts to take on the role of the leader, which so far has been his father's. Therefore, he tries to operate a coup d'état, or rather deals a blow in the contract by becoming the teacher and testing the old man. This reversal will be one of very few that does not work in the film precisely because it is not part of the father's agenda. Réda doubts that his father will be able to get them back on the right track, as is evidenced in his statement, "How do you know? You can't even read." Ironically, the father is literate in Arabic—a language the son does not know. In turn, it will require continued efforts on the part of Réda to manage to read between the lines of his multifaceted trip. Réda's calling his father illiterate does not trigger any violent response, for the previously stated reason that an aspiring hājj must keep his composure in all circumstances. Thus, the old man gets back into the car, buckles up, and his deceptively passive submission is matched by an act of uncompromising resistance. Réda's attempt to gain control fails due to his controlling attitude—a behavior that momentarily closes the door to dialogue between the two men. Remorseful, Réda gets back into the car and cajoles his father while pointing at the map: "Look, Dad. We're here and we have to get to Belgrade. If we backtrack to Zagreb, we can get on the freeway to Belgrade. Understand? Hello? Okay. We'll do as you want." The father refuses to look at places the son points to on his map, for the young man has tried to usurp the role of the teacher too soon while his father is still alive.

The two characters' various disagreements about the purpose of the trip, how it should be taken, and which route to follow, mirror the gap between the two generations regarding life choices. In those scenes, the two travelers act out their multifarious differences, be they generational, linguistic, or cultural. Following the road (*tarīq* in Arabic) is the way (*tarīqa*). It is an essential matter and an existential concern for the father, hence his constantly visible anxiety that taking the wrong physical road may lead them to the wrong metaphysical path, thus misdirecting their project of disimmigration. The spectator recalls that from the very beginning, the father categorically has refused to stop in Milan or any other city to go sightseeing, claiming that they are not visitors on this trip. Put differently, the father excludes the possibility of a trip *à la carte* (which in French conveniently refers to both the option of choosing and the map itself). He even refuses to follow his son's proposed itinerary, Réda's *carte à la carte* (map à la carte). The father knows the way to the origin, given that they will arrive at their final destination even if they never understand directions given by foreigners, and despite the old man's insistence on following side roads that, according to his son, do not exist on the map. These roads obviously do exist, but the son cannot see them even though they are right before him. Visiting European attractions would constitute a distraction from the purpose of the journey and would therefore defeat the purpose, as the father strives to divert his son's mind from Western matters and calls his attention instead to more Eastern interests. The father diverts his son east, toward Mecca, the direction that all Muslims face in prayer. Furthermore, in spite of his refusal to stop along the way on the grounds that they are not tourists, the old man (purposefully?) lets himself be talked into the touristic visit of a Muslim site, the Blue Mosque in Istanbul, for this Muslim site is compatible with the spirit of his disimmigrational teaching.

In the aforementioned scene where the father refuses to speak to his son because the young man had rebuked him with a sensitive remark, namely "How do you know? You can't even read," Réda starts the engine, drives on, and lets his father decide which branch of the splitting road to take. Later on, stuck at a fork, the old man looks up at the sky, and the spectator wonders if he is trying to make use of some knowledge of astronomy. After reading the signs from above, the father, who has the last word—in addition to the first, for that matter, since Réda will not be asked to express his point of view—decides that they will spend the night right there. Thus, the father has remapped the route yet again. The father's strategies on the mountaintop, as well as at the fork in the road, succeed in bringing Réda back to the wheel. The pillars of Réda's French education not only are put to the test but are also discarded when they prove ineffective. Indeed, the young man's reading skills are ignored. His ability to express himself in French and his rudimentary English do not allow him to make himself understood. When Réda stops the car to ask a local for directions to Sofia, the middle-aged man responds to Réda's question ("Do you speak French?") with *Da* (Yes). Instead of being rebuked by the stranger's obvious sign that he actually does not speak French, Réda formulates his question this time in English: "The way to Sofia, please?" Réda listens to the foreigner's long tirade in a language neither Réda nor his father can speak. The father then asks his son if he has grasped the man's directions to which the young man answers "No." This directs the father to respond, annoyed, "Well, then, what are you waiting for?" thus prompting him to keep driving. This scene, among others, furthers the old man's argument that his son's Western knowledge is without practical function. It is Réda who does not know how to read this kind of situation and therefore does not realize that he is wasting his time, because the foreigner is not going to guide him anywhere. Though the father does not read (the monolingual language of his son), he leads. An illustration of this is the money-changing scene examined by Mireille Rosello in her article "Ismaël Ferroukhi's Babelized Road Movie," in which the son, bewildered, watches his father nonchalantly change money illegally with a hawker, all through nonverbal communication.[32] The father is somehow a polyglot—he can interact with almost everyone they meet, in one way or another.

The old man excels at showing that he knows best by getting them where they need to go and by dealing with locals effortlessly. The father teaches his son by virtue of example. He successfully proves that his son's abilities to read and to speak "international" English, for instance, are not able to outsmart the old man's savoir faire. Even though Réda has been at the wheel, it is his father who has been steering all the way. This becomes evident in a scene after the travelers have crossed the French-Italian border and Réda insists on disobeying his father by continuing to drive late into the night. The father feels his authority is being threatened and so he pulls the handbrake while they are going full speed on the highway at night. It is not because he fears for his son's lack of sleep that the old man takes it upon himself to stop the car, since, as Réda tells his father, he nearly got them both killed. For the father, to risk death is preferable to losing control.

However, the progress that the old man hopes his son will make toward Arabness is threatened by the intrusion of Mustapha (Jacky Nercessian), a Turkish guide who, after offering to help Réda complete customs formalities, unexpectedly seats himself in the backseat of the car without being invited. With the arrival of Mustapha, the father's lead is put to the test. The Turkish protagonist volunteers French directions to his house—a place that was not on the father's map—and then to local sites of interest—a touristic deviation from the father's plan. The Turkish guide is regarded by the father not only as an unexpected distraction but also as a rude intrusion into his instruction. Mustapha has all the characteristics of an intruder as described by Jean-Luc Nancy:

> The intruder [*L'intrus*] enters by force, through surprise or ruse, in any case without the right and without having first been admitted. There must be something of the *intrus* in the stranger; otherwise, the stranger would lose its strangeness: if he already has the right to enter and remain, if he is awaited and received without any part of him being unexpected or unwelcome, he is no longer the *intrus,* nor is he any longer the stranger. It is thus neither logically acceptable, nor ethically admissible, to exclude all intrusion in the coming of the stranger, the foreign.[33]

By and large, the father was looking more and more relaxed as he and his son traveled further away from France. But Mustapha's arrival threatens to reverse the father's disimmigration tactic and return Réda back to France. Accusing Mustapha of stealing his savings is part of the father's plan to get rid of the undesirable newcomer. Mustapha's "strangeness" (read "intrusiveness") lies not so much in the fact that he is a Turk but rather that his binationalism includes Frenchness, which enables him to speak to Réda about his French ex-wife, thus resuscitating memories of Réda's French girlfriend and his ties to France. Up to that point, no other character was able to speak French to the two travelers. The Turk's incongruity manifests itself less in his liberal views of Islam than in the fact that the father begins to fear a reversal of methodology from a Francophone third party. Indeed, Mustapha encourages the young man to order a beer by telling Réda the story of a Sufi who had been seen drinking wine. Mustapha's anecdote implies that the Islamic faith does not prohibit the consumption of alcohol, but that it is excesses that it condemns. It is also Mustapha's recommendations of places to visit that lead Réda into the licentious milieu of a cabaret where he meets the belly dancer that he brings to the hotel, to his father's dismay.

Once more, the old man does not reprimand the son for what he views as a momentary deviation from the path. It is a break, not in the sense of a rupture or ending but rather as an intermission in his mission. What actually counts is that Réda continue tagging along. And this is exactly what he is shown doing in the very next scene. The father walks out of the hotel in the morning. Réda follows the patriarch, driving the car slowly, begging him to get back into the car and asking for forgiveness. In a moment of desperation, Réda decides to play the religion card, in order to rejoin his father on their journey. He exclaims: "Don't they practice forgiveness in your religion?" as if he were making explicit his understanding that religion is both a pretext and pretest for the success of a disimmigratory endeavor. But what Réda is oblivious to is that the old man's itinerary by foot has caused the son to follow him blindly by car all the way to the outskirts of the city. Réda's motor and fuel is none other than his father, who knows full well that he will get back into the car no matter what Réda says. Therefore, his packing his suitcase and leaving alone is just a ploy, for his son cannot allow him to resume the trip by himself. The young man's objectionable behavior is marginal to the essence and primary goal of the voyage, namely, to keep Réda embarked on a continued journey toward disimmigration.

Throughout *Le Grand voyage,* religious moments are used to present the viewer with a story about disimmigration, and this is especially so as the characters near Mecca. This film introduces two characters presented as prototypes, in that these two men, who can easily be compared to major symbols in the Muslim religion, are two leading personages in the concept of disimmigration. Indeed, in the context of hajj, the sacrifice of a lamb is a common ritual, commemorating the substitution of a lamb sent from God in place of Abraham's son. In the film, a lamb is bought in order to provide sustenance for Réda, who had been complaining that had his father refrained from giving alms, they would have had something to eat other than the egg sandwiches they had been having far too often. Shortly thereafter, the father exchanges a camera for a lamb. This transaction symbolizes a felicitous and long-expected trade, that of media for tradition, trading away their victimhood at the hands of Westernized culture and ritualistically transposing the status of victim onto the lamb—another scapegoat, so to speak. But the animal manages to turn tail and escape the men's grip. As a result, the slaughtering never takes place. Both the religiously mandated sacrifice and the slaughtering for the purpose of a more sustainable diet never occur. Basing his storyline on Muslim stock, Ferroukhi offers new possibilities through the disappearance of the sacrificial creature from the screen. This shifts the focus to the two default sacrificial scapegoats, thus offering the viewer a twist to the religious story. The slippage from one thematic or contextual layer to another is a trademark of the film. In accordance with the movie's signature, the religious narrative leaves room for another layer of interpretation of the plot, which has been woven throughout the film, that of disimmigration. Indeed, the father and the sons are guinea pigs (sacrificial creatures) for the cause of disimmigration. As pioneer characters, they attempt to enact a ritual cleansing of their status of émigrés and lead the way for generations to come. The father incarnates the messianic character who sacrifices himself to unburden the missed obligations of a whole generation. In so doing, he patches the hole in the intergenerational continuum of cultural transmission, which emigration to France has caused.

In turn, Réda is a volunteered sacrificial entity. He was forced to commit to this trip by coming with. He was "chosen" among two brothers, just as in the Islamic tradition Ishmael was selected over Isaac for the ultimate sacrifice, which would have consisted of Abraham's slaughtering of a son as the expression of his obedience to God, which Réda's father is about to commemorate symbolically, by severing Réda from his routine in exchange for a life-changing trip.[34] Moreover, Réda's act of driving is passive. In actuality, he does not drive but is driven instead. He is abducted in order to be conducted. He is a volunteered candidate, so to speak, "directed" to the sacred locus of sacrifice.

Shifting Gears: Migration in Reverse

Both protagonists are from North Africa, either by birth, in the case of the father, or through lineage, in the case of the son. Nevertheless, the film frames the trip to Mecca as a "return" in various ways, for both the father and the son. Indeed, the place they are about to set foot on, Mecca, is the city that the first community of persecuted Muslim converts left in the sixth century CE in order to live their new creed peacefully and to spread their religion. This event is called the *Hijra,* or *Hejira,* which means "emigration" in Arabic. Therefore, any Arab/Muslim who lives away from Mecca is by definition a migrant—not necessarily an economic migrant (émigré) but a diasporic individual. This condition is due not only to a historical connection and/or a religious affiliation but also to heritage. Traveling to Mecca is therefore a return to an origin. Since there can only be one origin, the only veritable homecoming Réda can undertake is to Mecca, regardless of his faith in God, which remains questionable. Indeed, the return does not have to be presented along religious lines. Being a Muslim, Réda is de facto a migrant/diasporic being—certainly not in relation to France, his country of birth—but undoubtedly to Mecca, the place of Hijra, the site of departure of his ancestors.[35] The men's voyage is a return to what is both Arab and Muslim, since what is known today as Saudi Arabia is the country of origin of Islam, as well as of the Arab Diaspora.

By dying in Saudi Arabia, the father comes back home, for the Ka'aba is God's home (*bayt Allah*). The father and the other pilgrims attest to this return as they approach the holy site, chanting:[36]

> Here I am, O Allah. Here I am.
> Here I am. No partner hast Thou; here I am.
> Truly the praise and the beneficence are Thine, so is the Kingdom
> No partner hast Thou; here I am.

Réda comes back home as well. It may be argued that in the context of North African immigration, the expression "return home" applies exclusively to migrants who settled in France and had planned to return to where they came from after their stay abroad. This seems logical; nevertheless, it is not unusual for *Beurs* to express this type of nostalgic return in analogous terms. *Beur* literature and cinema have provided us with representations of such views, including Houda Rouane's novel *Pieds-Blancs* (2006) and Mehdi Charef's 2002 film *La Fille de Keltoum / Bent Keltoum (Keltoum's Daughter)*. Réda's journey is also a return because, while he is not a practicing Muslim, he is a cultural Muslim. Though this assertion might be challenged by Réda himself, the young man has inherited Muslim practices and, even if he should choose to deviate from them, he will still be assumed by his community and the world at large to be a Muslim.[37] Furthermore, as an Arab, Réda's place of origin can be traced back to Saudi Arabia where he is destined to return in a physical fashion by way of a symbolic journey.

Reconnecting the son to Arabia is an act of disimmigration, a return to an essential belonging and, as such, a remolding of identity. The old man comes back in order to retrace the path of his predecessors, through the pretense of the ancestral ritual of the pilgrimage and the historical displacements of his own people. The father reenacts a historical story through a spiritual ritual, which, in the context of global migration, is a reverse act of migration. In spite of his alleged cartographic illiteracy, the father's directional instructions enable him to withdraw his son from France's grasp by redrawing the geographic itinerary of Arabs from the Arabian Peninsula to France in the context of nineteenth- and twentieth-century migrations from the Maghreb. He traces his trajectory of reverse migration from France where Arab migration ended, to the Arabian Peninsula where it started. He also does this in order to inscribe his own imagined direction of flow, which aims at dismantling deep-rooted trends and preconceptions. Ferroukhi's intention is to play with the idea in order to provoke his audience to rethink Maghrebi migration and migrants, as well as *Beur* descendants, in light of an imagined ex-centric migration, in which France would be out of the picture.

We will see in the following chapter that the conception of an ex-centric migratory pattern not only is possible but is in fact already taking place. This situation becomes clear in the context of *Le Grand voyage,* which is unique in that it is an original departure—both physically and conceptually. The death of the father, which occurs in the next to last scene, represents a significant topical innovation in *Beur* and Maghrebi filmmaking as well. North African travels through Eastern Europe, the Near and Middle East, is also a thematic novelty in *Beur* and banlieue cinema, which may begin soon to tackle another type of "new migration," as experts have called it—that of European nationals to Syria and neighboring countries at war, recruited for the *Jihad*. The same is true for hajj. As Michel Cadé rightly remarks, "The fifth pillar of Islam is rarely evoked in French cinema other than by its name, hadj, employed occasionally in the characterization of a few pious characters, or more recently as a secondary plot in *Dans la vie*. So, making the pilgrimage the subject of the film [*Le Grand voyage*] was audacious to say the least."[38]

The film is to be commended for the ex-centric scenario it presents. Indeed, instead of focusing on the experiences of North African migrants and their descendants in France, it chooses to focus on unusual (eccentric) experiences at the margin of the ex-centered traditional migratory poles of France and the Maghreb. *Le Grand voyage* revisits questions of identity by placing the story alongside the axis of France and Saudi Arabia, two highly symbolical and historical nodes in this regard. France not only is removed from its privileged status of point of arrival for Maghrebi immigrants, it also loses its status of "center" in all senses of the term. Indeed, Mecca is at the center of the film via its symbol, the Ka'aba where the father and son are headed. In turn, contrary to the majority of *Beur* films thus far, *Le Grand voyage* does not take place exclusively in France. Instead, from the very first scenes, this film follows two protagonists as they keep driving away from the French hexagon. All in all, France has turned into merely a place to leave.

The amount of time devoted to France is minimal, as it appears only in the first few minutes of *Le Grand voyage*. Ferroukhi could have opted to film a father and a son starting their trip from a Parisian banlieue; instead, Réda and his family are residents of a village located in southeast France. *Le Grand voyage* is therefore conveniently excused from allotting more time to France—the two protagonists drive a few miles before arriving in Italy—as if the director wished to convey the message that France has already taken up enough space in the men's lives. As a matter of fact, once the two men have left France, the film never shows them back in the French hexagon. Whereas France is hardly visible, Mecca is omnipresent in the lives of all the characters, even in those who do not partake in the journey, for they know and speak of it. Mecca is mentioned from the beginning, and from that point onward it becomes increasingly present as the characters disimmigrate in their travels toward it, until finally it appears on the screen. It is ultimately shown exclusively and unusually close, to the point of being magnified by its own magnificence. Indeed, the father is attracted to the Ka'aba in the heart of Mecca like a mesmerized *amant* (lover), pulled by a kind of *aimant* (magnet), to the point of being oblivious of his son. The latter tries in vain to get his father's attention. The old man follows his fellow-pilgrims while remaining deaf to his son's farewell, which starts as a statement and turns—through intonation—into a question posed twice: "I'll leave you here. See you tonight. See you tonight?" The statement begs a response, but instead it turns into a rhetorical question, for his father never replies. In symbiosis with a group of men and women, who move forward in a centripetal fashion, as if swallowed by an invisible force, the father walks on, with his undivided attention on the Ka'aba, in a scene that could well be the director's vision of a soul called to (re)unite with his Creator.

In 2001, Yamina Benguigui released *Inch'Allah dimanche,* a film in which Zouina (Fejria Deliba), a young mother, leaves her relatives in Algeria to join her émigré husband in France. She is accompanied by her two young sons and her daughter, as well as her mother-in-law. The film starts with a shot of the port of Algiers bathed in an almost blinding white that spreads from the sun, to the walls of the Haussmannian buildings lining the lower boulevard of the capital, and finally to the ferry. In the next scene, the vivid whiteness is replaced by the dull grayness of St. Quentin, the small French town where Zouina is to reside. Gray is the color of everything from the clouds to the station's clock to the van in which her husband arrives. Interestingly, in the two films, final destinations are depicted in a different light, literally and figuratively. Whereas in *Inch'Allah dimanche,* France offers a shady welcome, so to speak, it is Mecca's white that greets the newcomers in *Le Grand voyage.* For Réda's father, the crowded religious site, the endless flows of people, and the bright whiteness of the pilgrims' garments reflecting a scorching sun are not seen as burdensome as France, which the two men left perhaps forever. While Mecca is depicted as crowded, it is also presented as a place of easy and liberating flow. The people are numerous, but they are shown walking without bumping into each other, with no need for directions, at peace with themselves.

The shot of the Ka'aba in *Le Grand voyage* is unique in that Ferroukhi obtained special permission to film the holy perimeter from inside. The showing of the Ka'aba is common in televised religious programs across the Muslim world but not in commercial features—let alone in a film coproduced with a Western country, France, which, to top it off, was intended for an eclectic audience across nationalities and faiths (and lack thereof). Ferroukhi's project of inviting Mecca into the film is a sign of Mecca's welcoming of Réda and his father into her womb—and tomb, in the case of the father—thus reasserting her legitimate claim of motherhood. In Arabia, the two men are stripped of their label of France's émigrés and invited to become like everybody else, Arabia's returnees. The old father is an émigré-turned-émigré, but given that he is a returnee he is actually an émigré-turned-native. So is the case for Réda in the sense of his Muslim heritage. Like all other pilgrims, including Saudis, the father is clad in conventional attire. He trades his Western suit for the customary pilgrim's two pieces of white unsewn material to be tied around the body. Through this act, he also signifies his acceptance of his new identity—of hājj (an honorific title and a much coveted status among Muslims)—which supersedes his previous identity of economic migrant. His ritualistic act of shedding his old garment symbolizes his parting with his status as France's immigrant. Though, administratively speaking, he is a foreigner in Saudi Arabia, he is there as a returnee to the house of God where all pilgrims share the same rank. The sartorial transformation signals a change of status not only from that of sinner to that of hājj but for characters such as Réda's father, from émigré in France to ex-émigré out of France. Réda's resistance to this change and Mecca's welcome is evidenced by his entering the Ka'aba's vicinity with his cargo pants and yellow T-shirt, clothes he would wear back in France. The young man stands out as atypical in the homogenous crowd of pilgrims in their near-identical outfits. The son's attire allowed him to blend into French/Western culture, but in this setting it actually sets him apart. This scene asks a set of questions in relation to the concept of identity, namely, what happens when you are socially simulating to fit in and then are thrown into a totally distinct social arena where your mimicked behaviors in fact make you different because they were not your organic behaviors to begin with (but rather copied in order to homogenize)? This reversal can cause a great identity crisis. How do you behave? Do you identify with your old behaviors or do you strive to imitate the ways of the new setting?

The old man leads his son into a process that consists of reintroducing him to his Arabness, to which he is entitled. This project runs counter to Réda's outlook and cultural upbringing, as imposed by the media and various French institutions. The *bildungsfilm* is a way to recenter the lost son. As a matter of fact, we are shown that in Saudi Arabia, the center of the Muslim world, Réda is lost among the pilgrims who chant in unison while they circle the Ka'aba peacefully; meanwhile, he is unable to revolve harmoniously like those around him, and instead he physically struggles through the crowd, calling for his father: "Excuse me. Excuse me. Excuse me. . . . Out of the way! Excuse me. I'm looking for my father. Excuse me! Let me through! Excuse me! I'm looking for my father! Let me through. Let go of me! I'm looking for my father. Let go of me! I'm looking for my father!" In this scene, the dialogue is limited, but each statement is repeated a few times, and each repetition helps to take the deceptively simple text to a symbolical level. The young man cries out that he is searching for his father three times. He obviously is looking for his literal father, but his desperate cries reveal the deeper, figurative levels of his search. Paraphrased, Réda's statement first signifies that he is crying out for the land of his fathers, and for a connection with those around him. Then, it implies that the only link he has with his land is his father. And lastly, it connotes that Réda is looking for what his father represents or what he has brought him here for: disimmigration. The son is unable to communicate with pilgrims, nor is he able to commune with them. He does not speak the linguistic and spiritual languages of this plural Other, who speak in one voice by repeating the same religious formulae as a united entity. Réda being lost in the Ummah authorizes the director to show what is lacking in Réda. Indeed, in the Ummah or Community he is supposed to belong to, he neglects the "common" and "unity" to which he is supposed to adhere. Instead, Réda is by himself, missing in his attributed community while feeling himself a hostage of it. He begs, "let go of me" while he is shown surrounded and unable to move about freely. At the same time, he begs for the Ummah's forgiveness. As he aggressively makes his way through the crowd, he relentlessly asks to be "pardoned" as he tries to push people aside. Réda becomes aware that he is misbehaving and that he has misbehaved all along—hence his disimmigrational journey. Now he is about to miss his father, who is missing and will soon be missing forever. This trial scene is to encourage the young man to enter the (Muslim) Community via a payment.[39] The disappearance of his father—a representative of the Community—is a symbolic sign of his pressing contribution. By the same token, Réda is "hosted," or embraced by the Ummah, in that he is surrounded by a crowd that does not do him harm. The pilgrims are unperturbed by the presence of Réda, even as he fights against their circumambulation of the Ka'aba. Ultimately, he cannot change their flow and must move according to their motions. The young man's struggles against the crowd highlight the paradox of his marginal position in the Muslim Community. The pilgrims think of him as belonging, and they accept him into the holy perimeter even as he resists them. But the scene also indicates to the viewer that Réda has begun his own process of reverse migration. He is alone now after the death of his father, who passes to his son the torch of disimmigration, the lesson he had been teaching him throughout their journey together. In the next shot, Réda is taken away by two men in uniform. One could easily first think that he is being escorted to jail by two officials through a dim corridor, but one soon realizes that the two men are part of the staff and are taking him to the local morgue so that he may identify his father, who is lying on the floor with other deceased pilgrims.

Just as in Benguigui's *Inch'Allah dimanche*, *Le Grand voyage* includes a scene early in the film in which relatives see the two travelers off as they expatriate. This well-wishing sequence is expected in Maghrebi cinema that focuses on the experience of border crossing and exile. Departure involves members of an entire family or community because an individual departure is a communitarian operation, as it deprives the group of one of its constitutive elements. However, one of the differences between the two cinematic narratives is that *Inch'Allah dimanche* is concerned with a nascent immigrant community in France whereas *Le Grand voyage* revolves around an established Maghrebi community and its French children. Another crucial difference is that the farewell sequence takes place in Algeria in *Inch'Allah dimanche* and in France in *Le Grand voyage*. Furthermore, while both farewells are of a communitarian nature, they are of different sorts. In *Inch'Allah dimanche,* the community weeps. In *Le Grand voyage,* though there is a palpable anxiety in the community concerning the outcome of a potentially eventful road trip, many are elated that the old man is on his way to accomplish a holy act. Indeed, in *Inch'Allah dimanche,* a mother and her daughter part in tears, separated by the recently implemented 1974 French Family Reunion Law that allows only the daughter and grandchildren to emigrate in order to reunite with the head of the household. The old mother is shown behind the bars of a fence at the port, as if she were in prison. A customs officer pulls the daughter away from her screaming mother, who finally gives up and faints. In *Le Grand voyage,* leave-taking is not imposed upon the father. It is celebrated as a willed departure.

In Ferroukhi's film, the migratory phenomenon is filmed in reverse at various levels. The film starts with a good-bye scene in France and ends with the arrival of the travelers in Saudi Arabia. Besides being shot backward, in the sense that we are presented with a farewell scene at the beginning of the film and a greeting shot near the end, the migratory act appears as an event that is meant to turn the concept of migration around. The film originates at the historical end of this case of Arab migration. It works its way back to beginnings in order to initiate the ending of misconceptions surrounding issues of migration. With this trip comes a revisiting of the concept of migration itself, for the émigré is not who he is "supposed" to be, namely, a labor-migrant who is "seen merely as a working body, a being without history, culture, or professional qualifications."[40] Never in the film does Réda express his wish to become a "labor-migrant," though the region he lives in is home to a large community of North African blue-collar workers. Instead, his insisting on taking the *baccalauréat* exam is an indication that Réda is aiming at securing a better future for himself. Most likely he is hoping to take on a nonmanual profession, reaching the higher status of white collar, which the French society often fails to equate with the *Beur* and Maghrebi communities.

The old man will attempt to reverse the spell, the curse, and the direction of Maghrebi immigration altogether. The project takes the shape of a derouting process. And yet, his father must be *dérouté,* as the French has it, namely, "unsettled," for he moved to France for the promise of a better life for his children—the original idea behind the Maghrebis' migration to France in the first place was indeed a search for better living conditions for themselves and their families. To reconnect his son with his roots is a natural dream, but what—logistically—is the father's new plan for Réda? Where does he want him to go once his bonds with France are broken? And do what? The film does not provide the answers to these legitimate questions. It simply poses them and lets the father exit the narrative and leave his son's life hanging. Though not distinct, the derouting plan to replace an unsatisfactory situation unfolds in various ways, for the father ordains their route by saying that they will not follow the map. Therefore, the old man destabilizes his son's sense of orientation by disorienting him in order to re-Orient him, so to speak. By derouting a migratory scheme, the father also deroots it through his choice of Mecca instead of Morocco. In so doing, the father not only undertakes a preventive conservation of what is left of his son's Arabness but also shows the viewer that his son may not be misconstrued as being part of a generation of immigrants. To deroute is to rewrite. It is also to re-map. In this light, the old man rewrites his own story and the history of emigration. He paves the way for new discourses to emerge. The character of the father deconstructs a debasing rhetoric in order to better position his son, or to place him in a more comfortable situation by having him embrace his Arabness or at least let go of his exclusive Frenchness, which he views as hostile and/or inhospitable. This destabilizing method is meant to shake the young man out of his status of *Beur,* which is often amalgamated with that of Maghrebi migrant.

The father brings his son back into a new center, away from the illusions that his status as *Beur* has woven, back to a place where he can make an informed decision about his own life—whatever that may be. The idea is a meditative one, that is to say that instead of making decisions from momentum, to instead move to a place of centeredness, the place of pivot where Réda may reflect on his options and make his choice accordingly. The father's initiative is explained by the fact that immigration decentered the father and his family, turning them into marginalized individuals in French society. It rejected them to its periphery, both literally (the banlieue where the family lives) and figuratively (their cultural status). In what I dub "para-community," the father reappropriates his marginalization by marginalizing himself further.[41] He leaves France before France kicks him out completely. Put simply, he kills two birds with one stone, so to speak, in that his anticipatory and preventive extreme measure is associated with his religiously mandated pilgrimage, which sets the stage for his ex-centeredness. Mecca is the center for Muslims both spiritually and physically. All of the pilgrims focus their undivided attention on the Ka'aba and literally gravitate around it.

Resetting the Countdown: *Désimmigrance* and the Zero Degree of Migration

The experiences of these two protagonists are those of the generations they symbolize. Indeed, whereas the father is not named, Réda also happens to be the name of the main character in a previous short film directed by the same director. And it so happens that both films tackle the issue of *Beur* identity among Franco-French individuals and Maghrebi parents. The death of the father seems to have a broader implication. It is an indication that the generation of Maghrebi immigrants is dying and that their children are left to fend for themselves. The latter are compelled to choose their destiny between an inherited past and a future that is certainly uncertain but dominated by a globalized Western world. When Réda is filmed in fetal position next to his father's corpse, which he has just identified, it is a clear sign that Réda is being reborn. He does nothing but cry, like a child in the first moments of its life. It is as if the director wanted to convey the unfolding of a case of metempsychosis, not of a person but of a thought, the message of a leader being passed on to the next of kin. It is now up to Réda to take the lead and give migration, integration, and identity a new beginning, a new meaning, a new direction.

Stirred, moved, and sad, Réda's rigid composure and naïve perceptions of who he and his father were have been shaken up. It is only after death has closed the father's eyes that Réda's open in their own awakening. In the scene following the father's death, Réda gives money to a beggar—an act for which he had previously scolded his father. Then Réda gets back in the back seat of a cab as if his new journey may require stops along the way, during which the young man will put into practice the teachings of his late father. Réda is no longer the driver, signifying that his training has ceased, and he has reached the end of his lesson in disimmigration. Neither totally part of the community yet, nor excluded from it because he has entered the sacred perimeter of the Ka'aba, Réda is an illustrative example of Derrida's *destinerrance*. The message indeed is that the young man is destined to err—both words are contained in the philosopher's neologism, along with "wandering," as Derrida makes clear in *The Post Card*—rather than follow blindly the French way and the way to France. Réda has experienced a mysterious epiphany. His head leans slightly out of the cab's window, his eyes are closed, and his hair flows freely in the wind. This image shows Réda in the momentary peace of catharsis, before the next obstacles of his life unfold, wherein he will have to decide what to do with the lessons he has learned and how to reconsider his own identity.

Ismaël Ferroukhi and Hassan Legzouli (see chapter 6) present us with immigrants who are no longer immigrants not only because they have passed away, but also because they are buried outside of France. Before they passed on, these aging individuals insisted via their eccentric requests to remove their immigrant status by returning to a symbolical, spiritual, and original "home." The deaths work to constitute a new schema, as if death were the only way out of a vicious and fallacious cycle.

In these closing notes, I would like to examine what else the powerful concluding scenes of *Le Grand voyage* may tell us. Is the parting of the Arabophone Muslim father with his Francophone French son in Saudi Arabia a commentary on the possible renewal of a Muslim inner self? Or could this be a comment on the symbolic rebirth or revival of French Islam, or simply the sudden interest of Réda (and every spectator he represents) not only in the religion of the father but also in his language and culture? How will the son identify himself with regard to his heritage and inherited religion? The death of Réda's father marks the end of a cycle and the closure of the paradigm of the "first" generation of émigrés. It is after the two relatives have stopped migrating that the film delivers its message, when an instance of ex-centric migration has taken place. The father's soul has migrated to other horizons, and his body has relocated to a new country. Disimmigration is a return to the ground zero of North African migration, whereby a man who finds his last home away from France is leaving his son stranded, as if to offer him the possibility of keeping his distance—physically and/or otherwise—from his country of birth. The pilgrim is presented as a possible model to follow, a messenger who speaks in a coded fashion. As for the son, he has been selected to speak the language of the father, that of disintegration and disimmigration, in other words, the subversive language of dissent. The affecting ending of the father may allow for Réda's rebirth.

This presentation of a potential new host place may be interpreted as a condemnation of the recent drastic closing of borders, which turn erstwhile host countries into additional stones to Fortress Europe unable (or unwilling?) to offer hopes of a better future, not only to prospective migrants from the other shore of the Mediterranean but also for the established Maghrebi community in Europe, as well as to many of their constituents in limbo between identities. *Le Grand voyage* urges us to consider the pressing need for a discourse not about immigration or so-called second, third, and fourth generations of immigrants, but rather about the sense of disbelonging among French citizens and residents that leads more and more individuals toward disimmigration.

2　"Burning the Sea"

Clandestine Migration across the Mediterranean in Francophone Moroccan Illiterature

> The Mediterranean is a fracture . . . because it is meant to be one and because it is sailed to and fro by warships aligned against civil rafts . . .
>
> —Ali Bensaâd, "La Méditerranée, un mur en devenir?"

OVER THE LAST four decades, a series of French anti-immigration laws have caused many Maghrebis hoping to immigrate to turn to Spain instead, first as a country of transit, and more recently, as a possible country of settlement. After Spain entered the EU in 1986, however, it too began to enforce stringent immigration policies. In 1991, these laws ended the Moroccans' privilege of entering the country without a visa. In 1998, Spain implemented the Sistema Integrado de Vigilancia Exterior (Integrated System of External Surveillance, or SIVE), a technologically advanced surveillance apparatus that lines the Spanish coasts. By establishing this electronic wall, European authorities hoped to fight clandestine immigration into Spain, as Spain has become a gateway for immigrants to make their way to other European countries.

Since the 1990s, there has been a sharp increase in literary accounts that center on clandestine migration from North Africa to destinations across the Western Mediterranean.[1] The prevalence of this theme at the end of the twentieth century coincides with the closing of Europe's doors to new human migratory flows.

Illiterature: At the Fault Line or in the Front Line?

The "militarization" and "fortification" measures put in place in the Mediterranean basin have forced migrants to travel along clandestine routes.[2] Accounts of Maghrebi clandestine migration to Europe are broadcast widely in print and electronic media. Concurrently, fictional accounts on the matter published in French have grown considerably; literary analyst Katarzyna Pieprzak aptly writes that "clandestine migration has produced a new terrain in Moroccan literature."[3] Interestingly, as social scientist Jørgen Carling has pointed out, "unauthorized border-crossing in the Mediterranean region has received extensive media coverage, but little academic attention."[4] In this chapter, I will examine Francophone literary representations of clandestine migration from North Africa into Spain. This growing body of literature I propose calling *illiterature*.[5]

As Carling remarks, although the label *illegal* is avoided by most international agencies and many academics, it is the "standard term in Spanish media and politics."[6] Carling lists a number of adjectives in circulation that designate unconventional migrational patterns such as *irregular* and *unauthorized*. In his article, he opts for the second term. In this chapter and throughout the book, I will employ *clandestine*. I call the previously unidentified new terrain of writing *illiterature* so as to make a deliberate compression of *illegal* and *literature*, in order to reappropriate illegality, as well as to highlight how the characters of this subgenre circumvent anti-immigration laws. Additionally, illiterature draws attention to the issue of clandestine emigration originating in the global South and particularly African countries, which in some cases complicates the government-sponsored images of these places as tourist havens. I will focus exclusively on the case of North Africa. The character and voice of illiterature unfolds, moreover, in the unpacking of its name. First of all, the literature carries "ill"-ness at its core, for it often features sickly characters before, during, or after a journey. Its Mediterranean authors, whether they hail from the northern or southern rim of the sea, show a patent empathy for a Maghreb caught in countless ill effects of globalization. Tahar Ben Jelloun, for instance, in *Partir* introduces us to the character of Malika, who works as a *fille-gambas* (prawn-girl) in a local factory and whose health deteriorates as she processes a product that is destined for the world market. The homonym *île*-literature ("island"-literature) refers to the socioeconomic isolation felt by many (North) African youth who would risk life and limb to desert the "island" for the chance of a better life abroad.[7] This homonym also denotes Europe's isolation to the point of becoming an island—a point of view shared by Bensaâd: "Europe . . . cowers into a paranoid and Eurocentrist vision where it sees itself as a "fatal island" in an ocean of misery. . . ."[8] For the time being, *il*-literature ("he"-literature) is gender-specific. To date, Laila Lalami's book, published in English, *Hope and Other Dangerous Pursuits,* constitutes a rare example of fiction on clandestine migration produced by a Maghrebi female writer. This confirms that illiterature is, so far, a male-dominated domain. Lastly, *illiterate*-ture teases out the phonetically close *illiteracy* of many migrants to France that prompted *Beurs* to write about the migratory experiences of their parents, the difference being that, in illiterature, the experiences of clandestine migrants have replaced those of legal émigrés for the most part.

Representatives of Moroccan illiterature include Youssef Amghar's *Il était parti dans la nuit* (2004), Moulay Hachem El Amrani's *Hmidou el emigrante* (2001), Nasser-Eddine Bekkai Lahbil's *Le Détroit ou le voyage des vaincus* (1995), Ahmed Bouchikhi's *Le Cimetière des illusions* (2006), El Driss's *Vivre à l'arrache* (2006), Hocein Faraj's *L'Aller et le retour* (2001), Rachid El Hamri's *Le Néant bleu* (2005), Salim Jay's *Tu ne traverseras pas le détroit* (2001), Youssef Jebri's *Le Man-uscrit d'Hicham, destinées marocaines* (2007), Youcef M. D.'s *Je rêve d'une autre vie* (2002), and Hamid Skif's *La Géographie du danger* (2006). It is worth mentioning that, because of its primary concern with Mediterranean clandestine crossings, il-literature also features other national literatures, such as Algerian, Tunisian, French, Spanish, and Italian.[9] Indeed, Algerian writer Boualem Sansal, in *Dis-moi le paradis* and *Harraga,* and Tunisian Fawzi Mellah, in *Clandestin en Méditerranée,* both tackle the topic. The phenomenon is addressed in novels written in Arabic as well, such as Moroccan Youssef Fadel's *Haschich*. We will see later that *Beur* literature has also begun to explore the issue of Mediterranean clandestine crossings. In addition, Spanish illiterature is booming. Among Maghrebis, Moroccans have taken the lead in literary productions surrounding clandestine intercontinental crossings. Ironically, many of the fictional narratives imagining the hidden pas-sage claim to compete with the "factual" renderings of the phenomenon that circulate in European mass media and, more recently, in Maghrebi newspapers and television programs. Various literary productions have denounced these "factual" accounts for serving as fodder for conservative positions with respect to the control of "illegal" migration in the Mediterranean.

By looking at the works of three Moroccan Francophone writers, Tahar Ben Jelloun, Youssouf Amine Elalamy, and Mahi Binebine, I will examine how Moroccan *illiteraturists* have reacted against, and offered an alternative to, monolithic narratives in mass media and politics concerning clandestine mi-gration.[10] Through an analysis of three of their literary works, I intend to show that this particular subgenre of migrant literature is an instrument of political expression, in its denunciation of the criminalization of Moroccan immi-grants, the dehumanization present in the coverage of clandestine migration by the European and Moroccan press, and the "official suppression of discourse of the clandestine."[11]

Before beginning my analysis of particular works of illiterature, I will outline the underlying geopolitical forces at play in the region, for these have influenced illiterature in general. Indeed, the crucial location of the Mediterranean—between a rich Europe and a poor Africa—as well as the highly politicized and ideologized status of this sea and its surrounding territories, no longer as loci of exchanges but rather as sites to control, need to be examined to better understand what illitera-ture depicts and to what it reacts.[12]

Building New Borders to Consolidate Old Contested Identities

Spain's agenda to fight clandestine immigration on behalf of Europe was undertaken in part for identitarian purposes. Indeed, since it was also meant to be an "official closure to the discourse of Spain's 'difference' in Europe, exemplified in the French saying 'Africa begins at the Pyrenees,'" it has been a determined exclusionary identitarian struggle that has affected North Africa(ns) and the region at large.[13] The saying implies a "negative image of Spain as barbaric, uncivilized, and more akin to Africa than to Europe."[14] In this light, Europe's current anti-immigration agenda has provided Spain with an opportunity to frame a new identity at national, European, and international levels. In short, the Iberian Peninsula has used its ongoing fight against unwanted immigration to boost its Europeanness. This project was undertaken to expand Europe's border from the Pyrenees all the way around Spain's coastline in order to include its southern *comunidades autónomas,* notably Andalusia, a highly symbolic region, since it was the stronghold of Al-Andalus, a Muslim province in southern Europe from 711 to 1492. This southern region has suffered an additional layer of differentiation due to its struggling economies, which rely heavily on "first sector" activities such as agriculture, plus its alledgedly stronger ties with its historical and culturally Muslim past and supposed Berber identity.

SIVE not only marks a physical border along Spain's coasts where there used to be none, but it also stretches its functionality beyond the "belted" land. As cultural theorist Iain Chambers states, "Today, individual states and the European Union propose a complex system of filters and channels that stretch outward into extraterritorial space, both on the waters of the Mediterranean Sea and over the horizon into the Maghreb."[15] Ben Jelloun argues that SIVE is an insidious form of control that uses all possible avenues to achieve its objectives: "an electronic surveillance system along its beaches, with infrared and ultrasound equipment, ultra everything, along with automatic weapons."[16] Ben Jelloun's mocking description of the "ultra-everything" surveillance system conveys the idea that all means are put together to fight clandestine migration as efficiently as possible. Boualem Sansal remarks in a similarly ironic fashion that the most powerful walls may be those that do not resemble physical walls: "Not all [walls] are made of reinforced concrete. Luckily, surveillance satellites, electronic devices, biometry, laws, and campaign speeches make it possible to erect some that are invisible and therefore more efficient."[17]

Achille Mbembe confirms that "various centers of power might have authority over a single place, which might itself fall under the control of another place that was nearby, distant, or even imaginary."[18] The Strait of Gibraltar is a stretch of water surveilled by Spain (in concert with the EU), which exerts its control via the "distant" and "imaginary," and yet "nearby" and real SIVE. The latter acts as a phagocyte on the Moroccan shore, fending off foreign elements by intruding all the way into the African continent, thus ingesting the particular identities of its dreaded neighbors because "Europe . . . frequently feels secure only when purged of its 'foreign' bodies."[19] Mbembe adds that "these borders could shrink as a result of military defeats or be expanded through conquests or acquisitions."[20] Because of its present-day ruling of Ceuta and Melilla, two territories located in the northern Morocco, Spain has traced a continuation of its land ownership over the sea and into Morocco.[21] It has done so with the help of an electronic wall, as well as a steel and concrete wall, that surrounds Ceuta, which makes this coastline—along with the United States–Mexico border—one of two militarized borders in the Western world where no actual war is taking place.[22] Thus, it seems relevant to affirm that just like Spain, which has been a gateway to Europe for clandestine migrants from North Africa, the issue of clandestine migration has been a gateway to North Africa for Spain, and immigration has been used as a pretense for Europe to become involved in North African matters and sovereignty, a subtle point of entry into foreign affairs.

Morocco continues to advocate the "return" of Ceuta and Melilla, justifying its claim with the remark that it is no different than Spain's own petition with respect to its hopeful reintegration of Gibraltar. Up to this day, the two Spanish enclaves continue to negatively influence binational relations.[23] Is Spain adamant about retaining these two autonomous cities in North Africa because this situation allows it to install an additional physical border—not on continental Spain but rather in Morocco—as a reinforced layer of control? Nabiha Jerad argues that "the Mediterranean has become the first border post of Europe."[24] The border has indeed been displaced. After shifting from the Pyrenees down to the southern tip of the peninsula, it is fair to say that the border is continuously pushed as far south as possible, all the way down to the other side of the Mediterranean. This remote external border doubles as a layer of protection of Spain's Europeanness and, via the ultramodern wall, a way for conflicts, contested identities, and independentist claims to be kept away from the peninsula. The ongoing tensions that surround Ceuta and Melilla are cultivated by both countries. For Morocco, they distract international attention from its disputed occupation of the Western Sahara. For Spain, they justify an escalating militarization of the region.

The stakes are high, and Spain's presence in, around, and beyond its national confines are substantial, as displayed by SIVE, boats patrolling the sea, and escalating performances of power in the area. Contentious issues are influenced by Spain's presence in the Mediterranean. Thus, the sea has become an experimental space where decisions, debates, and laws are tried out in order to establish Europe's view of what the global North wants and what the global South will have to accept. A case in point is the long series of altercations between Spanish and

Moroccan fishermen and a number of diplomatic faux pas following disagreements on fishing agreements, protocols, and quotas. There was also the 2002 incident that took place on the uninhabited islet Leïla, located a few miles away from the Moroccan coast.[25] A small group of Moroccan soldiers pitched a flag of their country on the islet, allegedly because it was a hub for terrorist and contraband activities in addition to a stopping place for clandestine migrants. This act triggered the anger of the Spanish government, who framed the enterprise as an encroachment on their sovereignty, for they also claimed ownership of the "rock." The conflict resulted in North versus South alliances, which expressed an almost unanimous European condemnation of Morocco on one hand and an almost total support of Morocco's action by the Arab League on the other. The crisis ended with Spanish military forces dislodging the Moroccan Navy. This event reinforced the notion of a subregion, which acts as a lab site for the expansion of virtual and onsite presence, in other words, "imaginary" and yet "real" neocolonial European rule, in what Mbembe calls "interlaced spaces."[26]

Jean-Philippe Stassen's 2008 cartoon (Figure 2.1) is an original illustration showing the Moroccan and Spanish flags very close to each other. One effect of such a configuration is to stress the geographical proximity of the countries, as the accompanying text does as well. More importantly, given that these flags are placed where contested islets and enclaves such as Leïla, Melilla, and Ceuta are, the map subtly and effectively heightens the question as to where Spain ends and where Morocco begins. The reader is led to wonder what lands are owned by each country, and whether or not the kingdoms actually own shared property. Spain and Morocco once envisaged building a bridge between the two continents.[27] On June 16, 1979, the Spanish and Moroccan kings signed contracts that expressed their intentions of setting up a future infrastructure that would link both continents. In 1996, it was decided that a tunnel would be preferable to a bridge. Trains in the tunnel are scheduled to operate in 2025. In the meantime, it is SIVE that is in place. In turn, the strait has become a place of disputed propriety for some and a zone of power demonstrations for others.[28] As a country formerly depicted as a subaltern in a giant federated Europe, Spain now has the double responsibility to keep pace with the EU and to show its ability to fight clandestine immigration from Africa.[29] Spain's eventual inclusion into the EU after various failed attempts comes with a heavy sacrifice to which it has consented. In its new role as "guardian" of Europe's borders,[30] and in exchange for its inclusion in a supranational entity, Spain has inflicted a performative power grip upon its southern neighbor.

The Mediterranean has emerged as a privileged site for exploring global dynamics, containing both proximity and distance, constituting a link but also an obstacle, and a barrier. The lived consequences of the relentless European intrusion into North Africa, the constant European scrutiny, and the continued

Figure 2.1 Jean-Philippe Stassen's map of the Mediterranean, which focuses on the Strait of Gibraltar and contested territories. Used with permission.

discursive and military fragmentation of the Western Mediterranean have all inspired a new wave of literary accounts about clandestine migration. I contend that these narratives provide us with new means for binding the region together by bandaging a fractured physical, geopolitical, and discursive entity with accounts that advocate the connection of multiple Mediterraneans.[31]

Marginal Literatures: Ill Literatures

Illiterature relates to *littérature-monde* (world literature), a recently formed genre that has mobilized a considerable number of Francophone authors from outside the French métropole.[32] Indeed, this genre was a revolutionary vision that forty-four writers had and for which they wrote the manifesto "Pour une 'littérature-monde' en français."[33] Among the contributors are well-known names such as the aforementioned Ben Jelloun and Sansal, as well as Maryse Condé, Edouard Glissant, Nancy Houston, Alain Mabanckou, Gisèle Pineau, and Abdourahman A. Waberi. The collaborators advocate abandoning the "official francophonie," which according to Waberi "is nothing other than an appendage of the Elysée, deaf to the mutations of modernity," and therefore "is dying a beautiful death, for lack of sincere and popular adhesion from both shores of the Mediterranean."[34] The manifesto's signatories denounce a geographical divide, which stigmatizes their peripheral position vis-à-vis the French métropole and their ensuing relegation to the status of mere *annexés francophones* (Francophone-annexed individuals). In other words, they condemn the presence of a strict separation within the literature of French expression built along controversial identitarian lines, from which emerges a neocolonial project that establishes a segregationist boundary for writers from outside metropolitan France.[35]

In 2003, Winifred Woodhul acknowledged a burgeoning divergent trend in the Francophone literature of the Maghreb: "why should we persist in segregating the Francophone world from the rest of the planet in our thinking about literature and culture, particularly when the most interesting North African writers of our time are expressly drawing connections between North Africa and other parts of the world, and when so many North African literary scholars are living and writing in countries outside the French speaking world?"[36] She compellingly proposes that French, Francophone, and postcolonial studies rethink their positions in these terms:

> I believe that recent North African writing suggests some new directions not only for French/Francophone studies but for postcolonial studies generally, which have, by and large, focused on relations between a colonized or formerly colonized space and a corresponding imperial or neoimperial metropole, drawing on the centre-periphery model favoured in political theory of the 1960s and 1970s. In the age of transnationalism, it seems more fruitful to shift our sights and to look at both minoritarian writing's relations to an array of

"metropolitan" locations and its relations to other minoritarian spheres, that is, relations of margin to margin.[37]

Littérature-monde challenges the reader to think of literature in terms of a world stage, and not the author's country of origin, hence its name. In a globalized era where the world opens itself to some and closes its doors to others, the hyphen—what the French call *trait d'union* (union mark)—between *littérature* and *monde* unravels the various links that the world establishes with its surrounding environment. Due to its usage as a connector of the elements on both sides of the sign, this mark is used to convey more than a rapprochement between France and the world, because, in this case, it also highlights an obvious separation and the difficult merging of geopolitical entities. It draws attention to the marginal, to the borders that still separate those who hail from the "wrong" side of the sea, and to the growing wall that is being built.[38] The hyphen thickens as the borders stiffen. Internal European borders have progressively dissolved; simultaneously, the European countries have been exerting control on countries to the south in order to gain a semblance of national agency, prerogative, and control (previously given up by EU member states in exchange for a newly borderless confederated entity), thus creating a highly delineated external frontier. While the EU continues to include new members on its eastern front, it has expressed reservations about including Turkey and other Muslim countries to the south, and it invites itself into the environments of peripheral countries by proposing various partnerships, unequal commercial deals, and neocolonial monitoring.[39] Both littérature-monde and illiterature strive to subvert the assumption that they are facets of some kind of a *littérature-immonde*, in that non-Franco-French literatures are relegated to the opposite of *monde* (world)—*immonde* (both "local" and "contemptible"). This stringent separation of what is from the métropole and what comes from the ex-colonies manifests itself in various ways, one of which is the shelving in French bookstores of works of littérature-monde in French in exclusive areas under labels such as literature of the Maghreb, the Caribbean, South-East Asia, and sub-Saharan Africa. Just like the ill-shaped divisive hyphen, "*île*-ness" and "ill-ness" are part of illiterature's core and décor. Indeed, illiterature displays the Maghreb's illness, how it is sick of being turned into Europe's quarantined island (*île*). One of the preoccupations of these two genres, especially in the case of illiterature, is the fragmentation of the Mediterranean into many Mediterraneans kept separate.

Nowadays, it is fair to say that one of the Mediterranean Sea's Arabic names, "the Sea of the Romans/Byzantines" (the Sea of Europeans), is quite apt. So is the name used by Russell King, namely, "the European Mediterranean": "A . . . question is the extent to which the anthropology of the Mediterranean is really an anthropology of the European Mediterranean. . . . This leads to yet another related question—the validity of the existence of the Mediterranean (or the European Mediterranean) as a distinct cultural region. Judging by recent debates ... the jury is still out on this issue."[40] In the current conjecture, "the Sea of the Romans/Byzantines" (read, the Sea of the Other) is the Arabic equivalent of King's "European Mediterranean" and could easily be translated thusly. The middle way inscribed in "the Mediterranean Sea" is being gradually replaced by the "European Mediterranean," which is given full force in Europe's attempts to dispossess the South of its share of the sea.

Clandestine migrants would find the three common appelations—Mare Clausum, the Sea of the Romans/Byzantines, and the European Mediterranean, as well as the one I propose, Mare Vostrum—fitting, since they reflect the ongoing materialization of the sea into an exclusively European property. At the same time, by separating the political and media divisions of the Mediterranean into subblocks, or "Mediterraneans," within global North and global South, ex-centric writings set out to unfracture the sea. I would argue for the consideration of the use of the term *Afro-Mediterranean* as a complement to *Euro-Mediterranean,* which examines the sea from the viewpoint of the northern shore. In my examination of the Afro-Mediterranean, I turn my attention to how the Mediterranean is lived from the opposite vantage point. Europe has been denounced for trying to co-opt the sea by all means, from the political, to the economic, and the cultural. By means of ex-centric productions, the novelists discussed in this chapter invite the reader to rethink the concept of Mediterraneanness. King qualifies the Strait of Gibraltar as one of these "mini-Río Grandes," whose physical location coincide with what I have called "blocks."[41] He has remarked that this notion (as developed by Montanari, Cortese, and himself) has continued to be evoked in political debates and newspaper articles dealing with European migration.[42] King adds that "within the Basin there are several 'mini-Río Grandes' where short stretches of sea separate societies with very different levels of material wealth, opportunity and quality of life."[43] He warns against the overuse of this expression on account of its divisiveness and suggests that "whilst not wanting to deny the *realpolitik* of a Eurocentric, anti-immigration rhetoric, it does contravene to a large extent both a deeper history of Mediterranean movement and identity and the experiences and aspirations of today's migrants who want to be relatively free to 'come and go' within 'their' Mediterranean space."[44] As we have seen, my use of the term *block* refers to a recent geopolitical creation, whereby critical regions of the Mediterranean carved under the discourse of clandestine migration have been stripped of their Mediterraneanness and turned into European neocolonial possessions, whether discursively, virtually, or militarily.

The Strait of Gibraltar forms another "island" where disputes in the enclaves, islets, and the sea have fragmented the area into additional subblocks that thicken a discursive, military, and physical border. While littérature-monde "shows that literature from France is a mere islet, which rustles, intones and creates in French in the middle of an archipelago of French expression,"[45] illiterature, a *littérature-mer* (sea-literature) par excellence, reveals that France—and French, as I will discuss later—is showing signs of shrinkage into an "islet" in the current geomorphology of Western Mediterranean human migrations and literary creations. Illiterature is a *littérature-mer* in that the Mediterranean Sea is a recurrent element in the narratives. Crossed, imagined, loved, haunted, or hated, the sea is a central entity. Some of the stories unfold exclusively on or near it. In actuality, illiterature demonstrates that France is no longer the center in an ever-growing number of these new narratives. As opposed to the migrant literature of the 1980s, characters are not focused on migrating to France but rather to other destinations, such as Spain. Migratory patterns are no longer simply a straight and smooth line between a center and a periphery; this pattern has deteriorated due to France's parting with its tradition of being a welcoming host country for North African newcomers. Instead, through its state-sponsored institution La Francophonie, France strives to retain its prestigious status as a linguistic and cultural center for the world, so long as it is able to preserve its territorial distance.

Both littérature-monde and illiterature teach us that we have reached the end of a paradigm. Indeed, as the following excerpt from the manifesto indicates, there is no center and no periphery:

> In due course, it will perhaps be said that this was a historic moment: in autumn 2006, five of the seven French literary prizes—the Goncourt, the Grand Prize for Novels of the Académie Française, the Renaudot, the Femina, and the Goncourt for High School Students—were awarded to foreign-born writers. A random coincidence, among publishers' fall catalogs, uniquely concentrating talent from the "peripheries," a random detour before the channel returns to the riverbed? A Copernican revolution, rather, in our opinion. Copernican because it reveals what the literary milieu already knew without admitting it: the center, from which supposedly radiated a franco-French literature, is no longer the center. Until now, the center, although less and less frequently, had this absorptive capacity that forced authors who came from elsewhere to rid themselves of their foreign trappings before melting in the crucible of the French language and its national history: the center, these fall prizes tell us, is henceforth everywhere, at the four corners of the world. The result? The end of "francophone" literature—and the birth of a world literature in French.[46]

Illiterature echoes the various debates taking place in Europe on the political and artistic scenes such as the one initiated by "peripheral" artists who published the 2007 manifesto "Pour une 'littérature monde' en français," claiming that the garnering of France's most prestigious literary prizes a few months earlier by foreign-born writers is proof that France has become a literary and cultural ex-center—a claim that is meant to justify their request for dropping the misnomer "Francophone" for the more fitting "world literature in French" (littérature-monde en français).[47] This document has impacted the ways in which postcolonial scholars are thinking about the place, nature, function, and reception of artistic and fictional productions from French ex-colonies.[48]

The point behind littérature-monde is that the recent works of literature written in French that have garnered massive recognition have originated from places commonly called the "peripheries," which have now proven to be a new center. And according to the manifesto, this is not "a simple vagabond detour," but a grand change, a "Copernican revolution." Illiterature holds a similar ex-centric/eccentric view with regard to the state of contemporary migratory trends in the Western Mediterranean. These trends have shunned the old center, and in doing so have created patterns of decentralization, which in turn have destroyed the notion of any "center" whatsoever; there is no longer a locus of power and control as such. As Arjun Appadurai posits, "the new global cultural economy has to be seen as a complex, overlapping, disjunctive order that cannot any longer be understood in terms of existing center-periphery models (even those that might account for multiple centers of peripheries). Nor is it susceptible to simple models of push and pull (in terms of migration theory)."[49] Works of illiterature, an indicator of these shifts of migratory patterns, were still marginal three decades ago. However, since the late 1980s, the theme of clandestine migration has garnered the attention of many writers from the old periphery, among whom is the 1987 Prix Goncourt recipient, Ben Jelloun.[50] In Partir, as well as in the works of other writers, whom I will be discussing in the following sections, France is presented as a migratory destination of increasing unpopularity even among students who had planned to remain in France after their arrival. Indeed, the Maghrebis who obtained visas a few years ago to study in universities and institutes of higher learning had to face difficulties in securing a job due to a circular issued by Minister of the Interior Claude Guéant on May 31, 2011, which drastically restricted the recruitment of new foreign graduates. On the other hand, since the turn of the past century, Spain has found itself becoming one of the only options for desperate Moroccan migrant hopefuls, for its coasts are more easily reachable by the most rudimentary means.

Burning the Sea

In illiterature, the liminal space of the beachscape often replaces airports and seaports as expected exits in this new age of increasingly select emigration to Europe. Ben Jelloun's title Partir, which means "to leave" and has been published in English under the title Leaving Tangier, is the closest French equivalent of the Moroccan Arabic hrig, although brûler (to burn) translates more accurately the common practice of burning identification documents before undertaking the sea crossing, in order to render repatriation challenging for European authorities. This word also conveys the figurative act of "burning the road" (in this case, the sea), and of illegally "burning up" kilometers in one fell swoop.

Hrig as the means of emigrating clandestinely northward is internationally thought of as a recent phenomenon, due to extensive Western mass media coverage, but according to various historians, it dates back to 711 CE, which marks the arrival of Berber general Tariq Ibn Ziyad in present-day Spain and his decision to burn his ships, making it impossible for his troops to backtrack, thus giving them no choice but to battle valiantly in exchange for the promise of riches and honor in the newly conquered land. Gibraltar, "the Mountain of Tariq," is named after him. Given that the term *burning* is also used to designate the clandestine crossings of terrestrial borders, I called this chapter, in addition to the 2009 article it is based upon and the symposium I organized in 2013 on the topic, "Burning the Sea." I propose the phrase *burning the sea* to specifically discuss clandestine maritime journeys. As for *harragas* (burners), also spelled *harraga* and *harragua,* it is the neologism used in the Maghreb, as well as by French media, to refer to individuals who emigrate clandestinely in search of more promising opportunities.[51]

In Ben Jelloun's 2006 novel *Partir,* the protagonist Azel obtains a visa to enter Spain with the help of his wealthy Spanish lover, Miguel López, while other characters are left only with the possibility of emigrating clandestinely. Elalamy's 2000 novella *Les Clandestins* (published in English as *Sea Drinkers*) recounts the stories of twelve men and a pregnant woman found washed ashore in Bnidar, a small town in northern Morocco. In each of these works, the respective writers trace a narrative of escape and migration. Binebine's 1999 novel *Cannibales* (published in English as *Welcome to Paradise*) depicts North African and sub-Saharan individuals whose life stories are told in the form of flashbacks as they hide at night on a Moroccan beach, waiting to leave for Spain on a small fishing boat.

Fictional examples of the diversity of harragas include Elalamy's Abdou, who is an unemployed college graduate; Ben Jelloun's Azel, who holds a law degree; and Siham, who as a female is not the stereotypical burner (i.e., male). When Azel asks his neighbor Malika what her professional plans are, she responds "Leave," to which Azel retorts: "Leave? But that's not a profession!"[52] Malika's answer to Azel suggests the extent to which the desire for change has made leaving an end in itself. Many of Ben Jelloun's characters are "obsessed by the idea of leaving, of fleeing this country."[53] Malika's words sound like a profession of faith, where the aspiration of leaving is turned into a kind of mission or all-enveloping cause. Jerad writes: "People from the southern rim speak about crossing the sea as a *harq,* a 'burning.' How could someone burn water? This violent metaphor contradicts the natural image of the water that extinguishes fire. . . . Those who succeed in getting past the barriers become clandestine wanderers whose future is uncertain."[54] It is no coincidence that the name of the smuggler in *Partir* is Al Afia, which means "fire" in Arabic.

This oxymoronic desire to burn the water of the Mediterranean, which I call *leavism,* is generally understood as the obsession with leaving the country someday. In fact, a majority of Moroccans share this obsession; according to a 1998 survey, "72 percent of the population wished to emigrate."[55] Diverse pressures push Maghrebis, from farm workers to the professional classes, from unaccompanied minors to pregnant women, to become harragas and leave their country behind. Journalist and historian Zakya Daoud provides information as to why the rate of leavism is so high: "there are . . . those for whom a refused visa makes them feel confined, as if they were being locked up, those who worry for not having papers . . . athletes who vanish while traveling abroad for a contest, students who remain there after their studies. According to Unesco, Morocco has the third highest rate of all countries in the world whose students go abroad to study and decide not to return. Out of 300,000 students, 45,000 are overseas. Hardly 10% will return to their country."[56] Sansal concurs that leavism is not the exclusive opium of the poor; burners do not always leave to flee hunger and poverty: "*Harga* is no longer an individual and marginal phenomenon that used to throw some young unemployed people on the roads of clandestine emigration to reach Europe . . . it has become a complex and multifarious mass phenomenon that affects . . . everyone, rich and poor, unemployed and workers, young and old people, women and men, modern and traditional individuals."[57] Sociologist Smaïn Laacher has a similar view: "the individuals who are the best endowed in terms of symbolic resources (social position to maintain, faith in the future, etc.) as well as material resources, undertake the longest and the most dangerous of journeys."[58] A feeling of confinement is often at the root of leavism. This sentiment is shared by a wide social spectrum; even the elite are affected. The migration of the most educated and privileged contributes to a major brain and currency drain: "I see that individuals supposed to be free or who would like to become free, or at least remain free, can no longer leave with a visa to take a breath of fresh air some place other than their old colonies ruined by tribal wars and separatist groups—they also have to have a great mind, a well-endowed wallet, and a confirmed return-trip ticket."[59] *Leavists* may indeed be well off and possess a comfortable profession at home.[60] Their departure is a response to the closure of a body of water that Arabs traversed freely during their Golden Age. Nowadays, these "individuals supposed to become, or at least remain free" are asked to stay home. Harragas' leavism is also a feeling and an act that denounces *hogra,* which means "spite, injustice and humiliation accompanied by cynicism."[61] Its shuffled Arabic trilateral roots and its transcription in the Latin alphabet establish a visual proximity with *hrig* and *harga.*[62] I would like to suggest the existence of a potential layer of embedded meaning linking *hrig, harga,* and *harragas* to *hogra*. Utilizing multiple levels of meaning is a common practice in spoken varieties of Maghrebi Arabic, where new words are sometimes infused with irony and sarcasm, two street and social remedies to despair and ennui.

In the 449th issue of *TelQuel*, Moroccan experts, including sociologists, psychoanalysts, and lawyers, provide diverse views of what the concept of *hogra* covers. The author of an article on hogra acknowledges that it is difficult to translate the term accurately or in a single word.[63] But the cover illustration says it all: a drawn man lies in the street, his face pinned down by a police officer's shoe. In the same issue, the authors quote Moroccan sociologist Abdessamad Dialmy, who asserts the following: "in any traditional society where one is only a subject, hogra is a structural and structuring element."[64] The cover image reflects what the journalist claims is a daily reality that is discussed everywhere and concerns everyone in Morocco, but the article argues that Algerians are also victims of hogra. (Dialmy's assertion can be applied to the Maghreb generally.) As I will demonstrate in chapter 5, it is a case of humiliation that undoubtedly triggered the Jasmine Revolution in 2010. Semantic and phonetic similarities between *harga* (clandestine immigration) and *hogra* (humiliation)—though coincidental—are at the heart of *hrig*, since it is not only economic reasons that push people to burn their identities, so to speak, and migrate without papers. A forgotten but crucial push factor in the dynamics of clandestine migration is the feeling of injustice among Maghrebis that comes from confinement to one nation and the "systematic human devaluation" at home,[65] thus "in cinema, as well as in music, our artists use hogra as a source of inspiration."[66] For this reason, it is not surprising that Noureddine Lakhmari director of the Moroccan film, *Casanegra*—which evokes migratory plans as far north as Sweden—should link, through a subtle interplay of words and images, the issue of *harga* with *hogra*, stating that in Morocco, one's value is proportional to his salary, even if there is no sacrifice to his dignity. The idea that hrig is an act of resistance in the face of injustice has been discussed by scholars such as Taieb Belghazi and Slemnia Bendaoud. Bendaoud seems to agree that hrig is not always undertaken for economic reasons: "Harragas . . . are also recruited among university professors and businessmen. . . . They decided to leave because they are convinced that in their country they are not in a position to bear humiliations any longer."[67] Leavism is an act of extirpation from a "hierarchy of mobility,"[68] in which "citizens of the Western world usually enjoy the widely held liberal principle of being free to choose a place of residence and of employment . . . [whereas] citizens of certain other countries who migrate for specific purposes are often refused this right."[69] Just like the followers of Prophet Muhammad who emigrated in secret in order to escape persecution back in Mecca, harragas leave in secret. Modern-day migrants resort to a secret way of leaving because if they happen to be caught by national or foreign authorities, they face deportation and then a trial, imprisonment, and police brutality back home. Harragas are also secretive about their project because families often try to prevent them from leaving the beach. Clandestine migration's official name in Arabic is "secret emigration" (*hijra sirriya*). This is one reason why I claim that irregular migration should not be called *illegal*. I find the use of the adjective *clandestine* not only more fitting than *illegal* but also more appropriate, especially because *clandestine* retains a major element in illiterature, namely the plight and dire living conditions inflicted onto characters condemned to hide. This word choice thus sheds light on one of the consequences of anti-immigration laws (one seeks to become invisible in the country of arrival) instead of stigmatizing the clandestine migrant as criminal ("illegal"). Also, until not long ago, Maghrebi clandestine migration was indeed hidden. In countries such as Morocco and Algeria, there was a state-imposed ban on depictions of this phenomenon.[70]

It is interesting to note that the colloquial neologism *harga* is also phonetically close to *hijra* from standard Arabic whose trilateral root is [ر ج ه] (*ha, jim, ra*), and means "emigration."[71] In 622 CE, Prophet Muhammad led his first followers on a hijra to Medina, fleeing the persecution of Meccans.[72] This constitutes the first emigration undertaken by members of the Ummah (Muslim Community) accompanied by their religious leader. *Harga* and *hijra* both share the notions of persecution and secrecy. The idea that in our modern era prospective harragas envisage a journey to flee hogra (institutionalized humiliation) is necessarily conveyed by this semantic commonality between harga/hrig (clandestine migration) and Hijra (historical migration), which are conflated in *Partir*:

> He calls himself Moha, but with him you're never sure of anything. He's the immigrant without a name! This man is who I was, who your father was, who your son will be, and also, very long ago, the man who was the Prophet Mohammed, for we are all called upon to leave our homes, we all hear the siren call of the open sea, the appeal of the deep, the voices from afar that live within us, and we all feel the need to leave our native land, because our country is often not rich enough, or loving enough, or generous enough to keep us home. So let us leave, let's sail the seas as long as even the tiniest light still flickers in the soul of a single human being anywhere at all, be it a good soul or some lost soul possessed by evil: we will follow this ultimate flame, however wavering, however faint, for from it will perhaps spring the beauty of this world, the beauty that will bring the world's pain and sorrow to an end.[73]

This quote implies that hrig is another form of hijra, a call to which many feel compelled to respond. As for the conceptual correspondence between *hogra*, *harga*, *hrig*, and *hijra*, it feeds into a historical and religious legitimization of human migratory flows in Islam-based cultures. Indeed, one *Hadith* demonstrates that the Prophet himself urged his community to travel far. It states, "Seek knowledge all the way into China if need be."[74] In Muslim societies, the propensity to set off to new lands not only is permitted but is in fact also framed as a religious command: "Seek!" This mandate helps us to understand Ben Jelloun's advocacy for free movement and his insistence in his writing that we are all immigrants, a claim he makes for instance in his fable titled "Le dernier immigré" (The Last Immigrant). In this fable, the Berber Mr. Mohamed Lemmigri is the last migrant to leave France. The departure of Maghrebi migrants engenders a linguistic hijra, namely, the disappearance of over a hundred commonly used words of Arab origin from the French language. The catastrophic outcome of the return home of immigrants enables the writer to attribute to the head of state the following statement: "*After September 11, some said: We are all Americans! Today, I say:* 'Koulouna 'arab! *We are all Arabs!* 'Koulouna mouhâjiroun.' *We are all immigrants.*"[75]

While Europe increases the sophistication of its coastal technological shield, clandestine migrants continue to embark on pateras. "Their name comes from 'pato' (duck) because these boats were used for duck hunting in the south of Spain."[76] This Spanish word has come to mean "little boats." These vessels are also named by the Spanish and Moroccan press as "boats of death," "boats of shame," "pateras of despair," and "floating tombs."[77] These monikers highlight the fact that globalization and tough immigration policies have transformed hopes into coffins. The Mediterranean, a traditional site of exchange and human migration between cultures from both shores of the sea, has been reduced to a cemetery. The embarkations lead many to their last home, for pateras capsize frequently, as is the case in Elalamy's *Les Clandestins,* and it has been reported that smugglers throw passengers into the sea when spotted by coastguards. The passengers who know how to swim will try to make it the last few yards to the shore. As for the others, they will drown and disappear in a sea-cemetery: "Azel has decided that this sea has a center and that this center is a green circle, a cemetery where the current catches hold of corpses, taking them to the bottom to lay them out on a bank of seaweed."[78]

The Strait of Gibraltar is an ambivalent site on many different levels in *Partir:* "He knows that there, in this specific circle, a fluid boundary exists, a kind of separation between the sea and the ocean, the calm, smooth waters of the Mediterranean and the fierce surge of the Atlantic."[79] Additionally, in Ben Jelloun's novel, harragas call the Mediterranean Sea "Toutia, a word that means nothing, but to them she is a spider."[80] Just as the water is conceptualized in oppositional terms ("calm" and "fierce"), the spider has the dual ability to kill and assist:

> she is a spider that can feast on human flesh yet will sometimes warn them, in the guise of a beneficent voice, that tonight is not the night, that they must put off their voyage for a while.
> Like children, they believe in this story that comforts them and lulls them to sleep as they lean back against the rough wall.[81]

The sea or Toutia is a provider of both good and bad. She advises the young men on the best time to embark on boats, lulls them to sleep, or lures them into her web. Interestingly, Miguel (Azel's Spanish lover), shares a phonetic proximity with *mygale* (mygale spider), which frames him as a dual character, a provider of goods as well as the agent of a luring process that leads to an act of cannibalism. This choice of name shows Ben Jelloun's harsh criticism of neocolonial Orientalist prostitution practices—that sometimes tourism hides another face, that of prostitution rendered possible through an Orientalist-type interest in the region. As I will discuss later, Azel is not spared authorial criticism; he comes across as a reverse sexual tourist, a version of the *bezness* (gigolo).[82]

Promiscuity involves bodily proximity; as for Azel and Miguel's country, they too almost touch. The short distance that separates the two continents, which could otherwise pass as a detail, is often mentioned in works of illiterature. Ben Jelloun writes that Spain is fourteen kilometers away. The number fourteen is a determining factor in the migrants' plans for leavism. Laila Lalami opens her novel thus: "FOURTEEN KILOMETERS. Murad had pondered that number hundreds of times in the last year, trying to decide whether the risk was worth it. Some days he told himself that the distance was nothing, a brief inconvenience, that the crossing would take as little as thirty minutes if the weather was good."[83] The kilometric indication even gave the name to a Spanish film by Gerardo Olivares: *14 kilómetros*. Why do illiteraturists compound the magic or tragic number fourteen? Their intention is to bring to our attention the psychological effect that the number of kilometers has on future harragas. Fourteen resonates as a mantra, a word of encouragement, and a means of escape for some, whereas for others, it is nothing but an alluring curse: "Is the magnet that attracts us fully responsible? A fourteen-kilometer long magnet in the Mediterranean?"[84] The strength of attraction of the magnet is matched by, or is proportionate to, the "tyranny of geography" inflicted on Maghrebis to whom "time space compression" has been denied.[85] The "green circle" that Ben Jelloun refers to in *Partir* could well be just a reference to the color of the sea. But given the many Muslims who have sunk into this mass tomb, Ben Jelloun implies that the color of the Mediterranean cemetery is a symbol—not that of hope, as one would expect—but that of Islam, whose symbolical color is green. Ben Jelloun's message is clear: the Mediterranean has been turned into a trap to keep Maghrebis at a distance.

Candidates to hrig come to view the Strait of Gibraltar as a frustrating geographical impediment that prevents a union with the continent to the north, complicated further by the installation of SIVE, the sea's sieve. Ben Jelloun tackles the subjective, and sometimes distorted, view that Moroccans benefit from the propinquity of the Spanish coast, which can be seen on a clear day. The closeness is presented as an optical illusion that magnifies the unequal regional institutional dynamics, which entice harragas toward a kind of Eldorado—literally, "that which is golden." Eldorado is symbolized in *Partir* by the gold-colored mint tea that the young characters drink in Café Hafa in Tangier while they watch the glistening lights from Spanish Tarifa. Attracted to the sweet beverage, bees get so close to the liquid that they drown in it, an omen for future human tragedies. The attraction generated by this Eldorado contrasts with a strong disillusionment expressed in many testimonies of clandestine and nonclandestine migrants once on Spanish land. The poor working conditions, the low salaries, the precarious status of migrants, and their minimal rights are all factors in the too-often belated realization that the grass is not always greener on the other side, that "Spain [is] somebody else's Utopia."[86] The sea is reduced to "a great river" as "it appears on a late Roman map, the Peutinger Table, where the sea is grossly elongated. Gulf, river and sea are imaged as varying extensions of the same medium, not conceptually divided as they are in modern geomorphology."[87] This minimizing argument about the attainable distance is a major topic of discussion for potential burners as well as for smugglers. The latter present the strait as a narrow body of water and use the short distance to convince candidates to take the perilous journey. In spite of the danger of traveling northward, pateras are often packed with desperate individuals eager to "burn" the body of water between Moroccan Tangier and Spanish Tarifa.

In *Partir,* the *passeur* Al Afia inspires only fear and disgust among the harragas.[88] Though illiterature generally elicits sympathy for harragas and condemns smugglers lured by profit, it ultimately attributes the human cost to a closed coast. The so-called Mare Nostrum, traditionally seen as a flourishing site of exchanges, is portrayed according to the antagonism surrounding the line dividing the global North from the global South, which Bensaâd qualifies as a "fracture."[89] In *Les Clandestins,* Elalamy employs the sea figuratively as a backdrop against which he foregrounds the fractured arm of a drowned harraga, buried in the sand, twisted like a bird's wing. Ben Jelloun treats this notion of fracture through his implication that any Mediterranean crossing causes an inevitable splitting of the self. The writer warns against resulting forms of dehumanization. Indeed, in the earlier extract, the reader will notice that even though the name Moha exists as such, it is a half-name, that of Mohamed. Ben Jelloun's characters are warned of the possibility that they will lose a part of themselves in the process of displacement from one place or culture to another. Moha is a truncated version of Mohamed because Moha the madman actually hides the wisdom and lucid vision worthy of a prophet.

Moha is not the only incomplete name in *Partir.* Azz El Arab's truncated name, Azel, is another one. It betrays a lost identity, for it does away with the "Arab" in him when he puts himself into the sexual service of a European man. This symbolic emasculation—the name resonates both in Arabic and French with the feminine term of endearment "gazelle"—translates into the character's sudden impotency and foreshadows the actual slicing of his throat in Spain. One can find an analogous literal and figurative dismemberment in *Cannibales* where Mourad has nightmares in which his limbs are being pulled off by praying mantises or his body is being eaten up piece by piece by his Portuguese boss, for whom he works at a Parisian restaurant. He dreams that his head is presented to his employer on a pillow. Through the course of the narrative in *Partir,* Azel becomes increasingly disconnected from his family. Moreover, his murder at the hands of Muslim extremists and his detachment from religious tenets could also mark the end of his membership in the Ummah. Finally, his occurrences of impotency give him the feeling that he has lost his sexual organs. This view is supported by Ben Jelloun's commentary on the feminization of Azel, which parallels the West's Orientalist feminization of the colonized Maghreb(is). Azel is among the happy few who did not have to enter Spain in a life-threatening way. However, his migratory act caused him to constantly risk his life and to hide his identity. Though one may first envisage Azel's Spanish lover to be an empowering asset, since he facilitates Azel's entry into Spain, the reader soon realizes that the seductive dynamics do not benefit the Moroccan character. It is Azel who is the loser in this game, as is implied through the image of an innocent gazelle that is the victim of a venomous *mygale* spider. Indeed, he feels belittled and used, and his humiliation culminates when his Spanish benefactor has him dress as a woman to entertain his friends.

Ironically, the protagonist himself explains that Azz El Arab means "crème de la crème," the upper crust of the Arab nation. However, *Partir* conveys the idea that the character is not deserving of such a prestigious attribute; instead, he exemplifies another embedded meaning in his name: the verb *azz,* which is related to leaving. The notion of leavism—this strong desire to leave no matter what, which the title of the novel reflects—is thus inscribed into his name, in other words, his identity. Just like Malika, Azel has lived to leave. The verb *azz* also connotes the idea of disappearing, vanishing into thin air, of taking one's life. This derived meaning has inspired critics to make a connection to the persona of the martyr and the kamikaze, a recurrent theme in Maghrebi literature, music, and cinema since the 1990s. This kamikaze parallel was common in the decade of violence during the Algerian civil war and has resurged recently in response to the West's stigmatization of the Muslim world as a place of terrorism. The harragas are well aware that many perish during the crossing and that "Europe . . . is not *paradise,* it does not have anything to offer them."[90] And yet individuals often state that they would rather take the chance to reach "a bearable step toward a better elsewhere," than to stay where they have no hope for a better future.[91] It can be argued that leavism is a response to *dégoûtage.* This Maghrebi word (literally "disgust") derived from the French is used extensively by Moroccans to express a feeling of boredom due to lack of employment and social infrastructure. On a symbolical level, though Azel will be murdered, *Partir* shows that it is he who brought about his own downfall by being consumed by an easy but oppressive existence. His forced subordination sets off this downfall, which first takes the form of psychosomatic troubles and an existential and metaphysical questioning, then his rejection of what he came to Spain for, and finally his murder. Azz El Arab, literally, the one who brought the Arab community up in esteem—and ironically, due to the ambivalent meaning of *azz*, the one who was stripped of his Arab identity—allows the reader to decipher Ben Jelloun's insinuation that emigration is a complex and a multilayered reality—an exodus shaped and dictated by global inequalities.

Does the Mediterranean See? Is Mass Media "Covering"?

With the rising presence of satellite TV, Moroccans have become eyewitnesses to clandestine crossings. The footage first came chiefly from media outlets in nearby European countries, as a passage from Binebine's *Cannibales* reveals: "Réda stopped in front of a shop-window where televisions were for sale. I joined him. . . . I laid eyes on the set, which was broadcasting a Spanish program. One could see policemen retrieving bodies from the water that were inflated like balloons: a man with a child held close to him by a piece of material, two black men, a white man and a woman with untied braids. One had trouble discerning their faces."[92] This passage conveys the idea that this human tragedy has been downgraded to commercial entertainment and that the harragas have become a spectacle for everyone to see. The parallel made between undocumented migrants and "balloons" (an image that also haunts Elalamy's text) reveals a dehumanizing process in which the drowned are reduced to what I call "UFOS" (unidentified floating objects). The footage's *chosification* (thingification) of harragas—a term I am borrowing from Aimé Césaire—demonstrates the notion that the southern countries are not noticed.[93] This is further exemplified in a postcard Azel sends back to his country: "*You know, from Morocco you can see Spain, but it doesn't work like that in the opposite direction. The Spanish don't see us, they don't give a damn, they've no use for our country.*"[94] This quote indicates that Morocco becomes visible to Spain only in a virtual fashion, through television programs and surveillance systems, when its migrants attempt to reach the North, at which point they are perceived only as a threat to Europe.

Harragas are often reduced to nonhuman things framed as a menace to the security of the region. Additionally, the statistics quoted by the press further the transformation of harragas into persons of "nonidentity" whose arrests are continuously announced by the Spanish authorities, and their drowned corpses shown on television. Sociologist Düvell remarks that it is only recently that in Europe the topic has freed itself of a certain kind of censorship. And yet, states still influence the discourse of research: "Writing and researching clandestine migration is no easy task. In Europe, where it was often considered a taboo topic often too hot to touch . . . this only changed during the late 1990s. But the topic is highly politicized, and states, and indeed most of the wider literature prefer to see clandestine migration within the framework of security concerns . . . some practices apparently eschew well-defined methods of developing migration typologies and uncritically use discursive concepts instead, as with the expression 'illegal migration' which frequently turns up in academic language."[95] Some of these discourses "follow a political agenda and have political purposes, such as ringing alarm bells," and this alarmism "contributes to a sense of threat and panic, fueling *angst* amongst the host country."[96] Consequently, the synecdochal patera, a "Spanish" boat, is now construed as an uninvited means of transportation, and an object launched onto the Spanish shores as if in attack. Anthropologist Liliana Suárez-Navaz remarks that "alarmism is used to stir up old fears of a silent invasion of the Iberian Peninsula," which reanimates xenophobic sentiments expressed by Spanish characters in *Partir,* who stigmatize the *Moros* (Moors) as Muslim invaders capable of a second *Reconquista.*[97] The foreigner takes on the role of the intruder, a scapegoat in political campaigns to explain societal ailments and to justify radical protective initiatives. In this era, mass media have become for many twentieth- and twenty-first-century citizens a primary provider of information. It is undeniable that mass media have an impact on societal conceptions about immigration, especially when they relay or advocate tendentious political positions. One is led to wonder what the Spanish media's role and responsibility have been in the dissemination of "new racism" in the "new Europe" and especially in Spain where, as Daniela Flesler argues, it is "publicly articulated and accepted in social and political spheres . . . not only by the right, but by the whole political spectrum."[98] In Spain, the widespread use of *Moor* to designate a Moroccan migrant is indicative of a problematic conflation of identities, namely the North African migrant as an eighth-century conqueror.[99]

But as political scientist Catherine Wihtol de Wenden notes, current anti-immigration propaganda is not supported by statistics: "the idea of a horde of clandestines ready to invade Spain and Europe is more fantastical than real. Since 1990, in the Algeciras area, Spanish authorities arrest no more than a thousand clandestine migrants per year."[100] Düvell concurs that while "many sources claim to be certain about the worrying nature of the phenomenon, its extent is only guessed at, the terminology is blurred and its impact on economy and society is often unknown. Instead, assumptions inform the discourses. Indeed, the issue is highly politicized and emotionalized."[101] Düvell adds that, "quantitative data is either absent or of poor quality. By their very nature hidden populations are difficult to quantify. . . . Existing figures are often either implausibly low or unbelievably high."[102] The number of harragas is by definition unknown, and one is often left to resort to estimates instead, which vary purposefully among "both protectionist and humanitarian actors."[103] Aware of this problem, Daoud's following estimate presents relevant data with utmost precaution: "Who can count those in the underwater cemetery, which according to Spanish statistics in 1999 was home to 3,450 cadavers? The more plausible statistics claim from 200 to 1,000 attested deaths for the year 2000. According to others, we should have reached 8,000, in other words 3 a day since 1990. The estimates of Atime, an association of Moroccans residing in Spain, claim that between 1997 and the first half of 2001, 3,924 died and 1,500 disappeared."[104] Jørgen Carling explains why data can also be easily misread: "figures are sometimes, but not always, presented separately for migrants apprehended 'in boats,' 'on beaches,' and 'in the inland,' and the latter group may have resided in Spain for a long time before they are arrested. In some cases, figures also include migrants who were 'detected but not intercepted.' Finally, most figures are based on apprehensions by the Guardia Civil, a joint military and civilian police force, and usually exclude apprehensions by other agencies."[105] Estimates are provided by various sources on both sides of the Mediterranean, and they often help to justify European anti-migration policies and are designed to show to European states that Maghrebi governments are joining their efforts to curb clandestine migration. As Carling insists: "A few notes of caution are required regarding the use of media reports as sources. First, media reports do not always feature the quality control that is integral to academic research. Second, reader accessibility may be given priority over attention to detail; for instance, statistical definitions might be ignored. Third, it is not always easy to see how the political context influences media reporting, and to interpret the coverage accordingly."[106] Experts state that the data are not always reliable and that media "facts" often fuel widespread misconceptions. All these factors produce an equation, suggested in this section's title with a play on the double meaning of the word *covering*. Echoing Edward Said's use of the term, *covering* means both media coverage and covering as a means of constituting reality through powerful discourses representing harragas in ways that shape perception and practice, while obfuscating the power constructs that underpin and sustain them. In this articulation, through mass media, depiction masks true description.[107]

From Liminality to Criminality

An examination of the language surrounding clandestine immigration unravels a common criminalization that is intended to shape the target audience's judgment. Indeed, clandestine migrants are referred to in Spanish media by the term *ilegales*. In France, the Arabic term *harraga(s)* cohabitates at times interchangeably with *sans-papiers* (undocumented migrants) and *clandestins* (clandestine migrants).[108] Clandestine migration is often called *l'immigration irrégulière* (irregular immigration) and applies to undocumented migrants regardless of their means of arrival on French soil. Though the Spanish term establishes an obvious link between unauthorized immigration and illegality, the French is seemingly less indicting. However, the idea that irregular immigration patterns may disrupt regular ones reveals an underlying call for reparative and punitive measures. This implication is not an innocent one. It feeds on a claim of abnormality and justifies a remedy for a malady suffered by a sane society attacked by an invasive foreign object, in this case, the burner.

As for Moroccan media depictions of clandestine migration, they can be overly cautious, as pointed out in *Les Clandestins* when, after the corpses of harragas were found on the beach, the tragic news spread all over the country, while the voice on the radio announced only that

"Two careless swimmers were drowned near the little town of Bnidar."
That's all.
"Two careless swimmers."
Voilà.[109]

Following the media hype over the drowning of the "first" harrag on November 1, 1988, and the capsizing of three pateras in one day in the summer of 1992, constant international pressures (imposed chiefly by France and Spain) forced the Alawi kingdom to incriminate hrig. Both sides of the issue decry the loss of human life, but while the European countries view the solution as prohibiting hrig, the African countries believe that the answer lies in more lenient immigration policies. In "La tragedia del Estrecho," Spanish photographer Ildefonso Sena Rodríguez, who took the picture of the first known harrag, explains that his photograph triggered an abundance of media coverage of clandestine crossings into Spain, which contributed to the imposition of such pressures on Morocco.

Recently, Moroccan media has capitalized on the government's overwhelming success in reducing the number of *hargate* (burnings). Media outlets, such as those of Moroccan television (especially RTM) or the dailies *Al Alam* and *L'Opinion* have, more than others, adopted the official antihrig discourse. In Ben Jelloun's *Partir,* the protagonist Moha says, "I, too, am on fire. I burn like this paper that does not tell the truth, that says all is well, that the government is doing everything it can to give work to our young people, and that those who burn up the straits have succumbed to wild despair. . . . Here, gather up the ashes of the news I just burned: there's lots of it, fake news."[110] Ben Jelloun's madman corrects the media's account by perspicaciously critiquing the newspaper. In this regard, the printed text of illiterature constitutes a different sort of coverage, such as that of the more nuanced Moroccan weekly, *TelQuel.*[111] It thus functions as replacement identification papers—new papers—free of the institutional criminalization of hrig, as voiced by an official earlier in the story: "This is the last time! Hey you, cameraman, come over here and film these bodies! All Morocco must see this tragedy! It has to be in the evening papers—too bad if it spoils people's appetites!

We've had enough! *Basta!* We're sick of it! This must stop. Morocco is losing its strength, its young people! Where's the police chief? Get him here right away. We're going to seal off the coasts!"[112] This *mise en abyme* points to a general demonization of hrig. In the age of globalization defined by a growing number of human movements around the world, the northern Mediterranean countries have engaged in a systematic control of the Mediterranean and have dragged those located on the southern rim into their project. As a result, there seems to be a consensus among Moroccan parties, associations, and media that hrig should be condemned. The Mediterranean has become a reverse panoptical site of control whereby harragas are tracked down and prevented from arriving and leaving. Indeed, governments on both sides of the sea have monitored the body of water to make sure that those who hail from the global South do not reach the North. To this effect, a constant deterring parade of warships and coastguards is summoned to the Sea of the Middle in order to enact the grip of reverse panoptical power, where the margin controls the center, namely, another eccentric form of ex-centeredness.

The improvised documentary film in Ben Jelloun's novel impugns Morocco's state-sponsored media coverage of clandestine migration while suggesting that literature may be a powerful channel to challenge cover-ups. The 1990s saw the rise of *cinéma d'urgence,* a filmic genre made popular among Algerian filmmakers to recount and condemn the horrors of the civil war that bled the country. Simultaneously, Moroccans were in turn developing illiterature, yet another type of *littérature d'urgence.* Farida Boualit explains that this literature of urgency "was launched by the Algerian writers themselves in order to stress the concomitance of facts and their writing, in other words the imperative is to make reality and fiction coincide in time."[113] The presence of this *documentaire d'urgence,* or documentary-type of writing, in Ben Jelloun's *Partir* is also made possible because illiterature, to some extent, shares the referential aspect of many works of literature of urgency and accounts for the need to "denounce and demystify violence."[114]

Writers have rushed to fill the void in state-suppressed Moroccan accounts of hrig and to react to Western television reports that focus on the macabre effects of the clandestine passages and that enflame fears of conquest. In spite of its mission to inform, mainstream media, concerned with the "big picture," often transforms clandestine migrants into anonymous outlaws plucked from the sea. Indeed, from the early 1990s, the depiction in the West of clandestine migration "captured the public imagination as a problem."[115] Similarly, depending on the amount of harragas found by the Moroccan authorities, the encounter may inspire a "catchy" headline such as "Moroccan Navy Makes Big Catch," which likens individuals to fish, "a catch" to be taken dead or alive.[116] Answering such accounts with an ironic eye, illiterature systematically rewrites and reverses their dehumanizing effects. For instance, in *Les Clandestins,* Elalamy writes, "there below, scattered about the sand, a strange kettle of fish. Fish so big they may have been human, God forbid, they look human, dear God, like people, they *are* people! And oh my God, they're our people!"[117] Common parlance undertakes a resembling biological deformation, albeit particularly disturbing, for derogative denominations do not pertain to the realm of fiction and are instead circulating referents specific to the areas and modes of travel used by clandestine migrants. As d'Ors explains, harragas are referred to as *atún* (tuna).[118] The persistent trope of rehumanizing the dehumanized illustrates the political stakes of illiterature. Elalamy's repetition of the words *human* and *people* restores not only the harragas' humanity but also, with the use of the possessive adjective, their community, in contrast to mass media coverage that limits itself to repeating a uniform (and uninformed?) animalizing or objectifying *vue d'ensemble* that numbs intellectual and affective attention. Elalamy, Ben Jelloun, and Binebine's solution to the paradox that fiction authenticates reality while the media fictionalizes it, is what one could call *literary reporting,* namely the conversion of flawed or neglected facts into *bio*-logical details, where the dead are not merely bodies but rather deceased individuals with a name, physical appearance, family, and community. Literary reporting aims at reporting, literally speaking, and not figuratively via numbers and statistics. This technique is symbolized in *Les Clandestins'* "burning" of the distance between the harragas and the discursive voice. The narrator approaches what calls for a closer look (the fish) to reveal what it really is (human beings). This gesture is too often discarded by journalistic coverage in favor of quantitative data and qualitative designations, which cause a sort of detachment, yet another form of distance.

What Is in the Picture When Illiterature Documents Harragas?

In his excellent study, "The Global Mediterranean: Literature and Migration," Dominic Thomas asks the crucial question, "What then might be the potentialities of literature in humanizing these experiences [of clandestine maritime crossings]?"[119] He convincingly argues: "Confronted with media images and statistics on death tolls attributed to Mediterranean crossings, one has to reflect additionally on the limits of empathy and tolerance and how literature can articulate such frameworks, particularly as a way of countering the claim by the authorities that Europe is being invaded and that the fabric of societies is being eroded."[120] Illiterature comes to the rescue of the undocumented migrants by giving them its own papers while it brings light to a phenomenon that is untraceable. The media stories that envelop the migrants are likely to be invented because of the anonymity of the drowned; in the absence of the departed to tell their real story, journalists may speculate histories that, in the end, stifle the memory of the dead. In *Les Clandestins,* a French weekly goes so far as to *defocalize* (in all senses of the term) the drowned harragas, by publishing a photograph with the following caption: "WHAT A PRETTY LITTLE BEACH!"[121] The picture was selected among 137 others taken that day of harragas and surrounding environmental elements. The accompanying caption transforms itself into a monstrous missed epitaph, for instead of capturing the main story, it turns an open-air cemetery into an attractive tourist site.

Images may miss their mission of representation, as is the case in Binebine's televised coverage where faces cannot be made out and identities are obliterated by superimposing paratextual or paravisual data. This type of coverage and obliteration thus inscribes a trace of collective death in lieu of a trace of the individual dead. There certainly are many unknowns in the clandestine migration equation. Official narratives reveal many x's and y's. The photographic image, which often flaunts a scientific component, an archival status, and the function of tool, in the search for historical truth may become archaic, especially when used as a commercial, decorative, marketing item. Readers are then presented with a task: each time they leaf through works of illiterature, they are invited to uncover and re-cover living and dead bodies between the pages. In the case of fatal hrig, we are enjoined to lay its victims to rest. Thus, this literature also memorializes the dead just as it legitimizes them.

Illiterature counterbalances the cold vision, filtered, for instance, by the eye of a camera through what I call a "discorpsing" discourse of harragas, which discloses "un*ID*entified" subjectivities. Through the medium of fiction, authors bring to life the unspoken words of the departed, those who have been claimed by an illusionary Eldorado. Once the migrants' bodies have left national waters and have therefore "trespassed" (as the French *trépasser* has it, "passed away"), they become unidentifiable to the locals and even to their families. In Elalamy's novella, the failed crossing disfigures the dead harragas. The mother, who rushes to the beach to find her drowned son, reidentifies her loved one, whose face has been eaten up by fish. Her act is one of re-collection—to be understood as the act of retrieving what is hers and of remembering the one who is long gone. The sea (*mer*) refuses the harragas. In turn, the mother (*mère*) seeks to re-fuse with her child—who is mere refuse to those on the European shore—to reclaim their bond, as in Binebine's *Cannibales* where Nouara holds her toddler tight under a flipped patera to keep him warm. From there, she bites a threatening dog to death for fear that the animal might alert his master to their presence. The only evidence of clandestines in most mass media coverage is in the form of anonymous corpses that *la mer* sends back to Africa, *la mère-patrie* (the motherland). This image is reappropriated by works of illiterature to show that these ex-centered individuals are left abandoned at the margin of the motherland embodied by the liminal space of the sea.

From Intercontinental Crossing to Interdisciplinary Bridging

Why do illiteraturists claim verisimilitude or feel the need to claim that their work of fiction is the unaltered rendering of a true story? Certainly, media is a competing force. Newspapers and television coverage is visually appealing and up-to-date; in a consumerist society, media has the advantage of being more easily and quickly consumable. A writer of fiction has to make a different claim in order to compete for the telling of the same story. The writer therefore claims omniscience and truth; through fiction, the real facts are revealed and the media's story is corrected. While the newspaper may be able to give the blow-by-blow account, fiction purports to give the story behind the story, complete with characters, motivations, and plot. In this sense, fiction "uncovers" the dehumanizing fiction of the media, revealing the individuals behind the phenomenon.

Some authors have played the role of reporter in order to fill gaps of information in their stories. The Tunisian author Fawzi Mellah, for example, attempts to explain clandestineness as he experiences it firsthand. Mellah, who is also a scholar and reporter, has opted to offer his own view, not in a newspaper article but rather in a fictional account titled *Clandestin en Mediterranée,* which was published in 2000 in France. In his novel, Mellah explicitly states that he writes as an insider, both as a Tunisian and as a passenger of a clandestine crossing, which takes him and other "real" clandestine migrants from Tunisia to Italy, then to Switzerland and France. The author's professional affiliation can be viewed as a disqualifying element in his claiming the status of "clandestine in the Mediterranean," since in his real life he is able to enter Europe as he pleases. In order to counter such criticism, Sansal, who is permitted to travel to his characters' fantasized Europe, opens *Harraga* with a disclaimer stating that the story is entirely real: "This story would be a most charming one if only it were the fruit of imagination. . . . But it is true, from one end to the other, the characters, the names, the dates, the places, and thus, it just tells the misery of a world which no longer has faith or values, one that can only brag about its escapades and profanations."[122] The novel joins the myriad writings that compete with *actualités* (daily news). This disclaimer may not be entirely true. Furthermore, an author may be less informed than a reporter who happens to witness hrig, but the rendering might come across as more real when framed as a "true" fiction that provides bio-logical details about the personhood of those involved. Though illiteraturists may be viewed as eccentric or ex-centered (not writing from the scene), the task of these *passerelles* (bridging agents), as one may define them, is challenging but praiseworthy. Their bridging efforts are multifaceted.

Illiterature is the site of many crossings, surely physical but also conceptual and academic. Whether they succeed or fail to burn the Mediterranean and reach the closed doors of Europe, many harragas will make it across a different border: that of Maghrebi and Hispanophone literature, as some already have. As I indicated in the beginning of this chapter, though not yet officially called thusly, clandestine migration studies are an emerging terrain, and harragas are not merely submerged migrants who make the news at local, national, and international levels, but they are also the main subjects of various literary works. Interestingly, this literary preoccupation is not solely the concern of Francophone Maghrebi novelists but of Spanish writers as well. Besides the aforementioned Spanish titles, one could cite Lourdes Ortiz's *Fátima de los naufragios* and Moroccan Rachid Nini's *Diario de un ilegal.* Nini's book is the first testimony in Arabic—it was originally published in the newspaper *Al Alam* under the title "Yawmiyyāt muhājir sirrī"—to recount the experiences of Moroccan immigrants in Spain. It is better known in the West in its Spanish translation.[123] Besides the Algerian Sansal's 2005 novel, the recent publication of several books that contain the term *harraga,* such as Moroccan Mohamed Teriah's *Les "Harragas" ou les barques de la mort* and Spaniard Antonio Lozano's *Harraga,* echoes the strong inscription of hrig as a key geopolitical phenomenon, a regional literary and linguistic institution, as well as an undeniable cross-disciplinary research terrain. Indeed, as Manuel Martín-Rodríguez writes: "the *patera* has become such a socio-symbolically charged signifier that it now stands as the key metaphor for immigration in daily life and in titles of books of both fiction and nonfiction, including Mahi Binebine's *Cannibales* (translated into Spanish as *La patera*), and Mario Gastañaga Ugarte's *Naúfragos: Pateras en el Estrecho,* among many others. Most dramatically, the symbolism appears linked to ritual sacrifice (by connecting the term with the 'pátera,' a dish used in religious ceremonies) in Andrés Sorel's *Las voces del estrecho.*"[124] The patera is an eccentric and ex-centering trope. Indeed, instead of taking Maghrebi and sub-Saharan migrants to France, the historically established destination, the patera has become for many a much-coveted gateway to peripheral-destinations-turned-centers in our contemporary era.

The bodies of clandestines have been reappropriated by novelists, as well as by Western media outlets. Because authors have used them as links in an attempt to forge a symbolic chain of an idealized inalterable united sea, harragas have redrawn the current Maghrebi migratory map to include Spain and clandestine migration. As a result, the new trend of Moroccan narratives that privilege Spain as a destination for prospective immigrants and, in turn, a thematic choice for authors, shows no sign of slowing, in part due to the culturally inscribed memory of those who have died to reach it. Spain and various third parties are becoming part of the history of clandestine Maghrebi human movements to Europe. The observation that contemporary hrig is no longer solely bipartite (i.e., a closed circuit between France and its ex-colonies in the North African subcontinent) is made clear not only in Maghrebi and Spanish illiterature but also in other illiteratures in the region. Illiterature, thus, invites us to assess issues associated with globalization, taking into consideration contemporary unconventional migratory patterns.[125] It also invites us to expand scholarship beyond national demarcations, in light of the presence of third parties, such as Spain and Italy, between the traditional poles of the Maghreb and France.[126] By "burning" the limits between national literatures, illiterature is likely to become a site where Spanish and Francophone studies meet. The same prediction can be made for Maghrebi-Italian scholarly encounters. Indeed, more Maghrebi works of illiterature (and clandestine cinema and music) portray Italy as a central place for hrig, thus leading to an increasing need for scholars in Italian and Maghrebi studies in particular, and the humanities in general, to share their research on the Mediterranean. The scholarship on the topic is central in migration studies and continues to expand in the social sciences, especially in economics, but it is just beginning to blossom in the humanities.[127] An interdisciplinary exchange beyond these two areas is destined to occur as well.

Marco Kunz argues that because Spain has become a country of immigration, a new generation of writers is soon likely to enrich Iberian literature:

> There still does not exist in Spain a real literature of migrants, if we exclude a few rare exceptions . . .
>
> The rich literary production of immigrants and their children in other countries can only lead us to predict that within a few decades, or even before, the same could occur in Spain: perhaps soon Spain's great immigrant *Bildungsroman* will be written and texts will appear that reflect upon issues of cultural clashes, ethnicity, transculturation, etc., which occupy a central position in many French and North American works, and also in the abundant criticism on this literature, but which the hispanocentrism of both the personal experiences of authors, as well as in their chosen narrative perspectives, have avoided until now. Also, it is possible that . . . in the future new men and women authors will appear, with non-Spanish sounding first and last names, but who happen to write fiction, plays and poetry that does not have any thematic relation to immigration. As of now, however, literature from Spain is so far from a relevant integration of the cultural pluralism the same way its society is.[128]

The experiences of migrants to Spain have become the source of artistic inspiration for their children, as is the case for *Beurs* in France. As Kamal Salhi rightly argues, "*Littérature-monde en francais* excludes the rich postcolonial literatures written in languages other than French," like Spanish (and Italian, for that matter).[129] It is one of the differences that illiterature has with littérature-monde in that the former has included in its fold narratives in languages other than French.

One can add another prediction to Kunz's, namely that ex-centered migratory patterns, especially clandestine migration, will shape coming scholarship of Mediterranean literature. As King argues, "what still seem to be lacking are studies on the new immigrants who are retexturing the erstwhile homogenous cultural fabric. . . . Research on new migrants-centred cultural encounters in southern Europe is beginning to emerge."[130] In contemporary Spanish literature, even hrig is being discussed. The recent encounters (both realized and missed) of Maghrebis with Spain have led several other Spanish authors such as Eduardo Iglesias, Gerardo Muñoz Lorente, and Andrés Sorel to tackle the topic of leavism.[131] Clandestine migration is becoming a major theme of Maghrebi writers in Spanish. In spite of Spain's "hispanocentrismo," this new direction is to be expected because of this specific form of migration to the Iberian Peninsula. One of the burning questions that come out of these sociocultural changes is the following: Will the Spanish *Beurs,* who as of yet—unlike the French *Beurs*—still have to be named, tackle the same topics? One may also rightly wonder what aspect of migration the Spanish *Beurs* will address. We can foresee that they too will become bridge-makers. Some will hold the *qalam* (Arabic for "pen") to express by proxy the *kalam* (words/speech) of the departed.[132] As Martín-Rodríguez remarks, due in part to clandestine migration, nascent migrant Moroccan literature in Spain is likely to grow: "Moroccan migrant literature is still young and only includes a few titles. Nonetheless, in light of official data on immigration (to which one must of course add an unknown number of clandestine immigrants), it seems logical to predict that it will keep growing and developing in the country and language of adoption."[133]

What is more remarkable—another Copernican revolution perhaps—is that both Spain and the Spanish language have made it into Maghrebi Francophone literature. Ex-centric fictions give Spain more and more space in place of France, which is decentered to the point of becoming the ex-center in various Francophone works from and about the Maghreb. In light of clandestine migration, Francophonie is hispanicizing itself. Thanks to illiterature, what we have called Maghrebi Francophone literature (a body of texts in French that may contain Arabicized language, syntax, etc.) now includes Spain. For the first time, this country and its language are at the core of Maghrebi literature of French expression, which comprises what scholars still call Francophone texts—which they are, but their nature is changing though the name remains. This reality is also reflected in the unprecedented strategic use of Spanish in the works of Francophone Moroccan novelists, as Ben Jelloun shows in this passage from *Partir*: "*Ocupación actual:* Azel did not know what to put down. Out of work? Student? Tourist? Zero. . . . *Nombre, dirección y número de teléfono de la empresa para la que trabaja.* But he wasn't working. . . . *Finalidad del viaje:* to visit a Spanish friend. *Fecha de lle-*

gada and *Fecha de salida:* he really didn't know anything about his dates of departure and return."[134] Azel's understanding of the Spanish-language questions on the immigration document suggests just how intertwined Castilian and *Darija* (Moroccan Arabic) are for many Tangerines. The hybridization of the French text is also a means to "denationalize the French language," as per Mbembe's expression.[135] While Spanish inserts itself into works in French, illiterature welcomes another linguistic element, which makes Francophone literature a less Francophone entity. The originality lies in the fact that the very same Ben Jelloun, who is known for Arabicizing French prose and syntax, is taking his defrancophonizing endeavor one step further, one country further, and one language further. As for *Les Clandestins,* instead of the Spanish language or land, it is the Spaniard Alvaro who makes himself at home in the Francophone novel. He could be the reverse image of the Moroccan harrag, in that he has migrated southward and likely "legally." Furthermore, in contrast to the dead harragas, his eyes have not been eaten by fish and filled by the blue sea, they just happen to be "as blue as the sky." They single him out, as if to indicate that he is an original feature in Maghrebi literature of French expression.

The presence of sub-Saharan characters in illiterature is noticeable as well. In real life, Moroccan authorities (pressured by Spain) try to deter them from gathering near Melilla and Ceuta, which are common meeting places for those awaiting their journey across the Strait of Gibraltar. In *Cannibales,* there are two Malians. Sub-Saharan Africans share the ordeals of their neighbors to the north, but their added layer of marginality is symbolized in the novel by the fact that they hardly speak. Illiterature brings to light the plight of an entire continent, and through the pan-Africanist aspect of hrig, this fight of the fittest to reach the North. In illiterature, the migrants' differences are often replaced by feelings of empathy and solidarity. The harragas' Africanness takes the first seat on the patera, and hrig becomes a color-blind African issue, as shown in this passage from *Les Clandestins:* "Bodies all over the place, run up on the beach. Black ones, white ones. The sea had not discriminated. They all had their eyes eaten out."[136] Pan-Arabism was a rallying force during and immediately after colonial times, and, according to Kateb Yacine, it had the unfortunate effect of diverting the Arab world from the rest of Africa.[137] One might justifiably ask if in a neocolonial context, illiterature's pan-Africanism, or pan-Southism, is the new rallying term in the global era.[138]

Just as the poet was excluded from Plato's *Republic,* writers are traditionally excluded from international policy decision making. Amid the chaos, as conflicting regional interests turn the issue of "migrations of despair" into a disturbing "problem," Tahar Ben Jelloun, Mahi Binebine, and Youssouf Amine Elalamy seek to influence public opinion. Such literary engagement calls for debates that could productively influence future immigration laws, since Fortress Europe will not grant North African countries membership in the EU. Limited access is offered by means of partnerships and cooperation agreements, such as Euromed and French president Nicolas Sarkozy's project L'Union pour la Méditerranée, whose first meeting took place in Paris on July 13, 2008. The 2006 film *Indigènes* prompted the then–French president, Jacques Chirac, to adjust the pensions of colonial soldiers who fought for France during World War II. Will illiterature play an analogous political role in opening up possibilities for Maghrebi countries? This momentous new subgenre offers a response to the mass media "covering" coverage, susceptible to hijacking by discourses saturated with demagoguery. By contrast, fictional accounts help their readers better understand hrig. Like harragas waiting to cross the strait, more of these narratives are on their way.

3 Southward Road Narratives

How French Citizens Become Clandestine Immigrants in Algeria

Sociologist zygmunt bauman explains that globalization is about its effects on us versus our goals: "'Globalization' is not about what we all, or at least the most resourceful and enterprising among us, wish or hope *to do*. It is about *what is happening to us all.*"[1] Thus, as the common vision goes, a distinction between rich countries and less rich ones has been made, encapsulated in the appellations *global North* and *global South*. The effects of globalization unfold in the daily lives of people in these two spaces. At the intersection of the pressures of the local and the global, the term *glocal* has been proposed to describe the connections and relationships between various types of local and global businesses, organizations, and processes. This term, coined by Roland Robertson in *Globalization: Social Theory and Global Culture,* is often used to refer to local ways of dealing with globalized practices and products. The glocal should not be understood in simple terms and binary divides, such as a glocal North and a glocal South but rather as a multifaceted process with numerous effects within these two regions.

The ways the global affects the local and the pressures each mutually exerts upon the other can be seen in the very means that allow for "time and space compression": the internet, social media networks, and modern forms of transportation, shrinking the planet to a local village.[2] However, these are not accessible by all to the same degree, in the same way, in the same frequency, nor for the same purposes. Even within societies that are often considered in tandem, such as groups of developing countries, striking differences exist in the types of glocal attitudes and globalized behaviors. Therefore, the same way as there are various glocalities, there are multiple *globalizations*. This is the case because *globalization* is synonymous with the free movement of people hailing from the North while it is not for those from the South. In addition, there are various globalizations in that the effects are not of the same kind in all localities. The Maghreb is an entity that reflects a particular colonial legacy. Its three countries were colonized by France and they all have a special relation to the French language, maintaining particular connections with France through programs and partnerships. But that colonial past is a factor that makes the Maghreb different from other spaces in the global South, such as the Mashreq (Arab countries east of the Maghreb). The shared historical past and fight for sovereignty from the same imperial ruler is indeed a defining element in how the countries of the Maghreb see and define themselves in relation to the rest of the Arab world, Muslim world, African world, developing world, and the global South.

Furthermore, the local ways in which the Maghreb deals with globalization are also informed by local identitarian claims and local infrastructures that originate in the colonial era or were derived from them (the railways, for example). Aspects of the Maghreb's Islamic practices, such as Sufism and the institutionalization of historic *maraboutism,* its education programs and curricula, and the form of Arabic (mixed with French), make the Maghreb a particular locality. There are multiple distinct societies within the Maghreb, each with unique cultural mores and particular spatial configurations along gender lines and responsibilities. These distinctions vary from one country and region to another, from cities to villages, and within ethnicities and tribes. But particularities that span the Maghreb still differentiate the region at the local, regional, and transnational levels. An anecdotal yet revealing example concerns linguistic variations within the Arabic language that yield strong distinctions between Maghrebi and Mashreqi Arabic—though variants exist within these two umbrella terms. In this regard, Mashreqis often point out that they can easily understand each other no matter what country of the Mashreq they hail from, but they have a hard time understanding Maghrebis. This divide within language is indicative of an implicit split at other levels. Because I am arguing that cultural, historical, and geopolitical parameters make the Maghreb a singular reality, I seek to indicate this singularity in language. I propose to use the term *Maghrobal* to indicate the unique glocality of the area. To this end, I shall scrutinize the impacts of the global on the Maghreb through the prism of "return" or rather, "reverse" migration.[3]

In the chapter he contributed to *Return Migration: Journey of Hope or Despair?,* edited by Bimal Ghosh, Russell King writes: "Return migration is the great unwritten chapter in the history of migration. The historiography of migration studies has nearly always tended to imply that migration was a one-way process, with no return. Studies have focused on departure, the migration journey, arrival, settlement and "integration"; rarely on return. Often one finds, perhaps hidden in a footnote, the lament that "little is known of those who returned."[4] King provides typologies of return. He calls one of the types he identifies "ancestral" return, and examples of this phenomenon includes those "prompted by religious, political or ideological reasons, such as the 'return' of the Jews to Israel or the *Aussiedler* (ethnic Germans) to Germany."[5] The present chapter is interested in two films that play with representations of clandestine journeys originating in France and ending in Algeria. It should be noted that this concept is all the more original that the clandestine characters are French individuals, in other words citizens in possession of a passport that travels well. Furthermore, characters claim a desire to "return" to the Maghreb. But because it is often difficult for the "returnees" to trace their ancestral ties through concrete facts or because the validity is contested for historical or political reasons, the idea of the return can become highly problematic.

Of Hideaways, Duels, and Singular Dualities[6]

Il était une fois dans l'oued (2005) is the third feature film of French director of Algerian ancestry Djamel Bensalah.[7] Bensalah's previous films, *Le Ciel, les oiseaux et . . . ta mère!* (1999) and *Le Raid* (2002), each attracted over a million spectators.[8] Featuring Julien Courbey, a talented actor who was instrumental in turning Bensalah's films into major hits, *Il était une fois* clearly belongs to the category of highly successful commercial films.

Il était une fois is a comedy that centers on Johnny Leclerc (Julien Courbey), born in Porte de Clichy to white working-class parents (a Norman mother and an Alsatian father) and raised in the *cité* Paul Éluard in a Parisian banlieue. Johnny desperately wants to be regarded as an Algerian, an Arab, and a Muslim.[9] As a result, the film elicits laughter from the audience through the abundant use of stereotypes, from Johnny's overzealous observance of Islam to his passage as a stowaway on an Algeria-bound ferry, his settling in Oran, and his adoption of the invented name Abdel Bachir. Yet, as I will argue, the director's playful inversion of typical accounts of migration makes *Il était une fois* a site for original and provocative reversals of commonly held identificatory perceptions. Bensalah invites his audience to consider the idea of the "first" Franco-French clandestine migrant to Algeria by transposing the stereotypical archetype of the Arab grocer in France onto the "first" Franco-French "Arab" grocer in Algeria. Bensalah's use of stereotypes and parodies thus becomes instrumental in this filmic experiment in which characters switch typecast cultural roles in order to audition, rehearse, and perform new postcolonial migratory situations. This essay will therefore present Bensalah's road trip southward as a road map for the implementation of an experimental identity and a model for the reversal of common societal and cinematographic migration narratives.

While praising the originality of *Le Ciel, les oiseaux et . . . ta mère!* for its alternative representations of banlieue youth, Carrie Tarr convincingly argues that Bensalah's previous two films are characterized by thematic and structural crudeness. *Le Raid,* for instance, strikes for its "ludicrous, misogynist plot." In spite of "a budget of about £12 million" it is filled with "(not very impressive) visual gags and special effects, a surreal plotline . . . and obsessive toilet humor."[10] Similarly, *Il était une fois* features a tortuous storyline and a cascade of misadventures, as well as a muddle of ethnic jokes. At best, *Il était une fois* will entertain an audience aware of the film's ironical and satirical import. At worst, the film risks fueling firmly seated prejudices due to invoking these prejudices for the sake of humor.

The film's carnivalesque structure, however, enables it to perform multiple unexpected displacements and transformations. Johnny/Abdel Bachir's metamorphosis is literally set in motion when he invites himself into a new geographic and familial space.[11] He hides in the trailer of his best friend's parents and travels to Algeria along with his best friend, Yacine (David Saracino); Yacine's younger brother, Medy (Medy Kerouani); their father, Si Mohammed (Sid Ahmed Agoumi); and Moroccan stepmother, Kheira (Amina Annabi). Johnny piggybacks on the ritual summer trip that many families of Maghrebi heritage make from their European dwellings to North Africa. On the ferry, he befriends two other travelers, Nadège (Marilou Berry) and Nadia (Karina Testa). In an Almodóvaresque conflation of intertwined subplots, Johnny ends up marrying Nadège, and Yacine ties the knot with Nadia, who happens to be the young lady with whom his father had meant to arrange his marriage.

From the outset, we are taken aback by Johnny's astounding claims to be an Algerian, a Muslim, and an Arab. Franco-French Johnny fits the stereotypical image of white French *banlieusards,* who, along with their disillusioned *Beur* neighbors in the banlieues of Paris and Lyon have converted to Islam in *réislamisation* movements since 1985.[12] Interestingly, blond-haired Johnny also adopts a "*Beur* look"[13] and claims to be an Algerian. By introducing Johnny as a perplexing French-*Beur*-Algerian allegorical amalgamation, Bensalah deconstructs institutionally recognized identities. Johnny is a hybrid, not in the sense of ethnic *métissage;* rather he is performing hybridity in his own peculiar way. Ostensibly of northern French ancestry, he is a religious convert (a Muslim), culturally *Beur* and affectively Algerian.

Johnny's idea of his "original" identity and cultural destiny is presented as a parody of *Beur*ness. It is founded on a patchwork of excesses and approximations. A case in point is his unruly multifacetedness, which shows the dizzying range of possible identities between and within "French" and "Algerian." Johnny vaguely recalls being from "a small village [*bled*] between Algiers and Oran,"[14] but the Algerianness, Arabness, and Islamness he covets, originates possibly from second-hand objects (e.g., a drawing of "his village" purchased in a flea market), culturally reified linguistic usage (rudimentary Arabic words roughly interjected into French), and a Muslim education learned in situ, as is the case for many French converts.[15]

Still, it is not certain what Johnny's conception of Algerianness really is, and the viewer wonders if Johnny even knows himself, since he never really explains what it entails, uttering instead simplistic statements ("I am a *Djazaïri* [Algerian]"). Johnny's strong nationalist feelings make him condemn any association with France, as is illustrated by the following words he shouts at Medy on the soccer field: "I'm sure you bet on France, little bastard"—a position that causes Mr. Sabri to warn him: "Be careful, Johnny, you're becoming a racist."

Another revealing example of Johnny's ironic and troubling adoption of "racist" terms is when Mrs. Sabri, worried that Johnny might damage his skin on the beach from covering himself with cooking oil, advises the young man to be careful, to which Johnny replies: "Don't worry, Mrs. Sabri, this is genuine Arab hide, it don't fear the sun." The scene mocks sunburned Johnny's prejudices, how he equates machismo with natural toughness against inclement weather and believes that because he thinks he is an Arab, his physical body will follow suit. Johnny's statement of hiding under Arab hide—so to speak—is disconcerting since its comic aspect relies on his sincere yet ironic identification with a racist reification of the Arab body as having a "hide" like a (dead) animal, a hunted and traded object. He seems to be unaware of the disparaging nature of such statements, as if they were inscribed in his acquired cultural and linguistic baggage. Meanwhile, Johnny's adventure has something uncannily neocolonial about it. The film does not really problematize the fantasy that a French oddball would be welcomed like an Algerian hero. Johnny's smuggling into Algeria in the Trojan Sabri car and his taking root in a "deep-settler colony" may reanimate French colonial nostalgia.[16] However, Johnny's emotional identification with Algeria also facilitates what may be deemed, in the postcolonial era, a subversive proposition: Algeria as a desirable *colonie de vacances* (summer camp).

The film's subversion of the characters' sense of direction and the meaning attached to the "return home" also invokes the political history shared by France and Algeria. In a comical scene in which Johnny's parents get lost in Algiers while visiting him, the camera zooms in on the parents puzzling over a street sign that used to bear the name of a famous French writer, Anatole France. Following independence, it was renamed "Anatole Algérie" and translated into Arabic as "Anatole el-Djazaïr" (Anatole Algeria). This scene points both to the blindness of postindependence Arabization politics as well as the nostalgic myopia of contemporary French travelers to Algeria rendered by Mr. Leclerc's exclamation: "Anatole Algeria, there is no such thing!" Indeed, the Leclercs, who may be connected to colonial Algeria, miss the crossed-out former street name that appears on the adjoining wall, next to the one they are looking at. Lost, they are *à l'ouest* and literally *à côté de la plaque* (completely mistaken), as the French slang has it, in that they are standing next to the street sign (*plaque*). The street sign is a metaphor for unique postcolonial creations—French-Algerian Djamel Bensalah's Johnny being one of them.

The Sabris' journey includes driving to the south of Algeria to visit relatives, whom Johnny informs that his own village is "somewhere in the west." Untraceable to the familiar Algerian west or the American "Far West," Johnny's village is "lost," as in the French expression, "*être à l'ouest*." *Il était une fois* shatters the sense of direction on which its title seems to play. The American West of *Once Upon a Time in the West* (1968) is replaced with the Maghreb (the "West" within the Arab world). Besides, where we expected *ouest* in the title, we read *oued* (river). However, instead of filming a story set on the banks of a *oued*, Bensalah's camera follows the characters driving to the bled: from the French housing projects to a ferry on the Mediterranean Sea, Algiers, the desert, and then back north to Algiers, Oran, and Algiers again. The "oued" of the title is lost in the narrative. Using a false metonymic indication, Bensalah's substitution of the cardinal point in the title with a phonetically close location dis-Orients the viewer. By dislocating words and places, Bensalah destabilizes easy generic categorizations of his film and revisits notions of identity, territory, and migration, leaving them in a different place than where he found them.

As is the case of *Big City* (2007)—Bensalah's fourth feature set in the American West of 1880—*Il était une fois* can be described as a "Couscous Western." Its camp character is an obvious homage to Sergio Leone's Spaghetti Westerns, which enables Bensalah to overlay serious moments of postcolonial Algerian history with farce to advance seemingly far-fetched scenarios in his contemporary Algerian Far West.[17] *Il était une fois* uses a playful Western-style duel scene that parodies the Western genre with the extradiegetic clicking sound of guns and close-up shots that frame the characters' eyes. This duel follows the scene where Nadia refuses to comply with her male cousin's demand that she leave the male space of the coffee shop. When Yacine asks Nadia's cousin to treat Nadia with respect, her relative angrily retorts: "Watch your mouth, Frenchie [*Françaoui*]. Here you're not home. Here you're just an emigrant." Unlike Westerns, however, Bensalah's story is not set on a physical frontier but rather a symbolic one. It spans an imagined bled buttressed by the unknown, against which characters define who they are and identify "the Other." In this light, the "duel" illuminates existing perceptions about the supposed incompatibility of dual identities, in this case French/ Algerian. It also relegates the interlocutors into two firmly marked camps, with "authentic" Algerian constituents on one side and visitors (outsiders) on the other. While inclusion in national identity is refused to Yacine, Johnny is granted it—a fact that signals the film's unconventional handling of the spectators' expectations.

The arena of sports has become the theater where issues of citizenship, and of social and national inclusion, are played out. In the film, Nadia, Nadège, Yacine, and Johnny are playing table football, which prompts Johnny to resort to identitarian binaries. He accuses Nadège of playing like "a Breton chick who lost her papers." Ironically, it is he who is undocumented. He will also prove to play soccer poorly in a later scene. In the first soccer game between Algeria and France since the independence of Algeria, which took place on October 6, 2001 at the Stade de France, the predicted "friendly" nature of the event was unhinged by *Beur* fans, who viewed the dual event in "duelistic" terms. Fans booed at the playing of the French anthem and interrupted the match by intruding onto the (battle)field.[18] Bensalah's 2005 film, which takes place at the end of the 1980s, stages an anachronistic parodic "coda" to the historic soccer match in which Johnny is eager to participate by playing for the Algerian team.[19] During the table football match, Johnny's teammate Nadège urged him not to "pass the ball off to the back," Johnny proclaimed himself the embodiment of "Laldjéria" (Algeria), thus taking another shot at self-proclaimed Algerian assimilation, but he fails the test when time comes to prove himself on the soccer field.

In the "rematch" staged this time on the field, the flabbergasted on-site Algerian commentator denounces Johnny, who wears the Algerian jersey, as a traitor for heading the ball into the net behind him, thus mistakenly scoring a point against his own team and making the Algerians lose against the French. Had the commentator spoken in the local language, he could have used the heavily loaded *Harki*,[20] thereby acknowledging Johnny's "original" Algerianness by the very same act of denigrating it. Sensitive to Johnny's crying over his soccer failure, his Algerian hosts express sympathy.

Bypassing Johnny by Passing as Abdel Bachir

Annoyed by half-Alsatian Johnny and his infatuation with his story about being from Algeria, Yacine objects loudly: "You could perhaps be a bit German, but you will never in your life be an Arab." While suggesting that his friend has lost his mind (*perdu le nord,* as the French expression goes), Yacine's bitterness may come from the experience of not being able to pass as French in France nor as Arab in Algeria, where he is refused entry to a nightclub because of his inability to speak Arabic. Johnny, however, is admitted without question because he happens to know the bouncer Jean-Michel Tahar la Rochefoucauld,[21] who we learn was expelled from France. The inflated but incomplete Frenchness of the bouncer's invented name—it includes an Arabic first name—echoes the parodied Arabness of Abdel Bachir. Jean-Michel and Johnny's complicity enables the latter to become the star of the disco and perform in an "Arabian Nights" atmosphere. Yacine's stepmother's response to Yacine—"Why do you care? One is from the country where one feels the best"—moves the question of national identity beyond the clear delineation between jus soli and jus sanguinis and proposes a third route to citizenship, one that transforms a potential outsider into an insider.[22]

To assemble his Arabness, Johnny has to pass as someone else. He adopts the compound first name Abdel Bachir. The first element of his name starts with an *A* and the second with a *B*. Probably following the Roman alphabet, "Abdel Bachir" is not possible in any linguistically authentic or appropriate form because "Abd el" (the servant/slave of) ought to precede "Allah" or any of God's ninety-nine other names, but "Bachir" is not one of them. Johnny's approach to choosing his "Arab" name makes the viewer wonder had he chosen a third element, if it would have started with a C such as Cherif.[23] Johnny's perfunctory self-"translation" highlights his naïve belief that deidentification from Frenchness and passing as an Arab is as simple as ABC.

Bensalah both highlights and challenges the importance of naming in facilitating social and ethnic belonging and an integrated sense of identity. Before his migration to Algeria, Johnny feels overwhelmed with his *Françaoui* heritage. He is devastated to hear his mother's racist remark—after she calls his *hbaya* a "Shabbat outfit": "It's the same, they're both raghead's holidays."[24] Johnny is also humiliated in front of his *Beur* friends by his father's insistence that he return home to eat sauerkraut, to which he responds, "I'm a *Muslim,* I ain't gonna break my fast with pork." Johnny's suffering conforms to Charles Taylor's statement that "our identity is partly shaped by recognition or its absence, often by the *mis*recognition of others. . . . Nonrecognition or misrecognition can inflict harm, can be a form of oppression, imprisoning someone in a false, distorted, and reduced mode of being."[25]

In Taylor's terms, Johnny's anxiety to free himself from the "*mis*recognition of others" in the banlieue pushes him to flee the national confines of his "imprisonment." Algeria will become Johnny's escape from the French banlieue, a "wild" space of fractures of various kinds including familial and social. In order to be grafted back on to his imagined—in the Andersonian sense—but nonetheless real-to-him Algerianness, Johnny embarks on a ferryboat that transports him to Algeria. There, he uses a botanical metaphor to suggest that he has been cultivating the dream of a jus soli and the "return" to his "roots." Like an uprooted plant, Johnny's parents are accused of cutting him off from his stock: "I was ['picked up'] by French people. They don't know nothing about Algeria. Since I was a child, they did everything to cut me off from my roots." In *Il était une fois,* where no scenario can be dismissed, "picked up" Johnny could be making everything up, or he could be living a fairy-tale dream of being a changeling.

Johnny insists that his parents did more than deprive him of his Algerian roots; they inflicted upon him a degrading identity in France through their choice of name: "They gave me the name of a loser." Indeed, in the French popular vernacular, *beauf* and *Johnny* are synonyms and they both mean "loser" when used as a common noun. But rather than playing the role of the *beauf* in France, Johnny conforms to the image of the social type of the farcical "buffoon." In banlieue slang, *bouffon* is a greater insult. This characterization of the outcast is a victim of ridicule, as is the case of Johnny. For instance, in the opening scene, Johnny's *Beur* friends laugh at him when his mother threatens that if he does not obey her, he will "lose" more of his self: "J'te fais bouffer tes chicots" ("I'll make you eat your teeth"). In an interesting twist on the botanical metaphor of being "uprooted," the slang term *chicot* designates a stump (*souche*), which in French refers to a person's dominant ethnic ancestry.[26] Whether intended or not, Mrs. Leclerc's double entendre conveys the idea that she could separate Johnny from his roots (stock) by removing, along with his teeth, his ability to claim his Otherness. Johnny's mother's intimidation seems to confirm the possibility of a hidden Algerian connection that she is eager to silence, as her complaint to her husband betrays: "Hey, Pop, he just insulted our race again," to which the husband responds: "You son of a bastard."

For Johnny's future wife, Nadège, Johnny's Johnny*ness* makes him all the more attractive: "You're an out-of-place prince but you're a prince nonetheless." Nadège's comment about liking Johnny for being "out of place," in other words "*à l'ouest*,"[27] seems to confirm the notion that offset is a particularly privileged modus operandi in Bensalah's work. The originality of *Il était une fois* resides in its treatment of identity and emigration/immigration between France and Algeria. Bensalah questions normative accounts of emigration from south to north by reversing the direction of Johnny's clandestine migration. Upon discovering that Johnny had tagged along and embarked on the trip with neither passport nor ferry boarding pass, Mr. Sabri is outraged and afraid that his family might spend their month of vacation in jail. When the Algerian customs officer orders that Mr. Sabri's car be searched, the latter cries out: "But what are you looking for? A clandestine migrant, right? Eh? But who would think of coming to Algeria, except for us?" To win over the customs officer, the father desperately resorts to the rhetoric of the stereotypical perception of the northward flow of clandestine migrants institutionalized by mainstream mass media by betting on the common belief that entering Algeria illegally ought not to make sense.

The presentation of this belief is problematic, since it does little to contest the Eurocentric view of Algeria as essentially an undesirable place. Mr. Sabri's trick works: the officer has "nothing to declare" to Mr. Sabri, for the former trusts that harga originates strictly south of the Mediterranean. This verbal duel is short-lived, and Johnny is not deported in spite of his missing passport, thus becoming a *French* clandestine passenger. Bensalah therefore humorously introduces both the fact of the "first" Frenchman crossing into Algeria without identity papers, and the novel idea that he would want to do it.[28] Johnny's groundbreaking immigration is facilitated by a joke at Algeria's expense. Yet such jokes allow Bensalah's characters the mobility to change, challenging essentialist discourse on national and cultural hierarchies. Ultimately, the customs officer—whose normative thinking is his downfall—is revealed to be far more foolish than Johnny is.

Il était une fois proposes further reconfigurations, including those of gender power relations. In order to engage Yacine to Nadia, Mr. Sabri sets up a plot to prank his son into accompanying him to Algeria to escape a fictitious prosecutor.

After being lured into Algeria, Yacine tries to recover his passport from his father at night.[29] This subplot restages *Beur* narratives featuring female characters sequestered in Algeria by their families in order to sever the young women from a love or sexual relationship, as is the case in Aïcha Benaïssa and Sophie Ponchelet's *Née en France,* where the female narrator is sent to Algeria and her French passport is confiscated, or in order to force them to marry there, as in Jamila Aït-Abbas's *La Fatiha.* However, in Bensalah's male version of "forced" marriage, the engagement and wedding of Nadia and Yacine are made official with the consent of both characters. This outcome challenges negative Orientalist assumptions about marriage practices in the Maghreb. However, one possible criticism of this parodic subplot is that it is not pushed further than its comical value, comfortably reenacting the tradition of arranged marriage by representing it, in Hollywood fashion, as an essentially consensual "happy ending." The reversal remains mere social comedy, mockery without critique.

"Remakes" of Arab Grocers, "Authentic" Stews, and Arabicized Beers

In addition to flirting with social commentary, Bensalah's reversal of the typical migration patterns and of the identity of the *sans-papiers* (undocumented migrants) contradicts assumptions prevalent in Western mass media coverage of Maghrebis, including those who have settled in France. The archetype of the Arab grocer is a common French stereotype of the Maghrebi migrant who has "made it" in the local community by setting up a small business in France. The expression *aller chez l'Arabe,* which is firmly grounded in the French imaginary, has come to mean a visit to the local convenience store, usually open late at night. In the last scene of the film, Johnny Leclerc has become the owner of a small grocery store. Turning widely held French stereotypes on their head, Bensalah transforms the French national Johnny "Leclerc" into "*l'Arabe du coin,*" and in so doing, reduces the French chain of supermarkets Leclerc to a single corner shop. Even more startlingly, this Franco-French *épicier arabe* is located not in Paris, Marseilles, or any other French city or banlieue but rather in an Algerian metropolis.

The film's use of cultural stereotypes is uncomfortable, yet Bensalah's position remains ambiguous, since such clichés are revealed through the buffoonish demeanor of Johnny. Johnny's relationship to *chorba* (a thick stew), which he elevates to the gastronomic symbol of Algeria, is an illustrative example. When Johnny breaks fast with the Sabris back in France, he laments he was served a Moroccan soup: "Yum, your *harira* is good, Mrs. Sabri. But *I* am an Algerian, and I would have preferred a *chorba.*" Though it is consumed in Morocco, too, Johnny associates the chorba with Algeria, making it an arbitrary symbol of "authentic" national identity. Johnny's parochial comment leaves Mrs. Sabri smiling at his naïveté. This scene embodies the film's ambiguous posture, for Johnny is at once a prototype that disorients usual identificatory categories and a character whose search for authenticity reasserts stereotypical associations (chorba with Algeria).

In another scene at an Algerian restaurant in Algeria, Johnny comes to blows with the cooks when he finds the chef's chorba to be flavorless. To his great consternation, Johnny had been made to eat an industrial chorba that came from a packet of the multinational Maggi brand for sale in chains of supermarkets such as Leclerc. The chef's substitution of what Johnny considers to be the essence of Algeria with a cheap imitation of the rich national dish inspires in Johnny the hyperbolic statement: "This is the shame of Algeria." Johnny had tasted other chorbas before, none of which had lived up to his expectations. Rather than the stew's flavor, what aggrieves the character most is the realization that longing for a stronger tie with an origin conceived as "authentic" is never quite satisfying because it is as unattainable as the perfect chorba. Wanting to renationalize the recipe, Johnny energetically shows the local chef how to make an "authentic" chorba. Nevertheless, the personalized rendering of the stew boils down to an overly fixed and finally alienating identitarian quest, since the instructions he gives the chef are for a chorba à la Johnny.

The treatment of culinary identity is contiguous with the film's questioning of notions of authenticity, belief, and truth. Significantly, the viewer is left wondering as to the authenticity of Johnny's claim to be an Algerian. Yacine discarded Johnny's assertion as mere mythomania, alleging that Johnny's native Algeria is imaginary, inspired by a purchased drawing. Yet on the way to Oran, the car has a flat tire and Johnny comes across the very village from which he claims to hail. There, Yacine and Johnny meet an old man with disheveled hair, who states that he knew an Abdel Bachir, whom he identifies as Bachir el Moussaoui and Johnny's father. One is suspicious from the start, since the name *Abdel Bachir* cannot exist. Johnny, the new convert, agrees to buy the old man a beer in exchange for directions to his father's tomb but protests that the drink is *haram* (illicit/forbidden). The old man circumvents Johnny's interpretation of Islam by knowingly misreading the label "Heineken Lager Beer" as "Hnaken Ajer Kbeer" ("Here Lies a Tremendous Reward [in the Afterlife]").[30] He also reads the Arabic transcription on the tombstone as "Abdel Bachir el Moussaoui a.k.a. the clown," whereas it actually reads "*Qbar majhoul*" ("Grave of a stranger"—as is indicated in the French subtitle). With this example, Bensalah playfully suggests that identity is not—so to speak—written in stone.

In addition, *majhoul* also means "ignorant" and "unknown." The implication is that one does not know one's real identity. The fact that this Arabic pseudoname has another meaning, that of "nameless," demonstrates that Johnny's identity relies on approximate markers that make room for personal readjusting. The examination of its trilateral root *jim-ha-lam* (ل ه ج) suggests, by way of association, the additional notion of "foolishness," which introduces the idea that Johnny's quest could be linked not to a physical father but to a clan of fools. When the young men leave the mining ghost town, the old man puts on a clown's nose found on the tomb, as if to tell us that he has just fooled the two visitors and the audience by the same token. Although the old man's story seems nothing more than a tissue of lies, it does not completely eliminate the plausibility of Johnny's story. In encouraging Johnny to be an Abdel Bachir (i.e., a clown?), the old man enhances the farce, hails Johnny as a Harlequin, and complicates the material reality of the stories at play. Did he overhear Johnny's loud recounting of his childhood as the two young men walked through the ruins of the village? Or could Johnny be standing at the grave of his deceased biological father? This scene manages to unsettle the viewer's certainties (as well as Yacine's—who functions as a surrogate spectator within the scene) about Johnny's true heritage. Is the deceased clown a colonial, and Johnny, in Homi Bhabha's terms, a mimic—but in reverse? In other words, is Johnny not quite white but not quite Algerian-Arab-Muslim either? (After all, Johnny's idiosyncratic identity is ultimately an effective model of mimicry: in the end, he achieves his aim of integration). Even the tombstone, a traditional site of closure, leaves the identity of the *majhoul* who lies there open to speculation. No matter who is right, the cemetery becomes a place of free trade where the exchange of a *bière* (coffin) for a *bière* (beer) benefits all parties.

As Taylor explains, "inwardly derived, personal, original identity doesn't enjoy . . . recognition a priori. It has to win it through exchange."[31] Therefore, the telling of stories is primordial for Johnny. When dining with the Sabris' relatives, Johnny imposes his favorite joke, that of a soccer game between Morocco and Brazil involving a *djinn* (genie), which triggers delayed laughter. Perplexed, the grandfather of Mr. Sabri's future daughter-in-law qualifies the storyteller as "intelligent," a "*jenn*" (trouble-maker), and a "*mahboul*" (fool). Embarrassed, Mr. Sabri tells his interlocutor that Johnny is not a *mahboul*; however, they agree that he is "*ness ness*" (half-half). Contrary to his misleading French last name Leclerc (a homonym of Le Clair, "the Clear One"), it is not at all clear who Johnny is. Johnny is *Moha le fou, Moha le sage,* half a madman, half a wise storyteller, "endowed with multiple voices."[32] Johnny-Moha, the wise fool, is bequeathed multiple facets, for he is altogether Joha (the Arab iconic buffoon), a *jenn,* and a genie.

Identitarian Tourism

The French cineaste Tony Gatlif has directed documentaries, shorts, and feature films. His major titles include *Latcho drom* (1993), *Gadjo dilo* (1997), *Vengo* (2000), and *Transylvania* (2006). Yosefa Loshitzky remarks that "all of Gatlif's films deal with the life of Maghrebi (North African) Muslims in France or with Gypsies in Europe. Hence, they introduce the two major entities of European 'otherness,' the

Romany and the Muslim, into the ongoing debate about European identity and its historical and cultural roots."[33] Tony Gatlif's diasporic road movie *Exils* (*Exiles*) was produced in 2004 and earned him the best director award at the Cannes Film Festival. In this film, like in *Il était une fois*, a journey is undertaken from France to Algeria, this time by two young lovers. The woman, Naïma Tarouni (Lubna Azabal), is the daughter of a Harki. The man, Zano (Romain Duris), is of Roma descent, the child of *Pieds-noirs* (settlers of European descent). His ancestors lived in Algeria until the country gained its independence in 1962 when Pieds-noirs left the country en masse.

Mana Derakhshani and Jennifer A. Zachman explain that the film is not overtly political. But as they point out, it opens with the song "Manifeste," notable for "the political message of its lyrics."[34] Beginning *Exils* in this manner paves the way to certain readings of the filmic narrative.[35] Indeed, in the very first scene, while we are acquainted with the protagonists, an anarchic manifesto (penned by Tony Gatlif himself) that questions the efficiency of democracy in improving the lot of the powerless is shouted in English by a female voice and recited in Spanish by a soft male voice, first separately, then concurrently. The manifesto urgently advocates for the voiceless.

Ensconced in a tiny apartment high up in a multistoried building, the couple seems to escape the grip of time and space. They offer their naked bodies to the eye of the camera. Laying on the bed, Naïma eats melted Camembert cheese while Zano—also nude—stands in front of the window and stares at the city while sipping his drink before he extends his arm, waits a few seconds, and then drops the glass out of the window with a similar insouciance. Their distance from the earth signifies their feeling of disconnection from their roots. It is no coincidence that right after the director paints the suffocating atmosphere of their habitat—the banlieue, a symbol of urban marginalization in French society—that Zano makes the proposal: "How about we go to Algeria!" Naïma laughs at the unexpected offer: "What the hell do you want to do in Algeria?"

Shortly after the project is mocked, the protagonists find themselves on the road. Following a short scene on foot in France and another by train, the travelers arrive in Spain. There, the couple meets Leila and her brother Habib, both Algerian clandestines. Habib asks in Arabic what the French couple is doing in the area. Leila translates her brother's question, and Zano answers, "We are going to Algeria," which elicits laughter from the young Algerian man. Leila inquires about what they are going to do in her country and Zano contributes a piece to the puzzle: "We are walking to Algiers." Leila in turn laughs at this unanticipated answer. Zano's second response reveals an important element: that the journey will be undertaken on foot. Leila then translates to her young brother, giving him the opportunity to further mock the preposterous project. Habib and Leila are also walking, but the difference is that they are going north. The amused reaction of the Algerian siblings implies that such painstaking effort is only reasonable in one direction: north. Algeria is not a common destination for French travelers; the postcolonial nation did not develop a tourist industry and lacks the infrastructure of the two other Maghrebi countries, Morocco and Tunisia—common places for European holiday-makers. Furthermore, the film takes place during a still unstable Algeria that is slowly recovering from a decade-long civil war. Finally, a deadly earthquake has just taken place and subsequent tremors could potentially occur. But the spectator soon finds out that Zano, and eventually Naïma (whom he convinces) do not set out to visit Algeria with the idea of engaging in traditional tourism. Rather, Gatlif frames the trip as identitarian tourism that can only occur in a specific *lieu de mémoire*.

Zano and Naïma's encounter with Leila and Habib allows the director to disclose the French characters' motivations and the nature of the couple's identitarian journey. It is essential that the four travelers find themselves involved in a quest together, though their goals are each different. Indeed, these coincidences allow for a contrast between the respective intentions of the French couple and the North African siblings on their way to Paris or Amsterdam where they expect to enroll in a European university. This contrast serves as a backdrop for the series of ordeals lived by real denizens of the South. All four characters are in a state of need, fragility, and distress, albeit of varying extents, in that two of them fear being deported, whereas the other two do not need to worry about this potential outcome. Their marginality brings them together, adding to their easily knitted friendship already fortified by mutual cultural belonging. They have Algeria and France in common. The difference between the two pairs, and an important one at that, is that they are moving toward each other's country of birth.

As the quartet parts, Naïma gives Leila a phone number to call should she and her brother manage to make it to Paris. Surprisingly, their paths cross again, and on that second occasion, Leila returns the favor by entrusting Naïma with her address in Algeria. Zano and Naïma eventually benefit from the hospitality of their acquaintances' family. Leila writes a letter to her relatives back home indicating that she has sent two French people and asks that they treat the foreigners well. She mentions in her missive the reason of their journey in Algeria. In her words, they have come to "bring memories back," thus assuming that their "walk" is a leisure trip. It is significant that the French word for memories, *souvenirs,* as used in the case of Zano and Naïma's transnational journey, reflects multiple aspects of their trip. The term in the film signifies "memories"—and not the English meaning of *souvenirs* (a homonym in French and Arabic)—literal keepsakes from travel. Indeed, Zano will not bring the memorabilia that belongs to his family, which he will be presented in the house where his ancestors used to reside. Furthermore, the couple is never shown purchasing Algerian-made collectibles, yet both Zano and Naïma collect several experiences, which challenge them to deal with familial and cultural memory, and which, because of their intensity, mark each character indelibly, becoming souvenirs for the psyche, so to speak.

Naïma's question to Zano at the beginning of the film ("What the hell do you want to do in Algeria?"), which characterizes her early attitude of distrust, disdain, and distance, is left unanswered. Her question is ostensibly rhetorical and her snobbish amusement further silences Zano. But Zano's ellipsis in the dialogue has the impact of alerting the spectator to the eccentric nature of his project. Zano's reaction is to look through the window again, swaying his body back and forth to the beat of music, as if wanting to reach a state of trance. The film cuts to a hallucinatory vision of a crowd of Algerians walking in one direction under a scorching sun. The title of the film then appears in red capitals across this image of a growing flow of individuals on the go. Some are empty-handed, whereas others carry bags. Though we read *EXILS* (EXILES) in red, we see an *EXODE* (EXODUS) instead.

The official cover for the DVD available in France and English-speaking countries is the same: it shows Zano and Naïma against a black and red wall looking boldly straight at us. An alternative French cover of the DVD shows the complexity of exile through a resembling (para)textual multilayeredness (Figure 3.1). The title *EXILS* is printed in black and placed between an image of Zano and Naïma (at the top) and one of the exodus of Algerians (at the bottom). Though the film title is superimposed onto the images, the two groups of leavists show through. In addition, the photo of Zano and Naïma and that of the exiles-in-progress appear to be placed next to each other in a mixed-media, photomontage style. These graphic decisions convey the idea that many kinds of departures can be instances of exile and exodus. Certainly, the Algerian exodus has a different motivation than the young couple's journey of self-exile: the mass of people are leaving out of fear of subsequent earthquake tremors, whereas Zano and Naïma's travel is not caused by sudden external circumstances. The choice of black lettering—the traditional color of mourning in Western society in which Zano and Naïma live in—induces one to interpret the film as an attempt to mourn an exilic condition that has its roots in dark times, namely, colonization and the Algerian War.

Exile is commonly conceptualized as an individual departure, while exodus entails a massive or a collective departure. But could we conceive of exile as a type of exodus? *Exils* undertakes the juxtaposition of the two processes, right from the start. The film also juxtaposes—and at times superimposes—various types of leave-taking. In particular, *Exils* merges real and fictional journeys as Zano's "return" parallels Gatlif's own return to his native Algiers after a forty-three–year absence. *Exils,* like many of Gatlif's other films, are very personal. It can be suggested that this trip was an opportunity for the director to come to terms with

Figure 3.1 Alternative cover art for Tony Gatlif's *Exils*.

his family's exodus and his consequent sense of exile. It is not surprising that the story of Zano, Gatlif's on-screen alter ego, should aim to reveal what these two words have in common beside a prefix (*ex-*), by attempting to mend the gap between past exodus and present exile. The "present" exodus we see in the film, that of Algerians leaving their destroyed city in the aftermath of a deadly earthquake, is an indication that exoduses are part of a fate-stricken reality for contemporary Algerians and lead to exiles for them and future generations. The history of modern Algeria is riddled with tragedies that have compelled locals to leave their country: the Algerian War, forced and willed emigration to Europe, the "Black decade" of the 1990s, and a succession of earthquakes in the heavily populated area of Algiers. The association made between exodus and Algeria is obvious in *Exils* in that in this occurrence of exodus, an old limping stranger is waving a small Algerian flag. In the same scene, the excerpt of a song in Spanish played louder and louder repeats almost invariably, "Argelia, Argelia, Argelia . . ." ("Algeria, Algeria, Algeria . . ."). The episode of Algerians walking alone yet together in one direction, which was shown the first time at the beginning of the film when Zano had suggested leaving, appears again right after the train scene in Algeria. In that second instance, the diasporic couple elbows their way through a crowd. Their journey is against the grain, for they walk counter to the flow to the multitude. The strangers are fleeing the massive earthquake that hit the capital and neighboring coastal cities on May 21, 2003. Images of this contemporary exodus of people symbolizing human migratory movements northward presumably to better conditions, while the "northern" couple moves against the crowd southward, becomes a parable highlighting a paradox. Naïma's aforementioned laughter also signifies the seeming improbability of their reverse journey. Gatlif's recurring imagery of the exodus sets up Algeria as a space of constant exile/exodus, and thereby as an experimental site for examining issues of migration, identity, and globalization.

How do migration, identity, and globalization concern characters already settled in the North? In an intimate setting, Naïma offers information essential to the narrative but in the form of a fraught confession. Naïma talks privately with Leila who asks her new friend why she does not speak Arabic. Naïma replies, "Nobody taught it to me. My father didn't want to speak Arabic with us. He didn't want us to talk about his country any longer." When the French couple discusses scars on their bodies, Naïma refuses to explain the origin of one of hers. Later, when Zano catches her cheating on him with a Spanish stranger, she insists that Zano cannot understand her. She also tells him in confessional fashion that since she was a child she has constantly been displaced from one home to another. We realize that this trip makes sense for Naïma as well, for it will reopen her wounds, forcing her to face her past and question her conception of "home." Upon arriving at their Algerian host family's home, Naïma shares her epiphany with

Zano, telling him that she is a foreigner everywhere. It is revealing that she keeps eluding her Arabness. Her status as child of a Harki has caused her to feel excluded from a binary axis of identification. When Habib asks if *Naïma* is an Arab name, she responds, "Well, it's just Naïma." Then, when her name leads a stranger to inquire if she is a Muslim, she responds categorically, "No." These moments demonstrate that Naïma refuses to adhere to an imposed identity and her determination to keep her distance from a cultural and religious affiliation with which she is not familiar.

The young woman has suffered a profound feeling of uprootedness. To address and, by the same token, redress, this disconnectedness from her forbidden past, Naïma takes part in a trance. The director chooses to make the trance the longest scene in the film, thus heightening its impact.[36] His strategy suggests that substantial effort is needed to call up and transform latent trauma. Music becomes a therapeutic force, helping Naïma to bring out and release obstructive and heavy feelings. Zano is shown gripping Naïma as she moves in trance. Not only does Zano grapple with her as she shakes her body forcefully in the little room full of other bodies in trance, musicians, chanters, and witnesses, but Zano also supports her in her endeavor, becoming her symbolic backbone. The young man is the right person to hold on to, for he once confesses, "Music is my religion." In this meeting, where music allows men and women to temporarily do away with the gender divide that holds them apart in other quotidian circumstances, Zano also takes part in the trance. His double function as danc*er* and danc*ee* turns him into a sort of guru who dances his lover out of her traumatic self. In this long exorcism, Naïma is deeply shaken: she gasps for air, faints, sweats, and cries; her body convulses more forcefully than that of other participants. We can see how much Naïma has been scarred by how much is released in this process. Naïma breaks free and flings her hair and body to the beating of musical instruments and the hypnotic chants.

These collective trance and private confession scenes with strangers set the stage for a crucial moment of disclosure for Zano as well. Indeed, soon Zano's reason for the trip is disclosed albeit in fragments: the young man feels the urge to visit the country of his roots. But his connection with Algeria is envisaged through a moment of major disconnection, the exodus of Pieds-noirs in 1962, which occurred almost overnight. The young man touches upon the exodus, just enough for the spectator to situate his family's story.[37] Later in the film, the character further addresses this history and tackles issues such as anticolonization and torture when he explains the sufferings of his ancestor Ferdinand Boulanger, "the first teacher in the locality of Rouiba." In 1959, the French arrested and tortured Ferdinand in the prison of Algiers for being an "anticolonialist."

It then becomes apparent that for Zano this trip is about reversing a previous exile. He has a clear vision of how, why, and where to go in order to conduct this symbolic reversal. To erase its negative effects, he walks the itinerary taken by his ancestors, only the opposite direction. He exposes pieces of a childhood event to his companion; we are later given additional elements of the riddle and soon realize that Zano's puzzle is not very distinct from Naïma's. Indeed, the trance scene is a catalyst, and we understand that both characters are looking for the missing link in their life stories, which are intertwined with their ancestors' national history. Zano's intimate recounting of his familial story reveals to Naïma and the viewer that his father vowed to return to Algeria, but a tragic car accident took Zano's parents' lives. Therefore, for the young man, the advent of the country's independence coincides with a profound gap of information held by his transmitters of memory, his ancestors. That rupture with Zano's personal, familial, national, and cultural place of belonging caused him to stop playing the violin, a symbol of his attachment to his origins. Zano even buries the instrument in a wall before his journey to Algeria. Only when he leaves does he signal readiness to replace a symbol of his immediate ancestry with the materiality of his inherited past. To facilitate the unearthing of missing information and the completion of his quest, the director opts to have the new dwellers in Zano's family's house in Algiers keep the frames hanging on the walls as they were left in 1962. The Algerians who moved in shortly after the owners left even keep a box full of photographs of Zano's relatives. The young man's moment of catharsis happens when his silent past is given back to him in the form of visual testimonies. He is moved to tears. To be able to put a face on the genealogical tree releases him from the ghosts of the past and helps him live with a better understanding of where he comes from.

As for Naïma, her inability to speak her father's tongue comes with a layer of shame. Her father's refusal to speak his own language—a traditional conveyer of a vision of the world—barred her familiarity with her father's personal, familial, and national story and history. The brutal disconnection in the flow of her own narrative is soon to be addressed. Will it be deepened or mended? An ominous image appears to provide an answer—albeit one that requires interpretation. Naïma shares with her lover that she had a dream. In this dream—or nightmare given its gruesomeness—the path they walk is covered with blood. The couple reaches Algeria safely, so the dream does not portend danger for them. One can read the trail of blood as her subconscious longing for lineage and blood relatives, from which both characters have been severed. This nightmarish dream occurs on the eve of Naïma's birthday and behooves Zano to undertake a staged performance that shifts the diegesis into a symbolic framing in search for a symbiotic pact. The young man buys a bottle of champagne to celebrate his lover's birthday and performs an impromptu skit. At the base of a tree, he digs and unearths the bottle of champagne, wrapped like a corpse in a shroud, thus enacting the resuscitation of a resurfacing past. The release of unidentifiable buried feelings contained in a champagne bottle have the ability to pop open and pour forth something sweet and celebratory. Thanks to this moment, Naïma is willing to proceed forward, despite her former lack of enthusiasm—on various occasions, she voices fears and questions concerning the purpose of her participation in this journey. But now, instead, Naïma exults with shouts of "Well done!" and applauds profusely. Zano's project has been successfully accomplished to her satisfaction. Zano hands the bottle to his lover who brings it to her mouth, drinks some of the liquid, spits it out onto the young man, and hands the bottle back to Zano for him to have his share. The latter puts some of the champagne in his mouth and spits it back onto Naïma. The scene ends with the two of them in each other's arms, and Zano lifts Naïma from the ground, metaphorically raising her to higher expectations. The protagonists sketch a cyclic ritual in which they water each other to allow the other to grow, as they tread the symbolic red line of blood to Algeria. In a pantomimic enactment, the two youths unknowingly conjure up Naïma's dream in preparation for what awaits them on a seldom-trodden path, that of exile in reverse.

Props and Prompts

On two occasions, Zano is shown stopping in the frame of the camera and putting drops in his eyes. Gatlif's close-up, which by definition is a type of magnifier, indicates that Zano is doing something important, namely, opening his eyes, literally and figuratively by removing veils, filters, and other obstacles that could impede a clear and objective perspective. Though the young man is treating his eyes with a medicated liquid, his action is also an instructing measure urging us to keep our weather eye open, to not miss the meaning of each deceivingly simple gesture. Zano is here to see what he was not able to make out at an earlier age.

The comment that follows this eye-drop ritual suggests that while Zano improves his vision, Naïma feels her companion's trip is having the effect of worsening her lot; she complains, "You contaminate me with your bullshit." It is noteworthy that many scenes and gestures including the eye-medicating episode appear twice in the film. The choice to double up moments throughout *Exils* is a clear indication that each iteration applies once to Zano and once to Naïma. Binarism is a central feature. Each instance of the same image however is filmed with slightly different elements, as if to imply that both protagonists are on the same trip and after the same quest but with slightly varying expectations, determination, and outcomes. We shall see later that Naïma's experience is a relatively less satisfactory one. In the meantime, it is necessary to grant a place to Naïma here, which the director does not seem to give her in *Exils*. The lack of importance as an agent in the plot leads me to raise a few questions. Even in the powerful trance scene, it is Zano who supports Naïma. Yet trance is a place where women traditionally dominate. Why then is the young lady not allowed to be the flag-bearer of this culture? And is the trance really effective in changing Naïma's heart and soul? Her itinerary from angst-ridden to appeased woman is hackneyed, for the sought effect is reached too suddenly (a trance session suffices), as if overlooked until the last minute.

One could argue that *Exils* is ultimately about the director, so the focus is on Zano. Unfortunately, the result is that women are portrayed in this film—and in others of this corpus—as extras. Why is that so? Why does this artistic piece depict Naïma as an accompanying character versus a lead? I would contend this neglect presents an incomplete perspective on identity, culture, and migration. Perhaps new directions in Mediterranean cinema will rectify these gaps in gender representation. Meanwhile, Naïma voices her discontent at having to tag along, although she is not a particularly empowered voice. Réda in *Le Grand voyage* and Nordine in *Ten'ja* (discussed in chapters 1 and 6, respectively) are both male protagonists who are also reluctant to "accompany" their fathers; in the one case the father is alive and in the other he is dead. Though the trips are useful for the male characters, it is not evident that the journey has the same complete cathartic effect for Naïma. Indeed, she is shown smiling at the end of the trip, but she does so as she peels the orange and hands pieces to Zano; she has been returned to a secondary position as the one who feeds her man.

In this final scene, the title slowly reappears on the screen in large letters covering the entire screen to signify and intensify the end of the film. The imposing font and choice of red color call our attention: EXILS is an EXIT sign. It is a possible closure, provided we proceed forward on the journey. Like a stamp on a package or a neon sign, the title makes it impossible to mistake the focus of this journey. We are reminded to read the film as an attempt to reflect on the notion of exile. The sign appears after an open-ended closing shot, giving the title still more power to frame the preceding narrative. The open-endedness of the scene resides in the fact that it raises an essential question. In what looks like a romantic walk on a sunny day rather than a farewell visit, the couple is shown strolling in the local Christian cemetery where Zano's grandfather is interred. At peace with themselves, the protagonists smile and leave the area hand in hand, happily having accomplished their respective missions to "bring memories back" from the buried past, symbolized by the cemetery, which constitutes their final stop. The two characters are walking away, thus likely resuming their exilic condition. But the recurrent message of the film is that exile can be dispelled only if one remains close to one's heritage and its representatives. Therefore, in light of the message contained in "Exils," summed up by the song that draws the film to an end, it is not clear whether Naïma and her companion are heading back to France or not.

As Naïma sits on Zano's grandfather's tomb, the young man places a pair of headphones on the cross that towers over the burial site and in a touching gesture, he plays a *chaâbi*/flamenco track for his ancestor. The viewer hears the entire song titled "Exils," which also serves as background for the closing credits. What follows is an excerpt:

Solo & Choir:

Para cantarte nuestro dolor	In order to sing you our pain
Y rezarte	And pray to you
Y protegerte	And protect you
De aquellos que se quedan	From those who remain
Cerca a ti	Close to you[38]

Since it is ultimately for us that it is played, the musical content works in tandem with the filmic narrative, enriching it and giving it a sense of direction. The closing song speaks of the sadness that comes from rupture with one's country of origin and the necessity to maintain ties with it. Immediately after the singer intones, "And pray to you / And protect you / From those who remain / Close to you," "EXILS" appears, followed right afterward by the usual black screen that announces the end of a film. This sharp cut directs our attention to the line in the song that signifies that what remains, when all else ends, is the music. This line has the last word, which takes the form of a piece of advice, ostensibly for the young couple, to "remain close." Though *remain* can build on a nostalgic connection with origins, it adds to our uncertainty about whether or not they will return to their French banlieue. In that song, and in "Ceux qui nous quittent," which also forms part of the soundtrack, to remember the one who is missed becomes an important endeavor, because time has dissolved ties.

The song "Ceux qui nous quittent" states that those who leave always return to us. Its haunting chorus delivered by a breathy and powerful female voice echoing the sounds of painful cries is played over an exhilarating techno rhythm. The idea is that returns are unavoidable in that they exert an irremediable pull that ceases only when one takes the initiative to fulfill the need to investigate one's past. This message is an extra layer of narrative that is itself supplemented by female and male voices uttering words of advice in Arabic—a recurrent recommendation unfolds as they repeat "Don't forget . . ." followed by family members, such as "father, paternal uncles, mother, and maternal uncles," and ending with "origins." The human significance of music is central to the narrative, as it is in all of Gatlif's films. In *Exils,* music is a form of intratext; it is an inscription that teases out meaning in the scenes and plot, providing an additional layer of cultural information on the stories we are observing and explaining how these journeys affect identity formation, deformation (crises of identity), and reformation (quests such as Zano's and Naïma's). The soundtrack comprises an eclectic choice of songs that range from *bulerías* to *chaâbi* and *raï*. The music is given special attention because the songs comment not only on the overt messages of the film but also on its hermetic meanings. One of them is particularly relevant to our themes of exile and identitarian tourism.

Ambient sounds may appear incidental, but they are actually instrumental to the purport of the film and therefore require our attention even in cases when, or precisely because, the couple dismisses them or is not attentive to them. For instance, as soon as Zano and Naïma open the door of the train to disembark in Spain, they are met with an announcement that the train is headed to Madrid. The announcement is made in Spanish. Its foreignness (especially for Zano who speaks no Spanish) signals right from the outset that the film is full of learning opportunities with regard to Otherness and identity-related issues. Acting as a prop or an aside, the soundtrack helps find answers to questions such as Naïma's ("What the hell am I doing here with you without my cell phone?")—a question she throws at Zano and us like a riddle that needs to be deciphered. At the film's closure, music tracks layer on top of one another so as to provide as many answers as possible before the film ends. As Zano and Naïma sit in the Christian cemetery, one hears the *adhan,* the muezzin's call to prayer. The call does not clash with the song Zano plays on his Walkman.[39] The literal message of the call to prayer is overlooked and the assumption is that various traditions seem to speak together. These concomitant "sound tracks" put the protagonists in motion the same way the trance sent their bodies into the realm of the magical. This layered soundscape also signals the protagonists' encounters with cultural history (for Zano) and psyche (for Naïma).

Priceless Trips: Ferry Fares and Free Rides

As we saw at the beginning of this chapter, Johnny in *Il était une fois* embarks on a ferry without a passport or a boarding pass. The missing passport makes him a clandestine. The missing boarding pass makes him an outlaw, a criminal, albeit of a lesser kind. Not only does the young Frenchman set foot on the ferry and the Algerian land without permission, he also does not contribute to the local economy by failing to pay his dues to the nautical company. In fact, like Johnny, Naïma and Zano are also technically "stowaways" from the North, an appellation that "refers to hiding in a ship that arrives openly and lawfully."[40] The two Guardia Civil officers do not feel the need to check the vehicle in which Zano and Naïma are hiding, since the van is heading back to North Africa. The officers ask the driver for the van's documentation, which they glance over before letting him proceed with an exuberant politeness, as if grateful that he is leaving their country.

It is unintentional that the lovers embark on a Morocco-bound ferry. They find out the destination too late, when the ship is already at high sea. Through the device of the protagonists' boarding the wrong boat, Gatlif is able to shoot the clandestine passage between Morocco and Algeria. The director has often discussed his obsession with (representations of) danger, rough lives, and tough destinies. With the help of a smuggler, Zano and Naïma take an unauthorized path from Morocco into Algeria, rather than transborder transport. Though this path is unguarded at the time they take it, it is subject to patrol by the local authorities. This trail, in northeastern Morocco by the city of Oujda and the near Mediterranean Sea is known for being frequented by clandestine migrants and human traffickers. "What the hell! All this just to save 150 Euros?" Naïma exclaims when their bus breaks down in northern Morocco; we know then that Zano is to blame for getting them onto the wrong ferry, and that it is he who had them hide under a tarp covering the roof rack of a van.[41]

Before traversing the Mediterranean Sea, the couple also takes a train from France to Spain without paying, evidenced by Zano's warnings to Naïma when he spots a ticket collector on board. His plan is to travel for free. However, it should be pointed out that once they cross over to North Africa, the travelers never hide when they take public transportation, so one can conclude that on the other side of the Mediterranean they do pay their fares on local transport. It is interesting that it is in Europe that the protagonists cheat the system. One could argue that given their sparse savings, the duo complies merely because public transportation is cheaper in North Africa. However, the couple pays a major amount to the smuggler, who shows them the way across to Algeria. They assent to the smuggler's demand, "Give me the other half; it's 1,000 dirhams, okay?" As a thousand dirhams equals ninety-eight dollars, we see they are willing to let go of about two hundred dollars to be led on a short walk to the Algeria-Morocco border.[42] The protagonists took the risk of hiding on the roof of a van—which could have been searched by the authorities, for it was suspiciously overloaded—and of sneaking onto a train, all to save the cash that Zano hands over to the smuggler without even haggling. Since the characters do not appear to save their money consistently, their choices are more likely based on an unwillingness to perpetuate a capitalist system that does fine without their contribution. Conversely, perhaps they feel a certain allegiance and are more than happy to participate in the local—albeit parallel—economy?

Do ideological motives actually account for the couple's insistence on going for free? Personal critiques of the economic system might explain why Zano and Naïma seek to travel without tickets on European transportation. But the couple's motivation need not be of a grand nature. It may simply be that the two characters are not willing to pay for a means of transportation that does only that—transport them from one place to another. In the train that takes them to Spain, they are closed to the world that surrounds them. They both listen to music on their Walkmans. They do not speak to each other except when it is urgent that they get off for fear of being fined. Among the landscapes they barely look at, engrossed as they are in their musical universe, includes one that is blurred by rain being wiped off the train's windshield. The pouring rain is an opaque screen on the windshield and on the screen. This image of wipers moving sideways frenetically simulates the covering over of a site, as if it were not worth showing. The implication is that Zano and Naïma are impatiently waiting for a new type of scenery, synonymous with a different culture—searching for signs such as the sun, stereotypically associated with Spain and Morocco, that would confirm that they are closer to their destination and traveling in the right direction. The next scene shows a contrasting setting, which Gatlif portrays as alien, a land full of discoveries to make, one to master and understand. What is clear is that the French segment stretching from the Parisian outskirts to southern France, which represents about eight hundred kilometers of travel, takes only a few seconds in the narrative. The little we see of France's landscapes—a panoramic view of green fields separated by a rectilinear country road—evokes much of what the youngsters are hoping to avoid, namely, a predictable itinerary for their lives. Their sighting of the ticket collector after they have made it to the other side of the Pyrenees happens at a most convenient time. It jumpstarts the protagonists in their journey of self-discovery. As I have indicated in discussing other ex-centric films, these filmic journeys taking characters out of France possess a sense of urgency that translates into the minimization and swift erasure of the hexagon from the aesthetics and economy of the plots.

Modes of Transportation and the Maghrobal

The couple's trip is priceless not only in the monetary sense, but also in that it presents the protagonists with a once-in-a-lifetime experience. The modes of transportation Zano and Naïma utilize carry with them original cultural contacts, and Gatlif adamantly characterizes transnational transit as an essential part of the film and the characters' identitarian quest. Contrary to Zano's statement that he and his partner will walk to Algiers, they alternate between quite a few means of transfer in what Gatlif has defined as a "journey of 7,000 km by train, car, boat, and on foot, and 55,000 meters by film."[43] The director's insertion of various means of travel into the diegesis cannot leave us indifferent to their potential as bearers of meaning, symbolism, and cultural critique. They are the travelers' access to their new environment, a prism through which they experience the unknown countries, a vantage point from which we assess their navigation of this rigorous foreign encounter, and the lens through which the Maghrobal can be examined.

Buses, for example, are almost depicted in *Exils* as characters in their own right. Bus rides are hard to find and hard to handle. In the deserted Spanish village where they first meet the young Algerian clandestines, Naïma inquires about where they can get on a bus to Seville. She happens to ask the wrong people, since Habib and Leila are not from the area. The first time they take the bus, Zano and Naïma have no choice but to do so. After finding themselves in Morocco, they are shown in an intercity bus in which local musicians are playing their instruments loudly. The joyful atmosphere the musicians create only heightens the French passengers' anxiety. Adding to the mêlée, the bus driver tries to pass a truck, determined to race it. Excess is taken to the extreme with the superposition of the threatening and impressive horn coming from the truck that wakes up Naïma and startles Zano. Their apprehension climaxes as the truck, the bus, and cars fight for the same narrow road as their respective horns signal dangerous passing, which carves expressions of fears on the couple's faces and provides a stark contrast to the ongoing festive atmosphere. In this scene, the intradiegetic soundtrack unravels the position in which the global tourists find themselves when outside of their comfort zone.

Because Zano and Naïma are eager to find themselves in the right Maghrebi country, their bus trip in Morocco is lived as a painful adventure that elicits feelings of claustration and claustrophobia, and they move on to the next destination with much more trepidation. Disillusion overwhelms the characters throughout the trip, and modes of transportation become spaces where such epiphanies occur. A moment of disenchantment for the travelers takes place on the train ride in Algeria. The train enters the darkness of a tunnel and reappears bathed in light. It does not mark a transition from angst to release and happiness. Rather, it leads to further anxiety in the following scene. A comparable fade-in tactic is used on the ferryboat. Once the van is parked in the ferry's garage, the couple gets out, finding themselves in a dimly lit area. They climb up the stairs and emerge into the light. In the following scene, short-lived merriness again paves the way to sudden disenchantment as they find out that the ship is headed to the "wrong" place. These images of characters coming out of darkness to be met with a harsh reality different from one's expectations highlight Zano and Naïma's naïveté and the necessity for them to adapt to unfamiliar regional specificities.

Beyond the pragmatic aspect of making various logistical arrangements, the director incorporates modes of traveling into the very materiality of his narrative. Indeed, even a taxicab becomes the title of one of the film's chapters included in the DVD. In addition, the taxi gives its name to the title of a song, "Willy le taxi" (Willy the Taxi), which is part of the national musical patrimony. In Arabic, "willy" expresses frustration, feelings of damnation, regret, and impotence in the face of fate. Yet in French (or English, for that matter), the title communicates the idea that the cab is named Willy, thus turning this common mode of travel into a character endowed with a proper name. The shortage of cabs causes an entire crowd to line up on the street. It is as though the entire neighborhood has gathered there; the director suggests that an endless chain of individuals symbolizing the entire nation is standing quietly in a moment of silence to remember, perhaps, the casualties of the Algiers-Boumerdès earthquake. The way the strangers are filmed corroborates the idea that they are not just waiting for a taxi but are partaking in a singular collective ritual. Indeed, the locals first stand immobile with their heads turned sideways away from the street. When the cab irrupts into the charged scene, Naïma cuts in line. The cab is a rare commodity for the locals—which justifies the regional interjection "Heavens, the taxi!," whereas Naïma takes it for granted as she rushes toward it. Surely, her boldness emphasizes her light handling of local preoccupations and problems.

The level of cultural ease of the two French travelers, along with their expectations from the locals, which the viewer assesses through their facial, verbal, and bodily expressions, make room for a reflection on the Maghrobal as seen through the eyes of reverse exotic flâneurs. Naïma grows gradually tenser as the couple is repeatedly slowed down on their journey. By the time they set foot on Moroccan land, her port of entry into Africa, she is without makeup, looking like a tracked animal, distrustful of others. She clings onto Zano as the bus driver duels with the racing truck. On the train in Algeria, the camera does a close-up of her face as she bites her nails frenetically; Naïma is terrified, for she has realized she is in a country that she hardly knows. The presentation of locals using a modern means of transportation without the luxury that it is supposed to come with unravels a sharp condemnation of the uneven nature of impacts of globalized practices and of the quality of associated products. Traveling at a slow speed and packed with people, the old train can also be read as an indication that globalization operates with a double standard, or rather that there are various types of phenomena encompassed in what we commonly call globalization. Globalization is ostensibly meant to enhance lifestyles, whereas here it does not bring great convenience or comfort to people on the southern shore of the Mediterranean. Thus, one could definitely say that there is not one but several globalizations.

Zano experiences the Maghrobal (i.e., globalization in the context of the Maghreb) in a particular way. On the train, the young man sits on the floor next to silent strangers. In general, he enthusiastically embraces the unknowns of their journey as a learning opportunity and much-awaited challenge. Could Zano's open attitude be the sign that his objective is to blend in? Can one contend that he is merely a neocolonial Orientalist? Zano's exuberance recalls *Il était une fois* where Johnny argues he can feel Algeria in the air as the ship approaches the Algerian coast. Johnny peppers his speech with Arabic delivered with a heavy French accent. Likewise, as Zano sits by the open train door, he looks out (and smells the air?) before he shouts to Naïma, "We are in Algeria. *Hta al 'assima.* [All the way to the capital city.] Do you realize? All my family on my father's and mother's sides were born here!" (His diction of the Arabic sentence is such that Naïma, who learned the Arabic expression from Leila, feels compelled and able to correct him). The young man raises his voice, whereas his neighbors do not exchange words. Algeria, which he presents as his relatives' home, becomes his in what may appear to be a suspiciously neocolonialist attitude. Zano's attempt at Arabic begs the spectator to ponder whether Zano then is a self-proclaimed Frenchman-turned-native.

The foreigners' presence, especially Zano's, appears to be one that imposes itself onto local space. Indeed, in Algiers, a female stranger scolds Naïma as she comes across her clad in a light dress. Still under shock after the earthquake that destroyed the neighborhood, the angry female stranger argues that it is because of the condemnable sartorial appearance of people like Naïma that God has cursed Algeria. In order to appease the lady, Saïd (Zouhir Gacem), the Algerian guide, explains that Naïma is a foreigner. Naïma experiences harsh rejection due to her behavioral inflexibility. This presentation of a disparity of mores is echoed in another moment of *Exils* in which Naïma expresses her own brush-off of local cultural practices. After the dress incident, she does purchase a djellaba and hidjab but only wears them for a short time before uncovering herself. In a defiant gesture, she says she cannot take it any longer and flings both pieces in a Muslim cemetery, which land on a tomb. Her veiling the grave—a symbol of the past and the unknown—with her clothes portends her decision to keep haunting issues and daunting discoveries at bay for fear that they might emerge in her consciousness when she least expects it. It is a clear sign that Naïma is simply opposed to readjusting her clothes and identity. Overwhelmed by culture shock and unable to adapt to social standards of behavior, Naïma rejects situation after situation, confirming Saïd's statement that she is, after all, an outsider.

This episode is telling in terms of Naïma's lack of inflexibility when immersed in the local culture. In *Exils*, the Maghrobal is examined partly through the witnessing of the different forms of hospitality that the characters from the global North encounter in various localities. In many instances, hospitality is tied to gendered behaviors. Therefore, it is important to weave a gender analysis into the examination of glocal hospitality. The couple's welcome in this new, yet "familiar," place will include lodging, touring the city, and guidance all the way to the house where Zano's family used to reside. As for the couple's participation in a local trance ritual, it is not solely an opportunity for them to exorcise their blocks but it is also a significant illustration of cultural hospitality. A local Sufi group wholeheartedly welcomes the couple who is outside of their clan, language, and cultural practices. Indeed, the group's underground activity is carried out secretly from other locals, yet it is open to the two foreign travelers. Zano and Naïma eat with them from the same plate—a practice that is the epitome of cultural inclusion. More importantly, Zano is the only man who dances with women. Yet he is not kicked out when he starts moving his body frenetically to the sound of chants and music, though the trance practice is in this instance reserved for women. Zano's foreignness makes him an alien to politics of intrusion and affront. At the same time, his intrusion into the female circle allows him to disturb local rules that are temporarily adjusted for the sake of a foreign guest, who imposes more or less in spite of himself a configuration that suits his needs.

In Spain, the travelers witness what, at first glance, appears to be another case of cultural hospitality. The couple attends a flamenco show in Seville among dozens of tourists. The spectacle is performed for them and not with them. Attendees are portrayed as passive receivers of the cultural experience. As for culinary specificity, it is absent, for the guests drink beers that come from a bar that looks like any other Western bar. This commercial presentation of artistic products (music and dance) and alcohol, is in an imposing warehouse. Ultimately, this setting reveals itself to be very different from an authentic sharing of cultural traditions. The music and dance are rendered as entertainment intended for a foreign audience expecting an "exotic" experience. Instead of locals overseeing what is shared with outsiders, here, spectators control the manner and extent to which they experience this "culture."

For Zano and Naïma, some form of hospitality occurs each time they meet a stranger in a foreign country; their status as outsiders leads the other to treat them differently. In company of Algerians in Spain, the potential monetary component of various interactions is never stated. Habib and Leila help their friends by teaching them some survival Arabic and by inviting them into their modest lodgings on the agricultural domain. Even though Naïma provides Leila a French address if the two Algerians make it to Paris, we never see the siblings make use of the contact information. There is no implication that Zano and Naïma are somehow indebted to the Algerian siblings. Naïma offers this information on her own initiative, but compensation or reciprocity of services is not requested by the young Algerian protagonists.

In Morocco, the French characters find themselves challenged in their European view of financial exchange, as they benefit once again from "free" hospitality. When their bus breaks down, a teenager selling various little items asks the couple to buy lighters or pens from him. Naïma retorts that they do not need pens. She fails to understand that the point is not to purchase lighters or pens for need but rather to lighten his plight by buying novelties, in other words by undertaking an engaged act of consumption. In spite of the couple's unwillingness to contribute to the young man's business, the peddler provides them crucial news—"The next bus is tomorrow"—before he walks away. It seems that the travelers feel the need to follow the trail of free hospitality; the young bearer of news becomes an essential auxiliary. They benefit from the gratuitous assistance of individuals on foot. One should note that only North African characters are shown consenting to walk a stretch with the French couple to their next destination, even when in Europe. Indeed, no European character does the same. Given this trend, it becomes clear that a statement is being made, namely, that the Maghreb is harmed by global tourism—even the noneconomic type, precisely because it does not give back (enough). The French travelers also discover from their new acquaintance—whom they walk with without asking his permission—that the border that they are about to cross has been closed for four years. At first, Naïma considers this information to herald the irremediable end of their journey, but this obstacle is easily and quickly overcome again by the young native's timely and selfless offer of guidance. He knows a smuggler and proposes to lead them to him, and in this manner, the chain of hospitality takes the travelers from one person or place to another, allowing them to proceed with their plan. Surely, one could assume that the knick-knack seller might get a commission for referring the smuggler to them, but this is never mentioned.

The human trafficker is the only person we witness getting money from the French couple. Naïma clearly perceives this deal as inappropriate, for it does not conform to the type of hospitality they have thus far received from locals and have come to expect. In order to make her assumption clear, Naïma turns away from the smuggler, opens her purse carefully, and closes it before handing the missing amount to Zano instead of the trafficker. She never smiles at the stranger nor speaks to him directly—not even to thank him for his expression of good wishes when they part. Naïma's air of suspicion indicates her insinuation that the Moroccan businessman is stealing money from them, since he does not continue the romanticized politics of local hospitality. From her point of view, the payment is excessive and even inappropriate, given that all that the man did is walk them through an arid landscape. She perceives the physical effort to be her own, since they took an uneven route made of narrow paths and a dry riverbed strewn with stones. After all, they had followed Habib and Leila on foot through a desolate area of Spain—without consulting them either—yet they did not have to pay for the walk with their Algerian acquaintances. But they do not contest the smuggler's fee. The ambiguity of this scene reflects Gatlif's complex take on the parallel economy that oscillates between a condemnation of smugglers' networks and the benefits that a circulation of riches may have on impoverished areas expecting their share of globalized praxes.

Gatlif's Manifesto: "The Necessity to Speak for Those Who Have No ~~Voice~~ Choice"

Commentary on the pernicious aspects of globalization are visible in *Exils*. That the Algerian and other African characters must work in hiding and risk arrest at any moment is clearly depicted in the film and point to Gatlif's critique of the impact of global economic forces on vulnerable populations. "Passeport," an Algerian song audible during the scene in which a sub-Saharan migrant is taken away by law enforcement officers, elicits the viewer's empathy: its lyrics describe the effects of globalization on African emigration while the images show a discrepancy in the treatment of illegal employment on the basis of administrative status. Indeed, the African migrant is handcuffed and Leila and Habib escape a similar fate by hiding under a truck that is driving away. Zano and Naïma happen to be around during a surprise raid on an orchard that employs undocumented fruit pickers. The French travelers have taken part in an underground labor network, whose illegality is underscored further by the employing of children, whom we see in the truck on their way to work. Yet the couple walks around freely before and after the Guardia Civil officers stop them, not on the grounds of their illegal employment—which is overlooked—but in order to check their papers. Zano and Naïma are not anxious, since they are able to prove they are authorized to stay in Spain thanks to their Frenchness. As her passport is being checked by the Guardia Civil officer, annoyed Naïma even proclaims: "*I am French.*" This scene shows that the travelers do not "read" themselves as clandestines in the "legal" sense of the term at any point of their trip. Yet they do hide and they do employ illegal routes. Zano and Naïma arrive in Algeria without their passports being stamped by the local authorities. Thus, the protagonists enter Algeria clandestinely despite the fact that they are in possession of their passports. The Algerian song tells the story of opposite fates, that of a woman who left the country thanks to the documents she was able to procure and that of a man who stayed behind: "You had your documents issued / And you emigrated / You had your passport issued and you left / As for me, I love you and I'll try to find a way." The song comments on Zano and Naïma's position as "rightful" voyagers protected by their European identity, which travels well all the way to Algeria.

African workers have unquestionably boosted Spain's economy. In particular, Murcia and Andalusia, the agriculture-reliant regions of southern Spain, have been sustained on the backs of clandestine migrants. As Brown, Iordanova, and Torchin discuss in their work on filmic depictions of African migration to Spain, the demographic shift has benefitted the southern part of the country.[44] The region underwent a miraculous boom significantly facilitated by the presence of African laborers who have been willing to do the jobs that Spaniards turned down, toiling for low wages and with no rights or benefits. In *Exils*, no Spaniard is shown working in the Andalusian orchard and the two employers are Spanish and are not engaged in strenuous work. The area surrounding the orchard is depicted as deserted, a space for marginal people who have no other choice but to remain in this zone for work. To use philosopher Jacques Rancière's expression, these *sans-papiers* (undocumented individuals) are *sans-parts* (have no part) in the society in which they find themselves.[45] Migrants are shown as sharing dwellings in a ramshackle communal boarding establishment, where ironically their only right, namely water, is already a common good, for it flows out of open-air fountains. We see text graffitied on walls, signaling a message from migrants, perhaps an attempt to proclaim their rights. However, these expressions are not being heard/read, or rather they are misunderstood. Indeed, because the spray-painted text is in Arabic script, the potentially political message of the writing on the wall is lost. Being filmed from afar, it is even more easily disregarded. It is geographically distant and distant from our concern. In turn, the inscriptions are viewed not as meaningful statements but as mere graffiti—an illegal practice framed as a deliberate destruction of collective property, that of a potential host.

Exils also critiques the notion that these individuals, compelled to deal with the most humiliating of circumstances, are somehow disposable. In the film, a sub-Saharan clandestine is wearing a T-shirt sold in Spain, showing a black bull—a Spanish symbol—on red print. This garment is easily recognizable as a Spanish commodity, for it is sold to tourists throughout the country. One implication is that the migrant has no choice but to submit to his own exploitation. Despite his coerced participation in this system and the fact that he may be deported at any moment, he is wearing a national emblem of Spain. He uses his small savings to benefit the local economy while the latter uses him. Another connotation of the image then is that global dynamics force the migrant to reinvest in a system that oppresses him economically and therefore asserts its domination further by inscribing him in an insidious circle.

Once Upon a Time in . . . *the End*

Johnny qua Abdel Bachir takes his performance of self very seriously, while Bensalah's cinematographic tale suggests that all identity is to some extent a repeated parodic performance. This holds true for personal identity and for the film genre: *Il était une fois dans l'oued*—both the film and the title—are parodies of *Il était une fois dans l'ouest* and of the Western genre. Meanwhile, the excessive use of parody leaves us wondering where it ends. It also points to the unsettling uncertainties regarding origin and nationality and the relationship between the two, which are at the core of the film, as well as the repetition of the stereotypes (even if inverted) on which they rely.

Yet the excesses and the distance between illusion and reality in *Il était une fois* could be seen as one of the film's strengths because they allow the director to turn upside down a number of commonly held perceptions pertaining to migration and identity. Some of the many reversals in the film remain in the domain of fiction because the changeable nature of the figure of the clandestine in the region is hardly credible. Yet *Il était une fois* merits praise for its new perspective on the myth of the "return home." The comic register of the film, along with its open-endedness (announced by the title), allows Bensalah to create an integrated Algerian utopia. His use of the comedy genre stands in contrast to other *Beur* filmmaking, which tends to privilege "social realist" modes. It helps us to think through issues of identity construction by appealing to our imagination. Characters play out futuristic individualities and experiment with new ways of assessing their relationship to France and Algeria. As for Johnny, he reproaches France for his identity crisis in order to better approach his Algerianness. In emigrating to Algeria, he simultaneously abandons his French *cité* and his *Francité* (Frenchness). Johnny's comical character serves to propose a narrative *à la Bensalah* in which the notion of migration is toyed with in order to put before us a counter-prototype who, contrary to documented Maghrebi migrant workers, enters the host country in a clandestine fashion in order to undertake an identitarian quest. Before Johnny ever reaches Algeria, he climbs out of his hiding place on the ferry, stands on the deck, and stretches his arms out, making himself as visible as he can, ready to embrace his new adventure and residency.

The promise of this far-out narrative is derived precisely from the fact that it overlooks unsolved problems such as the clandestinity of Johnny's status in Algeria. We do not know if Johnny will remain Algerian during the civil war of the 1990s—for such a possibility is barred by the chronological limits of the film's plot. Nor do we find out if he will rediscover his Frenchness and go back to his "first" bled. *Beur* director Djamel Bensalah has turned his satirical lens back onto both Algeria and France in order to propose a unique way of viewing migrational identities. By returning to the decade (the 1980s) in which *Beur*ness was first being explored in France, and making Johnny the representative of an ingenious and unexpected prototype, *Il était une fois* reflects on the future of emigration, immigration, and integration, while also tangentially contributing to the ongoing questioning of the act of naming and misnomers such as *Beur*. In this film, Djamel Bensalah offers innovative takes on clandestine migration at a time when an increasing number of Maghrebi youths relentlessly dream of reaching the other side of the Mediterranean.

Analogous statements could be made about Tony Gatlif's *Exils,* especially with regard to Zano's utopian Algeria and the potential shortcomings of an open-ended diegesis. The close of this film allows us to imagine—improbable though it may seem—that the characters, too, have left an exclusive sense of *Francité* in the dust, by leaving their French *cité*. But their journey in reverse should ultimately make Zano realize that Naïma's laughter at the beginning of the film was intended to mean that Zano's roots are more in Europe than in North Africa. The characters' respective paths to reconstruct their personal stories are irreversible. In order to find the "reparative in narratives," in one's eclectic history, elliptic memory, and ex-centric identity, one has to follow an eccentric itinerary.[46]

4 The New Eldorado in Mediterranean Music

North Africa as a New Eldorado

Stuart tannock writes, "In the rhetoric of nostalgia, one invariably finds three key ideas: first, that of a prelapsarian world (the Golden Age, the childhood Home, the Country); second, that of a 'lapse' (a cut, a Catastrophe, a separation or sundering, the Fall); and third, that of the present, postlapsarian world (a world felt in some way to be lacking, deficient, or oppressive)."[1] Many *Beurs* consider "the Golden Age, the childhood Home, the Country" to be located south of the Mediterranean. Within this particular vision, it is not surprising that French nationals of Maghrebi descent should be nostalgic of a past, from which migration acts as the "cut, Catastrophe, separation or sundering, the Fall," which irremediably leads to "a world felt in some way to be lacking, deficient, or oppressive." As Tannock adds, "the nostalgic subject turns to the past to find/construct sources of identity, agency, or community, that are felt to be lacking, blocked, subverted, or threatened in the present."[2] Nostalgia and exile have long played an important part in *raï* music, but in the context of French raï music (and raï made in France) they have recently become popular tropes.[3] Recently, a series of *Beur* Raï n'b albums have positioned North Africa as a site of wealth and abundance. In this Maghrebi-French category, the Maghreb has replaced France as the gilded Eldorado. To combat negative depictions of the Maghreb and to advance the concept of a more welcoming and competitive North Africa, three DJs recently collaborated on a multivolume collection, which includes *Raï n'b fever*, *Raï n'b fever 2*, and *Raï n'b fever 3*. The reputation of the hybrid Raï n'b genre has enabled the labels to invite a great variety of artists to be part of this musical initiative. Some of the most famous names in raï, R&B, and hip-hop have participated in the project. Original songs even include tracks crafted especially for this musical style, as is evidenced by the dedication made to the DJs or the mentioning of the Raï n'b genre or even of a "Maghreb United"—a special rallying motto for the artists and for listeners in need of a sense of belonging south of the Mediterranean. Intended primarily for an audience based in the French metropole, the subject matter resonates with individuals disillusioned with France and nostalgic about an actual or imagined country of origin. Some of the songs partake in an obvious conceptualization of France as an ex-center, while others treat leavism as a worse evil and Europe-bound journeys as a dead end. For France-based listeners, the lived French experience is different from the Eldorado perceived by their North African counterparts. Instead, France is synonymous with the racism, alienation, and the towering, gray housing projects that outline the country's urban peripheries.

In this chapter, I will first examine a handful of tracks on three albums of Raï n'b music released in France. I will then turn to two Spanish-language songs. The first one, "Papeles mojados," is by Andalusian pop group Chambao. The second one is Manu Chao's "Clandestino."[4] This wide scope of music made and sung by artists hailing (by birth or blood) from countries located on both shores of the sea crosses not only geographic borders but also lines of genre and language. Because "Clandestino" and "Papeles mojados" describe the failed attempts of North African clandestine migrants (among others) to reach Spanish shores, in other words, a phenomenon that is taking place primarily in the Strait of Gibraltar, this music of clandestinity stages France as a remote ex-center in the remapped network of migration.

There are now many collections on the market that resemble the Raï n'b label, which, as its name suggests, is inspired by the American R&B genre.[5] Currently, French media chain FNAC keeps the albums under the subcategory Raï/RNB. The Raï n'b franchise comprises a considerable number of discs. *Raï n'b fever* (Sony Music Entertainment France), *Raï n'b fever 2* (Sony BMG Music Entertainment), and *Raï n'b fever 3* (Artop Records), were released in 2004, 2006, and 2008, respectively. Another Raï n'b fever album called *Raï n'b fever 3 L'Issonciel* (The Issenshial) came out in 2009. The latter is a sort of compilation in that the majority of the tracks are to be found in the aforementioned trio of *Raï n'b fever* CDs. The same year, a two-CD set of *Raï n'b fever 3* was released. It contains a few extra tracks, as well as the video clip for "Bienvenue chez les Bylkas." The deluxe two-CD edition, *Raï n'b fever 3 . . . même pas fatigué!!!* (Not Even Tired!!!) (Artop Records) came out in 2009. It is the one I will refer to in this study when I discuss *Raï n'b fever 3*. DJ Kore and DJ Bellek, along with DJ Skalp, popularized the Raï n'b genre with the production of the various *Raï n'b fever* CD sets. Aided by the commercial success of the first album, the DJ duo Kore and Skalp have become the most respected producers of Raï n'b.[6] In turn, the Raï n'b appellation has inspired playful derivatives, like the *Raï 'n' bled* and *Raï made in bled* albums found on the same shelves at FNAC. In the albums I discuss, Maghrebi raï artists collaborate with French artists of various origins from across genres (*Beur* raï, Maghrebi classic and pop-raï, reggae raï,[7] rap, and R&B). Most tracks on these albums feature duets and trios, and many of these collaborations are bilingual, with each singer singing in his or her mother tongue.

The second track on *Raï n'b fever 3* is called "Ya Mama." It is sung by the male singer Najim and the female singer Kenza Farah.[8] One would expect antiharga advocates—often attached to patriotic sentiments that may be at odds with leavism—to constitute a more conservative range of singers, and the vision to be woven into a classical repertoire. Instead, the duet appropriates images of clandestinity (boats, etc.) and recasts them to embrace a position that denounces this practice. Najim, who sings exclusively in Arabic, pleads: "Khuti . . . ngu'du fed-dzaier / Fel-ghorba twuder / Tsufri u tnahger" (Dear brothers . . . let us stay in Algeria / Overseas one loses oneself / There one suffers / And one is discriminated against).[9] To make his call more convincing, the singer shares his personal story: "Khtini men bote / Nebqa f-bladi" (I don't need the *bote* / I stay in my country).[10] Songs are fictional productions. One should always take pains to avoid a facile conflation of singers' biographies and their songs' messages even when lyrics are penned by those who sing them. Yet the practice among listeners is widespread. Some artists know full well that they serve as models and that their lyrics—misread as real-life stories—may influence the lives, behaviors, and beliefs of their fans. Najim is one of them, as he draws much of his inspiration from his biography. Born in Suresnes (in Hauts-de-Seine), France, of a French mother and an Algerian father, he was raised by his grandparents in Borj Bou-Arréridj, Algeria. It was only after he passed his baccalaureate exam that he decided to travel to France to reunite with his mother and to continue his singing career. Before then, in spite of various opportunities to live in France, Najim remained in Algeria where he was a choir leader at the age of six, sang at family occasions such as weddings and baptisms, and later in cabarets in major cities such as Algiers, Oran, and Sétif.

Bote is a word many use in Algeria for the unwieldy dinghies used for clandestine crossings (the patera in Spanish parlance), and the verse in which it appears is an obvious rejection of northbound journeys. The man promises that against all odds, he will make the journey with his beloved, taking the listener along for the ride. His plan is to travel from Oran in Algeria to Casablanca in Morocco. The female singer, singing in French, lays out the subsequent segments of the international trip, with stops in Oujda and Bejaia (Bonn). Inland territories are dismissed and a handful of coastal cities are selected for their resorts, popular with locals-turned-tourists.[11] Liminal spaces are transformed into touristic places and Kenza Farah urges us to pay a visit: "Viens faire un tour" (Come take a tour by home). Here is the picture she paints to entice the tourist:

Sur les plages de Boulémat	On the beaches of Boulémat
Sous un parasol	Under an umbrella
Un transat	On a chair
On prend le soleil	We bask in the sun
. . .	. . .
Sur le sable de Saïdia	On the sand of Saïdia
Avec les oncles	With uncles
Et les tantes	And aunts
Autour d'un thé à la menthe	Over a mint tea

The intrusion of Arabic words in the following French bridge: "Où les hommes parlent autour d'une chicha, où dans les cuisines ça sent la *chorba* et le pain kabyle de *yemma*) (Where men chat around a *hookah* and where in the kitchen it smells of *chorba* and the Kabyle bread of *yemma* [Mom]) exoticize the clichéd imagery of the romantic Maghreb. This imagery also needs to seem attractive to tourists and émigrés. However, these exotic settings are unlikely to seduce the native, who is more inclined to take them for granted, instead of as extrinsic items to look forward to. What sounds like a commercial also feeds into common stereotypes of the region, stripped of the common obsession with leaving that the seashore reinforces. Only a series of resorts remain and the beach is reduced to sun umbrellas, sand, and visitors tanning on beach chairs. It is a locus that inspires a vision of regional self-sufficiency.

The exoticized Maghreb is designed to appeal to those who possess a strong sense of national pride and reject leavism. Given the availability of such an enticing setting to locals, the song seems to ask, "Why would one want to trade the beauty of Maghrebi golden seasides with a European dystopia of grey suburbs?" Through the common association with "the sea and waves," Najim draws the picture of a Maghreb displayed in touristic brochures and official discourses, in which recreation is enjoyed in the company of friends and family. This Maghreb is directed in part to "contemporary diasporic subjects," who, as Daniela Berghahn and Claudia Sternberg explain, "tend to travel back."[12] For the locals—likely not Najim's primary audience—the song might be read as sarcastic in its rehabilitation of the Maghreb's image.

The Maghreb is envisioned as a spatial continuum, and from the start, the duet's proposed itinerary triggers suspicion. Given that the borders between Morocco and Algeria have been closed since 1994, in order to complete their journey, travel by air remains the best alternative, but this mode of transportation would disrupt the sense of Maghrebi continuity that the song attempts to establish, in that it would acknowledge the existence of a border, a marker of disruption par excellence. As a result, the song simply ignores the border between the two countries: visiting family members in both Algeria and Morocco becomes, in the imaginary cartography of the lyrics, an easy task.

"Bienvenue chez les Bylkas" (Welcome among the Bylkas [Berbers of Kabylia in *verlan*]) provides a portrait of an equally carefree Maghreb, one familiar to those expatriates locally known as holiday-makers (*les vacanciers* or *l'facances*). This track, which appears on the *Raï n'b fever 3* compilation, features Sinik, Cheb Bilal, and Big Ali, and begins and ends with a dialogue reminiscent of the film *Il était une fois dans l'oued* (examined in chapter 3). A man on a telephone asks his friends where they are going to spend their summer vacation in Algeria, and he is upset to learn that his comrades went without him. This section echoes a scene in the film but diverges from it in one important way: in the latter cultural production, Algeria is portrayed as a zone where one of the main characters is bored and looking forward to the end of his stay. What is clear, however, is that the *Beur* who did not get to vacation in North Africa is convinced he is missing out on the pleasures of a summer in the bled. In "Welcome among the Bylkas," Algeria is associated with Western modernity and comfort, home to a Sheraton hotel. There is a swimming pool, chicken fillo, and fresh orange juice. It welcomes people from the three countries of the Maghreb (from "Algiers, Tunis, and Oujda"). But as with *Il était une fois dans l'oued,* the song is a fictional framework that imagines a different Algeria from the material realities of the present. While the film capitalizes on reversals, the song superimposes Moroccan and Tunisian tourist cultures onto Algeria. The idea of a welcoming and idealistic homeland is a seductive option, but as in the film and various other cultural and artistic productions, *Beurs* have not found it easy to move from one unfamiliar home to another.

An additional reason for the song's idealization of Algeria stems from the CD's overt purpose of presenting a "Maghreb United."[13] In "Welcome among the Bylkas," as well as in several other songs in the Raï n'b series, the three countries are praised en masse: the singers usually name Morocco, Algeria, and Tunisia together; mention all the three nationalities; or single out cities from each nation. Obviously, such a view of a united Maghreb is illusionary and ignores local, regional, and national specificities. However ungrounded in current geopolitical realities, imagination is nonetheless the motor of fiction and makes room for digressions. Here, the "Maghreb United" is imagined as heir to *The Arabian Nights*—a shared and proud heritage for all Maghrebis. As if to drive home the point, the covers of the three CDs show the inscription "Raï n'b" resting on a shiny golden sword. While the sleeve of *Raï n'b fever 3 . . . même pas fatigué!!!* is less crowded with stereotypical Orientalized referents and artifacts, displaying only the compilation name against a black background, the first and second *Raï n'b* CDs include a brass oil lamp underneath.[14] On one of the record sleeves, the lamp is set on sand in front of a cobbled square. On the other, one notices a slight variation in that it sits on the cobbled stones at the foot of sand dunes. On both sleeves, a man rides his camel atop a towering dune. While the first CD—which is known to also be called "Version nomade" (Nomad Version)—displays a mosque, two minarets, and palm trees under the moon and stars, the only sign of modernity is a 4×4 truck (Figure 4.1). *Raï n'b 2*'s album cover presents an urban skyline in the background. The portrayal of the Maghreb as an exotic place is a marketing decision aimed at targeting a multicultural body of young consumers, presenting the illusion that the musical universe contained in the Raï n'b franchise endows the listener with the

Figure 4.1 Album cover art for *Raï n'b Fever*. © Mark093 (Facebook: mark093darkvapor); used with permission.

power to imagine themselves at the wheel of a luxurious 4×4 driving across scenery that promises endless enchantment.

A number of the songs in the Raï n'b series contrast the warmth of the Maghreb—its climate, foods, and cultures—with the chill of France. Such is the case in "Cholé, Cholé" included on *Raï n'b fever 2:* "Je me suis preparé onze mois pour un rendez-vous galant avec la chaleur" (For eleven months I have been getting ready for a date with heat), says Rappeur d'Instinct, featuring Reda Taliani.[15] In this track, a flawless vision of Algeria is painted, an overly optimistic depiction likely convincing only to those who do not have much familiarity with the country. For the residents of the global North, Algeria seems a remote and even glamorous location, offering its best in the summer days:

Une fois sur le soleil algérien	Once on Algerian soil
Je me sens loin	I feel far
Je me sens bien	I feel good
Chicha à la main	A hookah in my hand
Cocktail hawaïen	And a Hawaiian cocktail
Les bagages	Luggage
La plage	The beach
La traversée des nuages	Flying through the clouds
Les beaux visages	Beautiful faces
Les beaux paysages	Beautiful landscapes

By creating an imaginary Algerian Eldorado, the song diminishes France's allure and instead magnetizes the bled as a relaxing destination. The original homeland provides a "touche d'évasion" (hint of escape) as if the characters were "evading" a France that had become overwhelming. Rappeur d'Instinct defines this land as being free of suffocating limitations anchored in discriminations. It is located "beyond borders, check-points, and bouncers" in what is called Raï n'b fever—a musical space that allows entrance to those who are often denied access to European dance clubs. Though the song evokes a summer vacation in a country where checkpoints were part of the landscape, the possibility of a long-term stay is not excluded.

Conversely, for the native, Algeria does not provide the same dolce vita, as the song goes on to say: "Les cousines, pour elles c'est mariages forcés / Les cousins, champions du monde de mélanges corsés" (Arranged marriage awaits my female cousins / While my male cousins are the world champions of dope beats—hardcore mixes). These two lines prove an awareness of a double standard that differentiates between *Beurs'* view of the Maghreb as a site of leisure and the locals' experience of a tough life. The dichotomy that is established is between those who have (*Beurs*) and those who lack (native Algerians), which reinforces the notion of the songwriters' biased and subjective vision. The stark economic discrepancy enables the song to impart a different Algerian daily reality. But objectivity is undermined by an escalation of hyperboles: "Là-bas en boîte même à trente on rentre" (There *a whole thirty of you* can get into a club); "J'appelle un taxi, c'est tout mon bled qui se déplace" (I hail a cab and *all the village* rides); "C'est tout le village qui est branché sur un seul satellite" (*The entire village* is tuned to the same satellite dish); "Chaque jour on fête l'arrivée d'un nouveau né" (*Every day* we celebrate a birth); and "Ils veulent tous des cadeaux (They *all* want gifts) (my emphases).

An essentialist endeavor dominates in a few songs with the use of clichéd images to present the riches of the Maghreb. This type of Orientalizing gesture is not innocent and is reappropriated by the *Beur* artists, just like the bled they try to make their own. Other album covers have invested in what marketing specialists think will signify Arab culture to the prospective buyer, implying exoticism and dance music. Examples of such CD covers abound.[16] It is not surprising that *oriental* should be included in the name of many collections of this kind. On the covers of these albums there is consistently a silhouette of a female dancer, whose belly dancing promises captivating beats and folklore. The exaggerated telegraphic text that appears—in broken French—on the last page of the *Raï n'b 2* CD booklet traffics in a similar economy of reappropriation: "Mr Kore et Mr Bellek fait des sons qui tues, des tubes qui pace sur toute les télé, fait danser ta famille en arabe et en français, fait marché ton commerce avec la musique, fait revenir ta femme" (Mr. Kore and Mr. Bellek does killer sounds, hits that are heired on all T.V., makes your family dance in Arabic and French, makes your business success with the music, brings your wife back). As such, the over-the-top songs, where irony and self-derision are key, are not to be taken at face value.[17] They show instead an awareness of stereotypes, which they aim to debunk by piling them in one long sentence, making them appear even more incongruous. Such a recasting of stereotypes is at home in a set of compilations that feed upon well-known repertoires, tunes, and rhythms. The song "J'suis pas d'ici" (I'm Not from Here), included in the first installment of the *Rai n'b* CD series, is sung by OGB and Sahraoui, and features a rapped bridge and a chorus. The chorus is drawn from Maghrebi musical heritage, namely an excerpt from a famous hit, which proclaims (in Arabic): "Ma anich menna / Ghir el babour li jabni hna" (I'm not from around here / It's just the boat that brought me here). This displacement of responsibility in the face of the exilic condition is supplemented with a noticeable hijacking of a cultural phenomenon that justifies a claim of unbelonging. The original song refers to ferry crossings to France undertaken by parents and grandparents.[18] In "J'suis pas d'ici," released in 2004, the boat is no longer a ferry but a patera instead. Indeed, the mode of transportation is blamed for the unauthorized (?) presence of the migrant in France, where the newly arrived protagonist is surprised to find "papillons" (butterflies) instead of "papiers" (documents), the former being hard to catch and the latter hard to get.

As far as clandestinity is concerned, it is a topic that has expanded into *Beur* music partly as a direct result of raï singers' participation. Despite the seriousness of the life and death stakes of clandestine migration, artists have not shied away from experimenting playfully with the topic. Clandestinity is sometimes even featured in the titles of prominent songs. Cheb Mami's "Clando," featuring rap band 113 on his 2003 album *Du Sud au Nord* (From South to North, EMI) is a case in point. Another example is Rap singer Rim'K du 113's album, *Famille nombreuse* (Large Family) (Sony BMG Music Entertainment, 2007). The rapper cosings "Clandestino" with Mohamed Lamine and Sheryne. The artists have transposed the figure of the clandestine into the context of French society. Mohamed Lamine uses the French word *clandestin* to qualify Rim'K, whom he addresses in Arabic as an Arab endowed with a big heart. As for Rim'K, the French man of foreign descent prefers to call himself *clandestino* (an idiom he borrows from the Italian language just like *bambino* and *primo*, which he uses alongside the cultural references he enumerates: "Tarantino" and "Italian thug"). Interestingly, though he claims his Frenchness, Rim'K remarks that he has been pushed to its periphery (Italy) and the marginal space of the clandestine, like in the song "Clando," where 113 raps:

Mes parents sont venus ici pour forcer le destin	My parents came here in order to force fate
Mais en France on est comme un clandestin	But in France one is like a clandestine
Comme un clandestin	Like a clandestine
Qui vient de voir la Tour Eiffel pour la première fois	Who has just seen the Eiffel Tower for the first time

The reference to the Eiffel Tower illustrates the special place France and Paris have had on the imagination of African youth, as Dominic Thomas reminds us: "The symbolic value of France (and its capital city Paris, in particular), has informed the francocentrist quests of young African protagonists for generations."[19] Rim'K's place in the French society is being questioned due to his "thugness" (equated with clandestinity), which is commonly presented as incompatible with the Republican ideal of Frenchness. The artist establishes his ex-centric position without hesitation. At one point, he says that his first words, such as "*I love you,*" were foreign. He even professes that he has "un passeport international" (an international passport)—his music, which combines global hip-hop and raï.

Many songs in the *Raï n'b* compilations attempt to resist France's pull by voicing a bold ex-centrization of prevailing conceptions of France. To cite one example, in *Raï n'b fever 2*'s "D'où je viens," which features Tunisiano, Rim'K, Sniper, and Kabyle singer Idir, one can hear "Au bled, on dit la Tour Eiffel vaut mieux jamais l'avoir vue" (Back home they say one is better off not to have seen the Eiffel Tower). Interestingly, France is not mentioned by name, as if it were taboo. It is identified instead by its metonymical symbol. Not only it is best to skip a visit to the monument, one should also avoid speaking the name of the country it represents. This piece of advice does not foster antagonism toward France. Rather, it recognizes that to set foot in France is almost a guarantee of no return for visitors from the South, who may not be aware of the intricate identity politics that *Beurs* and Maghrebis face. That one is better off not to have seen France is a peculiar twist. It is a reversal of discourse, which the *Raï n'b* collection takes as its primary goal, in that it behooves "uprooted individuals" to "take pride in their origins" and to continue "to feel for their bled of origin." The bled becomes the place to be.

It is by pointing out the shortcomings of the other Eldorado that artists propose to promote the one that pervades all the Raï n'b tracks. The song cosung by Reda Taliani, Lim, and Samira on *Raï n'b fever 3* is titled "Raï-Kaï" (in reference to *racaille*, "scum"). Its title recalls the infamous appellation and officially established slur, since it was deployed by then-Minister of the Interior Nicolas Sarkozy in reference to Frenchmen of (North) African origins, whom he blamed in broad and blunt strokes for the major November-December 2005 uprisings, and proposed that the "scum" be washed away with a pressurized water gun (*au Karcher*) like an epidemic to be driven out of French society. The song hints at that episode: "In their opinion, we are all thugs." Indeed, Samira sings: "Ici c'est cho cho cho comme un clando au dépôt / Alors il faut faut faut qu'on s'en sorte tous" (Here, it's risky, risky, risky like for a clandestine in a detention center / So we all gotta, gotta, gotta get out of it). Via the persona of the French individual of foreign descent, the clandestine migrant is identified as another *racaille* who faces comparable repression ("A la téci y a trop d'ennuis et *l'houkouma* nous punit" [In the hood there's too many troubles and the government punishes us]). *Beurs* sympathize with family and friends from across the sea to the point of symbiosis ("we"). Lim dedicates the song to a certain audience: "C'est pour mes frères de la rue" (This goes to my brothers who live on the street). The fluidity of the genre creates a trans-Mediterranean affinity.

Mediterranean singers have complicated the way clandestine migrants are named by society, by reclaiming derogative terms. One such term is *clando*. As Virginie Lydie rightly indicates, "The word is imbued with spite and suspicion; it is a word that harragas themselves cannot stand, as they are ready to die for the only thing they possess: their adventurer's pride."[20] The word is short for clandestine and parallels the word *clodo*, which is a deformed version of *clochard* (hobo). A clando can easily be represented as the victim of an accentuated marginalization as the clando becomes a clodo. This terminology reflects the denigration of clandestine migrants, as described in the song "Rani m'hayar" by Houari Benchenet. Benchenet enumerates a series of travails that await the migrant who leaves his country to live as a *clandestin* (one of several French words in the song, which coincidentally cohabits with the metonymic Arabic expression *bla kwaghet* ("undocumented," literally, "without papers"): "turning round when witnessing a police raid," "having to hide in the basement each time there is a police control," and "finding solace only in bars and ending up *clochard*. The ex-centricity of the clandestine lies in his being marginalized from society: For having to sleep on a piece of cardboard, "I semmouni SDF" (They call me SDF [homeless]). In France and throughout the song, the unidentified "they" of the song use a wide spectrum of terms to convey nonidentity, a practice common in France that reflects a sophisticated jargon, newspeak. Classifying the migrant as *sans-*

papiers, or *sans domicile fixe* (SDF), *clandestin,* and *clochard* obscures his legitimate identity. *Domicile* here could refer not only to the individual's precarious living situation, but also to his feeling of exile. The blurring use of the impersonal "they" implicates all of France and reinforces binary oppositions of belonging and exclusion. As for the clandestine, the amputation of the title implies a certain loss suffered from the crossing, a cut that leaves a missing part. Such a wound festers in the psychological effects of a closed Mediterranean and opens the door to an antiharga rhetoric born not from ideology but from powerlessness. In fact, Benchenet argues: "exile is very tough. It's the worse calamity." The clando resists being romanticized and remains a Mediterranean vagrant.

Manu Chao's *Clandestino*: In Defense of the *Clans Sans Destin*

Manu Chao is the stage name of José-Manuel Thomas Arthur Chao, born in Paris on June 21, 1961, to a Galician father and a Basque mother. His family fled Spain after his grandfather was sentenced to death by the dictator Franco. The songwriter, raised in the Parisian banlieues Boulogne-Billancourt and Sèvres, was influenced by his family's hardships and artistic talent. Chao's maternal grandfather fled Spain on a boat, then he and his family found themselves in French *camps d'hébergements.* They finally emigrated to Algeria where they spent ten years before they moved to France again. His grandfather's political stance had a tremendous impact on the singer's own *musique engagée.*[21] Chao is known to be a strong supporter of proletarian sensibilities. His perception "as an anti-globalisation protester is channeled through the mediatisation of his sponsorship of various left-wing 'causes.'"[22] In a July 2007 interview in *Le Courrier International,* Chao condemned the pervasive tendency of mass media to draw easy conclusions, saying "I have been pigeonholed as the banner-bearer of the *altermondialist* movement because I demonstrated in Genoa and the 'alter' enjoy my songs. The press needed to find a top of the bill and it had to be me, but I am neither a symbol nor a spokesperson. I am a musician."[23]

The bulk of Chao's oeuvre is inspired by political situations and his protests cover a wide range of injustices. He has taken a stand on controversial topics, including hrig in the Mediterranean. Such is the case in the song "Clandestino."[24] Not so much a singer of world music—a label he qualifies as "neocolonial"—but rather of music of the world, Chao mingles languages and invites professional and amateur musicians to fuse their beats together. Chao's first solo album, *Clandestino* (Virgin Records), released in 1998, is also a model of generic hybridity—one that sold several million copies, and thus became a major best seller of "fusion" Latin music in the 2000s. Chao's Spanish lyrics and the term *clandestino* in the song (and) title all convey the ordeals of global clandestine migrants. In particular, they share the experience of having their presence criminalized. Chao's title track, "Clandestino," indicates that marijuana and clandestines are both branded as "illegal," a highly loaded term. He suggests that pigeonholing individuals with such labels frames them as transgressors, deserving of punishment, when their only crime is searching for a better place to live. In this light, Chao reminds us that it is not right to refer to human beings as "illegals," as the Spanish press commonly does. The message is unambiguous: harragas should not be irremediably locked in demeaning judicial language. These harragas are victims of metonymic freezing, as their origins in the global South (represented here by Algeria, Nigeria, and Bolivia) preclude their free movement across European borders. Smaïn Laacher explains that it is the fact that the harrag is thought of as "breaking into" the nation of the Other that gives authorities the impetus to harshly reject the newcomer.[25] "He is here whereas he should be somewhere else. He is present whereas he should, in all morality, be absent from the site."[26] This double-standard position on human migrations imposed by the global North is swept under the rug, and instead the would-be-migrant is demonized for breaking a law he did not create.

Me dicen clandestino	They say I am a clandestine migrant
Yo soy el quiebra ley	I am the outlaw
Mano negra clandestina	Clandestine Mano Negra
Peruano clandestino	Clandestine Peruvians
Africano clandestino	Clandestine Africans
Marijuana ilegal	Illegal marijuana[27]

The song's repetition of the word *clandestine* after the naming of global South nationalities insistently protests dehumanization: Africans, Algerians, Bolivians, and Peruvians are clandestinos, not *ilegales* like marijuana is. It is no coincidence that instead of pluralizing each national clandestine migrant, the singer points at an individual from each nationality. Indeed, singularizing is a humanizing effort in that it contrasts with images often seen in mass media of groups of anonymous people. As the camera zooms out to capture a phenomenon, it fails to delineate individual faces, emotions, and stories. Besides dehumanization, the clandestine migrant is animalized by way of association with a sea animal, the ray, whose flat shape conveys the invisibility that is necessary to navigate uncertain waters: "Soy una raya en el mar" (I am a ray in the sea). *Raya* is also a line. This indicates that the singer is playing with the idea of underwater borders where clandestines are kept away from the shore. In addition, it is important to note that *raya* is also a line of cocaine. As an inanimate substance, marijuana does not have to "hide." The insertion of marijuana into the list calls for a rehumanizing discourse of the clandestine. It also points to the consequences of our laws, policies, and language, and by the same token ridicules the term *illegal*. Speaking of pointing (fingers), the listener's attention is drawn to the fact that the accusing anonymous mass who reviles does so simply by using language that has acquired easy currency ("Me dicen") and in turn the harrag finds himself singled out as inevitably guilty ("Yo soy el quiebra ley"). Mano Negra, an alternative rock band of the 1980s, of which Chao was a part is included in the list of *ilegales*, reinforcing the idea that, for reasons the band endorses or not, illegal substances and a band with ideas can be harmful to powers in place—even if they do not intend to be.[28] In turn, people do not mean to cause harm by traveling, though they end up threatening the power élite. Their "illegal" action is everything but a determined act of breaking the law. Rather, it is the natural fight for survival, which takes criminalizing implications in the context of unauthorized transnational migrations:

Solo voy con mi pena	I wander alone with my sorrow
Sola va mi condena	My sentence wanders alone
Correr es mi destino	To run is my destiny
Para burlar la ley	In order to get around the law
Perdido en el corazón	Lost in the heart
De la grande Babylon	Of the Great Babylon

In this excerpt, *burlar* has several meanings that could work here including "to laugh at" and "to outwit." With this added layer provided with the use of *burlar* in reference to the law, the clandestine is presented as someone who spends his life running away (or in circles?) in a game of hide and seek with the law, which he laughs at in order to better cope with his fate.

The plight of Algerian, Nigerian, Colombian, and Peruvian harragas is clearly central to Chao's title song. The album cover bears a double-fold title. "Esperando la última ola" (Waiting for the Last Wave) is the second half (Figure 4.2). Red and green dominate the color scheme. Given the singer's tradition of attributing a political message to his songs and albums, the title of the album may target a part of the world where these colors are dominant on national flags. Due to personal attachment to Latin America, Chao could be referring to the countries on the American continent that he names. But of the two countries, only Peru has these colors. Colombia does not. Nor does Nigeria, the other mentioned country. Arabic is the only language other than Spanish used in the song, and the whitish background of the cover completes the tripartite color scheme of the Algerian flag, cementing the importance of Algeria to the album. The addition of a star in the middle of the second letter *A* in "Manu Chao" gives the final touch to the tableau, and is a recurrent sign on Chao's albums. This addition causes the A to possibly stand for Africa (with explicit references in the album to Nigeria and Algeria) or for Arabness; along with the crescent, the five-pointed star is one of the most common symbols for Islam. The mention of hrig in relation to the Spanish enclave highlights a notably absent country, namely, France, unmentioned as a

Figure 4.2 Album cover art for Manu Chao's *Clandestino*.

topographic reference; French—common in many of Chao's songs—is absent as well. Chao implies that in dealing with the struggles of harragas, omitting France and French is a deliberate act of decentralization by the French singer. Instead of old narratives common to (Northern) Mediterranean music—wherein Maghrebis sing about their (past/present/future) voyage to France—Chao offers a song that ties (North) Africans to Spain. This gesture acknowledges a deep and intertwined history cut short and implies that the North African harragas are heading toward Spain (a character dies in the Strait of Gibraltar): "Mi vida la deje / Entre Ceuta y Gibraltar" (I left my life / Between Ceuta and Gibraltar). The Maghrebi's crossing is a failed enterprise, and Spain becomes for the dead harrag a more remote destination than the one he was contemplating from the northern shores of

Africa. The harragas' need to conduct the voyage in secret underscores the daunting nature of the desperate, long-journey—an undertaking infinitely more difficult than in decades past, when migrant workers flocked to France with relative ease.

The man speaking Arabic at the end of the song instructs the listener how to track down a smuggler or middleman, the necessary intermediary in the burning project. Even if we assume that he is addressing a clandestine, his catchy, elliptic address ("Hey, listen") includes a broader group, for the song's message calls its diverse listeners to pay attention, as if we were all potential clandestine migrants. The address is doubly elliptic in that the song is cut short when the man speaking Arabic informs his interlocutor that the stranger he is going to encounter will give him something that seems crucial to the voyage, but is deliberately kept mysterious to us: ("will give . . ."). The song evokes a polymorphous being, casting the clandestino in multiple roles. In this spirit, the video for this song celebrates generational and ethnic diversity with the faces of migrants of different ages and races. Chao asks his listener to identify with the clandestine and close the gap between the self and the Other, center and periphery, belonging and exclusion. By addressing the listener directly, he transforms the listening experience into a learning experience, with the lyrics assuming the privileged role of instructor or informed newscasters. The complex but privileged binary relation between addresser and addressee is also a characteristic of the following song by Chambao.

"There Are No Migrants on the Coast" in Chambao's "Papeles Mojados"

Chambao is a Spanish band whose song "Papeles mojados" (Wet Documents) became a smashing success in 2008 when it ranked at the top of Cuarenta Principales (Spain's Top 40 chart). The band's international visibility increased when Chambao's lead singer La Mari (María del Mar Rodríguez Carnero) performed "Tu Recuerdo" (Your Memory), a duet with Ricky Martin, on *MTV Unplugged*. The song then became available on CD (Sony Music Latin, 2006) and DVD (Sony U.S. Latin, 2006), as well as on a CD/DVD combo (Sony U.S. Latin, 2007). "Papeles mojados" is the first track on Chambao's album *Con otro aire* (With Another Air, Sony BMG, 2007). The band recorded a subsequent version with Greek singer Helena Paparizou for the album *Vrisko to logo na zo* (Sony BMG Greece/RCA Records, 2008). At the end of the following year, Desalojo, a rock band from the Spanish region of Galicia, released their first album with the same title. It also includes a song named "Papeles mojados" in which the subtly addressed theme of clandestine migration becomes more obvious when the lyrics are compared to those of Chambao's. Desalojo's version, while musically quite different, shares a common language with Chambao's: *papeles mojados, hambre* (hunger), and *frío* (cold).[29]

Ululation

In Spanish:

Miles de sombras cada noche
    trae la marea
	Each night the sea brings thousands
	    of shadows

Navegan cargados de ilusiones	They navigate filled with hopes
Que en la orilla se quedan	Which remain on the shore
Historias del día a día	Everyday stories
Historias de buena gente	Stories of good people
Se juegan la vida cansados	They risk their lives, tired,
Con hambre y un frío que pela	Hungry, and freezing cold

Ahogan sus penas
    con una candela
	They drown their sorrows
	    with a candle

Pónte tú en su lugar	Put yourself in their shoes
El miedo que sus ojos reflejan	The fear reflected in their eyes
La mar se echó a llorar	The sea burst into tears
Muchos no llegan	Many don't make it
Se hunden sus sueños	Their dreams are drowning
Papeles mojados	Wet documents
Papeles sin dueño	Documents without owners
Muchos no llegan	Many don't make it
Se hunden sus sueños	Their dreams are drowning
Papeles mojados	Wet documents
Papeles sin dueño	Documents without owners
Frágiles recuerdos a la deriva	Fragile memories adrift
Desgarran el alma	Tear the soul[30]
Calaos hasta los huesos	Soaked to the bone
El agua los arrastra sin esperanza	The water drags them without hope
La impotencia en su garganta	Helplessness in their throats
Con sabor a sal	That tastes of salt

Una bocanada de aire les daba
    otra oportunidad
	A gasp of air gave them
	    another opportunity

Tanta injusticia me desespera	So much injustice causes me to despair
Pónte tú en su lugar	Put yourself in their shoes

El miedo que en sus ojos reflejan	The fear reflected in their eyes
La mar se echó a llorar	The sea burst into tears
Tanta noticia me desespera	So much news causes me to despair[31]
Pónte tú en su lugar	Put yourself in their shoes
El miedo que sus ojos reflejan	The fear reflected in their eyes
La mar se echó a llorar	The sea burst into tears

Chorus (repeated)[32]

"Papeles mojados" graphically describes the experience of drowning with such lines as "The water drags them out / Without a chance of survival," and "Helplessness in their throats / That tastes of salt / A gasp of air gives them another opportunity." The singer's voice is muffled at the end of the song when she declares that "Their dreams are drowning / Wet documents / Documents without owners." The muffled voice evokes death, and her diction, the shattering of a dream that death renders impossible. Indeed, in La Mari's regional pronunciation, the final *s* sound is often dropped. Her elongation of the *o* sound at the end of the last *dueños* of the chorus evokes the fading, sinking dreams of the harragas reinforced by the elongation of *sueñoooo* (dreeeeam), which vanishes in the process. The semantic field of drowning haunts the entire song, even extending into scenes that are not directly about drowning: the harragas "drown" their sorrows with a candle. The text also argues that the burners' "dreams are shattered" using the verb *hundir*, which can also mean "to sink." Various Spanish words in the song contain multiple meanings related to the idea of submersion that translations do not always capture. These double entendres normalize drowning and convey this omnipresent risk, as harragas grow accustomed to hearing this "everyday story" before tempting their fate.

Narrating the experience of drowning is a bold approach; "Papeles mojados" contrasts with media depictions of hrig that either dismiss the harragas' experience or categorize their crossing of the sea as an evil act, or both. In the song, the harragas are not called "ilegales." This choice reflects the band's determination not to use any of the terms society calls harragas, and at all cost to avoid reinforcing the cultural and political ideas they contain. The band chooses to call clandestine migrants in a peculiar fashion. "Papeles mojados" is structured to refer to them metonymically. Each time the following two lines are sung: "Many do not make it / Their dreams are shattered," the line "Wet documents" follows, signaling the disintegration both of the human beings and their identification papers. This choice impresses on the listener how mass media depersonalizes harragas and is also used to palliate biased conceptions. It is a common belief, and in actuality a widespread practice, that migrant-hopefuls burn their identification papers before they set off to sea in hopes of thwarting the authorities' attempt to identify them. However, the "burners" in this song have their papers. Technically, they are not *sans-papiers*—an umbrella term that encompasses people with varying legal statuses but which shows significant structural differences with clandestine migrants.[33] The Spanish term *los sin papeles* is quite similarly misused. It implies that obtaining papers is the primary motivation to come to Europe. By calling prospective migrants "wet documents," the music band first resorts to a euphemism in that the wet documents are water-logged from the journey. Identifying *sin papeles* as a misnomer allows Chambao to propose an alternate terminology.

The song complicates the picture further by not simply renaming but also praising the immigrant: harragas are qualified as "good people." The use of this adjective is anything but innocent: it inverts the current representation in society of the clandestine migrant as evil-minded in his attempt to evade the law. The public does not generally assume migrants to be respectable members of society, people they would gladly welcome into their community. Instead, migrants are assumed to be criminals, troublemakers at best. It is revealing that in the context of entrenched conceptions, standardized by common discourse, the band has to reassure the listener. The album was released the year following the 9/11 attacks—a time of heightened discrimination against Muslims around the globe. In that political context, parallels between clandestine migration from North Africa and "evil-doing" became pervasive and did much to shape public opinion. In contrast, "Papeles mojados" identifies the foreigners as "thousands of shadows." These shadows represent harragas in their immateriality. The word *shadows* opens the text in Spanish and serves as the subject for all the verbs that follow: "Thousands of shadows . . . they navigate." The invocation of haunting shadows implicates us in the deaths of the departed. To this effect, the song addresses the listener by gently inviting him/her to indulge in a redeeming act, namely, to "put [themselves] in their shoes." The line seems urgent, since it appears three times. It is almost a command, for to the imperative form of the verb is added the second-person pronoun singular *tú* as if to express informally: "you, *you* put yourself in their shoes," thus daring the listener to take the challenge.

The dare is, through the play of shadows, turned into theater, a game of shadow plays. This playful approach transforms harragas' arrival-to-come into an exaggeration. Even if there were to be an invasion, Chambao suggests, the intruders would be mere specters. Indeed, the memory of Muslim Spain (711–1492) is "fragile" and the returning conqueror is weak. Adrift at sea traveling by night, what kind of threat is he to Europe? As the song insists, the conquest agenda is mere myth, for most of the newcomers "do not make it." This undermines the wide assumption that burners are coming to Europe in great numbers. It is a false story, one in which the Muslim has historically been the bad guy, for the song indicates that the truth of the matter is "a story (or history!) of good people," whose motive is survival, not ideology, politics, or the settling of historical scores. The conqueror trades his usual identifiers of a horse, a flag, and regalia for the hunger and cold of a small boat. The menacing flotilla is reduced to a sad smattering of dinghies. The lines of torches advancing toward a city have been replaced by a candle, a symbol of peace. Besides, the burners are not fomenting war. Instead they are "gambling" away their own lives—not those of others.

The ululations that pepper the song could be mistaken for cries of joy, as Arab/Muslim women often ululate to express happiness. One could perhaps think that they are signs of victory, the celebrations of conquest. However, these "you-yous" are actually sorrowful markers of death in contexts such as these. It is customary for North African women to express these traditional cries of joy at the untimely death of an unmarried youth. The belief behind this seemingly contradictory practice of expressing joy in a time of sorrow is that the bachelor(ette) will marry in Heaven. In this light, the insinuation is that there are young individuals among the drowned. The ululation and the short poem that open the song contribute to it being an ode, a tribute to the harragas. The connotation is that harragas have been mistakenly identified. The residents of the other shore have made the Mediterranean shared space a no-migrants-land, leading many prospective migrants to "fear" the water that eventually "carries [them] away." The Darwinian logic of the survival of the fittest will irremediably apply, leaving no room for "hope," only a last "gasp of air."

Migrants are often equated with those who seek documents, and it is often assumed that these papers are obtained at the expense of nationals, who end up sacrificing jobs to the newcomers. Here, the song reveals that in his crossing, the harrag loses more than what he was supposedly going to gain: he loses everything, from his documents to his life and even his hopes, which remain prisoners of the shore. "Many don't make it," sings La Mari, implying that successful migratory endeavors have become less and less possible, and that even hopes struggle to get beyond the limits of the Moroccan coast. Rather than focusing on the coasts (where people depart and arrive), Chambao concentrates on the sea, where migrants frequently get caught. The expression "(Hay) moros en la costa" dates to the Muslim rule of the Iberian Peninsula. In *Política de España en África*, Gonzalo de Reparaz writes, "Felipe III saw to it that coasts be fortified by erecting towers in places where pirates used to land and by posting vigils who would warn the distraught villagers of *moors on the coast* so that they could flee and hide as well as they could."[34] At that time, there was great concern about Muslim pirates raiding the eastern coasts of Spain between Murcia and Valencia. Fear of these corsairs prompted locals to build towers from which they kept vigil over the shores—a mechanism that is a precursor to the contemporary Integrated System of Exterior Surveillance.

As L. P. Harvey demonstrates, "there was almost a Spanish psychosis related to the cry 'Moros en la costa' (the Moors have landed), but in fact there was no landing or any real threat on Spanish territory by troops from any Muslim power, no attempt to regain what had been lost."[35] The fear of the Moor gave birth to an expression that has come to mean the "coast is not clear." Guillermo Araya explains that the saying is in everyday use in Spain, and that "without knowing exactly why, we say, for instance, in colloquial Spanish, that such and such behavior is not Christian or, in order to refer in a generic fashion to the enemy, that there aren't (or there are) Moors on the coast."[36] Both literally and figuratively, the expression means, among other things, that it is not safe to leave one's hideout or undertake a project. Conversely, if the coast *is* clear, one may proceed with safety. In the expression "(Hay) moros en la costa" ([There are] Moors on the coast), a link between our coast (us) and moros (them) is implied. Rather than warning that the foreigners are on our coast, La Mari instead flips the colloquialism and testifies that there are no Moors in the historical sense. She marks the absence of moros, who have been replaced by the wet metonymic papers of the repeated song title, which act as a kind of place holder for the departed who do not hold papers. The song also reverses the narrative of the expelled landowner returning to reclaim his historical right to return, as the reality of the clandestine journey deflates this hyperbolic conquest narrative. A "second Reconquista" would be reduced to failure before ever reaching Spanish soil. The band thus corrects, or rather erases, a common belief and highlights a misconception. In order to challenge the vision of the dead Muslim migrants as "enemies," Chambao reminds the listener that the Mediterranean is no longer a site of conquerors, pirates, and corsairs, but simply of migrants who die more often than they make it. What Chambao sees is not the images imported from historical Muslim Spain, biased contemporary mass media discourses, or protectionist political speeches—all loci of confrontations. Rather, the band sees wet documents, a referent "without owners." Against the image of a heavily armed Moorish invader lies the deceased corpse of the migrant. Documents have become orphans.

But the main purpose of the song's disarming choice of words is to present the listener with a bold rebuttal of deeply derogatory visions of the sea's migrants. They are represented through human feelings that convey harmlessness: "the fear that his eyes reflect." Thus, Chambao maintains that fear of invasion held by inhabitants of the Mediterranean's northern rim is misplaced; it is the "Moors" who (should) fear what they might encounter at sea. The song states that the migrants' patera was filled with individuals carrying illusions. Their crossing was fueled by dreams. "Papeles mojados" resorts to the realm of the imaginary to invalidate the theory of invasion, making the case that it is a mere product of our imagination. The song turns the theory into a myth and transforms the "bad guys" into "good people." This choice transfers blame in the discourse of criminalization; indeed, it subtly points its finger at "us" by suggesting that the capsizing of a boat full of hopes and the "drowning of dreams" are cruel and unacceptable acts. Through his inevitable identification with the harragas' nonmaterial feelings, such as hopes and dreams, the listener is likely to feel guilt at his lack of involvement and action. If "even the sea burst into tears," how could the listener not be empathetic? The sea's role in this tragedy could be interpreted as either blameless or culpable: if the body of water cries, then it must be playing the role of the witness to a crime, and therefore the capsizing is not *its* fault. On the other hand, the sea could be shedding tears of remorse, for it is the property of Europe and therefore an accomplice to the North in "the tragedy of the strait." In fact, in chapter 2, the Mediterranean is sometimes described as conniving and spider-like in its schemes to trap African youth in its waters. Pointedly, though the masculine form is more common for "the sea" in Spanish ("el mar"), some novelists and poets have referred to it with a feminine pronoun "la mar" to convey specific meanings. In "Papeles mojados," the sea is a dangerous enchantress. While attempting to ascertain whether or not the sea is implicated in the tragedy, the song envisions ways to contribute to making a change.

The singer's authorial voice encourages the listener ("you") to imagine the harrowing situation of the clandestine and identify with him through its highly empathetic tone. The artist also endorses a bold discourse that decries the status quo. La Mari uses the first-person pronoun twice: "So much injustice causes me to despair" and "So much news causes me to despair." This technique has several functions. First, the deaths of individuals trying to reach the Spanish coasts are unfair ("injustice"). Second, just like the unfair drowning, the rendering from this phenomenon ("news") triggers feelings of frustration. Such a correlation indicates that in spite of "so much" coverage of the harragas, our passivity is making the singer lose hope (*desespera*). Her repeated use of "me" teases out a dichotomy between the singer and us, thus suggesting that we may be couched in too much indifference. "Papeles mojados" offers a rare, unwavering position with regard to leavism and clandestine migration, and we, the listeners, are urged to take a stance on the failed crossings.

"Papeles mojados" is original in its focus on the unfortunate outcome. It pleads on behalf of the departed and advocates identification with the subject (matter). For the subject *does* matter. This song rejects the preestablished national and communitarian European discourse by focusing on the predicament of the migrant. The band approaches this project in two steps.[37] The first step is the reassurance of the listener—necessary in order to make the audience consider a different approach to an issue of national concern. The fearful listener should feel relieved: the Moor is not on the coast, he has sunk in the depths of the not-so-straight way to Gibraltar. The burner will not burn the sea, for he and his patera will never arrive. Not necessarily condoning hrig, the song nevertheless emphasizes the humanistic nature of clandestine migrants, too often viewed as trespassers who show up uninvited. The idea is that they are good people, regular people, and that they should be welcomed, not abhorred. The second step is to convince the listener that a progressive position is more suitable. The use of the unambiguous adjectives studied earlier is a clear mark of this. "Papeles mojados" is not only a dedication to harragas but is also a hymn to the departed, a stele on a maritime cenotaph. The revenge of the dead lies not so much in that they have come to haunt the shores; rather, these figures resonate through the lyrics beyond national shores and reach an international audience. Muslim women's voices mourn with cries of joy, so to speak, the young men and women who lost their lives in the sea in order to guide them to higher shores. In so doing, they join Chambao in a trans-Mediterranean dedication to those who demonstrate to us that both globalization and the Mediterranean have failed in their functions as pathways to document-free mobility (for all).

Both "Clandestino" and "Papeles mojados" take place in the Strait of Gibraltar—the Mediterranean's primary site of fatal attempted crossings. Alternatively, the Rai n'b genre tackles clandestine migration mostly from the surface. Why is it so? Surely, it is not out of indifference, for even the harrag, referenced as the traditionally excluded symbol of the clodo in Raï n'b, is depicted with empathy. Rather, the distance expressed by *Beur* singers is chiefly explained by a geographical factor: passengers of rickety boats rarely wash ashore French beaches. One could imagine that if singers in France set off to sea to see the underworld for themselves in order to sing about it, they could potentially be mistaken as clandestines by various regulatory agents on both sides of the Mediterranean. Therefore, could the global singer be apprehensive of being the victim of racial profiling on the high seas? Could he fear being caught in the electronic "net" of the Mediterranean? Yesterday's rulers and conquerors are today's vagrants, corpses, and ghosts, and this shifting of fortunes implies a universality of the *hrig* experience: we are all involved; we could all be harragas. Musicians implicate themselves and their audiences to make this point and collapse the identitarian walls that inhibit sympathy, understanding, and hospitality.

5 Europe Bound

Shooting "Illegals" at Sea

Burning in the Age of Global Revolutions

On January 14, 2011, Tunisian President Aziz el Abidine Ben Ali fled Tunisia. Following the tragic death of protester Mohamed Bouazizi, demonstrations spread to various parts of the country, precipitating the Jasmine Revolution, the first revolution of the Arab Spring. Bouazizi was a twenty-six-year-old Tunisian man who set himself on fire in front of the Préfecture of Sidi Bouzid on December 17, 2010. Bouazizi's self-immolation was an expression of his despair at his condition as an unemployed college graduate. His irreversible act was a physical migration out of an unbearable plight, because both physical and symbolic burnings are called *hrig* in Arabic. The extreme gesture is an unauthorized crossing over into death where the promise of a better life or the end of an ordeal is imaginable. Indeed, suicide is a religiously condemned practice. For lack of better professional opportunities, Bouazizi had resorted to selling produce. He set himself on fire after the municipal police confiscated his merchandise for not having a proper permit. Eighteen days after his desperate gesture, the young man died at the Ben Arous Burn and Trauma Center, and his fate set the Arab Spring in motion. The emergence of this revolution and subsequent ones in the region is partly attributed to the energy and dedication of the citizens ready to die at the hands of the police state[1] to fight for justice and to denounce hogra.[2] Some, like Bouazizi, sacrificed themselves—in Bouazizi's case, it involved burning, in the literal sense of the term.[3]

In twenty-three days, the revolution led to the demise of a statesman who had ruled the country for twenty-three years. Exactly a month after Ben Ali ran away, an unusually high number of Tunisians had escaped from the area of greatest unrest. The climate of insecurity and uncertainty that reigned in Tunisia during and following the protests in northern Africa has caused Italy to experience unprecedented numbers of migrants. European media outlets such as *Le Figaro, Corriere della Sera,* and the *Guardian* reported that five thousand Tunisians had reached the Sicilian island of Lampedusa over a five-day period. The newspapers credited this massive exodus primarily to the slackening of controls by the Tunisian customs officers since the beginning of the protests. Undoubtedly, people were able to cross en masse because of lesser vigilance. The crossings were also successful due to clement weather, as well as the proximity of the island. Indeed, Lampedusa is situated closer to Tunisia than to Italy—140 kilometers (85 miles) from Tunisian shores and 244 kilometers (152 miles) from Pozzallo, the nearest town in Sicily. It also happens to find itself halfway between the southern coats of Italy and Sidi Bouzid, the birthplace of the Jasmine Revolution, which inspired thousands of individuals across North Africa and the Middle East to overthrow their authoritarian regimes.

A *Corriere della Sera* article with the headline, "Stop the Wave as We Did with Albania," featured Franco Frattini, the Italian minister of Foreign Affairs, declaring, "The government has decreed a state of emergency and our patrols have already been deployed off the Tunisian coasts. But that's not enough, we have to mobilize the Mediterranean countries that have ships, planes, and helicopters."[4] This political position supports the idea that peaceful acts of immigration require an intervention commonly considered as a response to a war threat.[5] On televised news, Italian Minister of the Interior Roberto Maroni expressed his concern and accused the EU of letting Italy cope with the state of affairs on its own, "as usual." His condemnation was rendered in the form of a cataclysmic preface that would justify interference in Tunisian sovereignty through the sending of Italian police officers to Tunisia in order to help contain the migratory flux—a statement that the spokesperson of the Italian government had qualified as "unacceptable" the very same evening on the television channel Al-Arabiya.[6]

The Italian government's plans, as laid out by Frattini, to use "ships, planes, and helicopters" to fight the threat, draw a dramatic image of an "attacked" Europe that must implement emergency measures and fight back. This histrionic reaction from Europe also confirms the idea I have developed thus far that clandestine migration in the Mediterranean has become a new trope in divisive discourses that refuse a vision of a united sea. These discourses ignore the necessity of tackling the socioeconomic and political causes of the phenomenon and instead advocate further confining measures that only add to the Tunisians' feeling of global injustice. As a matter of fact, a meeting of Roberto Maroni with Claude Guéant, French minister of the Interior, Overseas, Territorial Collectivities, and Immigration, led Guéant to claim that neither country has the obligation to take in new migrants. In accordance with this position, Italy began to repatriate Tunisian newcomers and to ship heavy logistical help to Tunisia in order to abet a government crackdown on leavism.[7]

Mr. Frattini said in his interview with *Corriere della Sera*, "Our predictions are dramatic. Right as the flow from Libya is stopped, Tunisia opens up, and the trafficking in human beings becomes *African*. Just think what would happen if the Egyptians started arriving tomorrow, the situation could create another Albanian situation."[8] Though Italy's coasts are not endowed with an apparatus of surveillance equivalent to Spain's SIVE, local officials have recently implied that they think similar sophisticated technology should be used. Bernardino de Rubeis, the mayor of Lampedusa Island, who described the rapid influx of migrants to the small island as being "out of control," said the Lampedusa crisis "needs a European response."[9] And though SIVE is a Spanish high-tech border control system, it has been implemented with the help of the EU, who had assigned Spain the task of becoming an efficient buffer zone. Maroni's claim that the state members of the EU have not helped Italy could imply that, since they assisted Spain, they should also be willing to help Italy gain back its "control," and that a SIVE-like shield would be welcome. Maroni specifically calls for the activation of a "Frontex mission," which, according to journalist Monica Guerzoni, who interviewed him, is to "detain boatloads of illegal immigrants in the ports of the Maghreb."[10] In line with the assertion that Italy was being neglected, Marine Le Pen, current leader of the far-right political party, Le Front National (FN), who was a candidate in the 2012 French presidential election, stated: "I also want to offer my support to the inhabitants of Lampedusa who have had the feeling of being completely abandoned."[11]

The French saga of political blunders climaxed when Michèle Alliot Marie, minister of Foreign Affairs, offered to help the Tunisian regime repress protests with the savoir-faire of French security forces. After weeks of criticism and pressure from across the political spectrum, the minister stepped down as a result of her highly reprimanded proposal. The French consul in Tunis, too, was harshly criticized for failing to help the French government assess the situation in Tunisia in a prompt manner. France was reproached for not showing support for the revolutionary movement in Tunisia. This explains why shortly after replacing Alliot-Marie as minister of Foreign Affairs, Alain Juppé made his first international trip to Egypt to express his support to the Egyptian democratic efforts. A few days later, right-wing L'Union pour un Mouvement Populaire deputy Chantal Brunel declared, "We must reassure the French about all migrating populations that would come from the Mediterranean. After all, let's put them back on the boats." Her statements were condemned by the entire French political establishment. In the French assembly, and in her presence, Prime Minister François Fillon clarified his party's position in the midst of FN's rise in the polls: "the revolts that are taking place in Arab countries trigger big hopes, but they also have consequences in terms of migrations, which we have to face and handle in a humane fashion, but also in a clear way. . . . Behind each migrant, there is a human destiny, which must be respected. Chantal Brunel made statements, of which we do not approve, and for which she apologized."[12] The prime minister added that "the far-right wing had been setting the media and political agenda" during those preelection times. Some experts argue that the French right felt forced to adopt a very conservative take on immigration in order to win the election. Some even contended that the French president specifically asked his ministers to launch two debates, the first on national identity and the second on the place of Islam in France, for strategic purposes. According to these claims, these debates helped increase the popularity of the FN's xenophobic theses. They propelled Marine le Pen to second place in the polls in the spring of 2011. Supposedly, Sarkozy at that time hoped to compete against Marine Le Pen in the final round of elections in order to stand a better chance of being reelected. A previous scenario explains such contentions made by French political experts. In 2002, Jacques Chirac ran against Marine Le Pen's father in the final electoral round. Chirac won the election with flying colors by getting the votes of a massive body of voters who were fearful of the establishment of a racist and xenophobic state. Those included citizens who had abstained from voting in the first round, as well as those whose ballot in favor of Jean-Marie Le Pen had been a "contestation vote."

In an interview aired on French radio station RTL on March 1, 2012, the week before Brunel's comments, Marine Le Pen was asked to express her views on the idea of sending back "des êtres humains sur des *barcas*" (human beings on *barcas*). Le Pen's brash response contained the following uncompromising declaration: "We certainly can push the boats back onto international waters."[13] On her controversial trip to Lampedusa, Ms. Le Pen told locals that Europe cannot handle immigrants and that clandestines should be turned back, thus reiterating her extremist views by stating that European navies "should go as close as possible to the coasts from where the clandestine boats departed to send them back."[14] In the context of contemporary risky, clandestine, and maritime northward crossings, Lampedusa is a place of choice in times of political instability. Depending on its handling of its clandestine migrants and the severity of future immigration legislation, which a changing Maghrebi geopolitical landscape might alter in unprecedented ways, Italy may soon play a more decisive role in European antiharga decision making. The country will most likely remain a destination for clandestine migrants unless Tunisia accepts Maroni's "unacceptable" proposal, which consists in patrolling the coast of Tunisia so that "when human traffickers see patrol boats one mile off the coast they won't send out the boatloads."

In contrast to relentless escalating political condemnations of clandestines aimed at portraying Europe through the trope of a fortress with feet of clay, on July 8, 2013, Pope Francis took his first trip out of Rome to Lampedusa where he explained that "the culture of well-being [which] makes us insensitive to the cries of others . . . leads to a globalization of indifference." In addition, Christopher

Hein, the director of the Italian Council for Refugees *Avvenire* claimed that the pope's visit was "an important gesture." As for the Vatican, it announced that the pope was "profoundly moved" by the dramatic issue. The morning of the visit, 166 migrants had been taken to Lampedusa. The previous day, a boat of 120 people had been spotted going adrift south of Porto Palo, at the southernmost point of the main Sicilian island.[15] In total disconnect with the antihumanitarian discourses preached on the island by politicians before him, the religious leader commended the inhabitants of the island, the humanitarian organizations, and the police officers for their "attention" to these "people on a journey to find something better." He also visited "the door of Europe"—a monument in the memory of the drowned—asked the victims for "forgiveness," and prayed "to make a gesture of proximity and also wake up consciousnesses so that what happened never happens again."[16]

"To Sea" or "Not to Sea," That Is the Question

In spoken Maghrebi Arabic, there is a verb *tbaHar,* which means colloquially, "to go to the beach." Coming from the root *ba-ha-ra* (ب ح ر), which relates to the sea, the verb means to take a dip, to spend some time by the waterside, or simply to go for a swim. The beach has changed status in some of the latest North African literary and cinematic productions. It is no longer a place of leisure and pleasure. Instead, it is a site where characters go to look beyond, namely, toward the Spanish coasts or Europe in general. In Tahar Ben Jelloun's novel, *Partir,* Moroccan characters are depicted sitting at Café Hafa in Tangier waiting for the Spanish coast to unveil itself at sunset when it becomes bright with lights before the gaze of prospective migrants. In Tariq Teguia's film *Rome plutôt que vous,* an unemployed young man takes his girlfriend to the harbor, and they both look at the sea while imagining what lies ahead.

While the see/sea homonymy does not exist in Maghrebi Arabic—since "to see" is *shouf* and "to sea" is *tbaHar*—there is a regional belief that nowadays one of the only ways for migrant-hopefuls to see Europe is to "sea." Thus the idea of emigrating and settling in Europe is conveyed through the notion that it is an innocent pleasure, one that should be taken for granted, or rather one that we should grant rather than take away. Many characters in contemporary Maghrebi novels and films look ahead: their eyes are directed northward, seeing, or at least trying to see, Europe from across the sea. In this light, the sea— that space that is between here and there, but that keeps harragas "here" instead of taking them "there"—has become for many, especially those in Maghrebi films about clandestine migration, a site upon which the dreams of the prospective harragas are projected, holding the visions of an imagined Eldorado across the water.

In this chapter, I will examine four films.[17] All of them propose the idea that in order to see Europe, one has "to sea"—not as in "to go for a swim," as it was routinely understood before Europe became a deadly obsession for many unwanted North Africans—but rather in the sense of to "traverse the Mediter-ranean clandestinely," or to burn the sea. France is not the host country it used to be, as is suggested by a few recently released North African films. *Visa*, also known as *Visa la dictée*, proposes that in the context of extreme legislation in Europe, prospective migrants are forced to turn their attention to alternative methods of expatriating. Their Eldorado seems close enough to make the hazard-ous journey worthwhile but in effect remains unattainable for many, as *Harragas* demonstrates. In *L'Enfant endormi*, the departure of men has left women alone back in the village, where correspondence with husbands, who just reached the other shore of the Strait of Gibraltar, is established through videotapes. The prison-like universe depicted in the VHS tapes conveys the idea that Spain, in its compliance with the stringent immigration laws of the EU, has closed its doors to "illegal" newcomers. The latter find themselves in a state of limbo, forbidden from moving forward or backward, "caught in a social, economic, and political situation that turns them into hostages."[18] *Bled number one* experiments with the notion of forced expatriation, teasing out the incongruity and the irreversible damage that deportation of foreigners causes for individuals who do not feel identitarian con-nections with their ancestors' homeland.

These four films constitute a new form of contemporary Maghrebi cinema: they deal with prospective and settled migrants in European localities, whereas previous films tended to focus on the migrant conditions in France. *Visa* paro-dies current EU Schengen border restrictions in an effort to show the mounting difficulties experienced by migrants from the South.[19] In light of such restrictions, *Harragas* tracks a group of migrants who, with their eyes on a new life in Europe, attempt a perilous crossing to Spain. *L'Enfant endormi* envisions the questionable fruits of such migrations to the Iberian Peninsula, depicting the irreparable ways in which families are split by stringent immigration laws. *Bled number one* fea-tures Kamel, a young man who has been deported to Algeria, where he was born. Kamel is forced to stay away from France; however, he does not identify with the Arab and Berber cultures, so he tries to find a way to return to France clandes-tinely through Tunisia. All these films are commentaries on the lack of rights and the shortage of visas granted to citizens and migrants associated with the global South.

Visatation, or, a Surreal Dictation for a Visa Application

Emmanuel Levinas and Jacques Derrida theorized the concept of visitation in their treatment of hospitality. Derrida called this crucial concept, based on the acceptation of the other without consideration of his face, "unconditional hospitality." While Levinas dealt with the interconnectedness of the notions of host and hostage (which inspires part of my analysis of *Le Grand voyage*), Derrida summons a third element, that of ghost or specter. The term *visitation* evokes the ethereal, a spiritual or religious component in common parlance. The same way as a visitant imposes its presence on us and demands our acceptance of an unannounced *face à face,* the individual is called to adapt himself to the coming of the stranger and the foreigner. In various religious traditions, the visitor is sent to try our commitment to a divine law of unconditional hospitality, deemed in the sacred texts to be an imperative when the traveler seeks refuge in our homes.

The intervention of the visa raises a number of issues in light of this belief system. I would therefore like to consider the visa in the realm of global hospitality, as it relates to both Western homes of the global village and the Maghrobal (the Maghreb in its relation with global practicies). Here I would like to focus on the mobility of individuals across borders—obstacles that are not compatible with the essence of a globalized world. The notion of *visatation* teases out a sociopolitical reality denounced in the films discussed here. Whereas the concept of visatation is constructed on the phonetically close "right of visitation," what I call *visatation* dissects the problematic disconnect between the demand for visits overseas and the scarcity of visas, which constitutes one of the major themes of the film *Visa.*

In Ibrahim Letaïef's thirty-minute narrative released in 2004, the characters are required to pass a dictation test as part of a new procedure for requesting the right to visit France.[20] The winners of this contest will be awarded a French visa, the duration of which will be determined by the number of spelling errors they make.[21] The dictation is ultimately to assess whether or not the applicant can meet French standards of assimilation. The main character is the illiterate forty-year-old Rachid Belhassan (Jamal Madani), who is looking forward to traveling to Paris, where his cousin lives. In the ten days he has to prepare for his test, he purchases the *Bescherelle* (a French conjugation, spelling, and grammar manual), a dictionary, Gustave Flaubert's *Madame Bovary,* Jean de la Fontaine's *Les Fables,* and a French cookbook. Rachid studies diligently and desperately, using all means available to him. In order to further immerse himself in the language, he forbids his family to speak Arabic, and even limits the television viewing of his wife, Leila (Jamila Chihi), to the French channel, France 2. Tunisian Rachid is infatuated with the idea of France and everything that relates to it. He clings to anything that bears its name as though it were an amulet that will have the magical effect of increasing his luck at the dictation contest. The first time we see him, he enters the consulate wearing a blue, white, and red scarf—the colors of the French flag—around his neck. He wears the same scarf when he reviews a grammatical rule outside at night, as well as during the examination. Rachid's obsession with France, has, according to his wife, taken center stage in his life and destroyed their daily routine. Leila hums the French anthem as she clears the table but does so to mock her husband's blind devotion to a country that does not seem to want him—something she would like for him to realize for himself. In the next scene, a recording of the anthem takes over while the camera pans across a room in the dwelling. The space is filled with merchandise and pictures of French icons that range from political leaders to stars, sites, and stores.[22]

At the church where he went to take French classes from nuns, Rachid ventures into the chapel and addresses Jesus, whom he prays to in French. He vows that if "Sidi Jésus" (Lord Jesus) helps him pass the dictation test, "I will celebrate Santa Klaus, Easter, and even Bastille Day! I'll shop at Tati, and take the metro. I'll be totally assimilated." In his confused conflation of French references, modern life, and Christianity, Rachid feels the need to add that he will also keep Lent. After a pause and a quick glance behind him, he confesses in a low voice that he only fasts during Ramadan every other day anyway. He thus suggests that he is willing and able to let go of his Muslim fasting practice for what he considers to be a French one if that is what it takes to pass the French language test. Rachid even insists that his family only eat French cuisine: "From now on we will speak French, eat French, and sleep French." The man demands that his wife cook *patates en papillotes* (potatoes in a foil parcel) and *bœuf bourguignon* (beef casserole cooked in red wine). Leila will even prepare a *cassoulet,* one of France's most traditional dishes. Bœuf bourguignon is cooked in alcohol and cassoulet commonly contains pork. Therefore, it is important to note that Rachid's notion of what constitutes a French meal involves two dietary elements that are proscribed in the Islamic tradition. While both dishes are usually conceived of as major components of national cuisine, Rachid's selection of these two from among a multitude of other possible culinary choices reinforces his compliance with the French Republican vision of assimilation, which professes a renunciation of communitarian practices and identities including one's religious affiliation. Rachid's problematic approach is emphasized by the fact that besides putting a nonnormative twist to the basics of Islam, he adopts a faith he equates with French identity. He even becomes an adept of French cuisine, not by taste but by task. Indeed, his stuttering while searching for names of French meals that he would like to try is evidence of his struggle to find the right food to sample in order to improve his French skills faster.

It is interesting that French cuisine is a major step in Rachid's preparation for the dictation. In becoming acquainted with France's cuisine, it is not Frenchness itself—implicitly blended in France's culinary tradition—but a visa to France that he is ultimately trying to acquire. Indeed, he never states that he wants to become French. It is not the quality of France's culinary tradition that the man is interested in but its potential to help him with the dictation contest. Rachid is under the impression that one may eat one's way to France. The viewer remembers that Brahim Farza (Lotfi Dziri), one of the applicants for a visa to France, had mentioned that "we" (meaning "us Maghrebis") make of the Arabic and French languages a "ratatouille." In this light, Rachid attempts to cook the French language into his very being. From then on, the French language transforms itself into food. When his daughter Michkette (Beya Boularés) tells Rachid that "dictée" is spelled with "deux e" (two *e*'s), she is sent off to her room, and her father starts repeating to himself "deux oeufs," as if imagining two eggs. Indeed, two *e*'s is the French homonym for two eggs (*deux œufs*). The father conveniently places two eggs in his word soup, and thus cooking becomes a mnemonic tool for the exam he is training for. His own linguistic ratatouille, a slop, contributes to a flop.

Rachid's method of French acquisition is mediated through the belief that what you say is what you eat, and what you eat is what you say. It turns out that in his uncompromising approach to test preparation, in which he mobilizes his entire family, he demands that meals be called by their French names. This is Rachid's miracle potion. The recipe for success is no more and no less than a combination of exclusively French ingredients. This explains why when he asks for a French cookbook and the saleslady (Myriam Benedotto) at the bookstore presents him with a cookbook on Chinese cuisine, he automatically rejects her proposition. Rachid refuses to mingle his French manuals and literary canon with a cookbook that does not feed into his exclusive relationship with France even if the cookbook is for his wife because Rachid has decided that his wife and daughter will assist in his endeavor to make his home a French-only zone.

Rachid's dedicated preparation is contrasted with the ludicrous process of the test itself. Mr. Bernard Dictot (Christian David) is a parody of Bernard Pivot, an icon in the French cultural landscape known internationally for his televised *Dictée,* a spelling test taken by candidates worldwide. Mr. Dictot is introduced by the consul in a lecture hall of the Faculty of Letters at the University of Manouba in Tunisia right before Mr. Dictot delivers the *dictée* from France. The parodic character is not present in the room because, according to the sarcastic remark of one of the candidates, he was refused a visa to travel to Tunisia. At high speed, Mr. Dictot reads the text aloud, which is infused with difficult vocabulary, complex grammatical structures, and rarely used verb tenses.[23] Earlier in the film, Rachid's uneasiness with the French language was noticed by one of the consulate's staff, who said snidely, "Celui-ci n'ira pas plus loin" (This one won't make it any further), indicating that the dictation will successfully carry out its insidious goal of preventing Rachid from setting foot in France. The mockery rapidly takes the form of an ominous prognostication. Seconds before Mr. Dictot's dictation begins, Rachid misinterprets fellow applicant Brahim's well wishing, "I hope you make no mistakes," which Rachid mistakes for a curse, "I hope you make a hundred mistakes," due to the homonymy in French: "J'espère que vous allez nous faire un *sans* fautes" misunderstood for "J'espère que vous allez nous faire *cent* fautes." The outcome of his performance thus becomes predictable for the viewer, who quickly grasps the film's important message, namely, that excessively cumbersome bureaucratic procedures have become tactics to slow regular migration.

Visa stands out for its visionary representation of what the French government (under both Sarkozy's and Hollande's presidencies) is leaning to establish, namely a change in its handling of visa-granting procedures in order to move from a country of "mass" to "select" immigration, which would favor the entry of highly skilled individuals to fill worker shortages in underrepresented professional activities. Contrary to the other films of my corpus, *Visa* does not concern itself with clandestine immigration per se. Nor does it show "illegals" at sea, or before or after the crossing. However, it does reveal that the Schengen space is closing its doors to regular immigration from its southern neighbors while causing a "brain-drain" in the Maghreb. It also conveys that such exclusionary immigration policies ineluctably lead desperate candidates to consider not-so-legal options, for we are shown that characters' high expectations and arduous preparations are met with a surrealistic sort of examination—one that is not merely selective, it is deterrent. The candidates are literally put to the test. It is a screening, a rite of nonpassage. In fact, in the scene where Brahim Farza reads the new regulations and the criteria for obtaining a visa to a group of men, which includes Brahim, one of the candidates thinks that it must be a joke. The men laugh. Shortly afterward, the same man spots a camera above their heads. The camera happens to be directed at them, which enables the man to use it as evidence to back up his claim by exulting that they are being filmed for the sake of "candid camera" (*la caméra cachée*). Ironically, the camera is not so candid (it is a surveillance appliance) or hidden (*cachée*) for that matter, because it has been spotted. As film scholar Yosefa Loshitzky writes regarding Europe's new strangers and others within, "Nowhere are these anxieties better articulated than in cinema, which both reflects and constructs societal attitudes, because, like architecture, cinema is one of the most public arts."[24] The filmic *mise en abyme*, which consists of a film within a film, magnifies anxieties to the point of ridicule, hence the men's laughter in spite of the zooming of "Panopticon Europe" onto their faces and application files.[25]

The camera is one tool among others that aims at monitoring Tunisians who intend to visit France in a legal fashion. The notification that is pinned on the board at the entrance of the French consulate makes it clear that another tool, a dictation test, has been freshly implemented in order to monitor the identity of the applicants through an already complicated process: "In accordance to decree 21/21, France reserves the right to verify the level of knowledge of any person who wishes to enter its territory, regardless of the reason of the visit." The men's humor is short-lived, and soon they come to deplore the surreal situation that they are facing. The assumption that migrants cross into Europe in order to look for a professional opportunity is challenged. Indeed, the targeted migrants are not only contemplating an authorized journey; they also happen to be of retirement age, and thus not looking for work. It so happens that retired Brahim is a well-educated individual who explains to Rachid that his seeking a visa is accounted for by nostalgia. He simply wants to *see* again the Paris he grew up in (my emphasis). This scene is also an obvious condemnation of the harshening of visa applications, which now also concerns temporary visitors. The educated man, whose French fluency and accent sound native, will not make it to France, for he made sixty-eight errors in the dictation. Neither will Rachid. As Brahim hypothesizes, "It looks like they don't want us there." This may well be a reason, but undoubtedly the impossibility of Rachid's leaving is due to his persistent clinging to the clichéd image of France as a perpetually receiving country. This was conveyed through his fixation on all things French. Back home, Leila laments that they only listen to France Culture on the radio. She reminds her husband that when they used to tune into Radio Tunis, she managed to learn English, Spanish, and Italian in addition to French.[26] Rachid's answer to her statement—which he makes sure to spell out in French—is as follows: "French, only French, I don't need Spanish and Italian! Europe will have to wait! Let me start with France!" The man's failing the dictation in spite of his uncompromising loyalty to France, its language, and its culture may be a sign that France is too narrow a destination target.

At home, he keeps making mistakes, which his wife teases him about. Leila uses those occasions to present her method as a didactic tool, not so much to help her husband with the right pronunciation of words but rather to teach him a few basic lessons. One of them is that she does not need to take French classes since she is obviously the better speaker. Another one is that if someone in the house is to give lessons, she is in a better position to do so. She seems to imply that the French visa is an opportunity that comes with a price.[27] In fact, after his return from his French class, Leila asks in Arabic if he wants more tisane, which Rachid mechanically translates into French by repeating slowly as if he were helping a child prepare for a dictation test. His wife then reveals that herbal tea "is recommended for digesting *zucchini gratin à la Bescherelle* sauce."[28] Rachid corrects Leila: "*Béchimel, Béchimel!* It's not that hard—repeat!" Leila seizes the opportunity to once again correct her husband: "*Béchamel*," she notes, causing Rachid to acknowledge his mistake and that Leila knows better. Through Rachid's unfruitful obsession with leaving for France, the director shows that the hopeful migrant excludes other countries that are likely to grant him a visa.

The director's commentary on Rachid's stubborn project seeps through subtle plays on words that Leila masters easily. Thanks to her corrections of her husband's mistakes, she offers Rachid an opportunity to come to grips with the doomed outcome of his unwavering dedication to France. For instance, when he returns from the dictation test, which he feels he has failed, Rachid has no appetite. His wife asks him why he does not eat the cassoulet, which, she remarks teasingly "is French cuisine." Her husband retorts that he is not hungry and does not like "crassoulet" any longer. Leila repeats a few times the right pronunciation of the dish while looking at her daughter, pretending she is teaching the term to her. The viewer is aware that Michket knows the word too well and that it is her father who is being taught how to pronounce it. The way Leila utters the vocabulary word in the form of detached syllables ("cassoul-et") is not only to mimic the way a teacher would slowly detach syllables in order to teach a young learner, but it is also a way for her to insist that her husband is reduced to a little (*-et*) *cassoul,* which in Arabic means a "stupid, obtuse, stunned person."

Brahim, too, is aware that other countries besides France have accommodated newcomers. He suggests that Rachid try his luck in the Gulf, for "the Gulf countries are in need of people like you and me." Rachid applies and during the interview he is taken aback when the official asks him to recite a chapter from the Qur'an (the longest one at that!), namely, the Sura of the Cow, which he has not memorized. Rachid offers to declaim another chapter—most likely a less daunting one—but the official refuses to hear any other and demands that he leave. While France's visa was tied to high culture symbolized by a text recited by an icon in French culture, the Gulf's visa is similarly attached to high standards—though of a different nature. Neither a learned individual in either language nor a scrupulously religious individual of either faith, Rachid is left to envisage other destinations, such as Spain or Italy, and the only migratory pattern that remains for him is clandestinity.

Harragas: A Boat Named Bote

Especially known for his commercial hits, among which are *Omar Gatlato* (1976), *Bab el Oued city* (1994), and *Chouchou* (2003), Merzak Allouache is a prolific filmmaker, whose much-critiqued work has dealt with a variety of significant cultural, political, and societal issues. His first feature, *Omar Gatlatlo,* scrutinizes the alienation of men in Algerian society. His fifth full-length film, *Bab el Oued city,* is concerned with the rise of Islamic fundamentalism. As for *Chouchou,* it focuses on gender identity through the role of an Algerian clandestine played by Gad Elmaleh.

Harragas (2009) was awarded a few international prizes including Le Prix Spécial du Jury, Prix Fipresci, Prix des Droits de l'Homme at Le Festival du Film de Dubaï, as well as Le Palmier d'Or and Le Prix de la Meilleure B.O. at the Festival de Valencia in Spain. *Harragas* is the story of nine men and one woman who get on a dinghy on an Algerian beach and head toward Spain. The crew consists of Algerians, both northern and southern (from "700 km away"), and includes a fundamentalist and a deserter named Mustapha. Worried that he will not be allowed onboard because he has not paid his passage dues, Mustapha kills the smuggler prior to the departure and later holds the rest of the passengers hostage at gunpoint.

My analysis of this film will try to tease out layers of interpretation through the study of language(s) both in the film and in the metatext of *Harragas'* official poster and DVD cover (Figure 5.1). It is important to see how the patera (fishing boat) is portrayed not only in film but also in paratext and publicity. These mediums can be essential, for they often provide a first sense of the film and reveal the director's or the film company's view of what clandestine migration is. As for *Harragas,* the patera is on the DVD cover, as well as on its promotional poster. On the image, the boat is full of passengers. One could argue that the blue sea, which stretches across the DVD cover and the surface of the poster, is a romanticized symbol of hope. The characters are on their way northward and the open sea promises to be their ticket away from a confining Algeria that they have left behind. It might, however, also be argued that the crowded and fragile dinghy in the immensity of the sea portends its demise.

Underneath the names of the coproducing companies, the film's title appears in French and Arabic. On one of the images, between the two titles, the viewer can read in smaller print: "A Film by Merzak Allouache." A subtitle is provided as an explanation in parentheses: "Partir à tout prix" (To leave at all costs), an expression embodied by the character Imène (Lamia Boussekine), the only female clandestine on board, who is the girlfriend of Nasser (Seddik Benyagoub). Both Nasser and their friend Rachid (Nabil Asli) had tried in vain to deter her from leaving. But for Imène, leaving is crucial. She says, "I don't want to stay one more day without you [Nasser] in this country—a country of misfortune and misery." The Arabic title is all the more intriguing, as the term *harragas* does not exist in formal Arabic. Therefore, it is logically impossible to see it in writing.[29] *Harragas* is only in use as such in Maghrebi Arabic, hence its unconventional spelling, which includes ڨ (*g*), an unofficial letter in the Arabic alphabet. *G* has been invented in the form of a ق with one diacritic point on top in order to transcribe words of a foreign origin and of spoken Arabic. It should be remarked that in Morocco, another letter is preferred.

The film title in French appears above the Arabic title. The French title is in solid, square, and equal-sized white characters. Following the smaller-print attribution, is the title in Arabic script. The Arabic text can be difficult to discern, drawn with thin wavering arabesques that could well be mistaken by a nonreader

Figure 5.1 DVD cover for Merzak Allouache's *Harragas*. Used with permission.

of the language for mere embellishment. Meanwhile, the French title is perfectly linear, seemingly undisturbed by the shifting aquatic environment. Conversely, the Arabic inscription looks distorted and almost transparent, as if about to be diluted in the water, engulfed like harragas.[30] What remains unscathed is the French film title, which dominates the poster and DVD cover, as if to suggest the inferiority of the Arabic language in the politics of marketing, semiotics, and aesthetics to appeal to the expected audience. The stranglehold of French funding has irrevocable impacts on filmmaking in the global South. In an interview on a bonus track of the French DVD version of the film, Allouache indicates that, while *Harragas* should have been shot totally in Algerian Arabic, a significant amount of French dialogue was required because of regulations imposed by the cofinancing institutions. The dominance of French impacts various decisions, such as casting, for instance; in *Harragas,* the cast was expected to be credible as French speakers.

These uneven linguistic power relations point to transnational economic, political, and ideological hierarchies and tensions between the North associated with the French title and the South associated with the Arabic. They also speak to a number of disparities at transregional levels. The letter *g* (ﭺ) is sometimes transcribed differently as ﻙ, for throughout the Arab world no agreement has been officially reached on a universal written alphabet across the Middle East and North Africa. For this reason, the film obliquely begs the following set of questions: Are harragas foreign in their own country? Put differently, are they *étrangers* (alien, as in "foreigner") and *étranges* (alien, as in "strange") at the same time? Then, is harga erased from the visible and formal power, just like colloquial Arabic is? Is the presence of harragas in a cultural production that aims at showing the nonexisting, the invisible, a way to draw attention to them? Is the transparent title in Arabic supposed to transcribe the clandestine status of the burners, namely that they must hide to the point of becoming transparent in the society they are about they enter, while the title in the Latin alphabet, bold, imposing, and the most visible script on the image, is a sign to Westerners that harragas are a threatening mass seeking to impose their presence and way of life? These questions are legitimate when one sees how much hiding is done in the film, such as the burners' di(sso)lution, and how taboo the crossing is, even though it affects all layers of Algerian society. As a matter of fact, the ex-officer in *Harragas* laughs at the entire crew by poking fun at the fact that both the hillbillies (*ploucs*) and the daddy's boys and girls (*fils à papa*) are all reduced to helpless clandestines.

The poster for Moussa Haddad's 2012 film *Harraga Blues* has striking similarities to Allouache's (Figure 5.2). It contains the title in Roman and Arabic scripts, and the Arabic consists of a faithful translation of the French. Similarly to Allouache's French title, Haddad's appears in white block letters. But unlike

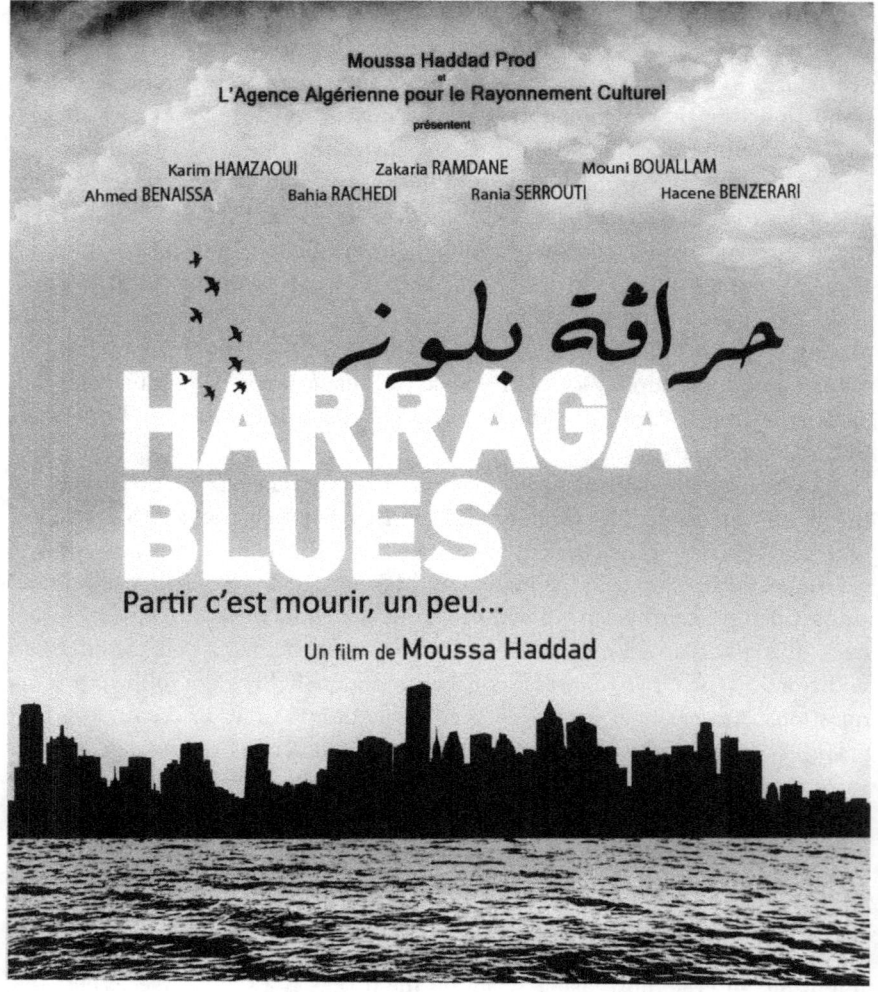

Figure 5.2 Film poster for Moussa Haddad's *Harraga Blues*. Used with permission.

Allouache's Arabic title, Haddad's is in black and it is printed slightly above the French, covering it at times.[31] The poster is also predominantly blue—except that Haddad's blue is mostly that of the sky, not of the sea. The French title is partially obscured by birds in flight. The image of birds soaring above a Western metropolis is evocative of freedom. And yet the tagline "Partir c'est mourir, un peu . . ." (To leave is to die a little . . .), followed by an ominous ellipsis, makes a clear allusion to death, thus foretelling that the film endorses an antiharga message. On the two posters, the selection of black and white for titles irremediably sum-

Figure 5.3 Ferryboat leaving the port of Algiers. Film still from Yamina Benguigui's *Inch'Allah dimanche.*

mons a discussion about languages (such as French) that overshadow others in the rendering of a local reality (clandestine migration between continents) for a global audience (living for the most part in Europe).

In a considerable number of literary and cinematic productions that were released in the last century that center on the theme of Algerian migration, the country of departure was Algeria and the country of arrival was France. This reality is illustrated in films such as the award-winning *Inch'Allah dimanche.* In this 2001 work by French-Algerian Yamina Benguigui, a ferry leaves the port of Algiers and transports its passengers to France. *Inch'Allah dimanche* opens with a historical note that tells us indirectly that the journey that the protagonist Zouina, her children, and mother-in-law are about to embark on is a state-sponsored immigration endeavor. In *Inch'Allah dimanche,* the ferry is depicted in a positive light. Shot from a low angle, it is portrayed as an imposing machine that leaves the port with its letters of nobility: the name, Zeralda, is displayed in Arabic and French (Figure 5.3). Proud and full of energy, the ferry sounds its horn as it pulls away, seeming to signal a happy event, the union of two shores. It is shining white, like a bride on her wedding day, and is also a marital connector for Zouina, in that it allows her to reunite with her husband.

Although the northbound ferry has been a common representation of Algerian migration to France, in *Bab el Oued city,* the maritime connector is off-kilter. The first time a ferry is shown in the film it is in reverse mode. It is heading to Algeria, as if the passengers had (been) returned. In another scene that shows a ferry, two brothers (Kader and Boualem), filmed among a multitude of anonymous bathers on the beach, discuss their future plans to leave the country. As they do so, the seemingly infinite sea lies before their eyes, and to symbolize the impossibility of them leaving, a ship in the distance progresses from one side of the screen to the other, from east to west. Though the ship may well be a trans-Mediterranean sea vessel that left the Algerian port, the extradiegetic viewer is led to believe that unlike the ferry in *Inch'Allah dimanche*, this one did not plan/is not planning to stop in Algiers. This is suggested by the fact that the sea vessel moves parallel to the coast, thus suggesting that regular migration out of Algeria is increasingly out of reach. While France—represented by northward ferries—has become more and more out of focus, and gradually out of the picture altogether, in the same shot a fishing boat crosses the screen. The little boat is more accessible, for it is shown closer to the shore. When the film was released in 1994, narratives of clandestine and ex-centric migrations were still marginal. Boualem will eventually get a visa and leave for France on the imposing ferry. The young man's departure occurs at the very end of the film. It marks a resolution in this character's life, but it also heralds the end of an almost exclusive focus on the ferry and the decline of a majestic mode of transportation, after which filmmakers tackling Algerian emigration, including Allouache, turned their attention to a different signifier, the more modest patera. The younger brother, who also expresses his desire to leave his country, may have to emigrate to a destination other than France. Furthermore, he will likely use a less conventional means of travel. The ferry as the primary mode of transportation of invited Maghrebi guest workers into France is still common. However, one can also witness a new development. In the last two decades, myriad films and novels relating the travel experiences of North Africans to Europe have reassessed this romantic vision. The ferryboat is replaced by the patera in many contemporary fictional narratives that relate the experience of migration in the Mediterranean. This reality is not unique to Algerian works: it is central in the Moroccan films *Mektoub* by Nabil Ayouch and *Et après . . .* (What's Next?) by Mohamed Ismaïl. These narratives tackle leavism and hrig from North Africa and both made the connection with Spain clear in 1997 and 2002, respectively. Spain has indeed been included as an integral part of Maghrebi literary and cinematic narratives and storylines, especially through the prism of clandestine migration and the patera as a connector.

Harragas exemplifies such a shift. The image of a ferry heading to France is rivaled by the dinghy headed to Spain. The majestic ferry, with well-clad passengers waving goodbye to those onshore, shares the cinematic space with fishing boats and dinghies that leave secretly. This ambivalent configuration is illustrated in a scene in *Harragas* where due to the failure of the dinghy's motor, the passengers are unable to move forward and are passed by a cruise ship. A few scenes later, the desperate passengers beg for help as another craft passes them. This time it is a fast Spanish boat. The film ends after a man leaves it, boards a rescue boat, and approaches the remaining four clandestines. The undocumented men express mixed feelings in a short amount of time. They first feel anger, calling the passengers of the craft "racists" (this mention does not appear in the subtitles of the French DVD). Then, when the Spanish individual gets close to them on his rescue boat, they rejoice, yelling, "Long live Spain," believing the man has come to save them. But the stranger simply stares at them from behind dark glasses. The viewer is left in suspense regarding the stranger's identity and the fate of the migrants.

Apart from harsh policies in France, another reason Spain has become the preferred destination for immigrants is because it is geographically closer to Algeria than France is. As Allouache explains, Italy is yet another possible destination, since Spain and Italy are relatively close to his country. Both peninsulas are geographically important in that they sit between Algeria and France, the historical destination of Algerian migrants. As for the Iberian Peninsula, it forms a constitutive part of the plot: the protagonists aim to set foot on it; some reach it, others scream its name. The smugglers transporting the passengers are eager to make frequent trips between the two Mediterranean shores in order to gain as much money as they can. In *Harragas,* the smuggler is nicknamed "mal de mer," literally "seasickness," but the name also implies that the old man is associated with the "evil" (*mal*) side of the sea. According to Rachid, who provides sporadic commentary on the plot, "Hassan-Seasickness" is an old sailor who'd lived overseas and been all over the world. Now he smuggles people to Spain. And his business is booming. He's from our neighborhood, too, but he charges us his usual rate. If money's involved, he doesn't know you. He'd charge his own mother." The smuggler Hassan is not too worried about the safety of his clients. When the person who supplies the boat requires one more week to ensure that it is seaworthy, Hassan dismisses his concern with an offhand remark, noting that if the motor starts, then it is in working condition.

It is mentioned in the film that Mostaghanem, the Algerian port from which the characters are setting off, is two hundred kilometers from the Iberian Peninsula. But when the clandestine migrants discover via a GPS unit that they are actually heading toward France, the reaction of one passenger is intriguing. At first, the extradiegetic viewer is not quite sure if it is a reaction of disappointment, panic, or horror. It may be that the character does not want to keep heading toward France, for this destination would lengthen the trip. Alternatively, the character's expression can be interpreted as fear in light of France's recent anti-immigration laws. In addition to advocating for them and spearheading some of them, it has passed additional restrictive laws for its own borders. Thus, by closing its door to migration further, France has thwarted its privileged relationship with its ex-colonies. This move has been viewed by some Maghrebis as a betrayal. These have called for a policy of reciprocity. Algeria now requires a visa for various Western travelers, including French nationals. France could have undertaken a series of official regulation procedures of undocumented migrants already present on its soil. But it was, along with Germany, one of the countries that vehemently condemned Spanish Prime Minister José Luis Rodríguez Zapatero for the regularizations he authorized.[32] The French have therefore been viewed as failing North Africans again. Thus, it is not surprising that the traveler would be horrified at the thought of the boat setting course for France.

The question of language in *Harragas* exposes many of the views and attitudes held by Maghrebis. For one of the passengers, speaking French reflects poorly on one's integrity. Some of his companions' socioeconomic backgrounds are expressed partly through their sartorial appearance and mastery of the French language. Their fellow passenger labels these travelers as bourgeois individuals who do not need to travel clandestinely—they could benefit from their parents' help and potentially get visas that way. In other words, their presence on the dinghy is preposterous. He implies that they should be on a ferry or a plane instead. For one of the characters onboard, his comrades' conversations in French make him feel excluded, causing him to say angrily, "Your French is Greek to me." He urges his fellow passengers to speak Arabic instead, since that is the language they all share. But another language comes into play here.

An important element in this film is Castilian. When they refer to the dinghy, the characters often call it a *bote*.[33] Therefore, in a sense they resort to Castilian Spanish. One could argue that this is a word of Algerian Arabic and then the point is moot. After all, many artists have called the vernacular they speak Algerian Arabic. This is the case of Allouache himself, in spite of the governmental refusal to officially acknowledge the importance of this vernacular. On the other hand, it is not certain that such artists would say that bote is necessarily Algerian Arabic, though this dialect is a *sabir*, a mix of idioms from various Mediterranean languages including Spanish. Indeed, *bote* is a term mostly used by Algerian harragas. In the film, *bote* and *flouka* (small boat), are used interchangeably. Just like other languages, Arabic has a varied vocabulary to refer to boats. Yet the formal use of a terminology about this regional tragedy is relatively scarce, and the victims of burning are left to use foreign idioms until the phenomenon leads to a national consensus on how to address it openly. A *bote* in Spanish is a dinghy, and it is exactly this foreign word that the characters use to refer to their means of transportation. This linguistic borrowing reveals potential political implications. Indeed, a subversive, alternative, or even foreign language may allow for the expression of a rebellious discourse looking to challenge the status quo.

One Spanish term in an entire film may seem quite minimal to draw conclusions. Yet not only is it mentioned a few times by various harragas, this is not the only foreign word used to discuss a local phenomenon. The voiceover uses the Spanish term *buque,* which means "ship" or "vessel." The word itself connotes a level of strength and durability that is clearly missing from the rickety boat on which the protagonists find themselves. *Harragas* is one of the first cinematic productions on the topic that uses Castilian in the dialogue, and since then, a few others have made the same linguistic decision. Beyond the linguistic choice lies an entire reality. Anonymous individuals borrow idioms that might sound subversive for those who are dismissive of the existence of that which they are naming and therefore giving life to. Indeed, words contain a view of the world, and if a particular view is dismissed by the powers that be, one way to express that view is by appropriating a word from a different language.

In chapter 2, I discuss criminalization, which is a recurrent question in the overarching theme of this book and is also conveyed through language. It emerges in *Harragas,* where one of the passengers of the bote ponders the dismal binary that is at stake: *"régularisation ou déportation"* (residency or deportation). Until the door to "residency" opens, the characters must find ways to remain invisible or mimic the ways of the settled immigrants in Spain in order to blend in. To this end, the first thing that Rachid does when he has successfully swum to shore is put on a suit and new shoes, which he had carried on his back in a tightly sealed plastic bag. The protagonists in *Harragas* are fully aware of the possibility of their being caught (in an unbearable situation). The passengers of the bote apprehend what they see as a potential nightmare. If the harragas are not "legalized," they will be deported by the Spaniards, drift back to Algeria, or be caught by the Moroccan coastguard. A panicked passenger paints a horrific scenario: "What if it's a Moroccan boat? Apparently, it's hell. They just beat you. Then they throw you in a camp and leave you to die like dogs." The narrator Rachid recounts his first harga, in which he and the crew thought they had reached Almería, Spain, but had unwittingly navigated back to Oran, Algeria. The dread of finding oneself at the starting point is not about wasting invaluable time, for as one of the passengers explains, if he is sent back home he'd burn again a thousand times. Rather, the harragas dread the consequences of their playing with fire. Allouache's characters are left with the following "options": (1) endangering their lives trying to swim the final stretch to the coast; (2) jumping into the sea to drown; or (3) remaining on the boat and risking death by sunstroke, dehydration, or starvation—the likely lot of the characters who stay behind. The choices are few and grim. One wonders if these undocumented migrants have any choices at all. Though one of the migrants argues that there are two possible outcomes for him and the crew (legalization or deportation), the viewer knows that there is a third possible end—death—for "in general, the highest death toll in one trip occurs at sea."[34] In all of these outcomes, the burners have no say. Death is conceived of as a better outcome than is falling into the hands of authorities back home. This paradox reflects the desperation of the harragas, and their fear of vindictive actions back home where prison time or torture are likely outcomes.

Filmmakers have tried to condemn these governmental disciplinary measures and polemical positions. Allouache explains in an interview that this is one of the reasons he made this film. The renowned Yasmina Khadra, the pen name of Mohamed Moulesshoul, an ex-officer of the Algerian Army, has himself harshly criticized the position of the government on this issue, which led to the February 25, 2009, law criminalizing harga. Khadra addressed the secrétaire géneral of the party in power, the National Front of Liberation in his piece, "Tout cerveau qui s'exile est un assassinat: Lettre ouverte de Yasmina Khadra à M. Belkhadem." Published on January 19, 2009, in the newspaper *Le Quotidien d'Oran,* his open letter states, "Each death of an Algerian from hard life is a crime; each brain drain is an assassination; each spark of hope that is put out is an act of treason; and each avowal of powerlessness on behalf of a decision-maker is a disaster. Then, which miracle ought one choose: that of redemption or that of resignation?" Khadra vehemently denounces the fact that officials condemn harga instead of making strong efforts to retain "brains" in Algeria. He also harshly decries the tendency of officials to point their fingers at the harrag as a scapegoat. Khadra theorizes about why Algerian youth burn and why the governmental position should not be one of excoriation, judicial harassment, and institutional punishment but rather one of understanding. The Algerian writer invites his reader to turn the tables by joining him in blaming decision-makers for not offering better opportunities back home, which he feels they owe to the disillusioned ones who have decided to leave: "If they [our youths] do not trust our promises, it is because you've never kept them." Khadra thus exhorts Mr. Belkhadem to seize the moment in order to implement prompt reforms that would end the deadlock in which the desperate youths—commonly labeled *hittistes* (unemployed men who spend their free time outside, "leaning against walls")—systematically become culprits for daring to think that they might find fulfilled promises on greener pastures. The ex-officer's explanation to the governmental official and by extension, the Algerian political system, is as follows: "It is because they [our youths] refuse to give in to violence, and because the fundamentalist underground networks no longer constitute reasonable grounds for basic demands that they prefer to offer their last hopes to fish and the fury of the waves."[35] This explanation establishes a link between one method of burning and another. In this simile, the reader will notice that the harrag-kamikaze is a pacific burner who throws his body into the sea's belly instead of throwing bombs onto bodies. He adds, "It is because they are lost that each night when the sea subsides they entrust their fate to a fiddled compass or a suicidal smuggler." Both the "fiddled compass" and the "suicidal smuggler" are present in *Harragas.* As a matter of fact, the passengers also resort to "entrusting" their fate to a fake GPS unit as well as to a serial killer.[36]

Because it is engrained in Maghrebi societies, because filmmakers want us to take a stand, because it has the same urgency as that of war, and because it is not going to be solved any time soon, Algerian *cinéastes engagés* have depicted the burning of the sea as a metaphor for glocal warring. The director researched the phenomenon of clandestine migration and cites statistics in his supplemental interview on the DVD. Whereas *Inch'Allah dimanche* opens with a note that explains that the film is going to show a reunion on French soil because of a new law that had been voted to allow familial immigration, *Harragas* ends with four notes on a black screen, listing in both Arabic and French numbers of dead clandestine migrants from Africa:

> From 1988 to February 2009 no less than 13,444 migrants died at the borders of Europe. 5,182 of them died at sea.
> In the Mediterranean Sea and in the Atlantic Ocean 9,500 migrants lost their lives.
> In the Canal of Sicily 3,163 individuals died between Libya, Egypt, Tunisia, Malta, and Italy, and 125 others lost their lives along the new routes between Algeria and the island of Sardinia.
> 4,399 people also perished offshore the Canary Islands and the Strait of Gibraltar between Morocco, Algeria and Spain. 2,232 of them are missing . . .

The data take on the form of a stele for martyrs who perished in the Mediterranean as is evidenced in the wording of the dedication that closes the narrative: "This film is dedicated to all the 'harragas' lost in the sea."

Bled number one: The Immobile Ferry as a Moving Metaphor

Films that have dealt with the issue of migration without tackling clandestinity per se have used the ferry as a symbol. Many more recent filmic narratives that have portrayed the South-to-North migratory experience have demoted the ferry. This ship may even be found replaced by a cargo ship. Indeed, because it is a merchandise ship, most of its length is an interminable lifeless deck.[37] Seen in films, posters, and DVD covers, it looks like a long decaying mass of rust. I argue that the cargo ship is a haunted version of the ferry, a signifier of a dead connector between the two shores. In recent films, the ship does not move. It has morphed into an empty shell that has come to a standstill. Worse, the ship may be sinking by the shore, as is the case in *Bled number one.*[38] The director of this film, Rabah Ameur-Zaïmeche, was born in Beni Zid in northeast Algeria in 1966. *Bled number one* (2006), whose English title is *Back Home*, is his second feature. It was the Sélection Officielle Un Certain Regard at the Festival de Cannes, and received the Prix de la Jeunesse. *Bled number one* is the sequel to *Wesh wesh, qu'est-ce qui se passe?* (Wesh, Wesh, What's Going On?) This first film was a commercial success. In 2008, the director released his third work, *Dernier maquis.* His fourth feature, *Les Chants de Mandrin* (*Smugglers' Songs*), came out in 2011.

As I indicated earlier, the ferry is another, and older, key metaphor in films about migration. I suggest that the abandonment of the ferry, its transfiguration, and its increasing disuse in North African cinema are indications of the repercussions of European antimigration legislation on the Maghreb. It is not uncommon for contemporary filmmakers to show a worn-out ship that has sunk or is washed up on the Algerian shore. In an endnote of chapter 2, I briefly commented on the image of the ship on the DVD and poster of *La Chine est encore loin* (*China Remains Far*) (Figure 5.4). On these, as well as on the DVD and poster of *Bled number one,* the boat is an old thing that no longer serves any purpose. As a matter of fact, in Ameur-Zaïmeche's film, there are two cargo ships docked next to each other, displaced like war remnants as if they had been attacked and deposed on Algerian land like mere burdensome spoils. This image reveals that regular migration is not going anywhere anymore. It is certainly not going to France. Like the characters in what may be termed "the cinema of clandestinity," the abandoned ships play the role of a rejected Other that cannot proceed further beyond the liminal space of the beach. Could these giant, and yet frail, steel monsters be indicators of contemporaneous positions concerning Maghrebi immigration to France? Could they be a vestige of postcolonial power struggles between France and Algeria? At any rate, characters, such as *Bled number one*'s Kamel, are not able to get on any intercontinental connector any longer.

In *Bled number one,* we learn that in accordance with the "double sentence" law in effect in France at the time, the main character Kamel, was deported by the French authorities to Algeria, after having served a sentence in France. A resident of Montfermeil, a banlieue east of Paris, the protagonist was charged with theft. Upon his arrival in Loulouj, his village of origin, Kamel—played by the filmmaker himself—meets his relatives. Most of them are played by members of his real family. In spite of a warm welcome, Kamel soon feels estranged as he learns about a country that he hardly knows. It is a country that is going through what is often referred to as Algeria's "dark years" or "dark decade" (a period of upheaval spanning the 1990s and early 2000s).[39] His village is prey to attacks from a group of vigilante men called Desperados. Though the parallel with the Western genre is obvious, the men's motives are of a different nature. They try to implement a puritan code of conduct inspired by religious precepts by tracking and terrorizing those who defy their rules. Kamel is on the side of the Patriots, an organized group of rebels. He is infatuated with Louisa (Meryem Serbah), with whom he shares a growing feeling of exclusion. Louisa is abandoned by her politician husband Ahmed (Ramzy Bedia), who kidnaps their son and leaves her stranded by the roadside. Her brother (Abel Jafri) is caught in an inebriated state by the Desperados, who threaten to slice his head off. He beats his sister Louisa for bringing shame

Figure 5.4 Movie poster for Malek Bensmaïl's *La Chine est encore loin*. © Unlimited.

to their family. Gradually, Louisa loses her sanity. She is on the verge of jumping off one of Constantine's suspended bridges when she is rescued by a group of passers-by. The anonymous men check her into a psychiatric hospital.

Ex-convict Kamel is severed from the country he grew up in. And as is common in cases of "repatriation" of French convicts of African descent, he was sent back "home" by plane. Kamel's passport has been confiscated. Ironically, the outsider is called "Kamel (de) la France" by local Algerians. The Arabic dialogue presents Kamel and France in a state of rapport. Indeed, "France's Kamel" furthers the irony in that he does indeed belong to France given that the French political and legal systems dictate his fate. But by no means can the deported Kamel convince his relatives that he is French any longer. Irony lies also in the fact that the Frenchman is evicted simply because of his ancestry, whose price he has to pay first with a jail sentence in France and then with his confinement to a country where he feels foreign, alienated, and imprisoned. The young man has been put under house arrest—the allegorical house of a country that is not his own. Without his French passport, his options for travel are drastically limited. The burgundy passport has indeed been portrayed in Maghrebi cultural productions as a miraculous object. Kamel is dispossessed of his French passport, which Maghrebis have come to call *le passe-partout* (the passkey). The French expression implies that the presentation of the burgundy document at border checkpoints grants its owner access and free movement around the world.

Surely, the protagonist comes across as one who lacks the freedom to move where he pleases. Kamel's incompleteness is depicted in various ways in the film; indeed, his name itself is ironic. In Arabic, the name *Kamel* contains the notion of completeness, yet deported, lonely, monolingual, and incapable of adapting, he is everything but complete. The soundtrack is another element in the film that indicates his incompleteness. Ameur-Zaïmeche has chosen a minimalist soundtrack. The score in *Bled number one* is essentially composed of natural sounds, like the overpowering wind that the camera does not mute (purposefully) and that highlights the destabilizing environment in which the story unfolds. Other background sounds include the ululations of women and the religious chants performed by men. For the most part, traditional sounds and local wind instruments have replaced the Western music commonly found in contemporary North African films, thus highlighting the task of Kamel's relatives who seek to bring him into their own cultural frame. They also try to teach him the fundamentals of their societal practices by emphasizing that he should not eat in the company of women on account of its sinfulness. This warning adds to Kamel's feeling of confinement, for he is also not allowed to frequent one half of the Algerian village. His loneliness is reflected in his lost gazes and awkward silences while in the company of the proverbial *hittistes*. In another scene, to kill time, the men play dominoes until they are interrupted by a visit by the Desperados, who throw the game off the table. Kamel's displacement is emphasized by the surreal nature of a scene that stands out due to the loud and jarring sound of the electric guitar of a French musician, Rodolphe Burger. The musician appears out of place, for he plays his instrument and sings while sitting on a hill by a lake at dawn next to a single attendee, Kamel. A few old women walk by, carrying bundles of firewood on their heads. They do not even seem to notice the surreal setting of the performance nor do they notice that Kamel has decided to follow them while the French musician continues to play. The old ladies walk by unperturbed, as if they were nonresponsive to the Western voice.

The call of the West is opposed to the call to prayer, another element of the film's soundtrack.[40] The musical guitar piece accompanies a sung text in English, which happens to be a rendition of William Blake's "The Little Vagabond," in which a line mockingly hints at the Desperados' hunt for drinkers of alcohol: "But if at the Church they would give us some Ale." The sung poem contrasts with the rest of the musical choices throughout the film, which are mostly "local." Kamel and Louisa's leavism is also expressed through English text sung in a melancholy fashion. For Louisa, in particular, this leavism is represented by A. Herzog Jr. and Billie Holiday's "Don't Explain." The female character is shown singing exclusively in English, as if for these characters leavism could not be conveyed effectively in French. Beyond the global nature of English and the influence of American cultural productions witnessed in Algeria, Louisa's choice of this language signals her search for a liberating alternative. She shuns the languages of an Algeria that isolates her in her societal roles and of a France that is unreachable. The unlikelihood of Louisa leaving Algeria is expressed in the scene where, upon her uttering, "I want to sing, that's all!" the call to prayer is heard in the background. This suggests that her wish is doomed to remain a dream, because a patriarchal society controls her fate. Her hopes of escaping the traditional society lead her only to a mental asylum, surrounded by barbed wire, even more trapped than before.

Zygmunt Bauman's analysis of globalization sheds light on Louisa's predicament. He argues that it impacts people differently. Some, like Louisa, are victims of forces they cannot control:

> The technological annulment of temporal/spatial distances tends to polarize [the human condition]. It emancipates certain humans from territorial constraints . . . while denuding the territory, in which other people go on being confined. . . . For some people it augurs an unprecedented freedom from physical obstacles and unheard-of ability to move and act from a distance. For others, it portends the impossibility of appropriating and domesticating the

locality from which they have little chance of cutting themselves free in order to move elsewhere. . . . Some can now move out of their locality—any locality—at will. Others watch helplessly the sole locality they inhabit moving away from under their feet.[41]

Louisa exemplifies one pole and her husband the other. The latter is characterized as an individual always on the go: he arrives in Algeria from overseas, drives his car around the village—whereas other characters are shown mostly on foot—then he leaves for France again. Louisa, on the other hand, sees her freedom limited. As Bauman's passage shows, at the core of this binary lies "freedom" and its opposite, "confinement to a locality." It is no coincidence that Louisa requests the right to sing; she is locked up in an institution where this is the only freedom she could have that does not require moving out of her locality. In another sequence, suffocating as well, Kamel asks his interlocutor at a café how far Tunisia is from Constantine. The young man learns that it is about 360 kilometers away—this number accentuates the claustrophobic image of a (vicious) circle in which the characters are entrapped . . . unless they have money. The ex-convict justifies his question with the claim that were he to stay in Algeria—a country whose language he understands but hardly speaks—he would go insane: "No, I'm going to crack up, I'm going to crack up, I can't stay here, I'll go crazy if I stay, I'm going to lose it, I swear!" The interlocutor proposes that he chew tobacco in order to dispel his *dégoûtage* (ennui). He goes on to say that if Kamel has the financial means, he can assist him in crossing over to Tunisia without a visa or passport.[42]

For Kamel, traveling back to France on a ferry from Algeria is not an option. This trans-Mediterranean transportation of choice in *Inch'Allah dimanche* and the 1970s has since exhausted itself or has simply been put to sleep by immigration laws. This reality causes Kamel to envisage crossing over to Tunisia, fathoming that he will increase his chances of returning to Europe from there. In chapter 3, I discussed *Exils,* in which a young couple treks through a neighboring country instead of embarking to France on a ferry. We are not shown whether they set out to Europe, but if they do, we are led to imagine that they choose to head not to France, but rather to Spain in which shots of open-air settings and carefree behavior contrasted sharply with boredom and the claustrophobic setting of a tiny Parisian apartment in a project. While *Exils'* Zano and Leila have the option to return home, in *Bled number one,* France does not want Kamel back. To this effect, the Desperados vigilantes who have taken it upon themselves to "protect" Algeria by terrorizing those they deem infidels, chat about Kamel as they play dominoes. One of them exults: "France is over." This assertion applies to Kamel—particularly since he was jailed there; however, the phrase "France is over" is one of the most important subliminal messages of the film and lends itself to other layers of interpretation.

One of these interpretations is that France as a destination is now out of the question for everyone. This embedded double entendre cannot pass unnoticed, especially in light of many times in the film when the word *France* is uttered. Indeed, when a relative asks Kamel to tell him a story about France—a country the relative may have been thinking about traveling to—Kamel remains silent. When the former asks him if there are jobs there, Kamel nods briefly and utters a timid "yes." But Kamel's bodily expressions convey the opposite. It is as if his providing a negative response would have demanded an explanation that Kamel was not in the mood to provide. In another scene, female characters interned at a psychiatric hospital in Constantine shout: "Long live France!" Sarcasm pervades their exclamations. Indeed, the patients do not seem to benefit from France's help. Because the ships that used to link France and Algeria have been assigned a slow death on the Algerian shores and because, as Khadra puts it, political impotence is spurring Algerians to offer "their last hopes to fish and the fury of the deep," "France is over." This phrase is a bitter verdict, a definitive expression of deflation, detraction, and demotion. In spite of the fact that Ameur-Zaïmeche's two boats are in bad shape, motionlessness, he portrays them as imposing and even threatening. Similarly, Bensmaïl's monster of steel is half-sunk, its stern is submerged in water, and its bow juts upward, as if wanting to jump onto the beach and leave the Mediterranean Sea (Figure 5.4). The boat is running away, for its utility as a transnational link is being questioned and so is the relevance of its primary destination.

Movement has come to a standstill. *Bled number one* aims for a crawling pace. The long shots of silent characters smoking, playing dominoes, or just wandering contribute to the feeling of *dégoûtage* that give many young Algerians the burning desire to emigrate. But the disillusioned population is aware that the beach does not imply departure. As a matter of fact, the only time the Mediterranean Sea is shown is when Louisa is accompanied by relatives to the beach. The young woman is thought to have become insane after her husband abandoned her and took their son away from her. "Possessed" Louisa is not sent to France for treatment. By way of remedy, the *fqih* (spiritual leader) encourages the family to take the desperate woman to the sea and let "seven waves beat her face." The characters do not even seem to notice the ghostly looking ships. No comment is made about them. The sea, once a symbol of hope and departure, is instead going to beat the lady in the face. Though the beating is supposed to bring about recovery, it is still, so to speak, a slap in the face. When the sea does not devour you, it beats you.

As for Louisa, she will not be able to leave for France, as the two leaning and motionless cargo ships lined up on the shore make clear. (One of them is in Figure 5.5 and two are shown in the film, but there may be more outside the camera's frame.) The vessels appear old and diseased. They are rusting. The unmoving boats

Figure 5.5 Kamel and Louisa at the beach by a corroded ship. Still from Rabah-Ameur Zaïmeche's *Bled number one*. Used with permission.

have been relegated to the Algerian shores, as if to signify that France is not sure what to do with them. Since France will not allow the old means of regular maritime crossings to resume, Algeria cannot operate the sickly looking boats. The director presents the once-moving ships as a burdensome yoke of history and immigration to France as a joke, an impossibility. Consequently, Algerian migrants journey elsewhere or back home.

Meanwhile, Ameur-Zaïmeche presents those who do migrate to France, like the father of the abducted son, as thieves who run away with a child, a symbol of Algeria's future. The blame is cast on France through the presentation of a problematic paradox. The French state "repatriates" individuals like Kamel for being criminals—though they have served their sentence on French soil—but then lets in other (more condemnable?) criminals such as Louisa's husband. Another implication of *Bled number one* and its contemporaries is that water is no longer a vector of movement. Instead, it is a stopper in the door to Europe. It is not the fluid element that allows for a flux of people, since the boat itself—this connector between shores—is stuck as though in quicksand. Whereas water is getting into the ship's hull on the poster of *La Chine est encore loin*, in *Bled number one* sand is advancing toward the boat as if to imprison it in a desert-like setting (Figures 5.5 and 5.6). And yet characters are looking forward to deserting their land. While the poster of *La Chine est encore loin* shows Algerians playing on the shore, obliv-

BLED
NUMBER
ONE

AVANT OU APRÈS WESH WESH

UN FILM DE
RABAH AMEUR-ZAÏMECHE

arte
VIDÉO

Figure 5.6 DVD cover of Rabah Ameur-Zaïmeche's *Bled number one*. Used with permission.

ious to the ferry-turned-cargo ship condemned to stop its traveling and therefore theirs as well, that of *Bled number one* depicts the beach as an almost deserted place. The DVD cover of *Bled number one* displays the outline of the country of Algeria, inside of which is Louisa's face, staring out (at us?) from behind the bars of her window. Below her is the abandoned beach and a ship boat on its shores. The sea and the boat are imprisoned as well, since they too are confined to the limits of the Algerian map. The only free individual is Kamel, who walks forth into the whiteness of the poster's borders. He walks with a smile, as if he were pleased to have managed to leave Algeria. But given that the dénouement of the film does not show Kamel making it back to France, the walking man might simply be the director who played the role of Kamel and was able to return to France after shooting *Bled number one.*

The Sleeping Child, or, the "Sleeping Penis" of Men on the Verge of *Demancipation*

Yasmine Kassari is a Moroccan-Belgian director born in Jerada, Morocco, in 1970. A former student of the Institut National Supérieur des Arts du Spectacle et des Techniques de Diffusion in Brussels, Belgium, Kassari made three shorts—*Le Feutre noir* (1994), *Chiens errants* (1995), and *Lynda et Nadia* (2002). In 2000, she released *Quand les hommes pleurent . . .* (When Men Cry . . .). This documentary, whose title in Modern Standard Arabic—('indamâ yabkî el rijâl . . .)—is a literal translation of the French, traces the phenomenon of contemporary Moroccan clandestine migration to Spain. Her first feature film, *L'Enfant endormi* (The Sleeping Child), a 2004 Belgian-Moroccan coproduction, was shown and praised in about fifty international festivals. The ninety-five-minute feature was awarded dozens of prizes including Le Prix du Public at Le Festival Premiers Plans in Angers in 2005, as well as Le Prix d'Interprétation for the combined performances of actresses Mounia Osfour and Rachida Brakni, and Le Prix du Meilleur Film Européen of the 2004 Official Selection of the Mostra of Venice. In 2006, *L'Enfant endormi* was screened in Moroccan theaters. The only professional actress of the cast, the Algerian award-recipient Rachida Brakni, plays a role in Coline Serreau's *Chaos,* as well as in André Téchiné's *Loin*—another film on Moroccan clandestine migration to Spain.

L'Enfant endormi illustrates the desire of a large number of North Africans to emigrate northward, which has been documented in various surveys. Maghrebis themselves are aware of the extent of leavism. The intermittent narrator in *Harragas* claims that if one were to take a survey in the neighborhood, one would find that 90 percent of the inhabitants wish to leave. But it is not simply the complex desire to leave that has brought Kassari to tackle the issue of hrig. Her place of birth, close to the Mediterranean Sea, may account for her being among the first Moroccan directors concerned with the depiction of what she calls "the new and massive immigration to Spain" that has become in a way a personal issue through her relatives' daily engagement with it. As the director explained in an interview with the Francophone Moroccan magazine *TelQuel,* it was the recent impact of leavism in both her home country and in her country of residence that caused her to embrace the topic: "We are in the early 1990s. At twenty-years old, Yasmine is 'marked by the new and massive immigration to Spain,' and stories about it, told to her by her aunt or a friend, reach her in pieces. 'Until the 1980s, before the accession of Spain into the European Community, the South-North border was the Pyrenees. Over a span of ten years, a wall of scorn was erected, rising as [Spain's] socio-economic level boomed.'"[43] It should be noted that the theme of hrig is not yet as widespread in Moroccan cinema as it is in Algerian cinema. Also, when Moroccan directors happen to cover this "new" phenomenon, they often set their cameras on Tangier, even though northeastern Morocco is home to a considerable population of harragas trying to reach Spain, as is evidenced in David A. McMurray's anthropological study, *In and Out of Morocco: Smuggling and Migration in a Frontier Boomtown,* and Kassari's film.

In an interview with Olivier Barlet, Kassari explains that Moroccan farmers are attached to their land and would rather stay than emigrate, but in this day and age where one tries to find ways to survive, the burning desire to go north has become an economic priority for a large number of people in the global South:

> OLIVIER BARLET: It is striking that every Maghrebi film is drawn toward this departure for other horizons. Is this incontrovertible? One has the impression that this structures society.
>
> YASMINE KASSARI: This is absolutely incontrovertible. If one wanted to change the country's situation, one would start with that. It's not only Morocco, but 75% of the planet! The whole world wants to come North.[44]

Barlet's assumption that in every Maghrebi film leavism is central to the narrative may sound like an obvious generalization. However, as scholar Valérie Orlando rightly indicates, "since 1999, films have taken up sensitive and formerly taboo subjects that were once forbidden territory."[45] Hrig is one of these subjects. Contemporary fictions, such as *L'Enfant endormi,* have given this issue greater space in their plotlines or have evoked it openly. In this narrative, after the leave-taking of many men from the village, two cousins Zeinab (Mounia Osfour) and Halima (Rachida Brakni) find themselves the sole caregivers of a blind grandmother. The difficult lot of women is rendered bleaker by having to raise their children under severe living conditions. Their motherly duties are one among many others. Some of their additional tasks are to cook and do laundry, as well as to work the land now that the hamlet has been emptied of its men. In other words, they take on chores in the private sphere in addition to those of the public sphere, which used to be the men's responsibility. The presentation of an arid land that yields fewer crops is one of the men's justification for his decision to leave behind his country, as well as his wife, children, and mother. The survival of those who are left behind is continually compromised by adversities: noncooperative weather, a labor shortage, a shrinking population, and a hostile human environment. The men who have chosen to stay are shown brutalizing women or bringing them trouble. But the film makes clear that these tensions are new and we sense that they are the result of external circumstances to the Berber village and culture. Capitalism and the ill effects of globalization on remote localities seem to be responsible.[46]

The dialogue in Kassari's film is in Arabic and Berber. The Arabic title is *El Ragued*. In all of its various international titles, *L'Enfant endormi* centers around a belief: that of putting a fetus to sleep. In other words, the decision of a mother to prevent it from growing and coming out of her womb until her husband comes back from Spain, where he went to seek a future for his family the day following the nuptial night. This belief-turned-practice is enacted by Zeinab. The young woman lives in a village of the Béni Chbel tribe in the region of Taourirt in northeastern Morocco, close to the director's place of birth. The ritual, which involves spiritual/magical steps to follow, has a historical and juridical legitimacy, as well as a strong social hold in rural areas. The director explains that in the countryside of eastern Morocco "everyone here firmly believes in [the myth of the ragued]"— that a child can be born a few months or even a few years after the average nine months of gestation. Whether thought to be the result of white witchcraft, possession, or trauma, or merely an act performed in order to protect women from repudiation for conceiving a child extramaritally and to allow a child to find a legitimate place in his mother's household in a society where adoption is not legally recognized, this myth—which has become even more popular in the context of male labor and clandestine migrations to Europe—has been institutionalized as a legal right granted to women by national jurisprudence.

However, *L'Enfant endormi* weaves the director's interest in the phenomenon of hrig through the prism of fiction, which she had started to address in her fifty-seven-minute documentary, *Quand les hommes pleurent. . . .* Though the future of the fetus rests on its father's fate, it is the father's fortune that becomes the main concern of a wife, an entire family, or a whole hamlet. It is interesting that the fetus is put to sleep, for though the purpose of such a practice is to awaken it later on, the viewer begins to wonder if the unborn being will meet a fatal end because the father himself may pass away or never return. Even if other men from the village who crossed the Strait of Gibraltar do not physically die, they still may never really penetrate the female universe, as in *L'Enfant endormi,* where the lack of cross-gender geographical interpenetration and the slow pace of the film are metaphors for the women's sexual frustrations. The spectator will never find out one way or the other, since the fetus will not be delivered before the movie's end. As Patricia Pisters explains, "After months and months of waiting . . . Zeineb decides to break the spell of the sleeping child. Without performing the prescribed ritual she opens the amulet, which means that the unborn child will die."[47] Thus, in a way, the fetus is sacrificed. Its place in life and in the economy of the narrative is diminished in order to allow for other sacrifices to come to light. The fathers' crossing over to Spain is only one of these sacrifices. Mothers are left behind and as a result they have to make many difficult compromises, such as giving up a regular pregnancy and a traditional livelihood. As Nancy L. Green argues about this type of migration, "it is [women] who allow men to leave. By doing the job in the bled, by continuing to work in the fields or to run a shop, women who stay behind often play 'men roles' during long months, if not years, while they wait for their husband's hypothetical return."[48] As Green remarks, women have often been mistakenly regarded as passive in the history of migration. In fact, they have either taken the trip themselves, or when their husbands decide to leave, they take care of demanding household chores. In *L'Enfant endormi,* their abnegation comes with additional responsibilities. They have to find ways to contact their estranged husbands. This mission leads them to change their customs and hone skills, which range from learning how to operate a camcorder, to spending their time looking for tapes, to traveling to a remote town to have a picture taken at a lab. Zeinab's husband returns the picture with a warning for his wife not to go to the city without his permission, for the city is viewed as a risqué place where politics of gender-divided spatial practices are looser and therefore considered as a potential threat for the absent father. As Valérie Orlando aptly puts it, Zeinab and Halima "decide to directly engage the camera, speaking openly to their husbands one to one. The lens becomes their weapon of confrontation, and filming marks the first step to their emancipation."[49] In turn, men are being de-*man*-cipated by being incapacitated and dismembered.

The sleeping child is the central symbol of the narrative. Its presence (in the form of an absence) enables the director to direct the viewer to empathize with women in the context of male clandestine migration. But there is another important reason to focus on the *ragued.* Indeed, whereas the Arabic title of *Quand les hommes pleurent . . .* was in Modern Standard Arabic (the language shared by the entire Arab world to express formal matters), the Arabic-language title of the film is in a local Arabic dialect. This is not insubstantial, for although *el ragued* is translated as "the sleeping child," it also covers another phenomenon that is rendered through the local vernacular (which allows the expression of intimate issues), namely, the sleeping penis. Indeed, *el ragued* literally means "that which is sleeping." The addition of the child in the title is inferred because of a known practice that is referred to in this way. But this name could well be pointing to something else. Indeed, the local language says of an impotent man that his penis is asleep. *El ragued* is therefore also an expression for a man who cannot perform sexually. The subtle metaphor institutes a correlation between clandestine emigration and female sexual frustration. This connection is further established through the depiction of a barren landscape and what Pisters calls "the waiting bodies of women," who are sexually unsatisfied or whose pregnancies are put to a halt.[50] Visible signs of Zeinab's pregnancy throughout the fiction could lead to questions about her fidelity in addition to her husband's virility if rumors of cheating were to spread. The possible sterility of husbands is suggested by statements made by various characters that the land has been yielding less and less and the harvests are smaller than in previous years. Halima's husband is nowhere to be found abroad, having left the other male migrants. As a result, his wife decides to ask for a divorce betting that he has "given up" (*smah*). What he has given up is open for interpretation, but Halima's extreme decision, while aware that it is very unlikely that she will be granted the divorce, is a strong sign that she will bring up male sexual inactivity, a major winning cause for divorce. The absence of rain has jeopardized the fertility of the soil the same way as men's leavism has endangered their virility and convinced others of their marital neglect.

This equation is posed in a highly symbolic moment of the film, namely, the celebration of Hassan and Zeinab's wedding. In the hamlet, men have gathered to dance and sing. The men form two lines facing each other. Some of them are holding *bendirs,* drums made of lamb- or goatskin, which they beat as they sing. Each line has a leader who is responsible for starting a new verse, which the rest of the men on that line will repeat before the other leader improvises a response. The chanting is accompanied by a collective dance that consists of one line moving toward the other in an alternative fashion. This configuration, though peaceful, mimics a symbolic fight as the men advance toward the others while they rival each other in verbal ingenuity. The image of chanting warriors is more relevant in this setting, for the two leaders, Ahmed (Halima's husband) and Amziane (her future supposed lover) have decided to confront each other through innuendos and escalating piques. The verses the two men craft are meant to articulate weaknesses in each other:

AMZIANE: I'm home and I'm doing fine / We can't expect any good from Spain

AHMED: I count on my own strength / To travel across continents

AMZIANE: You, illiterate one, think again / Even languages are beyond you

AHMED: You, literate one, your diploma molders in a cupboard / And you live at the mercy of chance

AMZIANE: If you really want to emigrate / Divorce your love, she's better off free. . . .

After Amziane calls Ahmed "illiterate," one who wants to "burn," and yet does not know foreign languages, Hassan remarks that the diploma of "educated" Amziane is moldering in a box while *he* gets to travel the world.[51] These devaluating remarks are tolerated on both sides, and the game goes on. It goes on until the conflation of "burning" and demancipation is made explicit: "If you really want to emigrate / Divorce your love, she's better off free." The insinuation that his emigration to Spain makes him unworthy of his manhood pushes Ahmed to violence toward Amziane: he darts forward in a vain attempt to beat his rival, as he is stopped in time by the group of men.

The evaluation of a man's virility through his capacity as a household provider is central in Kassari's film. Men's masculinity is challenged through a savvy reversal of accepted gender roles in Moroccan society. Husbands and wives send taped messages back and forth across the strait. Men's tapes take time to reach their wives back in the village. The viewer soon realizes that the delays are not due to a slow shipping method, but rather to the men's hesitation to send news back home, for there is nothing new to report concerning their quest for jobs in Spain. When the tapes finally make their way into the only VCR available in the village, all the female relatives gather and wait anxiously for the cassettes to reveal their contents (Figure 5.7). A man explains that they have been waiting to get their papers for six months. He and a friend deplore their incapacity to wire remittances to their loved ones. One of them asks his father to forgive him. He explains his being seated (unlike the other men, who are standing) by the fact that he was injured while looking for a job on his bicycle. His injury affects an obvious symbol of movement, his leg. Freud and Jung agree that the foot has a phallic connotation—a relation between the foot and sex that the English and French languages convey in one of the meanings that "prendre son pieds" and its equivalent "to get one's kicks" have. In addition, "leg"—*rijel* in Arabic—has the same root as *rajul*, "man" and *rujūla*, "manhood, masculinity, and manliness." As the film illustrates, the handicapped limb is equated with a crippled virility. Since he is seated, the man appears shorter than his fellow countrymen. A bird eye's view shot of the injured man enables Kassari to infantilize and therefore belittle him. Here again, the director is able to make a subtle connection between clandestine migration and the sleeping penis. "That which is sleeping" is a symbol of impotent men in the face of their barren destiny overseas. While one of them is reduced in size due to a disability, all the male migrants are reduced by the little television

Figure 5.7 Women waiting to watch the VHS recording that their sons and husbands made of themselves. Still from Yasmine Kassari's *L'Enfant endormi*. Used with permission.

screen, which frames them as cut beings. They all are dismembered in that only their upper bodies are filmed, whereas the women's bodies are shown in full.

The lower male trunk, commonly associated with masculinity, is truncated precisely because the director wished to show how these men were robbed of their virility. Furthermore, this cropping decision implies that the Moroccan men have not secured the permission to proceed with their lives and jobs abroad, hence their cut legs. In addition, the dark setting operates as a veiling of the men's faces, rendering them difficult to discern while their wives' bodies are in the light. The camera's focus on the men's faces, mouths, and eyes highlights the fact that some of the men remain speechless; they avoid looking at the camera, and their verbal interactions with their loved ones, including their wives, are scant. They just stand there. In turn, music fills the gaps. Its oppressive nature emphasizes the men's desperation, and the women's conviction that the migration of their male relatives has cut them in their dignity. The clandestines are portrayed as feeling uneasy as they are watched by their wives, to whom they can only confirm their inability to secure jobs or a stable life abroad. As for the injured man, he asks his father for forgiveness for not being in a position to wire money home that month. The immobile and unemployed husbands cannot hide because of their confinement to a small room, which is reminiscent of a jail cell. The celluloid's lens acts as a Panopticon, for the men know they are being watched but cannot see those who are watching them. The eyes of the two cameras (the director's and the villagers'), and our own—three audiences watching the embedded film within the

Figure 5.8 Women listening to loved ones sharing their news from the other side of the strait. Still from Yasmine Kassari's *L'Enfant endormi*. Used with permission.

film—capture the impasse at which the men find themselves. In order to magnify this deadlock, the director has some of the cast break the fourth wall (of the camera) while others try to escape (our gaze) in vain. Trapped, destitute, and desperate, like animals at a fair, the clandestines also appear like showcased criminals. Portrayed as passive and beat down, they are cramped together, huddled near a pot on a single burner gas stove in the kitchen—the space traditionally assigned to women. As the French saying runs, the men are "serrés comme des sardines" (packed together like sardines). The depiction of cropped limbs in lieu of active full male bodies produces not only dehumanization to the point of animalization, it also establishes a *de-man-cipation*. The television set's horizontal and vertical frame acts as a box, or as the bars of a cell, and this image contrasts with that of the wives who are free to be out and about in the village. Their entire bodies fill the camera's frame as they sit on the ground to watch their male husbands and relatives as hostage of their undocumented migrant status, and of their short video clips, which have become their only means of communication and information, or, as Halima would probably agree, disinformation (Figure 5.8).

Final Words: Of Other Worlds

The four films, *Visa, Harragas, Bled number one,* and *L'Enfant endormi,* from the three countries of the Maghreb (Tunisia, Algeria, and Morocco) express in seven languages total—namely, French, Tunisian, Algerian, Moroccan, Modern Standard Arabic, Spanish, and Berber—the plight of a large number of leavists, who are denied the legal right to see/sea Europe. In *Visa,* gullible Rachid's poor attempt at the dictation dictates that he cannot travel to France. Some passengers in *Harragas* will likely not make it to the other shore because the *passeur* is not a *passerelle* (bridging agent) to the imagined Eldorado but will rather be responsible for some of his passengers' passing away. As for the ship in *Bled number one,* it has lost its prestigious image of that which bridges two continents. Rusting feet away from the shore, the specter-like maritime mass does not even interest nearby bathers. And finally, *L'Enfant endormi* shows that the migratory pull often pulls families back home asunder. Surely, the village women are forced to recognize that the global village is too big of a concept to include their village . . . at all.

6 Heading Home

Post-Mortem Road Narratives

> It is perhaps at the occasion of the death of the migrant that one can grasp
> his real place with regard to the migratory space that he took up more than a
> generation ago. Standing on his feet or lying in a coffin, he will return to his
> place of origin where something stronger than him snatched him one day.
>
> —Yassin Chaïb, "Le Lieu d'enterrement comme repère migratoire"

> Born, or arrived in France at a very young age, schooled and brought up in
> France, they will have to work there all their lives, and they will die in
> France (and maybe unlike their elders, they will have tombs in France;
> because the conditions and reasons of a *post-mortem* repatriation,
> which is almost the norm nowadays, will have ceased).
>
> —Alain Gillette and Abdelmalek Sayad, *L'Immigration algérienne
> en France*

Perpetual Quests for "Homes"

The choice of burial place for French citizens of North African ancestry is a pressing issue not only because death is inevitable, but more importantly because for
Maghrebis and their children, burial cannot always follow rules of tradition, which
are essentially practical. Indeed, it is customary to bury loved ones in local cemeteries. It is logical that one should want to keep close to home that which is close
to heart. But this is not an inevitability for Maghrebis and *Beurs*. From the moment of their arrival in France and even more so when they realized France was
to become their "home," Maghrebis have had to ponder the question of what
was to be the final "home" for them and their children. Available scholarship in
the humanities, and in the realm of cultural studies in particular, has treated the
notion of home, uprootedness, exile, and biculturalism. But the notion of final
"home" has understandably not yet concerned scholars, for the generation of immigrants who arrived in France in the middle of the past century has just started
to pass away en masse. Questions related to their burial have been tackled in various
disciplines, such as sociology and (clinical) psychology, which deal with the practical and economic aspects of this phenomenon. One can only hope that the

humanities will catch up soon. This will become more likely when a higher number of fictional accounts and biographies are produced, thus provoking humanistic studies. Indeed, as of today only a few of these have appeared. A dead individual cannot by definition write the account of his own passing away, just as with illiterature the experience of the death of the other is often told by external "witnesses," humanists, writers, relatives, etc. But what the available literature and cinematography teaches us is that a reflection on the issue is taking place a priori. It is characterized by investigative journeys, the unknown, and rituals of initiation. According to writers and filmmakers, these narratives imposed themselves as an inevitable source of creative productions through personal confrontation with death. Put differently, these writers and filmmakers' experiences of the death of a loved one have led them to ponder the sensitive subject. Consequently, retirement, death, and burial sites have taken center stage in their fictional works. This emergence in migrant literature and cinema often concerned with questions of identity in the here and now is a significant move that is bound to raise a few important questions for experts. This is no new matter for the North African community based in France; indeed, the epigraph from French journalist Gillette's and Algerian sociologist Sayad's *L'Immigration algérienne en France* dates back to 1976. It highlights the essential and continual concern: will *Beurs* be buried back home like their ancestors? The quote starts with the expression of an objective vision: French citizens of Maghrebi heritage will pass away in France. It includes a statement introduced by "maybe" and framed by parentheses. The embedded hypothesis indicates that one is to expect the ending of a trend, which consists of taking the corpse of a family member to Algeria to bury it there.[1] Why do the authors assume that this practice is likely to come to a close?

Gillette and Sayad's prediction in relation to the burial place of *Beurs* appears to be marginal to the overall argument. Besides, its parenthetical status could mislead us into thinking it is merely an afterthought. In actuality, not only is it as important as the rest of the sentence, it also poses a crucial question, one I feel is the main element of the clause. The question of one's body's ultimate destination is more relevant now in France and is a less taboo topic. Though as a group they have not focused on the question of where to be buried, the younger people (i.e., *Beurs*) have died in accidents and succumbed to sudden disease. Therefore, families have had to confront the burial of these French-born citizens who did not necessarily have a chance to voice their choice of resting place. The writing of a will not being a common practice among *Beurs* and Maghrebis, the decision seldom relies on a tangible trace of one's articulated or unspoken wish. One's own death is a taboo subject and therefore often remains undiscussed until fate strikes. The individual is then only considered as a corpse to bury appropriately in order to facilitate the smooth passage of the soul to the other world. Indeed, in the Muslim tradition, the cemetery is a place where the dead will be summoned to resurrection on Judgment Day.

Expected behavior involves two aspects: Islamic law and land (fast inhumation in Muslim soil). A recent event highly debated in French, Algerian, and international media and politics has highlighted the issue of burial of binationals. The death of killer Mohamed Merah, a twenty-three-year-old French resident of a suburb of Toulouse, in the south of France brought the question of where to bury young Maghrebis to the public sphere and to the attention of Maghrebi immigrants, their children, and grandchildren. In addition, it has prompted French and Algerian governments to discuss the societal issue, which concerns them both. The young man made the headlines of numerous national and international news outlets for murdering seven people between March 11 and March 19, 2012, before he was encircled by RAID (Recherche, Assistance, Intervention, Dissuasion, a French antiterrorist unit) and killed. Among the victims were three French soldiers (two of Maghrebi ancestry and one of Caribbean origin), as well as a teacher and three children, murdered at the entrance of the Jewish school Otzar Hatorah in Toulouse.

In spite of Mohamed Merah's alleged wish to be inhumed in France, his father expressed his intention to fly his son's remains to Algeria so that they could be interred in his family's village of origin, Souagui. According to Merah's mother, the family hoped to bury their son in the bled to prevent his sepulchre from being vandalized; however, the Algerian government refused to authorize the burial in Algeria. Security and public order were the official reasons given for the refusal to issue a permit, but unofficial accounts spoke to the fear of Algerian officials that the tomb might become a place of pilgrimage for extremists. The mayor of Toulouse also tried to prevent the internment from taking place in his city, but after much popular resistance and confusion, the authorization to inhume the body in France was granted. Just hours prior to the internment, President Nicolas Sarkozy offered justification on the grounds of the terrorist's citizenship: "He was French, let him be buried and let's not engage in polemic with that."[2] The burial took place on March 29, 2012, on the outskirts of Toulouse in the section of the Cornebarrieu cemetery allotted for Muslims.

Cultural critics have shown that it has not been easy for Maghrebi migrants to find a new "home" in exile and for their French children to feel at home in France. Brinda Mehta has coined the expression *citoyenneté non partagée* (citizenship of disaffiliation), which pinpoints "the French Republic's tenuous negotiations of cultural plurality."[3] The search for a place of internment constitutes an additional quest for "home." In Merah's case, the burial site was refused to the individual, but entire communities have also been denied. Harkis are still not allowed in the bled, and some Algerian localities decline their inhumation. And for criminals of North African ancestry expelled from France, their only "choice" for final resting place becomes the country of their ancestors. Thus, families are not always presented with an option between national alternatives. In the struggle to either keep Maghrebi corpses in France, or to send them to

North Africa, religion plays a crucial role in the selection of the eternal home. Indeed, why is the question of burial place less of an issue for Portuguese, Spanish, and Italian migrants and their children? It is not that these communities have been in France for longer, or that associations with a "back home" have disintegrated. For the most part, the Portuguese, for instance, have kept strong connections of various kinds with the other country. Rather, these groups have Catholicism in common with French society; the respective societies of their ancestors are based on shared Christian principles and values. Feeling at "home" in a country therefore can be thought of as being a question of spiritual and religious compatibility. And the chosen place of burial is likely to reflect one's place in the society one lives in. In the case of a citizen who is torn between two countries engaged in a war or that share a still-vivid belligerent past, where to call home can be a question of patriotism. But for Maghrebis living in a predominantly non-Muslim nation, the matter, a source of worry throughout one's life, is also about cultural and religious continuity. The deceased may not have identified as Muslim. The truth of the matter is, however, that one is always buried by others. Relatives and friends will contemplate possibilities for the soul to "rest in peace" based on conscious and unconscious spiritual and religious grounds. Even if the deceased is atheist, if the relatives handling the body are Muslim, there is no possibility of cremation, as Islam does not allow it. In the case of European migrants and descendants of Christian background, preferences for burial practices and location can be religiously mandated, but they may not experience a conflict or be forced to make a difficult choice because France is a Judeo-Christian society. For people of these religious backgrounds, unlike for Muslims, religious questions in general may not present themselves with the same acuity.

Religious identity that is understood by the populace and major media outlets as "incompatible" with values or norms of the dominant country can sharpen feelings of marginalization. Some may expect *Beurs* to be more rooted in French society than Maghrebis are, and consequently that burials in France of the former are likely to become a trend. However, feelings of exclusion among the younger group can be stronger than among their elders, because *Beurs* may self-identify as French and expect equal conduct in the country they live in as the Franco-French, in contrast with their parents. However, this is often not a reality, as they are still perceived as foreigners by many of their countrymen. In discriminatory discourses at play today, Muslims are criticized for their religiosity, whether they happen to be practicing their religion or not. "Looking Muslim" is enough for assumptions to be made. On March 23, 2012, while still in office, Nicolas Sarkozy gave a highly controversial interview for the radio channel France Info, in which he pigeonholed so-called Arab-looking people, calling them of "Muslim appearance" regardless of the fact (among other similarly problematic ones) that skin color does not necessarily coincide with religion affiliation. Perhaps when the religious denominator ceases to be a factor of exclusion will *Beurs* feel that their bodies can finally elect a home in a cemetery in France next to, or even among Christian, Jewish, and nonreligious bodies.

To this day, there are only two exclusively Muslim cemeteries in France. The first one, inaugurated in 1937, is located in Bobigny, a town in Seine Saint-Denis, a northeastern suburb of Paris. The second public Muslim cemetery opened in Strasbourg in 2012. Some communal cemeteries, such as Cornebarrieu, have sections reserved for Muslims called *carrés musulmans* (Muslim squares). Twenty-three of them are to be found in Ile-de-France, which is mainly composed of the Parisian metropolitan area. This system should enable a higher number of French Muslims to lay their loved ones to rest in the country where "they were brought up and educated, and lived all their lives."[4] Nevertheless, the number of Muslim cemetery quarters is low compared to the number of Muslims living on the French territory—"seventy-five Muslim sections in the entire hexagon, needless to say it's derisory in light of the size of the Muslim population! Yet with or without reserved sections, experts on the topic agree that repatriations of corpses should likely remain the rule in the years to come. A sociological oddity."[5]

In an article published in the French newspaper *Le Monde* in 2012, Stéphanie Le Bars mentions that there are now two hundred such Muslim squares. Still, studies claim that there still is a significant shortage: "A survey done on the topic by the CRCM Rhône-Alpes in 2008 reckoned that 600 Muslim squares were necessary and deemed it indispensable to eventually manage to create a Muslim square in every city with a mosque."[6] As for the creation of other exclusively Muslim cemeteries, this endeavor is unlikely as of yet. Indeed, the cemetery in Strasbourg was made possible due to a unique situation in France. Still to this day, Alsace and Moselle follow the concordat regime, which is a special status— one that these two places in northeastern France enjoy that the rest of France does not. This region (Alsace) and this *département* (Moselle) were under German rule when the 1905 law was passed. This law marks the separation of church and state in France. Upon integrating the French nation in 1919, Alsace and Moselle were able to claim the concordat stemming from the 1801 concordat signed by Napoléon Bonaparte, which the Conseil d'Etat declared still valid in 1925. However, the concordat only applies to the Catholic, Protestant (Lutheran and Reformist), and Israelite confessions recognized by local law at the time. One major feature of the concordat allows Alsace and Moselle to take part in the financing of religious edifices. Socialist Party member Roland Ries, the mayor of Strasbourg, claimed that the opening of the second Muslim cemetery, for which the city contributed eight hundred thousand euros in order to ensure the realization of the project, aimed to give all religions equal rights and expand the concordat to religions not previously recognized by it.

But is the tradition of flying the corpse to the native land a result of the lack of "quarters"? Does this tradition account for local authorities' decisions to limit the number of Muslim sections? Certainly the scarcity of plots reserved for the Muslims of France could prove incorrect Gillette and Sayad's aforementioned prevision that more *Beurs* will be buried in France, unless the religious constraints become less of an issue for *Beurs* (and Maghrebis), who would resort to a final home in France to give their descendants easier access to tombs. The "derisory" number of Muslim burial sections may be interpreted as a lack of official acknowledgment on the part of French decision-makers of the Muslims' ties to France—and to the land, so to speak. This message—whether it is deliberate or not—could become a swaying element in the choice of a burial site "back home" for those who do not feel strongly about burying their relatives on one side of the Mediterranean or the other.

That there is only one exclusively Muslim cemetery in the entire country is another way for the republic to signal the Othering of its Muslim population. It is a way of signifying to this community that there is no place for them in the long run. After reminding the reader that France, with five million Muslims, has the most numerous Muslim population in Europe, Zohra argues, "To these men, women, and their children born here, France seems to be telling them 'go die somewhere else.'"[7] Though one might argue that things could change, the Maghreb-born population—consisting also of Harkis (a significant number of whom are both French and Muslim)—has been in France long enough for officials to remedy this dearth of plots. It is noteworthy that presidents and other officials with sensibilities across the political spectrum have spoken for the memory of Harkis who died when French forces were fighting Algerian revolutionaries. It is equally noteworthy that monuments have been erected in the honor of Harkis who died for France, and yet there are not enough cemeteries in which their children (Muslims or converts) can plan for a final resting place. Until recently, these individuals were considered as (the children of) "traitors" in Algeria. It was only on September 2, 2005, that President Bouteflika recognized that they should not be held responsible for the crimes of their parents.

More and more French citizens of North African descent have recently voiced their atheism or expressed their detachment and sometimes rejection of Muslim principles and rituals such as prayer and fasting during Ramadan. For these people, the place of burial, a priori, would be France or not matter—but again, it is the ones who outlive us who bury us. For some families of more or less devout Muslims, an important and newer aspect that has caused them to opt for a final home in France is distance. Now that the eventual return home has gradually receded into the realm of impracticality, *Beurs* have made France not only their temporal home but also their eternal one. In fact, French cemeteries are more likely to become the eternal resting place of a Muslim population that worries about leaving a legacy to their offspring. Indeed, the act of visiting tombs is condemned in mainstream Islam. Sepulchres are supposed to be simple, and local authorities do not hesitate to place a body on top of another one when space is lacking, in spite of the discouraged practice of burying various people in the same spot. Yet visiting the dead remains a common practice, and fewer and fewer Maghrebi families are satisfied with having the sporadic opportunity to visit the tombs of their loved ones on occasional trips back home.

The fact that Merah had voiced a choice for his own burial is not surprising in that he could have anticipated being killed after committing his crimes. On the other hand, his choice of France as his country of burial could appear surprising. Indeed, in the context of his murders of French nationals and his position with regard to France's political involvement in the Middle East, which he allegedly condemned by shooting individuals of Jewish faith and multiethnic soldiers—among whom were descendants of Maghrebi immigrants—one would expect that he would want to be interred in the land of his parents. However, Merah never resided in Algeria. But in spite of exceptions to this tendency, *Beurs* often choose France over the Maghreb as a place to live. One reason for this partiality is their familiarity with the French language and the feeling of alienation from the language and culture of the country of their parents. Conversely, this does not appear to be a determining factor in the choice of final home when this one is expressed openly in cultural productions tackling the topic, which revisit the tradition of flying the corpse back to the bled. In the novel *Pieds-blancs,* the main character voices a choice and makes of the book written in French a type of will in the image of a Western document where a last wish associated with a name is guaranteed fulfillment and whose aim is to grant the individual peace of mind.

Shopping for a Place to Die

Detailed statistics of individuals returning to their country of origin while alive are rarely published, but the phenomenon is a common, global reality and in fact can be encouraged by sending countries. Map 6.1 depicts country policies on return migration, which impact the sending and receiving countries at many levels. Mehta writes: "As *beur* literature engages with the sociological and political reality of Arabs in France, it is impossible to separate literature from the social text. Literature and sociology intersect in these works to provide a complex and creative sociopolitical document of lived experience. This literature thereby poses important questions about the multiethnic identity of France, the positionality of Arab-Muslims, and the French Republic's tenuous negotiations of cultural plurality amid this diversity."[8]

These considerations are indeed essential and have an impact on the literature of writers like Houda Rouane, who treats a subject that is haunting more and more *Beurs,* who weigh their options in light of their lives in France and their connections with the bled. The morbid topic of death is treated lightly in Rouane's

1.	MACEDONIA	16.	GERMANY
2.	ALBANIA	17.	DENMARK
3.	SERBIA	18.	POLAND
4.	BOSNIA	19.	GREECE
5.	CROATIA	20.	BULGARIA
6.	SLOVENIA	21.	ROMANIA
7.	HUNGARY	22.	MOLDOVA
8.	SLOVAK REPUBLIC	23.	UKRAINE
9.	CZECH REPUBLIC	24.	BELARUS
10.	AUSTRIA	25.	LITHUANIA
11.	SWITZERLAND	26.	LATVIA
12.	ITALY	27.	ESTONIA
13.	LUXEMBOURG	28.	GEORGIA
14.	BELGIUM	29.	ARMENIA
15.	NETHERLANDS	30.	AZERBAIJAN

Country policies on return migration 2005

- Encourages return of citizens
- Does not encourage return
- No policy
- No data

Map 6.1 "Country Policies on Return Migration 2005" from Russell King's *People on the Move: An Atlas of Migration.* Used with permission.

first novel, *Pieds-blancs,* published in 2006 in Paris. The French female writer of Moroccan descent paints the fascination for the Maghreb as a place to settle in in death. She expresses this desire to return to the Maghreb among those who are not from there in the context of a post-mortem trip. She says of the Moroccan town of Doukala: "But now I know if I'm not lucky enough to die there, I want to be buried there. It just dawned on me. Slowly, the feeling that I was home started to mess with my mind. Oddly, all my other projects, like visiting the Hassan II Great Mosque, going to Marrakesh, doing some shopping in the old quarter now seem superfluous to me. I've found a meaning to my visit: I've found my last home."[9] For the character Norah, to die in Muslim Morocco would constitute a blessing, a door to the sky. For her, this is a blessing also in that this is a rarity: not that many French citizens of North African descent "return" home, and many die in France. The newness of such a manifesto is indicated by its suddenness ("It just dawned on me"). As for its potentially whimsical nature, it is eradicated by its assured continuity ("Slowly, the feeling that I was home started to mess with my mind"). Given that the likelihood of her residing in the bled when her time comes to pass away is significantly small, her second-best option is to ask that her body be taken there to be laid to rest. This paragraph does not indicate that Norah went looking for a particular place to be buried. Nor is her voyage to Morocco portrayed as fieldwork of any sort. She traveled to Morocco on her break from school. In addition, this is not her first trip there. She therefore is used to the environment depicted in the novel. And yet, in spite of not being on a quest in vivo for her next home, she goes through a peculiar moment where she tests out the best place for her body once she has passed on. The common experience of tourist shopping is substituted with the unexpected search for a burial ground, inspired by her recollections of Moroccan cemeteries. The realization that her burial site has suddenly become particularly significant for her equates this epiphany to a mystical experience. It is backed up by the use of expressions such as "mess with my mind" and "now seem superfluous to me," which indicate a radical change of mind, a shift in the narrator's view of what matters. For the young lady, Morocco is no longer a place to shop for earthly satisfaction. Put differently, she has ceased to consider this country as a destination where she behaves as a tourist, in other words, a temporary guest. It has turned into a place in which to plan for postmortem peace.

Another passage confirms her strong desire to repose in Morocco:

> Cemeteries back home are fun because there you can find sellers of dry fruits, candy, nuts, popcorn, and fava or garbanzo beans seasoned with salt or cumin. Other sellers peddle junk, incense, rosaries, and framed prayers written in beautiful calligraphy, gerabs l'ma in colorful clothes wearing goatskin flasks full of water and brass kettledrums to drink from, and then goats, sheep, and beasts of burden, people clad in white or in color all over. It is especially for this that I would like to be buried there, in the warmth and in the midst of all this noise, of all these people, so that I ain't ever really alone and dead.[10]

The stated parameters informing her choice reside in the esthetic nature of cemeteries that take on a lively character. Though her portrayal is depicted in a comical fashion, which is the signature of the novel, it nevertheless makes its point. The narrator's claim is that Moroccan cemeteries are cheerful and colorful places. They are not the quiet, sober, and serious-looking loci they usually are in the West. Rouane's narrator wants everyday life to continue around her (body) so that she will not feel lonely. Norah contrasts this continuation that she seeks between this life and the afterlife with the disruption that her choice of Doukala will cause between her and her husband, who will be buried either in France or in Turkey, the country of his ancestors: "I've lived a love story I've never dared think of, and what's more, since Doukala, I've realized that when the two of us are dead, we won't be on the same continent. We'll rot in our separate corners."[11] It is interesting that this reflection should appear in a train of thought and not in a dialogue with Norah's husband, Souleymane. This illustrates that even within a couple's relationship, the place of burial is not discussed openly. It is left for (significant) others to figure out, as if it were their responsibility to guess what is right among the options that are left for them. In the case of diasporic beings, one would expect that this topic should necessitate discussion in that the place to reside in is not necessarily synonymous with the place to rest in. But what complicates this dual position is that the couple does not share the same place of origin. Upon the delicate topic of death is superimposed the intricate notion of togetherness in the afterlife. But one might desire not to be buried alongside one's partner in life. It might be that Norah is deeply aware that she and her husband have decided not to tackle the topic for fear that stating one's preference to part in death by being on separate continents might jeopardize their feelings of being a couple in this life. Instead of discussion, Norah chooses confession, not to her husband but rather to us readers. Literature provides a safe place for the narrator to play the guessing game, which is presented as a certainty, a sort of performative statement: "We'll rot in our separate corners." Norah's conviction is the outcome of her trip to Doukala. Her position signifies her unwillingness to compromise on her burial place, which she realizes will not include Souleymane. It is not so much that her husband is of Turkish origin that excludes the possibility for the couple to lay to rest in proximity. Rather, it is because Norah is aware that in spite of the variety of options that their French citizenship provides them, their decision will be narrowed to very few options—and perhaps only one. Indeed, Norah and Souleymane could spend the rest of their lives in France but also Morocco if they wanted to. Given their right to reside in any other member state of the Schengen space, they could settle in other European countries where they could eventually find a final home. Nevertheless, as Norah shows, the selection for them in death as a couple ends up being limited to two countries, Morocco and Turkey. This is due to familial, habitual, cultural, and religious reasons. The "norm," which Gillette and Sayad discuss, is one of cultural habit, family expectation, and communitarian tradition. Norah tells us her couple will follow the old school—the two countries on "different continents" presented as only possible contenders have Islam as the official religion of state—following their elders' modus operandi.

The fact that they will be inhumed in separate Muslim countries may be accounted for by their relatives' expectations to bring the corpse "back" home where its "roots" are. Rouane's character does not explicitly base her preference on religious views. She does not convey the idea that she must be buried in Muslim land in order to be at peace with her soul. Nor does she make an association between her last home in France and national betrayal. Even though Norah is never described as praying or following other pillars of Islam, in her daily living she asks for *halal* meat for her school meals, refusing to compromise on this religiously mandated practice. Norah then personifies the "cultural Muslim," following dietary rules out of habit. Not having been raised as consumers of pork, these Muslims may never have found the interest or inclination to change this custom but may yet not self-identify as rigorous practitioners of the Islamic faith. *Pieds-blancs* implies nonetheless that cultural Muslims such as Norah are still Muslims at heart and in heritage. Norah feels that to emigrate—let alone to choose France, the ex-colonizer, as the destination—is bad enough. To freely select France (for oneself or for a deceased) as the land to which to bury or "return" the body is further betrayal. Filmmaker and novelist Mehdi Charef, born in Algeria and raised in France, provides the flipside of the coin by framing his potential return as a betrayal to himself, which he calls "a failure": "The desire to return [to Algeria] scares me. What would bother me the most would be to tell myself one day when I am old: "well, I'm going back to Algeria. I want to die there!" This would be a return, therefore a form of failure. After all, I think that someone who has experienced exile should not return to where they came from."[12]

The conflation between the national and the religious in the case of Algeria has been particularly strong throughout history. The perception that dying on non-Muslim land is a sin has been woven into the national narrative in poetry and music. Thus, one expects the official rejection of France as the final resting place in contemporary Algerian artistic works. As Marie Virolle indicates, to die in the land of the colonizer at the end of World War I was religiously incompatible: "As for those who died at the frontline, they would never return. Even their bodies would remain in the land of [i]nfidels without a decent and Muslim sepulture."[13] In the context of postcolonial migration, non-Muslim territories remain the land of "infidels," but the deceased have the possibility of returning "home" and receiving a decent and Muslim sepulchre. This is precisely the wish of a Maghrebi retiree in Hassan Legzouli's *Ten'ja*. In this film, the protagonist Nordine buries his immigrant father in Morocco. When asked by a local why, the disenchanted French son exclaims, "He always wanted to be buried here."

Ten'ja: Enacting Closure

Born in 1963 in the village of Aderj, Morocco, Legzouli moved to Europe in the 1980s. He studied cinema in Belgium at the Institut National Supérieur des Arts du Spectacle et des Techniques de Diffusion, and later settled in Lille, France. He recently made another feature-length film *Le Veau d'or* (2011), which tells the story of a father who sends his seventeen-year-old son to Morocco in hope that the young man will settle down. The latter is adamant about returning to France before he turns eighteen so he may apply for French citizenship and reunite with his French girlfriend. In order to pay for the trip, he and his cousin steal a cow on a farm, which belongs to the king of Morocco. Legzouli made seven films before *Ten'ja,* namely, *Ailleurs et ici* (1990), *Coup de gigot* (1991), *Le Marchand de souvenirs* (1992), *Là-bas si j'y suis* (1993), *L'Ere du soupçon* (1994), *Chroniques d'un deuil ordinaire* (1997), and *Quand le soleil fait tomber les moineaux* (1999). Released in 2004, *Ten'ja* is the director's first feature film. It was produced by the French company Why Not Productions in conjunction with the Moroccan firm Videorama and TV channel 2M (Soread). The film was partly funded and supported by the intergovernmental agency of Francophonie. The support came in the form of "La bourse francophone de promotion internationale d'un film du sud," which is endowed with an eighty thousand–euro prize. The film is a seventy-five-minute piece in French, Arabic, and Berber. Among the various recognitions it collected is Le Prix special du Jury at the twenty-fourth edition of the Amiens International Film Festival.

Ten'ja is a pioneering work for its representation of return migration in Maghrebi cinema. Various films have tackled the return home as a dream that never comes true or that is frightening (e.g., Karim Dridi's *Bye-Bye*). *Ten'ja* presents a unique treatment of the concept of "return" migration.[14] This type of ex-centric journey is intimately linked to death and place of burial, an important nexus in this analysis. Legzouli's main character is the young Nordine Daoudi (Roschdy Zem), a self-employed taxi driver and the son of Moroccans. His father was recruited to work in the mines of Sallaumines, in Nord-pas-de-Calais. After departing for this region in the north of France, the miner never sets foot in Morocco again. For this reason, it might be remarked that *Ten'ja* too tackles the prospect of a return home formulated by Maghrebis that never actualizes, which illustrates well the dreamed return-turned-myth tackled by many filmmakers before Legzouli. However, what this film does that others do not is treat the theme of the return of the body of a migrant. Even Dridi's film, released in 1995, in which a dead Maghrebi corpse is being watched over in a banlieue of Marseilles, it is never shown on its way back home for burial. The "return" is not a minor element in the production's esthetics. It is a major theme, one that propels the narrative and mobilizes the protagonists, the director, and the extradiegetic viewers alike throughout the film. *Ten'ja* is precisely concerned with what I call the "methical return," which is the return home that is finally undertaken because it is lived as the only *ethical* option even if, and well after, it has become a *myth* for an entire migrant community abroad. The fact that reconnection with the land of birth takes place postlife does not cancel out the idea that this is a return. Indeed, given the father's resolute wish to be buried back home, the dream to return to the bled has been realized only post-mortem. In the widespread expression *return to the bled* used in French and Arabic by migrants to express their intention to go back across the Mediterranean, bled not only means "land, village, country"—according to its Arabic terminology it also signifies "the earth, the ground, the soil." With this in mind, the post-mortem return of the body to the land is the ultimate homecoming. Many Maghrebis wished to settle back home after a short stay overseas, but when the short stay transformed into a definitive stay and this project proved impossible, what counted for them is that their bodies be released from a lingering exilic condition. The aforementioned expression *return to the bled* refers to the land that gives birth and in religious terms the land, soil, earth that one eventually returns to—the most crucial meaning of the expression among the vast majority of North African expatriates. Wanting to be buried in Morocco after spending his entire life in France is a sign that the Maghrebi migrant had been eager to reconnect with his severed Muslim "roots."

From the first scenes of the film, we gather that Nordine's father has just passed away. We learn from his son that prior to his death, he requested that his body be inhumed in Aderj, his native Berber village, located in the High Atlas. *Ten'ja* depicts Nordine's trip to lay his father to rest where he was born. Along the way, he meets Nora (Aure Atika) and Mimoun (Abdou el Mesnaoui). Mimoun is a porter in a morgue, and Nordine meets him upon arrival in Tangier. The young man becomes Nordine's unofficial guide during his two short stays in this city on his way in and out of Morocco. Nordine comes across Nora stranded by the side of the road as he drives by one night. Kicked out by a rich businessman whose mistress she was, the young lady becomes Nordine's passenger and ends up accompanying him all the way to his father's village, thus becoming the Frenchman's second Moroccan guide.

As one prepares to watch the film, taking a closer look, one can discern the title in Arabic on the DVD cover. It is in a faded gray color. Being projected like a shadowgraph onto the sky makes it difficult to make out. Moreover, TENJA written in Roman characters in burgundy across the Arabic title makes the Arabic even less legible. The Arabic script is crossed over, and consequently, the meaning and sound of the title in Arabic, which is pronounced slightly differently from how it is uttered in French gives all the space and authority to the title in Roman characters, which becomes a homonym of *Tanja,* "Tangier" in Arabic. In spite of the film ostensibly being about a testament—given that *tenja* means "testament" in Berber, the language of Nordine's father's birth village—the film gives noticeable space to Tangier, a hub for pan-African clandestine migrations. The director explains in an interview in *Le Matin du Sahara* that Ten'ja is a legend, with which he became acquainted when he read "Le Fou de la Rose" (The Madman of the Rose), one of Mohamed Choukri's short stories.[15] As Legzouli specifies, the name of the film spelled in two words is what the biblical Noah exclaimed when he saw a dove with clay on its feet alight onto his ark. The arrival of this creature aboard the ark out of the blue was the indication that the land had presented itself—*Et-Tin ja:* "the dove has come"—an apparition that informed Noah that he had been saved from the flood. The subtext is interesting in that it signals a historically charged trend as well as a religious one that insinuates that the tropes of exile, return, and finding home are regional and even universal tropes.

The dominant title in Roman characters leads to potential equations between Tangier and clandestine migration, whereas the hidden Arabic title itself represents a personal and religious theme, that of the expected return of a Muslim to Muslim land. The ethereal title hovers over Nordine's face on the DVD cover like a shadow that haunts him, his father, and the Maghrebi community. For the latter, the responsibility to bury their elders hangs over them like the sword of Damocles. Once held back by economic constraints, the return to the homeland is brought into the foreground in the shared destiny of both Maghrebis and *Beurs* imposed by the arrival of death. As the director puts it, "The issue [of the burial in the land of one's origin] is an increasingly relevant one because this generation of workers who went to work in France in the 1960s is passing on."[16] The director also has stated that the film is based on a real phenomenon, inspired by the story of a friend of his. He mentions that coincidentally, one year after the director wrote the scenario, actor Roschdy Zem "experienced exactly the same story as Nordine, and went to bury his father in his Moroccan village."[17] He added that he wanted an actor who, having endured an analogous trial, was able to espouse Nordine's feelings and thus he was unwilling to shoot if he could not have Zem in the cast.

One of the most crucial questions that this reality brings is: What is the proper place of burial? Early in the narrative, the spectator realizes that Nordine's journey is out of the ordinary. Indeed, the officer at Moroccan customs inquires about Nordine's unusual decision to drive his father's corpse to Morocco. The man reminds Nordine that given that Air Morocco honors cheaper fares for Moroccans residing abroad, it would have been more convenient to transport the body by air. In *Le Grand voyage,* the son expresses a comparable confusion about the choice of transportation—why not just fly? Like Réda, Nordine is inconvenienced by the hurdles that his father's death in a foreign land implies for him, as is evidenced by his first reaction when his mother encourages Nordine to fulfill his duty to his father. The difference is that Nordine knows the reason for his father's wish to be driven back home. Indeed, he retorts to the official, "My father wanted to arrive in the manner he left, in other words, by boat. This was his last wish."

Legzouli's *Ten'ja* and Ismaël Ferroukhi's *Le Grand voyage* present intriguing parallels in their depictions of migrant experiences. The two films deal with the death of a father, interactions between the two male figures, and the uncertain future of *Beurs*. Both narratives evoke a ritual-focused return journey distinct from clandestine migration—a methical return, which is one that was not possible while the migrant was alive, but which his son considers as the right thing to do: the fathers migrated to France to provide a better life for their children; in turn, the children take their fathers to their lands of origins in the interest of attaining a peaceful afterlife. *Ten'ja* provides a representation of an ex-centric migration (namely, clandestine), but it is secondary to the geographic, cultural, and psychological process of return migration. As Legzouli himself acknowledges, there are strong similarities between his film and that of his colleague and fellow-citizen Ferroukhi. Legzouli discussed resemblances in an interview granted to Khadija Alaoui for the newspaper *Le Matin du Sahara*, especially with regard to "the relations with the father, perhaps because at the time we were both becoming fathers ourselves, perhaps because we were focused on the issues of the return, of one's attachment to the country."[18] Oddly enough, Mohamed Majd, a popular actor in Maghrebi cinema also known in the West for his performance as Réda's father in *Le Grand voyage*, is Nordine's father in *Ten'ja*. Thus this actor plays the father of bicultural sons and, surprisingly, an unnamed father in both films. This peculiarity turns fathers into symbols of an entire generation (Maghrebi migrant retirees) who bring *Beurs* to tackle the place of their parents' cultures in their lives and the place of immigration in their identity. Legzouli made sure to indicate that although he and Ferroukhi know one another, they were not in touch during the writing process of their scripts and thus were not aware of their respective ongoing projects. It is startling that the directors' contact with the reality of death should be the theme of choice in the films they released the very same year. This coincidence in contemporary Moroccan cinema is the sign of a trend and the presentation of a collective dilemma that concerns filmmakers for aesthetic and personal reasons.

The "Destination" Road Movie

Undoubtedly, *Ten'ja* is the journey of an initiate, a *bildungsfilm*. Even if the popular actor Roschdy Zem was in his late thirties in 2004, his character, who is twenty-six years old, is portrayed with quite a few infantilizing features in order to emphasize his coming of age on screen. When Nora asks the Frenchman if he is married, Nordine answers that he is not. His portrayal as a bachelor is meant to reinforce his youth, for in average Maghrebi families, not having wed after achieving professional and financial security is likely to trigger discord. Furthermore, not being fluent in Arabic and not conversant at all in Berber makes Nordine depend on others. Nora, herself raised in Morocco until the age of eighteen and aware of the impropriety, is shocked that Nordine plays a cassette

Figure 6.1 Nordine wrapping his father's coffin in a cardboard box, which reads "Fridge." Still from Hassan Legzouli's *Ten'ja*.

in the car while his father's corpse lies in the back. The linguistic and cultural awkwardness contribute to the characterization of Nordine as a young man. On a few occasions, he begs with excitement like a child for Nora to translate the lyrics of his father's favorite Berber song.

The lack of experience of *Beurs* with the transportation of a deceased relative by roadway and the nature of the response to this unusual situation are represented by uncertainty and suspense, which Legzouli manages to create for the viewer from the outset of the film via the use of ellipses. Such is the case when Nordine starts to answer the customs officer's question concerning the eccentricity of his journey by uttering "My father . . ."—but is interrupted by the entrance of an employee, who brings coffee to the officer. Information is conveniently suspended. The same goal is reached when Nordine and the local guide wrap the coffin tightly in cardboard in the back of Nordine's suv shortly before Nordine sets off (Figure 6.1).[19] The box has the ominous print on it, which reads, "REFRIGERATEUR" (FRIDGE). The director feeds the spectator's curiosity because he depicts the young man's preparing for the trip in the dead of night like a thief or an individual involved in esoteric rituals. It is only later that we find out that Nordine is simply hiding the corpse in the back of his vehicle. The peculiarity of this journey is highlighted further by Mimoun. As he establishes ties of friendship with Nordine, the perplexed local guide inquires, "He died in France but he wants to be buried here? You don't have cemeteries there [in France]?" Nordine's response was perplexed and resigned: "He wanted to come back home." The father's request reflects that the older generation of migrants conforms to the tradition of burial in the native land.

Unlike in *Le Grand voyage* where the father remains silent on these matters, the father in *Ten'ja* verbalizes his desire to leave and never return to France. In a scene that could be interpreted either as a spiritual vision or a delusion, Nordine chats with his father in the back of the van while Nora drives. The director commented on this scene: "Death is a vector in the story. I didn't want to focus entirely on the coffin, but its physical presence in the car allows for the first 'real' encounter between the character and his father. Both experienced the absence of words when the father was still alive, even if there was not really conflicts between them."[20] This surreal scene enables the two men to discuss topics they never tackled when Nordine's father was alive. As a matter of fact, when the father asks Nordine about Nora, the young man reminds his father that the subject of women is one they shied away from in life. The other taboo topic they discuss is the place of burial. Thinking that he may be suffering from food poisoning or typhoid and that he might die soon, Nordine jokingly proposes that they bury each other in their respective native bleds. The father, whom we see for the first and last time, promptly precludes this possibility in a more serious tone: "Ah, no, *I* am not returning to the North any longer." Will the son return? The old man's accented "*I*" establishes contrast and conveys the father's assumption that Nordine will indeed go back, that Aderj is a place for corpses only. The young man has difficulty finding the village. As a matter of fact, the village has been abandoned. Its cemetery is the only place that fills up with people.

Not much space in the storyline is devoted to France in *Ten'ja* and *Le Grand voyage*. Indeed, a minimal glance into the life in France of Réda and Nordine and his family is taken in order to provide necessary contextual background. Then, as soon as the journey is initiated, France disappears from the screen. In *Ten'ja*, however, Nordine has to drive through the entire French territory from the northernmost region of "Le Nord" to the France-Spain border. Still, an insignificant portion of the narrative takes place in the hexagon because the story is about taking a corpse to its final dwelling place in Morocco. Approximately one thousand kilometers are traversed in a few seconds. Despite the fact that the film belongs resolutely to the road-movie genre, the director opts to be selective in his rendering of the French segment. This emphasis away from the starting point of the journey reveals more than a plot exigency. As I pointed out in previous chapters, directors Djamel Bensalah and Tony Gatlif also make the filmic choice to minimize screen time in Europe. One could call their works "destination road movies" in light of the significant characteristics they share. They give minor space to the (European) place of departure and they convey that space in a negative light. In *Ten'ja*, the father dies when his family is spending their summer in a small trailer at the ill-named Berck beach in France (*berck* means "ick" or "ew" in French)." In *Il était une fois*, on top of the usual problems of the banlieue, the French fragment of the road trip shows a family stuck in a traffic jam without air conditioning. In other words, they cannot breathe and need to move forward rapidly to let some fresh air in. Their confinement in a car is symbolic of various limitations—their immobile social status and their small apartment in a ramshackle project—and causes the father to shout at drivers who are slowing down their plan to reach Algeria. In *Exils*, the protagonists make a decision to set off for Algeria purportedly out of boredom. The French portion of this film consists of shots of bleak rainy landscapes that emphasize the characters' sense of ennui. Subsequent segments in North Africa are depicted in contrasting light, oftentimes very positively (and simplistically). In these destination road movies, the arrival at the final destination is therefore imperative. "Point B" has to be reached diligently—before the father's death in *Le Grand voyage,* and on the coming Friday in *Ten'ja*. Death is another emphasis in that it presents *Beurs* with the opportunity to be confronted with the question of the burial place of their relatives first, and indirectly their own given that one conceptualizes one's death through that of others. This question imposes itself to the characters during their road trips through the surrounding landscape, land, and dirt—the potential setting of their last homes if they too choose to be brought back.

A major element of destination road movies is the importance of depicting the country of arrival. Legzouli lingers on the breathtaking beauty of the Moroccan places that Nordine drives through and his images are enhanced by a mesmerizing soundtrack of powerful vocal music. These visual and auditory features heighten the sense of enchantment of his story. The Berber song Nordine's father used to listen to is not only an abstract part of the auditory landscape, it also becomes a mechanism through which the son strives to come to grips with the old man's life. But the father's life narrative, which the camera and soundtrack attempt to reconstitute in pieces, essentially focuses on the target destination. Similarly, the absence of the French landscape illustrates the father's longing to leave the country where he spent the latter part of his life. Nora's reluctance to translate the love story in full and the gaps revealed by her "translation"—which is better qualified as a summary of only part of the song—also participate in this effort not to linger on the old man's failed covenant with the land that the song spells out in the context of the man's love for his land: "I promise that I will not forget you / That I will not abandon you / Make the same promise to me / I fear that you forget me one day." Make the promise not to "forget me" and to focus instead on the mission, which is to reestablish the old man's Moroccan ties.

While France is left quickly, Morocco proves to be difficult to enter. Indeed, when Nordine arrives in Tangier, the authorities refuse to let him proceed. Since he is traveling with a dead body, the signature of the medical examiner is required.

However, the doctor has left for a national holiday and will be back no sooner than Friday. Nordine objects to waiting three additional days. Moreover, his father expressed the wish to be buried on a Friday—the holy day in the Muslim world. This episode heightens the ex-centric nature of the trip. It is surprising to Nordine that the dead body should be a source of so much trouble. His exasperation can be understood in that he is simply carrying out a methical return. The object of contention is not a burden on the Moroccan economy or to the nation's political affairs. It is all the more puzzling to Nordine that this is the second time that he has trouble at the border. We learn that as a teenager he was refused entry to the country while on a school trip, whereas all his classmates were allowed in. Nordine explains to Nora that "since [he] was the only son of Moroccans in the group, the customs officers didn't let him in because [he] didn't have his [Moroccan] ID." It could be suggested that the officers are merely doing their job in not letting in an individual without a *carte nationale* (ID) given that European passports are not sufficient documentation for Moroccans Residing Abroad (Marocains Résidant à l'Etranger [MRES])—a name given to both *Beurs* and Maghrebis. But the director presents a critical perspective on the administrative procedure for crossing the Moroccan border. He depicts it as burdensome and illogical, given that a teenager was singled out; the nonsensical is further conveyed by the idea that Nordine's French classmates were recognized as more "legal" than he was. The Moroccan state's requirement that nationals living abroad must have an additional document in their possession may be a way to render entry more difficult for them and a way to emphasize the expatriates' foreignness. On the other hand, one could argue that this is meant to reinforce their Moroccanness by reminding the visitors that in the eyes of Moroccan law they are first and foremost Moroccan citizens. The Moroccan ID would then be a tool to establish a material pact between state-declared Moroccans who present European passports and their country of ancestry. In Nordine's opinion, the reason lies elsewhere. Indeed for him, his Moroccanness is obvious as evidenced in his response the second time he travels to Morocco by himself: "It's written in my passport," he answers disparagingly to the official who asks for his nationality despite having the passport right in front of him. The young man is aware that the agent is questioning his national or ethnic affiliation: "You have an Algerian accent . . . is your father Moroccan?" Nordine specifies: "He *was*. So what?" Then, the officer declares: "For us, you are Moroccan, sir." Nordine retorts angrily, "For me too, I am Moroccan." The dialogue on identity politics ends, and the officer allows the young man to resume the journey without the "required" medical examination.

The fact that Nordine is mistakenly thought to be an Algerian is a potential obstacle to his journey in that the search for undocumented Algerians on Moroccan soil is common. If local authorities mistakenly assume that Nordine is Algerian, he would face serious problems. Terrorist attacks (in Hotel Asni in Marrakesh in August 1994, supposedly planned by the Algerian intelligence services) led Morocco to enforce visa requirements on Algerian visitors. This decision led its neighbor to close the border, which *trabandistes* and clandestine migrants from sub-Saharan Africa, Algeria, and Syria cross near Oujda and Maghnia. The lingering enmity that reigns between the two countries is partly due to the unresolved question of sovereignty over the Western Sahara, which has prevented the reopening of the world's longest closed border (1,559 km). It is not so much the anti-Algerian sentiment that Nordine does not grasp but rather his attribution by locals as having an "Algerian" accent when he speaks. His encounters with his Moroccan guides make this element a visible one. The second time his accent is called out is in the company of Mimoun, who says, "What an Arabic accent you have, my friend!" Nordine angrily proposes that Mimoun stop commenting and in turn he will stop bothering him with questions. The third person to plunge a knife into this new wound is Nora, when Nordine begs her to teach him the song his father used to love, to which she replies, astounded: "In Berber? With your accent?" Annoyed, Nordine snaps, "Enough, I know I have an Algerian accent." Nora rectifies the misunderstanding: "No, it's not the accent of Algerians. It's the accent of immigrants. Since there have been a lot of Algerian émigrés in France, they have influenced the Arabic of Maghrebis." Nora's knowledge of the sociolinguistic dynamics of North African presence in France baffles Nordine, who learns that Nora went to the University of Casablanca. But not only is she aware of a sociolinguistic reality that Nordine may be ignorant of, her analysis highlights a unique perspective, which suggests that there can be an accent unique to Maghrebis abroad that was transmitted to *Beurs*.

Light (and) Language

An indication of the importance of language in the film is a detail to which Nordine himself has given much thought. Nordine and Nora dine at the home of Mr. Majid, who invites them upon finding out that Nordine is the son of a coworker in the mines of Sallaumines. When leaving the house of their host, Nora inquires about Nordine's taxi company's name emblazoned on the SUV: NORD'IN AUTO. Nordine is surprised his erudite travel companion does not understand the pun. "Your play on words isn't clear to me," confesses Nora. Adding hand gestures in an attempt to convey the idea behind the paronomasia, as Nora struggles to comprehend, the young man explains it is a combination of "auto" and "the North of France" where he lives—a merger that gives Nord-in-auto, a homonym of Nordine Auto. As he indicates, the company's name may have been inspired by the various sobriquets he was given when a child, based on his first name combined with mockery, derogatory terms, and proverbs: "Nordinateur," "Nerdine," and "Qui Nord Dine" (He Who Sleeps Forgets His Hunger, literally, Those Who Dine North). The last one, which is based on the expression *Qui dort dine,* almost sounds like a question (Who Dordine?) and impresses on the listener that Nora is inquiring about Nordine's identity. The scene is shot in the form of a Peripatetic lesson, whereby a teaching is provided as the learner and teacher are walking. Because it is dark at night, the protagonists have a gas lamp. Since light is the symbol of knowledge, this moment is meant to clarify things for Nora, and by the same token, to enlighten us literally and figuratively. It is also essential to point out that, ironically, Nordine himself may have not understood one important layer of meaning. Indeed, never does the young man explicitly indicate he is aware of the signification of his name in Arabic. This is still a language to master for the young man, and he is likely oblivious that his name means the "light of religion." Nordine is directly involved with death in that he brings the corpse of his father to the land. The young man facilitates passage from one world to another, namely, from material to spiritual life and from one side of the sea to the other. For Nordine, his name is a mere game of word play, whereas it holds a more symbolical significance in the economics of the film narrative. Indeed, while he speaks of puns, Nora holds the lamp, literally shedding the light on hidden meanings. Did she not say that the play on words was not clear? Through this dramatic irony, she informs us that Nordine's word play actually muddies the Arabic meaning. A native speaker of Arabic, Nora knows full well that her name is derived from the same root as Nordine's. *Nor* means "light." Therefore, not only does she hold light in her hand, she personifies it as well. Nordine's attempt to present himself as the witty one is challenged by an alter ego who has subtler cultural knowledge. Overtly, Nora accepts the role Nordine assigns her, but in truth she is amused by his behavior. She saves her knowledge, only using it in a practical fashion, lighting Nordine's way to his father's village and to consequent truths, which their companionship eventually triggers.

It is not clear what Nordine's level of schooling is. As for Nora, she is a graduate who became *diplômée chômeur* (literally, "unemployed graduate"), which according to her is "a specialty here." The neologism is not hers, but rather a common Moroccan expression often used by journalists to refer to a category of youth who have accumulated several degrees but are not able to find a job. The Moroccan paper *Le Soir Echos* dedicated an article to this phenomenon, and in particular to one of the sit-ins that these unemployed graduates held in front of the Ministry of Labor in Rabat.[21] The article even calls some of these desperate young people, "Kamikazes de la guerre contre le chômage" (Kamikazes of the war against unemployment). The piece transcribes statements made by some of the *diplômés chômeurs* present at the sit-in that day. The report indicates that the "kamikazes" will not hesitate to set themselves on fire in order to protest against their situation if their plights continue, thus making reference to Bouazizi, the Tunisian graduate who immolated himself in front of the préfecture of his town and set the Jasmine Revolution in motion. One of the interviewed unemployed graduates even praises the Tunisian man's act. According to Mohamed Darif, the political scientist whom Leïla Hallaoui interviews in the chronicle, this practice is known to have been used among unemployed Moroccans even prior to the Bouazizi case.

Nora's role is not to overwhelm Nordine with information that is not useful to his task. Nora and Nordine's paths cross so that each may assist in the other's quest. Nora's companionship is compensated by shelter in addition to the space and time to think about her future. The spectator suspects that Nora has grown fond of Nordine and that the possibility of an affair has been envisaged. Yet when the time comes to make that choice at the end of the film, they kiss briefly but she gently pushes him away and gets on the bus to Casablanca. Interestingly, Legzouli's Moroccan characters are not tempted by France. Likely aware of the growing desire between them, Nora turns down Nordine's offer to drop her off in Casablanca in spite of his insistence that it is on his way, explaining that she needs to be alone and will manage. Their respective missions now accomplished, Nora's presence by Nordine's side as translator of language and culture has become obsolete. No longer being able to wire her family funds monthly, she expresses anxiety at the prospect of her family finding out that she was not the civil servant she pretended to be. Yet instead of trying to convince Nordine to find ways to smuggle her into France, she argues that she will look for a job in Morocco. She represents the future of the young generation of Moroccans determined to counteract their fate as graduate unemployed.

Mimoun is not interested in journeying to France either. At the end of the film when Nordine presents him with a wad of cash, Mimoun shouts joyfully in English and reveals that his eyes are set on Australia, yet another ex-centric destination. The Tangerine has the last word, and it is not about France, nor is it spoken in Arabic or French. It is uttered in English, a language rarely spoken in Maghrebi films. In *Ten'ja,* which also tackles the ex-centricity of destinations at the margin of the Maghreb-France axis, this use of language makes sense. Moments after they meet for the first time, Mimoun asks Nordine to lend him money to travel to the remote country of his dreams. The Frenchman argues that he does not have the means. Throughout the narrative, Mimoun carries the picture of Joony, an Australian woman he is enamored with. But as he is about to part with Mimoun, Nordine insists that the fellow in love accept the dirhams he is handing him. Mimoun rejoices loudly, though the scene is all the sadder since we know that without a visa, the money will not get him anywhere—unless he plans a clandestine journey.

Figure 6.2 Nordine and his unofficial guide, Mimoun, waiting to retrieve the body of Nordine's father at the morgue in Tangier. Still from Hassan Legzouli's *Ten'ja*.

Heading for Clandestinity

The issue of clandestine migration, deceivingly disconnected from the film's primary concern with the burial of Maghrebi migrants settled in France, starts off as marginal to the storyline, but woven in as a secondary yet powerful theme, it eventually becomes more visible and audible. The first time we hear about hrig is at the morgue upon Nordine's arrival in Tangier. The phenomenon literally lurks in the background: speaking from behind a wall, the morgue employee talks about harragas. We overhear this man's statements while Nordine fetches his coffin. The same man, still invisible to us, asks Nordine his father's name so he can identify and retrieve the corpse. As the invisible man opens the wrong door, he interjects: "These are the harragas who arrived yesterday." The exasperated tone of voice indicates that these individuals have become overwhelmingly present. Nordine disregards this conversation, as he is impatiently waiting for one particular body, and volunteers details to speed up the search: "He is in a coffin." The attendant then says, as if relieved to have found the corpse among many unrecognizable ones: "Ah, Daoudi Slimane!" helped by the fact that this one has a name attached to it and has died a different type of death (Figure 6.2).

As the film unfolds, the extradiegetic viewer is gradually led into the realm of clandestine migration, to which eccentric Mimoun is tied. Indeed, we find that the young Moroccan owes a human trafficker 1,470 dirhams. This fact reveals that Mimoun is progressively paying for his future journey overseas. Nordine's guide is portrayed by locals as a madman who only causes trouble. It is interesting that

Mimoun's Australian friend is named Joony, a name which recalls the Arabic word for *genie*. This parallel conveys the idea that the foreign friend might be in a position to fulfill his wishes and that her picture, which he shows Nordine (but which we do not see), might be that of an imaginary being. His claim might be as fantastical as Franco-French Johnny's claims for an Arab-Algerian-Muslim identity in *Il était une fois*. Whether or not Joony exists, the film leads us to assume that Nordine eventually pays off his friend's debt to the trafficker one night while Mimoun is busy dancing.

Nordine seems to be unaware of the phenomenon of clandestine migration, with which his own path has clearly intersected. Not only does he not appear to hear the morgue employee mention the arrival of harragas, he also does not react when Mimoun tells him that he has to return to the morgue where "there are some harragas to put in the fridge" (my translation). It may be argued that Nordine simply fails to grasp what the discussion is about because of his limited level of Arabic. However, this hypothesis does not hold, as he interacts with his interlocutors in this language throughout the film. It is Mimoun who eventually brings the pervasive phenomenon of undocumented migration to Nordine's attention. For various reasons, it is not surprising that the director chooses the local Tangerine to be a mouthpiece on the topic of hrig. Given his engagement in the trafficking market and his own desire to travel to Australia, burning is central to Mimoun. Through him, Nordine better understands his friend's ex-centric project and is introduced to Tangier as the city of hrig par excellence. Nordine's deafness to the discussion of harragas is remedied in the last few minutes of the narrative. In that climatic moment, the director ensures that Nordine finally understands that the phenomenon exists. At dawn, the characters sit atop one of the most elevated cliffs in Tangier facing the sea. This site in particular is where burning is commonly discussed and can be observed taking place. Indeed, promontories in the city have been known to be locations where potential future harragas dream and talk about Europe as they watch the Spanish coast and its glimmering lights in the distance. Though Nordine did not plan to learn about hrig during his journey, he is guided to take a closer look at it.

On this field trip, Mimoun enjoys his impromptu role as a teacher. A young boy of about ten, not introduced to us, looks on smiling. The lesson starts with the story of "Mr. Seguin's Goat," Alphonse Daudet's tale generally taught in primary schools. Nordine knows it well, and it sounds out of place at first. One wonders if Mimoun is recounting the tale for the boy. But the latter is likely already familiar with it, and the lesson is not directed at the young character; rather, Mimoun directs his attention to Nordine. After warming up in a light fashion and having established himself as the voice of authority about to impart important knowledge, Mimoun changes the topic dramatically. Shifting to a serious tone and speaking in French, he proclaims, "We are going to see them soon." Using the

Figure 6.3 Nordine, Mimoun, and a teenager sitting on a promontory facing Spain. Still from Hassan Legzouli's *Ten'ja*.

mysterious object pronoun "them" devoid of any antecedent, Mimoun arouses Nordine's interest and piques ours by the same token. Nordine slips further into the role of student. Indeed, while the young child listens without asking questions as if everything already made sense to him, confused Nordine asks, "What?" Then Mimoun retorts, "the lights of Europe." His response brings the spectator's attention to the topic of transnational attractions. The conversation reveals Nordine's unfamiliarity with leavism. Legzouli establishes a didactic environment for Nordine with the aim of addressing the lacuna in his understanding of local realities— teaching him what the local Moroccan child present in the scene already knows. Generational and linguistic boundaries are overturned in the aesthetics of the scene by the director's adultization of the child and the infantalization of the adult. After declaring that the lights of Europe are on the brink of apparition, Mimoun flips his prophecy: "No, I don't think we'll see them"—literally, it is very unlikely that we see them. The social outcast's sudden retraction is ironic and reflects a common insight, namely, Europe's ideas of "freedom, equality, and fraternity" inherited from the *Siècle des lumières* (the Age of Enlightenment, literally "the Century of Lights") stand in contrast to contemporary double-standard practices in the domain of immigration, and thus remain far (Figure 6.3).

An additional discussion of burning happens behind Mimoun's back. On Nordine's last night in Morocco, he and Mimoun enter a bar. While the latter dances, the former takes the opportunity to ask Zilachi, the smuggler, if he is the one who runs the cynically named "Algeciras-Tangier Shuttle." Easily identifiable by his yellow raincoat, the smuggler is seated at the counter. Instead of wondering why a stranger is addressing him in Arabic and French about his illegal activities, the trafficker confirms. The latter even asserts a biblical basis for his operation: "Yes, I follow the path Noah took, but in the opposite direction." He then offers justification for his act: "Because the flood is presently on this side." Zilachi is not condemned by those around him, who perceive the man as an individual who takes his fellowmen to a land of better opportunities. For Nordine, the smuggler's justification of his activities inspires a satirical remark: "Noah is a bestseller here." Nordine indirectly challenges the man's legitimization of his cupidity by pairing a historical/religious reference with an overtly capitalist one, thereby highlighting the merely economic motive of Zilachi's business.

The following day, Mimoun's mission to accompany Nordine to the port of Tangier—the final checkpoint before the latter may return to Europe—has been accomplished. The guide asks the visitor to take his Moroccan passport. Mimoun explains that if he keeps the piece of ID on his person while making his journey abroad, if he is stopped, he will be sent back to Morocco. The discussion on hrig becomes so pressing that we are left with no option than to take a seat in the car with them and witness Mimoun's symbolic burning. This dialogue between the two men is shot in close-up in Nordine's car. Legzouli monopolizes our attention and sight, signifying that nothing else should distract our viewing. Thus, the director literally zooms in on the topic of clandestine migration. It gradually becomes a crucial theme in the film—from being a topic in the background, to that of Mimoun's daily life as a porter in the morgue and a leavist, to the lesson on the cliff and the transactions that Nordine is personally involved in at the site of the border. When the latter opens the door, our attention remains on Mimoun. Like the passersby, we watch with surprise as he sings out, raising his arms and shouting, "God is in Australia, God is everywhere we are. Joony, Joony, I see you. Joony, Joony, I see you." These potentially blasphemous words do not attract condemning eyes. After all, for fellow city-dwellers, Mimoun incarnates folly. Even the customs officer knows who he is, calls him by his name, and asks that he get out of Nordine's van. He checks the traveler's passport, then leaves, not worried that Mimoun will try to slip away, likely assuming that he is too insane (or not enough?) to seize the opportunity. Nor does the officer interfere when he witnesses Nordine and Mimoun giving each other items they are trying to rid themselves of in haste, namely a passport and money. All these transactions occur right in front of the officer standing in his booth. The officer's lack of vigilance is due to his awareness of Mimoun's intention of traveling south to Australia instead of north to France.

Precisely when Mimoun's intention is made clear, Nordine's becomes obscure. The last shot of *Ten'ja* shows Nordine driving no further than the entrance to the port of Tangier. There, the camera focuses on his smiling eyes looking back in the rearview mirror, perhaps cheerful about his new bonds in

Tangier or perhaps mocking us? Legzouli confirms that this conclusion was meant to be open to interpretation: "As far as the film ending is concerned, the idea was to not lock everything up, to let the spectator do his job, and end the film in his head."[22]

Practical Considerations

Between 1923 and 1956, Tangier had the status of international zone. That period has often been depicted as a time of easy access and mobility, creating a crossroads among cultures, languages, and people. Indeed, the Beat Generation, hippies, and the elite from abroad sojourned in this international zone. American literati such as Paul Bowles, William Burroughs, Ernest Hemingway, and Truman Capote paid visits or expatriated there. Tangier was also a place where criminals were sent(enced) away. Nowadays, for many, Tangier represents a porous border in the context of clandestine emigration. Valérie Orlando explains that the "New Morocco" is the period following the Lead Years (under the dictatorial rule of King Hassan II), initiated by his death in 1999.[23] Representations of Tangier in *Ten'ja*, among other films, focus on the rigidification of mobility into the "Lead Years Morocco" slightly softened in the "New Morocco" and on Tangier as the emphasized locus of leavists. In being required to justify his right of entry into the kingdom, Nordine becomes aware that these are hurdles symptomatic of a bureaucracy that marks its presence from the very start by slowing down and complicating the passage.

Nordine is aware that he could get by without jumping through official hoops and that rules can be adjusted through bribery or eloquence. This is why he stands his ground and this will prove effective. Later, Mimoun confirms Nordine's certitude that obstacles and procedures can be worked around. This critique of border administrative practices with regard to MRES is not new. They are not exclusively Tangerine, but previous cinematic and literary representations of the first contact with Morocco often took place in the Herculean city. Netherlands-based Moroccan writer Fouad Laroui treats this issue with caustic humor in his novel *Méfiez-vous des parachutistes* (1999) by depicting a Kafkaesque scene where an average MRE is suspected of being a spy for carrying a notebook containing notes about the character's readings of Western writers such as Vladimir Nabokov, Jorge Luis Borges, and Victor Hugo, and a picture of the Russian writer. Through wit and a savvy use of behavioral techniques, the narrator turns the interrogation in his favor. Bureaucracy is one of the few topics that Legzouli takes issue with by contesting its corruption and illogic. As film critic Will Higbee points out, "The only problem experienced by Nordine concerns irregularities surrounding the paperwork for transporting his dead father's body."[24] It is all the more striking that before and after the transnational passage, the journey goes smoothly.

Higbee rightfully remarks that "the SUV Nordine drives through the breathtaking scenery of the Atlas Mountains partially insulates him from these same sociopolitical realities that might destabilize idealized notions of home and return."[25] One wonders if the aforementioned shortcomings (the main character's lack of involvement in the country's socioeconomic deprivations, and romanticism) of the film account for its mitigated success. As Higbee mentions, Legzouli's portrayal of Morocco has triggered negative comments from Moroccan critics such as Loubna Bernichi, who accused the director of exoticism in *Maroc Hebdo International*.[26] Legzouli ascertains that he made sure not to indulge in aestheticism.[27] "*Ten'ja* attracted only modest audiences upon its release in France (just under twenty thousand spectators in a nine-week run)."[28] Critic Qods Chabâa argues that this figure is not on par with audience numbers for other Moroccan films dealing with emigration and does not reflect the recent popularity of this particular subject matter both in the West and Morocco.[29] Could *Ten'ja*'s slow pace explain its smaller audiences? Or could the fact that this is a first film play a part? Or is the culprit the director's critical eye set on the uncomfortable border crossing? Indeed, Legzouli's negative depiction of the tough admission into Moroccan land could be taken at face value by some critics. Though the director's intention could well be to portray Moroccan customs as reflective of a burdensome national bureaucracy, one could also interpret the passage at the border as a necessary trial for Nordine, a rite of passage, and a port of entry into an unknown environment. The passage cannot go smoothly because Nordine's memories of his first aborted passage into Morocco have left marks. Nordine's second trip is successful in that reconciliation with a country and culture has occurred even if no real conflicts existed. This approach condones the vision that in spite of the border officer's ultimate acquiescence, Nordine cannot simply be suspected to be an Algerian, then called Moroccan, and finally feel welcomed in one of his homes. His biculturalism, his poor Arabic skills, and his estrangement from the country he visits for the first time slow down an automatic acculturation. Lastly, the film's lack of commercial success in France and critical acclaim in Morocco may be explained by the less attractive elements for European audiences (such as an opaque title, a focus on the poetic aspects of the narrative, the landscape and the—foreign—languages, the lack of action and special effects), and themes that literally ring close to home for those in North Africa. Though *Le Grand voyage* also tackles the death of a Moroccan man, it was a blockbuster; however, the father dies outside the Morocco-France axis, which allows us to feel detachment from the narrative, for death in remote Saudi Arabia acts as an emotional buffer. Conversely, *Ten'ja* forces the viewer to confront a more likely—albeit complex— return to the southern node of the France-Morocco axis. The film thus reminds the spectator of a continuum between the two homes for Maghrebis. By the same token, it forces *Beurs* to consider the ineluctable outcome, that of the passing on of Maghrebis, the methical returns they might have to undertake, the adjustments their children must make, the memories they are to collect, and the burial that will take place.

Ten'ja simultaneously deals with two types of ex-centric migration. Legzouli literally and symbolically interweaves (methical) return and clandestine migrations. Critics have widely described *Ten'ja* as a film on filiation and mourning. The film is first and foremost a representation of "return migration"; the director himself describes it as such, emphasizing the link to the land(s): "This film results from the need to create a link between two lands that are particularly dear to me, Morocco of course, but also the North of France, where I have lived for twenty years."[30] When he speaks of lands and roots, he also means the land in which Maghrebis have lived, loved, and led long lives. In his commentary, the director traces the history of mine exploitations in the North of France and reminds us that various influxes of migrations have configured this region. He explains that in the 1950s, a military official by the name of Felix Maurat went to the Middle and High Atlas to recruit young fit men whose papers were confiscated. The selected individuals had to sign short-term contracts, permitting the employers to not grant the foreigners the status of miners, which would entail the payment of compensations. Though Legzouli's reading gives preeminence to cultural roots, according to him they are "not automatic." Thus, as his automobile displays across continents, Nordine is "first and foremost a Nordist."[31]

This filmic narrative addresses a historical abnormality and has the potential to redress it. Indeed, the director provides a critique of an ethnically based discrimination against individuals who devoted their lives to a country, which in turn failed to bestow its recognition upon them. *Ten'ja* may or may not trigger changes in the economic, social, and political powers of Maghrebis—who, it must be noticed, do not yet have the right to vote at local elections if they do not have French citizenship in spite of repeated electoral promises made by left-wing candidates and no matter how long Maghrebis resided and toiled in the hexagon. However, *Ten'ja* and *Pieds-blancs* achieve a daring representation across genres of a taboo topic and are likely to contribute to a discussion in the public and private spheres among Maghrebis and *Beurs* of an economic, social, and religious reality that is now on the table: death in Europe resulting in a major dilemma, namely, repatriation or burial in non-Muslim land.

Conclusion

"White Sea of the Middle" or "Wide Sea to Meddle In"?

The Other Continent

The works discussed in *Ex-Centric Migrations* provide a vision not solely of the other but of the other continent as well. Maghrebi works that treat the notion of clandestinity have presented the European Eldorado in its declination from "a country of light" to a land of disillusionment. It is the latter vision that has been the focus of the contemporary cinematic, literary, and musical productions examined here. In response to the old notion of Eldorado (the French one), which bred mythical stories that emigrants brought with them on their short visits back home, artists have crafted a "new" Eldorado—the Maghreb. The latter construction is a core theme in music such as Raï n'b and in films such as Bensalah's *Il était une fois dans l'oued*. This conception of the "new Eldorado" tackled explicitly via musical and cinematic representations is an original one, which lies in sharp contrast to the portrayal of the global South as a place that individuals desire to leave.

The dream of return is not new. It has been voiced by North African immigrants from the moment they left their countries. This dream was expressed in response to the immigrants' feeling of exile, which is commonly referred to as *el-ghorba* (which can also be spelled "el ghorba," "al-ghorba," or "al ghorba").[1] But the vision proposed by the works that advocate a "return" to the bled is an innovative one in that it is attributed to the children of these immigrants. As I attempted to explain elsewhere, el-ghorba is the purview of the immigrant community still attached to the bled emotionally and otherwise, mostly through language and culture. *Beurs,* in turn, whose testimonies and narratives have often expressed a linguistic and cultural disconnect from the country of their ancestors, can still be nostalgic for the country of their roots. However, because a feeling of alienation presides and their experiences differ from their parents', it is not the same el-ghorba that they feel. Indeed, el-ghorba implies the leaving of one's country and the longing to return to it. For *Beurs* who never crossed the sea, it is the feeling of *désappartenance* or disbelonging from their country that forces a strong pull toward an idyllic vision of the bled. This cultural disbelonging and resulting identitarian quest can involve a romanticized vision of the *pays pas natal.*

This vision reveals itself in *Beurs'* behavior, particularly in the ways they portray their position in the society in which they live and how they conceive of the way of life overseas. In Raï n'b and in Bensalah's comedic film, the longing for the "new" Eldorado back home is presented mainly through humor. It is as if such an idyllic depiction of the Maghreb is not (yet?) credible and the only way to conceive of its possibility is through humor and imagination. But as Brinda Mehta convincingly argues, imagination is a driving force.[2] Mehta also asks the important question, "How and why do literature and other forms of aesthetic expression provide . . . writers with an enabling narrative to imagine the (im)possible?"[3] Dominic Thomas makes the compelling claim that "literature provides the space in which to imagine new social configurations, to reflect on the local and the global, the individual and the collective."[4] Finally, does fiction not sometimes influence and preempt reality?

The fact that this romantic vision of the Maghreb as an Eldorado is treated with some amount of detachment by way of humor does not foreclose on its possibility. North African and European creative works have often resorted to comedy in order to tackle serious and even tragic situations. The plight of *Beurs* in banlieues is at the core of Raï n'b and Bensalah's narrative. The experience of deprivation is so widespread and entrenched that the notion of the Maghreb as a pleasant place to live is understandable. Racism, for example, would not be the norm in this new Eldorado, and discrimination, if present, would not be of the same nature as the one experienced daily in Europe. It is no coincidence that many of these works speak not only of beach and sun, local cuisine and hospitality, but also of respite from police controls. All these elements paint the picture of a paradise within reach, right across the sea. For Maghrebis, the idea was that you have to go somewhere else to find paradise. For *Beurs,* there is the feeling that paradise is a matter of "return," a turning back to what was overlooked, forgotten, run away from. Paradise was right here all along.

Another "unfathomable" scenario shown in film is that of diverging migration, in which Maghrebis and/or *Beurs* leave France for a destination in the South other than the Maghreb where they (or their forebears) originated. Seemingly improbable, this narrative is effective in the symbolical message it conveys; this divergent itinerary experiments with ways to extirpate the "migrant" status of both Maghrebis and *Beurs.* Not only does it reveal the multidirectionality of actual migration, this narrative also gives agency to both groups, allowing them to take the proverbial bull by the horns and put an end to labels and misnomers. In the current context of Islamophobia, this message is timely, as it challenges *Beurs* to proactively reappropriate identity and heritage.

A Mediterranean *Vivre-Ensemble?*

A great number of academic studies on the Mediterranean have engaged with the premodern era. Because of my focus on the Mediterranean through the examination of present-day harragas who attempt to make it to the other shore, I have used societal debates, media coverage, and artistic responses as my source material to analyze what Mediterraneanness has come to embody for various entities, from desperate migrants to powerful nation-states. The singers, writers, and filmmakers of both European and Maghrebi ancestry I have examined reflect on maritime crossings and the persistence of hrig in our globalized world. These works critique the hijacking of mainstream hegemonic analysis of current events. In particular, European and Maghrebi artists challenge the privileging of the EU's and the nation-states' concern for control, identity, and security over an understanding of the historical and economic roots of migrants' actions.

This study has in part attempted to show how the theoretical tools introduced in this book lay the foundation for an emerging field that examines a region often defined principally by human migration. These tools are reproducible and reusable in this branch of scholarship that is itself a form of ex-centric and eccentric migration across disciplines. I have argued that the Mediterranean has become a locus for theories and actions of exclusion reinforced in a post-9/11 geopolitical climate, especially in Spain where the topos of invasion is the most common among the nations of Western Europe due to its engrained historical memory of Moorish invasion. Neo-imperialist European laws ensure that North African nations are not able to influence the fate of their constituents. European and North African artists not only point to the impacts of restrictions on mobility on burdened southern countries but also propose their visions of a coming-together across the Mediterranean, an urgent *convivencia* or *vivre-ensemble* (co-existence or peaceful togetherness) in a region benefitting little from globalization.

In 1993, EU member states gave up national agency and control in exchange for a confederation without internal borders. As Zygmunt Bauman indicates, "In order to retain their law-and-order policing ability, states had to seek alliances and voluntarily surrender ever larger chunks of their sovereignty."[5] Since the 1970s and even more so since the clandestine migrations of the 1990s, European countries have individually and collectively striven to exert prerogative over countries to the south to gain a semblance of national agency. According to Eurostat, in 2011 (following the Arab Spring), the rate of immigrants to Europe from various Arab countries in civil unrest flared up. For instance, there was a 92.5 percent increase from Tunisia. The enthusiasm that European member states had expressed at the onset of the Arab revolutions quickly evaporated and led Schengen participants to consider stronger anti-immigration measures. The European Commission suggested that temporary adjustments be made, such as permitting certain states to close their internal borders, in addition to allowing the use of drones to track down clandestine migrants at sea and inside the Schengen zone. The European Commission's Frontex already had the most technologically advanced means at its disposal to limit the influx of immigrants. The Arab uprisings and its associated immigration pressures allowed the European Commission the cover it needed to appropriate expenditures and launch a program already conceived in 2008, namely Eurosur. Matias Vermeulen and Ben Hayes came to the conclusion that: "The Eurosur system and the development of 'intelligent borders' represent the cynical response of the European Union to the Arab Spring. These are two new forms of European control of borders [. . .] to stop the influx of migrants and refugees (completed with controls even within the Schengen space). In order to achieve this, the Ministers of the Interior of a certain number of countries are even willing to accept the violation of fundamental rights."[6] Despite cooperation agreements permitting Frontex ships to patrol far beyond the Mediterranean, such as the coasts of Senegal and Mauritania, the Italian government was in favor of tough actions following the uprisings. This was largely due to the threat of uncontrollable surges of migrants to the island of Lampedusa, whose hosting capacity is estimated at eight hundred; nonetheless it had experienced the arrival of thousands. In February 2011, Frontex launched Operation Hermes to assist the Italian border guards. The Dublin II Treaty rankled the likes of Italy and other southern European countries in that it stipulated that undocumented immigrants and visa "over-stayers" apprehended in any of the member states could be sent back to the country of arrival in Europe.

It is interesting to note that control has not been exerted along visible border lines. Rather, specific regions have been identified as needing special control. In the eyes of "Panopticon Europe," such regions include North Africa and particularly the common sites of departure for clandestine migrants.[7] Thus, buffer zones such as Spain and Italy have seen their responsibilities increased as the police of the New Europe. The duty of these nations to preserve the Europeanness of Europe, and by the same token their own, has been followed to the letter. By assigning this task to these southermost countries, "white" Europe has constantly requested the southern states to prove their sameness. The irony is that these regions, especially Spain, are in some ways culturally connected to North Africa more than any other part of Europe. These states fight to prove their difference from the Moors, when in fact history reminds us that Spain is embedded in Moorish culture. It is intriguing how anti-immigrant policies around the world are based on a historical amnesia. Narratives of diverging migration not only challenge the idea of northern Europe as the promised land, they also remind us of historical linkages that contemporary political boundaries try to make us forget or deny.

What Is in a Name?

The title of my conclusion asks whether the Mediterranean is the "White Sea of the Middle" or the "Wide Sea to Meddle In." I have tried to show the dichotomy between, on one side, the need to monitor and militarize the sea in order to reinforce the external European border controls, and on the other side, the dream to restore the Mediterranean as a place of free movement of peoples. In the Arab world, this sea is the central element of an atlas, literally and figuratively. As is customary on the maps used in the Maghreb, the continents of Europe and Africa are positioned on either side of the Mediterranean Sea. The name "White Sea of the Middle" (or White Middle Sea) sprawls across this body of water in Arabic script.

When I was a child, every late summer my parents and I would pay a visit to the same travel agency in downtown Oujda, Morocco, to purchase ferry tickets for our drive back to France. I recall that when my parents' turn to talk to the travel agent came up, I hung back to stare at a map of the world pinned on the agency wall, since in France I never had the opportunity to see one labeled in Arabic. I remember reading names of countries and hunting for differences from maps I had studied in France. With the basic knowledge of a junior-high student, I even tried to make sense of the choice of colors used to delineate certain types of blocs. What became obvious was that the map had not been manufactured in Morocco. Yet markers had been afixed to this map to rectify certain "errors." Beginning my investigation with the country I was in, I noticed a piece of tape placed on the Western Sahara covering up the line representing the border between Morocco and Western Sahara. The travel agency was under the obligation to make sure its maps represented the region accurately, according to the instructions of the Moroccan state. These markers stood for Morocco's claim to this disputed territory to its south. King Hassan II instigated the peaceful Green March on the contested territory of Western Sahara in 1975 after Spain ended its rule there. Hassan II was adamant that the Western Sahara was a natural continuation of Morocco, so signs of a Western Sahara as a separate entity were to be erased.[8]

Beside these amendments to the map, I remember my curiosity was also piqued by the Arabic name *al-Baḥr al-Abyaḍ al-Mutawassiṭ* (White Sea of the Middle). For the first time, I began to make sense of the appellations I had used in French (Mer Méditerranée), Spanish (Mar Mediterráneo), and English, of a "Mediterranean" derived from the Latin *mediterraneus*. Though in all of these languages, *Medi* and *terranean* accounted for *middle* and *land*, absent was the color *white*, which the Arabs had given the sea. The idealized vision of this site made explicit by the color, synonymous with harmony, was inscribed all the way into its name. As I repeated the long Arabic name in my head on the way home, I was drawn to the centrality of the sea, which sounded more obvious and significant in Arabic, as the term for *middle* is the last word in the phrase. For the boy I was, this word sounded grand. I found out over time that the Mediterranean continues to be a source of pride for Arabs and often appears in popular stories of their Golden Age. Much later, I realized that local and diasporic writers and artistic works of clandestinity had been influenced by these notions of white, centrality, grandeur, oneness, and wholeness that I had been intrigued by as a child, raising not a fixed idea of region or identity as previous generations may have constructed but a more malleable terrain, purposely retaining uncertainty.

What White?

When reading illiterature, watching ex-centric films, and listening to music tackling clandestinity, I started to wonder if having witnessed, as a child, individuals trying to burn over to Europe made me notice it in various works, all the way to a scene or a line, or even in the hidden meaning of a word. Why was it that years later, I repeatedly found myself coming across works about clandestinity? As I have revealed in my study, this topic has inspired an entire genre of film, music, and literature, and has left its mark on the vernacular. Everyone in the Maghreb knows the meaning of words such as *hrig*, *harragas*, and *harga*. Clandestine migration is a phenomenon that affects everybody back home, in host states, and in the Mediterranean in general, and it has been made a familiar phenomenon through stories told by family members to each other, through North African literary and cultural productions, and through European mass media depictions, all of which make visible what official narratives are reluctant to address. In hope of creating public awareness and eliciting action on the part of authorities, a number of Moroccan nongovernmental organizations have emerged, such as the Association of Friends and Families of Victims of Clandestine Immigration, Pateras of Life, and the Moroccan Association of Human Rights.[9]

Despite these rays of hope, in these circumstances, it is no wonder the Mediterranean has become the locus of death in various contemporary narratives. *Ex-Centric Migrations* identifies death as a through-line in southbound and eastbound journeys as well. Departure from life is the lot of fathers in the films that open and close this study, and it is as if France were deemed responsible for these departures. The father in Ferroukhi's *Le Grand voyage* dies in his attempt to leave France and after sacrificing his life toiling away in the hexagon. The father, by his initial migration, is also instrumental in his children's loss of linguistic and cultural heritage. In Hassan Legzouli's *Ten'ja,* the father, too, is portrayed as having sacrificed his life and his identity to France, where he had been swallowed up to the point of never returning to the bled alive.

An outstanding trait of these destination road movies is that it is the demands of male characters that instigate the journeys. Such a salient feature leads the viewer to ask why the intertwined themes of death, burial, and transmittal of memory should be the purview of male protagonists alone. In both films, the wives of the dead or dead-to-be men stay behind in France, leaving the assigned sons to undertake the diverging or return migration. Such a generic oddity could be accounted for by the fact that traditionally women do not attend burials. In *Ten'ja*, Nora is present for prayers but she does not accompany Nordine to the actual burial site. Daughters are not contenders in the diverging or return journeys either. It could be that the directors reflect the patriarchal system they live in and that burial is an affair of men. By heading to their *bières* (tombs), the old men are hoping to bury the *Beurs* in their sons and help shape the image of a new Maghrebi male.

The notion of death throughout this book brings up the question of burial sites for the generation of Maghrebis who are now dying. Death is inevitable, present in each migratory journey. But before the actual burial takes place, the body has to find a place in a Muslim section of a French cemetery, in the heart of the Arab nation, or back home where *Beurs* might never want to be buried. As Nordine makes clear in *Ten'ja*, the father wanted to come back home the way he left, namely, by boat—a choice Nordine does not necessarily approve of. But granting this last wish is the least that *Beurs* can do for their parents, the older generation that was forced to give up on their dream of journeying back home while still alive. In crossing the Mediterranean in the original form of transport, the characters enact an exorcizing ritual, cleansing the wounds of migration via the waters of the White Middle Sea. It is interesting to note that the cleansing of the dead father should be filmed in *Le Grand voyage*. Indeed, this common practice of preparing the body for its final home is undertaken by the son, who, according to the Muslim rite, washes his father's body. In doing so, he rubs off what the old man has come to Saudi Arabia for—his status of *émigré*. The white shroud Réda's father is enveloped in symbolizes the idea of making white, clean, and new his stained past of migration, by returning in death to the original land. In *Ten'ja*, another narrative of reversing the steps of migration, interestingly, the officiantes of Nordine's father's funeral are all in white. And finally, in contemporary works that focus on clandestinity, the "white" of the White Sea of the Middle takes on more tragic tones, foreshadowing the collective shroud that envelops harragas.

Many films discussed in this book start in France and end in the Maghreb. While one would expect protagonists to return to their country of birth except for Johnny whom we see standing in front of his Algerian corner store in the company of his family, all the characters are shown walking, driving, or being driven away in the closing scenes of the films. This happens after a death or upon leaving a dead person. But the extradiegetic viewer is left to wonder if a logical scenario—

that of a return to France—is envisaged by the directors, or if by ending the film overseas, one should contemplate whether the fatherless children will follow a less straightforward itinerary, take a detour, or simply stay away from France altogether.

Erasure of France, Visibility of the Mediterranean

Concurrent with the erasure of France from these narratives is the visibility of the Mediterranean. Shots of the typically idealized countryside and cityscapes of France are shortened or minimized in many contemporary Maghrebi films. In Merzak Allouache's film *Harragas,* passengers panic when they find out that their boat has been drifting toward France. France recedes to the background of fictional works. Implied in these works is the idea that currently, migrants are no longer welcome in France—the traditional host country that previously welcomed generations of African newcomers. In response, characters turn their backs on France literally and figuratively, happy to journey to Spain and Italy instead of proceeding further north to the historical destination of Maghrebi migration. France is not present in the novel *Partir* by France-based writer Ben Jelloun. In this novel, we see it sidelined through the use of language. In the pages of his novel, French is forced to cohabit with a new language, Spanish, after already coexisting with Arabic.

In *Ex-Centric Migrations,* I have departed from the well-known dyad of the Maghreb and France. This binary has been documented profusely in the media, in politics, and in academic scholarship. It is even entrenched in Maghrebi vernaculars. Until recently, when people would say, "so-and-so emigrated" or "so-and-so lives overseas," it was implied that the person had settled in France. France is even personified in the countries of the Maghreb such as Algeria—an ex-settler colony—as exemplified in "'France' came right up to our doorsteps; we were living at the Sidi M'hamed Aberkane *zaouia* . . . 'France' came and burnt us out," "Once again 'France' arrived and burnt the whole place down," and "And then the corn—before the French burnt us out, we gave it to the mill, then we kneaded the flour."[10] Here, France represents the soldiers sent by a government, a military supplied with artillery, as well as the authorization to subjugate and destroy entire Algerian villages. But the personification of France is not solely the ambit of Djebar's work, nor is it restricted to the colonial era. When the colonizer France left in 1962, the postcolonial nation tried to remove the memory of her presence by changing names of streets and towns, such as Bône (now Annaba), Bougie (now Bejaia), and Philippeville (now Skikda), and by restoring the use of Arabic in the educational and administrative systems. But France came back. Or perhaps she remained in the unconscious of many Maghrebis who continued to dream of living on French soil, through politics and aesthetics of seduction, which the vernacular and popular works of art have been able to pinpoint by giving France the traits of a seductive female. Algerians, Moroccans, and Tunisians alike have contemplated France as their final migratory destination. Many migrants have felt the draw of familiarity, and often proficiency, with the French language, and also the presence of a strong Maghrebi community in France. Relatives, friends, or members of the same villages may be present to make the transition easier, allowing newcomers to find assistance during the first months following their arrival. Whether the people come legally or as clandestine migrants, they may be helped with finances or in finding a job, and may even be integrated into an established professional network or microeconomy.[11]

Despite these tangible draws to France today, media reports, as well as the recent artistic corpus have pointed to the ever-growing "popularity" of peripheral destinations for Maghrebis. When these new narratives explicitly mention the names of ex-centric destinations, they force us to revisit assumptions about migration and lead to a deconstruction of the language itself. Now, when someone says that "so-and-so emigrated" or "has gone overseas," they might be referring to any number of destinations or places of settlement. New stories of the Maghrobal then catalyze a shift in the vernacular. The 2008–2009 worldwide economic crisis has forced us to reexamine our assumptions about global immigration patterns. Since the crisis, we have seen a reversal in migration patterns whereby countries traditionally characterized as "sending countries," such as Brazil, have gained immigrants from "receiving" EU countries. As of late, we are seeing the trend of many Spaniards leaving their country in search of economic opportunity in Latin America. But most importantly, Spain and France (both recipients of migrants from the Maghreb) have experienced a similar phenomenon with regard to North Africa. Indeed, for the first time, mass media have covered the migration of Spanish and French nationals to Morocco to flee unemployment back home and find a (temporary?) professional position in the Moroccan kingdom. Such articles recognize that this destination to the south has been popular among European retirees who have elected Moroccan locations for the cheaper way of life and more clement weather. It is also a well-known fact that Europeans and Americans often purchase real estate in Morocco either as an investment or for a second residence, but it is noteworthy that sudden and drastic changes of lifestyle have been witnessed among Western youths that involve ex-centric North to South migrations.

In 2012, France 24's program *Une Semaine au Maghreb* broadcast a documentary about sub-Saharan clandestine migrants from countries such as Cameroon and Guinea living in the Moroccan capital, Rabat.[12] Morocco has been one of the top five "sending" countries in Africa in 2010. In the televised clip, an official of the Conseil National des Droits de l'Homme confirmed this reality by indicating that four million nationals reside abroad, but he stated that his country had just become the country of immigration for individuals who until now had regarded Morocco merely as a place of transit. The documentary claims that there are between ten thousand and fifteen thousand sub-Saharan migrants living in Morocco. It indicates that national institutions have yet to undergo considerable changes in order to improve their respect of the United Nations' International Convention on the Protection of the Rights of All Migrant Workers and Members of Their Families.

Each in their own way, the works I have examined provide a commentary of the power relations at play in, around, and about the Mediterranean Sea. In the novels, films, and songs that deal with clandestinity, commentary often takes the form of an engaged criticism of the fact that this sea, deeply symbolic, has become closed to many peoples coming from the South. We are shown that the borders of Europe do not start on land but rather in the waters of the Mediterranean. Some artists have demonstrated that the military and electronic presence of Europe is sensed still beyond the sea on the southern shore, in North Africa. Yet these contemporary Maghrebi artistic expressions—individually and collectively—challenge Fortress Europe, reminding the world audience that the Mediterranean can be a creative site, not merely a restrictive one. The White Middle Sea can be a space where old cultural ties can be rekindled, different pathways can be attempted, and a new conception of the region can be explored.

Notes

Introduction

1. I indicate *Beur* in italics to convey the idea that this controversial name is meeting its decline, for it is in competition with other terms in circulation in France. The new terms include *Rebeu*, the reverse (*verlan*) for *Arabe*, and the up-and-coming *Rabza*. I italicize *Beur* as if it were alien in the life and vocabulary of those thusly designated. In fact, a novel written by Soraya Nini, a female *Beur* writer, bears a revealing title: *Ils disent que je suis une beurette* (They Say I Am a Beurette). My italicization of the derivatives of *Beur* (*Beurette, Beurité,* etc.) will therefore aim at restituting to them their quality of strangeness and of foreignness (*étranger* meaning both foreign and strange). I do not recall ever being classified as a *Beur* in the part of Normandy where I grew up, but was called *Algérien* by strangers labeling anyone looking Maghrebi "Algerian." The mass media, which were instrumental in perpetrating the name *Beur,* currently uses the coded term *les jeunes* (the youths), which encompasses a wider group of foreigners and French citizens of (North) African descent.

2. In this book, I will use *migration* mostly in its singular form as a generic category in order to refer to the act of moving across borders. It is certainly not to suggest that there is only one type of such journeys, since there exist various patterns. The choice to singularize is mostly for the sake of simplicity and partly to acknowledge a universal propensity of humankind to travel around freely and move from place to place. The various writers discussed here argue that people should be able to migrate the same way their characters move from one pair of hands to another across borders, in spite of national and linguistic lines, beyond laws and religious affiliations, and against criminalizing discourses.

3. "Maghrebian," "Moghribi," and "Maghribi" are other spellings. Though one could argue that "Maghribi" is a more fitting translation, one that scholars have come to privilege more and more lately, in this study I will employ *Maghrebi,* which many North African writers, artists, and commentators continue to use.

4. Lorcin, *Imperial Identities,* 17.

5. Map 0.1 shows that, in 1973, France was the main destination for Algerian and Tunisian migrants. France was one of the top three destinations (along with Belgium and the Netherlands) for Moroccans.

6. This category also encompasses the migrants themselves who return to a country where they are seen as émigrés. A large number of studies, mostly sociological, have been done on the topic with regard to southern Europe, but too few humanistic analyses have been undertaken, especially on the Maghreb. Two of these rare studies are Richard I. Lawless, A. Findlay, and A. M. Findlay's *Return Migration to the Maghreb* and Godfrey Gunatilleke's edited volume, *Migration to the Arab World.*

7. Rosello, "Beur Nation," 13–24.

8. As we shall see in the conclusion, the global crisis that began in 2008 has redefined some of the migratory dynamics between Spain and Morocco in unexampled ways, making Morocco a new destination for Spanish and other European citizens in search for employment.

9. Parati, *Mediterranean Crossroads,* 16.

10. Frontex was established on October 26, 2004. Frontex's mission statement stipulates that it "promotes, coordinates and develops European border management." It is virtually impossible to locate accurate figures. Not all individuals are counted in transit to Europe or upon arrival, nor are all of the bodies of dead migrants found of those who go missing. Some sources have found these numbers to be grossly inaccurate and underestimated actual figures, perhaps by as much as a factor of three. More numbers are quoted in chapter 2 and the conclusion.

11. *Hrig* and *harga* are synonyms and can be used interchangeably. Both terms derive from the Arabic root expressing actions and notions dealing with fire. *Harraga* means both "female clandestine migrant," and the non-gender-specific plural "clandestine migrants." To avoid confusion, I will add an *s* to signify the plural form, as some writers, filmmakers, critics, and scholars have done. Whenever possible, I will employ *harga* in reference to Algeria and *hrig* in reference to Morocco. When discussing clandestine migration in general with no specific attention to any country of the Maghreb, I will select either.

12. Noiriel, *A quoi sert "l'identité nationale,"* 146. Since its creation in 2007, this contested ministry took several names, such as "ministère de l'Immigration, de l'Intégration, de l'Identité nationale et du Codéveloppement" and "ministère de l'Immigration, de l'Intégration, de l'Identité nationale et du Développement solidaire" before it was abandoned and the question of immigration was given back to the ministry of the interior.

13. Ibid., 142.

14. Ibid., 146.

15. Ibid., 140.

16. Ibid., 143.

17. Düvell, "Clandestine Migration in Europe," 480.

18. In chapter 2, I will discuss the importance of this parallel between clandestine migration and illness.

19. In spite of German Green Member of the European Parliament Ska Keller's doubts, "I don't see how a border control agency can all of sudden [sic] turn humanitarian" (Nielsen, "EU Migrant Mission"), Frontex claims this dual mission through its development of the system Eurosur, launched shortly after 366 migrants died in the vicinity of Lampedusa on October 3, 2013, whose goal, according to European Commissioner of Home Affairs Cecilia Malmström, is to "make an important contribution in protecting our external borders and help in saving lives of those who put themselves in danger to reach Europe's shores" ("Cecilia Malmström Welcomes").

20. Though dinghies and other faster, smaller boats, such as motorized inflatable watercrafts are being used, they are still often referred to as *pateras*, a Spanish word that has lost its original meaning of "fishing boat" or "boats for ducks" to mean boats used for clandestine passage. The much less frequently used term *cayuco* is also in circulation in Spanish media as a synonym of patera, mostly in the context of clandestine crossings happening in places other than the Strait of Gibraltar.

21. Martín-Rodríguez, "Mapping the Trans/Hispanic Atlantic," 215.

22. Green, *Repenser les migrations*, 51.

23. In *Ex-Centric Migrations,* translations of literary excerpts as well as news clips, cartoons, and transcribed film dialogues are mine, unless official translations and English subtitles exist, or if indicated otherwise. As for translations of song lyrics, they are exclusively mine.

24. Silverstein, *Algeria in France*, 224.

25. See Robertson, *Globalization*.

26. Appadurai, "Grassroots Globalization and the Research Imagination," 6.

27. Bensaâd, "La Méditerranée, un mur en devenir?," 111.

28. Sassen, "Migration Policy."
29. Chambers, *Mediterranean Crossings*, 25.
30. Harland-Jacobs and Wigen, "Guest Editors' Introduction," ii.
31. Horden and Purcell, *Corrupting Sea*, 10.
32. Ibid., 11.
33. Another crucial comprehensive book to consult on the Mediterranean is Jocelyne Dakhlia's *Lingua franca*.
34. Quoted in Horden and Purcell, *Corrupting Sea*, 21.
35. Chambers, *Mediterranean Crossings*, 36.
36. Ibid., 13.
37. Ibid.
38. Ibid., 36.
39. Horden and Purcell, *Corrupting Sea*, 12.
40. Ibid., 11–12.
41. Chambers, *Mediterranean Crossings*, 12.
42. Horden and Purcell, *Corrupting Sea*, 21.
43. Ibid., 17.

1. *Disimmigration* as a Remedy

1. Born in 1962, Ismaël Ferroukhi directed the short film *L'Exposé*, winner of the Kodak prize at the 1993 Cannes Film Festival, and the feature *Les Hommes libres* (*Free Men*), released in 1992 and 2011, respectively.
2. Cadé, "Hidden Islam," 48.
3. Fox, review of *Le Grand voyage*, 95.
4. The pilgrimage to the holy sites in Mecca, Madinah, and surrounding areas constitutes the fifth pillar in Islam. Any Muslim whose finances and health allow is obligated to under-take the journey at least once in his or her lifetime.
5. This question is all the more relevant as migrating to Saudi Arabia is not an easy task and the mobility of foreigners in the country is highly monitored.
6. In order to reproduce the phonetic difference in Arabic of the two central terms *pilgrim-age* and *pilgrim*, as well as to differentiate them in my text, I transcribe the former as *hajj* and the latter as *hājj*. A female pilgrim is called *hājja*.
7. Contrary to *Ten'ja* (2004), a film I will discuss in the closing chapter, *Le Grand voyage* does not show the repatriation of the father's body to his country of birth.
8. Derrida, *Monolingualism of the Other*, 60–61.
9. Toler, "Interview with Filmmaker Ismaël Ferroukhi," 35.
10. Fox, Review of *Le Grand voyage*, 95.
11. A parallel should be drawn with François Dupeyron's *Monsieur Ibrahim et les fleurs du Coran* (2003), a film in which a father and a son travel eastward to Turkey, a landmark for Su-fism. *Monsieur Ibrahim* portrays a Muslim father, who is a corner shop owner—we shall see in chapter 3 that this profession has often been attributed to North African men (*épiciers arabes*). Just like in *Le Grand voyage*, the old man takes his non-Muslim son (here a Jewish "adopted" teenager) on a road trip to a land where there is no turning back for him since he, too, dies in his final country of destination. Additionally, the two films conveniently end in the new land in an attempt to leave the sons' homecomings as hypothetical. This filmic choice manages to create a mirror-image scenario lived by the immigrant fathers in France where their returns

home were slowly turning into an impossible dream. Finally, the two fathers bring their sons to their countries of "origin" (one to a historical origin, the other to a spiritual one). Conversely, in the final chapter of the book, we shall see that it is the now-adult sons of Maghrebi immigrants who drive their deceased fathers to their lands of birth.

12. Appadurai, *Globalization*, 55.

13. Derrida, *Monolingualism of the Other*, 14.

14. I write "Arabia" instead of "Saudi Arabia" because the father's project is not concerned with a modern geopolitical entity, in other words, an Arab country among others, but with the place associated with Arabness and historical Islam.

15. *Immigrances: L'Immigration en France au XXe siècle.*

16. While I use the term *disimmigration* exclusively in this chapter to discuss "diverging migration," it is clear that the three types of ex-centric modes of traveling examined in this book are instances of disimmigration in that they showcase journeys that do not fit in our common conceptions of migration taking place between North Africa and Europe.

17. Sayad, quoted in Chaïb, "Le Lieu d'enterrement comme repère migratoire," 16.

18. Charef, "L'Idée de retour me fait peur," 170–171.

19. Jerad, "From the Maghreb to the Mediterranean," 49.

20. Ibid.

21. As noted in the introduction, the term *flow* is ideologically charged in that it has been used in mass media and political discourses when applied to supposedly "mass" movements of migrants. Thus, I will intentionally avoid it. When I use it—as I do here—it is chiefly to remark that a conscious effort has been made by a character, an author, a director, a singer, etc., to undermine its negative connotations.

22. *Reversal* comes from the Latin verb *revertere* (to turn back).

23. Sayad, *Suffering of the Immigrant*, 232.

24. However, the viewer witnesses the unfolding of a wide range of instances of mutual understanding. For instance, instead of discarding the picture of Réda's girlfriend, he replaces it in his son's bag. Furthermore, regardless of Réda's denial, the father might even be convinced that the phone call he was charged for at the hotel was made by the young man to call Lisa. Finally, the father walks in on his drunk son in the company of a cabaret dancer. Though the father is undoubtedly at odds with his son's behavior, he chooses to remain silent and leave it for the son and for us to assess his gesture, which might be one of acceptance. Again, being outside of French geographical limits presents the two men with a novel setting that allows for a new scenario in which old feelings of resentment are attenuated and compromises are made possible.

25. Noiriel, *A quoi sert "l'identité nationale,"* 62.

26. This theme is central to Karim Dridi's film *Bye-Bye* (1995).

27. *L'facances* derives from the French "Les vacanc(i)e(r)s" (holiday[-makers]) and is used by Moroccan residents to identify expatriates and their European-born children who often spend summers in Morocco.

28. Toler, "Interview with Filmmaker Ismaël Ferroukhi," 34.

29. Réda is French. He has no accent and adheres to French values and the French way of life. He is the ideal example of an "integrated" French person. It is to be acknowledged that the actor Nicolas Casalé is Franco-French. Ferroukhi's choice of a native Frenchman was most likely intended not only to accentuate the two men's differences, but also to signify further that in the French secularist model, in order to be considered French, one ought to speak, behave, and look like one.

30. It is appropriate to tackle transnational politics of seduction through the use of allegories that resemble personifications in Arabic, because the Arabic language allows the enuncia-

tor to easily refer to the impact of various types of power relations, including colonial, postcolonial, and neocolonial, in this way. Assia Djebar uses this common rhetorical device in her novels in the loaded context of French occupation and the Algerian War of Independence. Oftentimes this is what she does when she employs *France* where *the French* is expected. In *Fantasia: An Algerian Cavalcade,* women's testimonies include "Then they brought some human bones: remains of certain people who'd 'worked' with France" (134) and "To tell you the truth, since he'd been working with France, I was afraid of him" (149).

31. Finally, it should be remarked that the close word *ridda* means "apostasy from Muslim belief"—of which Réda could possibly be suspected.

32. Rosello, "Ismaël Ferroukhi's Babelized Road Movie," 270.

33. Nancy, *L'Intrus,* 1.

34. The next section of this chapter will deal with the idea of reversal, but I would like to point out for now that even the father's choice of the sacrificed son runs counter to the Muslim tradition, in that for Muslims it is Ismaël who was about to be slaughtered, since God commended that Abraham sacrifice his oldest son and Ismaël was Abraham's first-born child. As a matter of fact, after Réda's brother was caught driving under the influence, the father chooses Réda as his chauffeur at the last minute as if alcohol was a disqualifying factor and the older son was definitely a lost cause, not eligible for "salvation," so to speak.

35. In 622, Prophet Muhammad and the first Muslims fled Mecca, where they were persecuted, and settled in Medina. The Muslim community holds this migratory episode as a major moment of its history and a crucial component of its essence. A *Hadith* (saying attributed to Prophet Muhammad), which I discuss in chapter 5, indicates that the Messenger of God encouraged migration among his followers to remote lands. The Ummah is therefore conceived as a community of migrants.

36. The Ka'aba is an almost cubic building made of stone, which in the Islamic tradition, was first built by Adam and rebuilt by Abraham and his son Ismaël. It is believed that its construction was ordained by God, and that there is a copy of the building in Heaven. Every year at the same time, millions of Muslims gather to circumambulate it.

37. Indeed, the film does not show an ex-communicated Réda. Furthermore, as his father must be aware, non-Muslims are not allowed in the sacred periphery of the Ka'aba. Though Islamness is not easy to assess, the act of taking Réda to the holy sites testifies to the father's belief that his son is a Muslim, not a practicing one, perhaps a cultural one, but in any case, the bearer of this identity as imposed on him by the community.

38. Cadé, "Hidden Islam," 47.

39. For a discussion of the notions of *communitas,* gift, and debt, see Esposito, *Communitas.*

40. Jerad, "From the Maghreb to the Mediterranean," 49.

41. For a discussion of *para-communauté* (para-community), see Abderrezak, "*Halfaouine—l'enfant des terrasses.*"

2. "Burning the Sea"

1. Films and songs concerned with the experiences of North African clandestine migrants also boomed at the end of the last century. They continue to be released at an increasing rate. A discussion of some of these cinematic and musical productions will follow in the next chapters.

2. Bensaâd, "La Méditerranée, un mur en devenir?," 99.

3. Pieprzak, "Bodies on the Beach," 104.

4. Carling, "Unauthorized Migration from Africa to Spain," 3.

5. I first coined this term in a shorter version of this chapter, "'Burning the Sea': Clandestine Migration across the Strait of Gibraltar in Francophone Moroccan 'Illiterature.'"

6. Carling, "Unauthorized Migration from Africa to Spain," 6.

7. Scholars such as Braudel have argued that the Maghreb itself is an island between the Mediterranean and the Sahara called "cette autre Méditerranée" (this other Mediterranean). For further information, see Bensaâd's article in which he shows that projects to fill the Sahara with water brought from the Mediterranean Sea had been contemplated by Ferdinand de Lesseps, who obtained permission from the Khedive of Egypt and Sudan to construct the Suez Canal. In addition, one should note that since the ninth century the Maghreb has been referred to as *Jazīrat al-Maghrib* (Island of the West).

8. Bensaâd, "La Méditerranée, un mur en devenir ?," 104.

9. For migrant literature in Italian, see Parati's *Mediterranean Crossroads*.

10. I will designate the novels by their French titles (*Partir, Cannibales,* and *Les Clandestins*), but the excerpts are from the translated novels (*Leaving Tangier, Welcome to Paradise,* and *Sea Drinkers*).

11. Pieprzak, "Bodies on the Beach," 104.

12. The majority of this chapter examines the crossing of the Mediterranean in and around the Strait of Gibraltar because most of the novels discussed are Moroccan, and they deal with the crossings undertaken from the northern shore of Morocco. However, Maghrebi crossings may take place at various locations, such as, from the Western Sahara toward the Canary Islands and from Tunisia to Italy.

13. Flesler, *Return of the Moor,* 11.

14. Ibid., 20.

15. Chambers, *Mediterranean Crossings,* 4. One can therefore argue that SIVE allows a form of neocolonization of North African space justified by the call to stop clandestine migration.

16. Ben Jelloun, *Partir,* 34.

17. Sansal, *Harraga,* 165.

18. Mbembe, "At the Edge of the World," 27.

19. Chambers, *Mediterranean Crossings,* 13.

20. Mbembe, "At the Edge of the World," 27–28.

21. In 1912, France agreed to the Spanish rule of the northern regions of Morocco and the retention by Spain of Melilla and Ceuta, which it had held since 1497 and 1580, respectively. The number of clandestine migrants arriving in the Canary Islands, an autonomous community located west of Morocco, increased markedly in the first years of the new millennium.

22. Bensaâd, "La Méditerranée, un mur en devenir?," 111.

23. In 2010, the two statesmen, José Luis Rodríguez Zapatero and Mohammed VI, met in New York to try and improve bilateral relations rendered critical, in part because of the burning issue of sovereignty over Ceuta and Melilla.

24. Jerad, "From the Maghreb to the Mediterranean," 61.

25. Isla Perejil (Parsley Island) or Islote Perejil (Parsley Islet) are its Spanish names.

26. Mbembe, "At the Edge of the World," 28.

27. The bridge was never built. In its absence, desperate attempts to cross the Mediterranean northward have taken place. Binational discussions and plans have often been replaced by skirmishes, which then shifted into accusations that try to justify the abortion of the project through the trope of clandestine immigration, which, as Taieb Belghazi finds, is often linked to drug-trafficking and terrorism. See Belghazi's "'Economic Martyrs.'"

28. Many view the armed incident over Leïla Island as a demonstration of force rather than the safeguarding of economic interests or the protection of nationals, since Leïla Island—whose Berber name is *Tura* (Empty)—is indeed empty.

29. Additionally, Spain has been strongly discouraged from regularizing the status of clandestine migrants on Spanish soil. The EU harshly criticized the regularization measures of the then–Spanish president of the government, José Luis Rodríguez Zapatero.

30. On this topic, see the first chapter of Flesler's *The Return of the Moor,* where she quotes various critics and writers who make this clear.

31. As Horden and Purcell explain in *The Corrupting Sea,* the Mediterranean as an object of study itself has suffered from a fragmentation: "The sea, its islands, and the countries that surround it, communicate across it, and share its climate, still seem to many historians to be far less worth studying as a collectivity than is Europe or the Middle East, Christendom or Islam. These, not the Mediterranean, form the major units of enquiry and determine the characteristic orientation of more specialized research—with damaging consequences for intra-Mediterranean comparisons. For all the frequency with which it is referred to (or simply invoked on title pages), Mediterranean history is a division of the subject of history as a whole that has yet to achieve full articulacy and recognition" (15).

32. This concept is not to be confused with "world literature" in the Anglo-Saxon context. Hence writers such as Alain Mabanckou refer to it as *littérature-monde en français* (world literature in French).

33. Released in *Le Monde* on March 16, 2007, it appeared in *World Literature Today* in 2009. It inspired *Pour une littérature-monde,* a collection of essays edited by Michel Le Bris and Jean Rouaud and published in 2007 by Editions Gallimard, one of France's major presses.

34. Waberi, "Écrivains en position d'entraver," 70.

35. For a discussion of littérature-monde with one of its signatories, see Abderrezak, "Entretien avec Boualem Sansal."

36. Woodhull, "Postcolonial Thought and Culture in Francophone North Africa," 217.

37. Ibid., 218.

38. The walls around Ceuta and Melilla were the focus of international media attention in September and October 2005 when customs officers shot eleven individuals, who tried to climb the barbed wires that separated them from Europe. Norah, the main character in Houda Rouane's novel *Pieds-blancs,* qualifies this "wrong" side of the Mediterranean as the "real side of the Mediterranean" (160).

39. As I will discuss in chapter 5, the French and the Italians discussed the possibility of jointly sending coastguards along the coasts of Tunisia to contain the clandestine crossings of Tunisians following the Jasmine Revolution.

40. King, *Mediterranean Passage,* 11.

41. King writes, "From the early 1990s on, the Mediterranean began to be viewed as Europe's 'Río Grande.' . . . Rufin . . . pointed out that, if anything, the development gap between the northern and southern shores was greater than that between the United States and Mexico. And in contrast to the relative ease with which the American Río Grande can be sealed and patrolled by frontier police, tracker dogs, fences, night-vision cameras etc., the Mediterranean is by its geographical nature a much more open and complex frontier to monitor." *Mediterranean Passage,* 8.

42. The idea for the term was inspired by Jean-Christophe Rufin's pioneering use of the epithet in the context of the Mediterranean.

43. King, *Mediterranean Passage,* 10.

44. Ibid., 9.

45. Waberi, "Écrivains en position d'entraver," 72.

46. Simon, "Toward a 'World-Literature' in French," 54. It may be worth noting that some critics have pointed out the irony in the fact that the manifesto proclaims the birth of this new literature from the point of view of the center, that is, prizes originating in metropolitan France—and most of them are indeed granted in Paris, the center of the center.

47. For a discussion of debates that followed the granting of major literary prizes to writers from the peripheries, see Thomas's article, "The 'Marie Ndiaye Affair' or the Coming of a Post-colonial *Evoluée*."

48. The Winthrop-King Institute for Contemporary French and Francophone Studies at Florida State University in Tallahassee organized its 2009 international conference around it. Invited speakers included signatories of the manifesto. The title of the event was "*Littérature-monde:* New Wave or New Hype?" The call for papers started thusly: "The manifesto published in 2007 in favor of a 'Littérature-monde en français' raises new and challenging questions about current trends in writing in French."

49. Appadurai, "Disjuncture and Difference in the Global Economy," 51.

50. Tahar Ben Jelloun is the first Moroccan to be awarded this prize.

51. It can be argued that the word *harragas* features a redundancy reflected by the addition of the mark of the plural *s* to a word that is already in its plural form. This explains why Slemnia Bendaoud's *Harraga"s": Ces éternels incompris!* puts the *s* within quotation marks even if some publishers, like Edilivre, removed these marks. However, as noted above, because *harraga* happens to be the feminine form too, I use the word with an *s* to make an important distinction. *Harrag* (one who burns) is the singular form of *harragas* and the masculine form of *harraga*.

52. Ben Jelloun, *Partir*, 92.

53. Ibid., 18.

54. Jerad, "From the Maghreb to the Mediterranean," 61.

55. Carling, "Unauthorized Migration from Africa to Spain," 11.

56. Daoud, *Gibraltar improbable frontière*, 219.

57. Sansal, in Abderrezak, "Entretien avec Boualem Sansal," 341.

58. Laacher, *Le Peuple des clandestins*, 46.

59. Sansal, "Où est passée ma frontière?," 165.

60. I coined the term *leavists* on the model of, and as a response to, that of *hittistes*, an "Algerian" word, as comedian Fellag would call it. The term, which literally means "those leaning against walls," designates men who spend their time "holding up" walls.

61. Caubet, *Les Mots du bled*, 12.

62. In this chapter, I will mention both terms when the phonetic element of the two words is necessary for my discussion. Otherwise, partially in order to avoid potential confusion between *harga*, *hogra*, and *harraga(s)*, I will employ *hrig*.

63. Mrabet and Layachi, "Système hogra," 37.

64. Ibid., 39.

65. Caubet, *Les Mots du bled*, 19

66. Mrabet and Layachi, "Système hogra," 41.

67. Bendaoud, *Harraga"s*," 7.

68. See Bauman, *Globalization*.

69. See Rawls, *Political Liberalism*.

70. For all these reasons, throughout the book I will employ *illegal* in specific cases, for example in quotes or when I want to draw attention to the implications of its use by institutions, agencies, etc.

71. Common transcriptions include *hijrah* and *hegira*.

72. This Hijra is the most famous one, but technically the first one occurred in 615 CE after Muhammad advised his followers, who were victims of persecutions in Mecca, to seek shelter in the Kingdom of Axum, ruled by a Christian king.

73. Ben Jelloun, *Partir*, 263–264.

74. This Hadith inspired the title of Malek Bensmaïl's film, *La Chine est encore loin* (2008). Though the film focuses on recent Algerian history, the title makes clear that because of modern travel restrictions on individuals from North African countries, there still is a large gap between leavism and actual leave-taking. Furthermore, the official poster of the film shows a wrecked ship—signaling a migratory dead end—next to Algerians confined to the beach. Because of limitations on a global scale, in order to follow the Prophet's injunction, migrants have been forced to undertake their journeys in a clandestine fashion.

75. Ben Jelloun, "Le dernier immigré," 24.

76. Jay, *Tu ne traverseras pas le détroit*, 51.

77. Belghazi, "'Economic Martyrs,'" 88.

78. Ben Jelloun, *Partir*, 13.

79. Ibid., 5.

80. Ibid., 4.

81. Ibid., 4–5. The dual framing of the sea is a recurrent element in illiterature. The following passage from El Hamri's *Le Néant bleu* is an illustrative example: "The sea is loyal, even if it is unpredictable. It is always there, waiting for you, lulling you, offering itself to you, giving you life, for it is the source of it" (65). The reader will notice that the verb *lull* appears in both El Hamri and Ben Jelloun's texts.

82. This type of gigolo is the topic of Tunisian filmmaker Nouri Bouzid's *Bezness* (1992). I use the adjective *reverse*, since Azel comes from the global South; traditionally it is tourists from the global North who practice sexual tourism in Morocco, as indicated in various works, such as *For Bread Alone*—Paul Bowles's 1973 translation of Mohamed Choukri's *Al-khoubz al-Hafi*.

83. Lalami, *Hope and Other Dangerous Pursuits*, 1.

84. Jay, *Tu ne traverseras pas le détroit*, 10.

85. See Blainey's *The Tyranny of Distance* and Harvey's *The Condition of Postmodernity*.

86. Santaolalla, "Ethnic and Racial Configurations in Contemporary Spanish Culture," 62.

87. Horden and Purcell, *Corrupting Sea*, 11.

88. Instead of the English *smuggler*, it is the italicized *passeur* that is used in the English translation of *Partir*.

89. Bensaâd, "La Méditerranée, un mur en devenir?," 99.

90. Sansal, in Abderrezak, "Entretien avec Boualem Sansal," 341.

91. Ibid.

92. Binebine, *Cannibales*, 213.

93. See Césaire, *Discourse on Colonialism*.

94. Ben Jelloun, *Partir*, 71.

95. Düvell, "Clandestine Migration in Europe," 485.

96. Ibid.

97. Suárez-Navaz, *Rebordering the Mediterranean*, 55.

98. Flesler, *Return of the Moor*, 5.

99. Flesler remarks that ex-Prime Minister Aznar used the term in English in his Georgetown speech in which he stated that "'Moors' are to be seen as a constant threat to Spain's sovereignty and unity . . . based on the interpretation of A.D. 711 as a violent invasion of Spain by the Moors" (*Return of the Moor*, 57).

100. Wihtol de Wenden, *Faut-il ouvrir les frontières?*, 75.

101. Düvell, "Clandestine Migration in Europe," 480.

102. Ibid., 486.

103. Ibid., 480.

104. Daoud, *Gibraltar improbable frontière*, 220.

105. Carling, "Unauthorized Migration from Africa to Spain," 7.

106. Ibid., 4.

107. See Said, *Covering Islam*.

108. As I mentioned earlier, harragas are known to burn their identification papers. *Sans-papiers* are literally individuals "without papers." These two appellations, however, refer to two distinct groups since the latter also applies to individuals who may have become "paperless" after being "legal" immigrants for a long time in France following the passing of a new immigration law, or the expiration of their visa or residence card.

109. Elalamy, *Les Clandestins*, 103.

110. Ben Jelloun, *Partir*, 140–141.

111. For a compelling analysis of *TelQuel*'s role in contemporary Moroccan society, see Orlando's *Francophone Voices of the "New" Morocco in Film and Print*.

112. Ben Jelloun, *Partir*, 21.

113. Boualit, "La Littérature algérienne des années 90," 35.

114. Ibid.

115. Súarez-Navaz, *Rebordering the Mediterranean*, 56.

116. Jay, *Tu ne traverseras pas le détroit*, 44.

117. Elalamy, *Les Clandestins*, 94.

118. D'Ors, "Léxico de la emigración," 57.

119. Thomas, "The Global Mediterranean," 147.

120. Ibid., 150.

121. Elalamy, *Les Clandestins*, 131.

122. Sansal, *Harraga*, 11.

123. It has recently been translated into Italian and been published under the title *Diario di un clandestino*. Once again, the use of *illegal* in Spanish is revealing. Just like in Italian with *clandestino*, the original Arabic title emphasizes the clandestinity of its character, not his illegality.

124. Martín-Rodríguez, "Mapping the Trans/Hispanic Atlantic," 215. Nonfictional studies include *Literatura y pateras*, edited by Dolores Soler-Espiauba.

125. One should perhaps resort to the plural form *globalizations* given that this phenomenon unravels at various speeds in the region.

126. Ben Jelloun's *Les Raisins de la galère*, *Le Labyrinthe des sentiments*, and *L'Ange aveugle* are concerned with the Maghrebi-Italian connection.

127. Düvell, "Clandestine Migration in Europe," 484. Humanistic scholarship on this theme has so far garnered more attention in North African universities than in those in the West.

128. Kunz, "La Inmigración española contemporánea," 136.

129. Salhi, Editorial, 169. Also, see Talbayev's compelling article on the place of Maghrebi literature written in languages other than French and Arabic (2012).

130. King, *Mediterranean Passage*, 11.

131. See Iglesias's *Tarifa, la venta del Alemán*, Gerardo Muñoz Lorente's *Ramito de hierbabuena*, and Andrés Sorel's *Las Voces del Estrecho*. Spanish theater has also taken on the topic of hrig, as evidenced by Jerónimo López Mozo's play *Ahlán* (*Welcome*), in which a Moroccan migrant reaches Spain on a patera and is soon disillusioned when he is not greeted with the welcome he had been expecting.

132. Such novels already exist, such as *El Diablo de Yudis* by Ahmed Daoudi.

133. Martín-Rodríguez, "Aztlán y Al-Andalus," 36. One should note the use in this passage of the term *clandestines* instead of *illegals*. Spanish scholars have been more careful with this qualifier than Spanish journalists have.

134. Ben Jelloun, *Partir,* 65. Ben Jelloun and other Francophone writers have granted Italy a central place in their literary works and have by the same token made the Italian language a component of their works. For more information, see, for instance, Esposito, "Neapolitan Baroque."

135. See Mbembe, "At the Edge of the World."

136. Elalamy, *Les Clandestins,* 94.

137. "The ideal of pan-Arabism does not concern me. . . . This (ideology) is what made us fail Africa, for instance. This is why we, North Africans, we turn our backs to Africa" (Yacine, in Caubet, *Les Mots du bled,* 172).

138. One should remark that in spite of various attempts to bring Africa together under one banner, especially during difficult historical times with extracontinental powers, Africans too often conceptualize Africa as at least two entities (North and sub-Saharan). Once again, the focus of this book is on Maghrebi harragas. However, numerous studies have shown that other Africans are often part of the burning process.

3. Southward Road Narratives

1. Bauman, *Globalization,* 60.

2. See Harvey, *Condition of Postmodernity.*

3. The notion of "return" usually entails a physical departure from a so-called country of origin. This however, can be inadequate, because individuals (as well as characters depicted in literature, film, and music) sometimes claim a migratory identity through the projection of their parents' or grandparents' experiences onto their own lives. This projected, or imagined, journey, in these cases, becomes formative to their North African identity.

4. King, "Generalizations from the History of Return Migration," 7.

5. Ibid., 10.

6. Parts of this section are reproduced in slightly different form from my article in *Screening Integration* edited by Sylvie Durmelat and Vinay Swamy by permission of the University of Nebraska Press. Copyright 2011 by the Board of Regents of the University of Nebraska. The article has been published in French under the title "L'intégration sens dessus dessous: Il était une fois dans l'Oued de Djamel Bensalah."

7. *Il était une fois dans l'oued* has not yet made its appearance on the Anglo-Saxon market. The French title can be translated as *Once Upon a Time in the River.*

8. Of these, over 870, 000 spectators were in France alone.

9. Ernesto Oña's *Mohamed Dubois,* released in 2013, also presents the figure of a Frenchman, Arnaud (Eric Judor), eager to take on the identity of an Arab and a Muslim. Just like in *Il était une fois dans l'oued,* Arnaud cuts ties with his family, adopts an Arabic name (Mohamed), and tries hard to integrate into *Beur* and Maghrebi communities.

10. Tarr, *Reframing Difference,* 171.

11. For the sake of clarity, I will use *Johnny* except when I discuss the implications of his assumed name, *Abdel Bachir.*

12. Kepel, *Les Banlieues de l'Islam,* 353, 376.

13. "Wearing Adidas sneakers, prewashed boot-cut jeans in line with the fashion of the time, a T-shirt . . . and gel in the hair . . . accentuating his speech with ritual formulae in a brand-new Arabic language" (ibid., 371). The color of Johnny's hair could be the result of a common practice in the banlieues in the 1980s of dyeing one's hair blond.

14. *Bled* used both in French and Arabic can be translated as "location," "village," "countryside," or "country of origin."

15. As Gilles Kepel explains in *Les Banlieues de l'Islam*, the *réislamisation* of banlieues in the mid-1980s brought forward the practice of an Islam different from that of the Maghrebi immigrant community.

16. In "The Angel of Progress: Pitfalls of the Term 'Postcolonial,'" Anne McClintock identifies various types of colonies such as "settler colonies," and "deep-settler colonies." The latter includes Algeria "where colonial powers clung on with particular brutality" (88–89).

17. The film was made in 2005 but conveniently takes place at the end of the 1980s just before the Algerian civil war raged. Antedating his film allows Bensalah to avoid incorporating tragedy into his comedy.

18. For compelling analyses of the 2001 game, see Rosello's *France and the Maghreb* and Durmelat's *Fictions de l'intégration*.

19. The 2001 soccer game is also central to Mahmoud Zemmouri's 2006 film *Beur, blanc, rouge* in which Julien Courbey also plays a leading role as a working-class soccer fan. In Zemmouri's comedy, Courbey's character supports the French team but attends the match wearing a jersey and a scarf printed with the Algerian colors, which interrogates the fixity of national identity even in a high-stakes situation. Thematic similarities of Zemmouri's film with Bensalah's include the presence of an *épicier arabe*, a road trip to the Algerian south (undertaken in the form of a daydream), and the administrative complications that Algeria-bound characters face at customs.

20. *Harki* (plural: *Harka* in Arabic and *Harkis* in French) is a Muslim Algerian who fought on the side of the French during the Algerian War of Independence. See Hargreaves' *Immigration and Identity in Beur Fiction* and Mireille Rosello's *The Reparative in Narratives* for a thorough discussion of Harkis.

21. This name, modeled on famous seventeenth-century moralist François de la Rochefoucauld, points to a continuum between France and Algeria that Johnny rejects by refusing his French name entirely.

22. From the Latin, jus soli (right of the soil) is the principle by which one can claim citizenship. The *Code Civil* "stipulates that the child born of foreign parents at least one of whom was born in France is French at birth (known as 'the double *jus soli*')" (Silverman, *Deconstructing the Nation*, 142). Conversely, Algerian citizenship works on the principle of jus sanguinis, literally "right of blood," or genetic inheritance of citizenship. Consequently, Johnny has to have Algerian parents to become Algerian, hence his insistence that his parents are not French.

23. This burlesques the belief inherited from colonial times that patronyms in the Maghreb are comically lengthy.

24. *Hbaya* is a light robe-like garment.

25. Taylor, *Multiculturalism and "The Politics of Recognition,"* 25.

26. *Français de souche* signifies "Franco-French."

27. The other meaning of the expression contains the idea of being *à côté de la plaque*, a sign that the director is pulling our leg to better displace constructions of various types, such as linguistic, identitarian, and geographic.

28. The DVD cover reads "the first clandestine passenger to Algeria."

29. The passport is important in this scene and in many other recent films. In Tariq Teguia's *Rome plutôt que vous*, it is a main object of speculation. When the policeman refers to it as the red passport, the characters know exactly what he is talking about. In the French DVD, "red passport" is subtitled as "French passport," but it actually should have been translated literally as "red passport," even if the document is actually maroon. The European passport circulates in red in common parlance for practicality and the associated insinuation that it is both a "hot"

and prohibited item. The protagonists are aware that this is not exclusively a French passport, since they are not necessarily looking to reach France but any country that has that color of passport. In effect, the main character had mentioned that he would travel to Belgium or "even the Netherlands, since it is nice out there as well." This highly coveted commodity is the pass to ex-centric travelability that goes in all possible directions.

30. Depending on how the vowel sound in the main word of the sentence is pronounced, it could also mean "Here lie big baked bricks" in Modern Standard Arabic.

31. Taylor, *Multiculturalism and "The Politics of Recognition,"* 35.

32. Urbani, "Entre humour et dérision," 40.

33. Loshitzky, *Screening Strangers,* 42.

34. Derakhshani and Zachman, "Melodies and Landscapes," 59–60.

35. Shortly afterward, a subtle discussion of Zano's soapbox, his ecologist philosophy, is presented through Naïma's amalgam between *idées bio* (organic ideas) and *idées écolo* (eco-friendly ideas).

36. When looking at Gatlif's filmography as a whole where questions of (lack of) identity are central, it is evident that scenes involving musical performances tend to be extended in his work.

37. That year, those who were associated with French colonial rule, including Pieds-noirs, were forced to leave the new postcolonial state.

38. The booklet included in the CD released in France contains inconsistencies in the transcription, as well as errors in the translation of the lyrics.

39. In this moment, Naïma is appeased and smiling. The first time we hear the call to prayer in the film, the young lady was expressing exasperation with her djellaba and hidjab (veil), which she refused to wear any longer. This difference attests to the protagonist's reconciliation with values she categorically refused to accept before.

40. Carling, "Unauthorized Migration from Africa to Spain," 5. The sociologist contrasts this case of "illegality" with "unauthorized entry by sea," which "refers to voyages for the purpose of unauthorized entry" (ibid.). See his article for a grid offering a detailed categorization of "literal unauthorized border-crossing," which is "just one aspect of what is variously referred to as 'irregular,' 'undocumented,' or illegal immigration and residence" (ibid.).

41. While the ferry company Trasmediterránea was only operating one regular line to Algeria (to Oran) and the Almería-Ghazaouet line (from Spain to Algeria) was inaugurated in March 2003 just prior to the release of the film in 2004, all of its shuttles to and from North Africa were concentrated on Morocco. Yet Zano assumed Algeria to be the only possible destination from the Spanish port they embarked on because Algeria is the only place on his mind.

42. As per currency rate calculated on April 13, 2012, for January 1, 2003.

43. Gatlif, in Marsaud, "Retour d'"Exils' en Algérie."

44. See Brown, Iordanova, and Torchin, *Moving People, Moving Images.*

45. See Rancière, *Dis-agreement.*

46. See Rosello, *Reparative in Narratives.*

4. The New Eldorado in Mediterranean Music

1. Tannock, "Nostalgia Critique," 456–457.

2. Ibid., 454.

3. Raï originated in the region of Oran, in northwest Algeria in the beginning of the twentieth century. Representatives of this musical genre generally hail from Algeria and Morocco.

Some of them now reside in Europe and propelled "raï made in France." The raï made by *Beur* artists is sometimes called French raï.

4. Rap artist Rim'K also has a song called "Clandestino" on his 2007 album titled *Famille nombreuse* (Large Family).

5. The *Urban raï* (EMI) series has many commonalities with the Raï n'b model. Some of the featured singers, such as Zahouania, Kenza Farah, and Cheb Bilal, appear on various Raï n'b CDs.

6. The DJs and producers Kore and Skalp are responsible for the first CD. Skalp quit the duo and Kore was joined by his brother, Bellek. Both worked on the second and third opuses.

7. J. Mi Sissoko and Cheb Tarik sing a duet, "Reggae raï fever," celebrating this genre.

8. In 2004, Najim released the successful album *Kount enhawes* (Aladin/WMO/Cheikh Music) and, in 2007, *Saba* (EMI/Virgin), on which he cosang with illustrious singers such as the raï diva Cheikha Rimitti. Kenza Farah was born in Béjaïa, Algeria, in 1986 and grew up in Marseilles. In 2007, she released her first album *Authentik,* which became an immediate success. She also has collaborated with famous singers such as Idir and Cheb Mami.

9. *Overseas* is *el-ghorba* in Arabic. Though this term can also be translated as "abroad," it has come to mean France, until recently. With the emergence of other preferred migratory destinations, one could rightly expect the appellation to regain its official meaning, which is intrinsically linked to the notion of exile. As for "One loses oneself," I could have translated it thusly: "One gets lost," but in light of the national incompatibilities that these lines attempt to highlight, it becomes clear that the song does not eschew a *geographical* confusion, but rather an *identitarian* one.

10. I will return to the concept of the *bote* and its linguistic implications in chapter 5. On a different note, in the same Raï n'b album, iconic raï singer Zahouania sings "Amitiés sacrées" with TLF. In this song, TLF argues: "Ça fait du bien de se sentir bien accueilli à ta sortie du ferry" (It feels good to be greeted warmly when getting off the ferry). I will discuss the symbol of the ferry in chapter 5, too, but in the meantime, one should remark that it is depicted here in a positive light. The southbound ferry does not trigger coastal or deep-sea police apprehension. Finally, this mode of transportation shares space in the song with a highly coveted toy for summer holiday-makers, the Jet Ski.

11. My reluctance to use the term *domestic tourists* is due to the fact that domestic tourism is not a common practice among Maghrebis. This reality led the Moroccan Ministry of Tourism to launch marketing campaigns and to propose incentives such as reduced hotel rates to encourage Moroccans to visit their own country.

12. Berghahn and Steinberg, "Locating Migrant and Diasporic Cinema in Contemporary Europe," 14.

13. This happens to be the name of Rim'K's 2010 opus. On this album (Frenesik Industry/AMD, 2009), "1001 Problèmes" is a track sung by Tunisiano and Cheb Bilal, where Tunisiano argues that *Beurs* have inherited the violence of "Sarkoland" while he laments that he, like his generation, is commonly viewed as an alien, or as he puts it, "objet volant pas très identifié" (quasi-UFO), thus playing on the *étranger* nature (simultaneously foreign and strange) of the unknown whether it is a UFO or a marginalized subject.

14. The lamp is also present on the DVD cover of *Il était une fois dans l'oued,* which is full of stereotypes.

15. A popular track with the same title was released a few years earlier, and several covers since then, including one by Nordine Marsaoui. Marsaoui's is a revisited version in which the famous bridge claiming "Algerians are dangerous"—in reference to the civil war that they raged against their own—becomes "Les Algériens gentils / Ou les Marocains aussi / Ou les Tunisiens tani" (Algerians are kind / Moroccans are too / And Tunisians as well)" in the track spelled

"Chouli Chouli" in various collections, such as DJ Malik's *Raï' rnb night* (MLP, 2006) and DJ Kim's album, *Mariage à l'orientale* (Wagram, 2010). Marsaoui's original cover is a hymn to the Algerian soccer team, Les Fennecs, in honor of its qualification for the World Cup that year. The expression "Cholé, cholé" is a local colloquial invention based on the truncated French expression "Cho les [Algériens]" ([Algerians] are the bomb).

16. Such is the case of *La Discothèque orientale* (Vols. 1 and 2, EMI Arabia, 2004), and *La Plus grande discothèque orientale* (Vols. 3 and 4, EMI Arabia, 2008 and 2006, respectively).

17. Credits do include what a purist would call typographical errors, which were made deliberately. This paragraph is definitely a facetiously crafted Franco-Arabic potion for success, situated beside the same lamp that adorns the front cover, ready to fulfill the listener's wishes.

18. There have been many covers of the song. Sahraoui did one with his then-wife, Cheba Fadela. Kouider Bensaid and Hanini have also sung the title.

19. Thomas, *Africa and France*, 162.

20. Lydie, *Traversée interdite!*, 21.

21. In the song "Denia" ("Life" in Arabic), included in Chao's 2001 *Próxima estación*, Chao and Idir mourn for Algeria: "This life is haunted with lies / Poor Algeria / My heart beats for your gaze / Poor Algeria."

22. Lebrun, "Banging on the Wall of Fortress Europe," 717.

23. Fernandez, "Rencontre avec Manu Chao avant la sortie de son nouvel album *La Radiolina*," *Le Courrier International*, July 31, 2007.

24. French singer Florent Pagny sings a cover of "Clandestino" on *Baryton, gracias a la vida* (AZ, 2012).

25. Laacher, *Le Peuple des clandestins*, 23.

26. Ibid., 79.

27. The inclusion of marijuana in the blacklist—even though it is "illegal" and not "clandestine"—conveys the idea that the consensus in Europe is to fight against harragas, because they are noxious to our well-being, like illegal drugs are.

28. Mano Negra was a group of singers and musicians from diverse ethnic backgrounds. Their albums often contain tracks in several languages, including the hit "Mala Vida" (in Spanish) and "Sidi H'Bibi" (a cover of a famous Arabic song). Some of their songs can be viewed as particularly subversive.

29. Desalojo's region of origin is known for the capsized boats of local fishermen. If applied to the Galician context, the song draws a transregional and transnational commonality that is indifferent to geopolitical differences.

30. The word *desgarrar*, in "desgarran el alma," merits closer analysis. It was likely chosen not only for its rhyming effect, but to create a vivid image of a brutal blow dealt to the soul (the migrant's, ours?).

31. Chambao's lyrics are scrupulously crafted to have various layers. The word *noticia* has a double meaning. Here, the fact that desperate migrants are dying at sea is one way to understand the term "news." Another obvious interpretation is that the narrator of the song feels overwhelmed, not by the amount of news—for the song advocates for more information on the phenomenon—but rather by the monolithic type of news that she hears, sees, and reads. This kind of news is detrimental to the burners' cause, because it does not show compassion toward the migrants, nor does it seek to eradicate the injustice that causes the sea to "burst into tears."

32. At the beginning, and before the repeated chorus toward the end of the song, are poetic pieces containing Arabic words. These two passages tackle ideas found in Spanish in the rest of the song. Chambao's "Papeles mojados." Written by Maria Del Mar Rodriguez Carnero. Published by Colores Nuevos/BMG Eleven Spain. Reprinted with permission.

33. Laacher, *Le Peuple des clandestins*, 19.

34. Reparaz, *Política de España en África*, 175.

35. Harvey, *Islamic Spain, 1250–1500*, 325.

36. Araya, *De Garcilaso a García Lorca*, 45.

37. The chorus is sung by the lead singer and her male backups, Toni Romero, Toni Cantero, and Jose Marín.

5. Europe Bound

1. For a comprehensive study of the Tunisian cinematic critique of the police state, see Lang's *New Tunisian Cinema*.

2. An explanation of this concept is provided in the introduction and chapter 2.

3. Because of the religious anathema that lies on it, suicide is a marginal form of death in Islamic-based societies. And yet, as indicated in an article of the French paper *Le Monde*, there has been a "recrudescence of suicides in Algeria." The article recounts a similar story to that of Mohamed Bouazizi in that on January 26, 2012, Hicham Gacem who was forbidden to set up his stall of glasses, set himself on fire and died from his injuries. Protests that confronted hundreds of young Algerians and the police ensued. *Le Monde*, "Recrudescence de suicides en Algérie," February 3, 2012.

4. Guerzoni, "Fermare la nuova ondate come facemmo per l'Albania," *Corriere della Sera*, February 13, 2011.

5. As *Le Courrier de l'Ouest* remarks, "Mr. Frattini preconised the 'Albanian model' in order to resolve the issue of Tunisian refugees. In the 1990s, when thousands of Albanese refugees came to Italy, Rome deployed, with the agreement of Tirana, military ships in the Albanese waters, thus stopping migrant traffickers." "Débarquements massifs de Tunisiens à Lampedusa," February 14, 2011.

6. In early March, he told a parliamentary committee: "We believe there are about 1.5 million illegal immigrants in Libya, some estimate even 2.5 million." The wide-ranging estimate, the fact that it is a belief, and that the source is unidentified, highlight the enunciator's intention to instill feelings of fear.

7. "Italy, France to Block Migrants Leaving Tunisia," Al-Arabiya, April 8, 2011. For an explanation of the concept of leavism, see introduction.

8. My emphasis. The minister's claim, that there exist two continents that the Mediterranean Sea is not able to separate but should, is also based on the allusion to the fact that his urgent request to act was supported by the fact that the latest movement of Tunisian clandestine migrants is part of a Maghrebi immigration that carries sub-Saharan Africans as well. His idea is that clandestine migration to Italy should be stopped—in spite of the moral obligation to give shelter to refugees fleeing a country where their lives are in danger—because it may inspire a future "flow" of clandestine migrants from the Machreq. The reader will notice the dramatization via the evocation through the rhetorical device of alarmism. Indeed, the minister's "predictions" throw into the same basket potential migrations from countries such as Egypt—which was going through its own revolution at the time the interview was done—as well as other "African" countries where demonstrations and social unrest had started.

9. "Tunisian Migrants Land in Italy," Al Jazeera, March 2, 2011.

10. Maroni's statement that clandestine migrants should be prevented from leaving the African coasts appears in the trailer of the documentary *Mare Chiuso* (2012), which showcases the testimony of a few Eritrean clandestines who live in a camp in the Sahara after being "rescued"

in the Mediterranean and then sent back to Libya. Another short clip shows Silvio Berlusconi walking alongside Muammar al-Gaddafi in addition to the piece of a speech in which he addresses the deportation of African migrants to Libya. The following data appears in the documentary against the shot of water: "Since 2009 about 2,000 migrants have been intercepted in the Mediterranean by the Italian navy and pushed back to Libya. The majority of them were asylum seekers coming from war-torn countries."

11. "Marine Le Pen Visits Lampedusa," France 24, March 14, 2011.

12. Deschamps, "Fillon désapprouve les propos de Chantal Brunel," *Public Sénat,* March 9, 2011.

13. "Interview with Marine Le Pen," RTL, March 1, 2012.

14. "Marine Le Pen Says Europe Can't Handle Migrants," *The Telegraph,* March 15, 2011.

15. "Le Pape à Lampedusa," *Le Monde,* July 8, 2013.

16. "A Lampedusa, le pape dénonce la 'globalisation de l'indifférence,'" *Libération,* July 8, 2013.

17. Though this chapter does not examine Spanish and Italian films, one should be aware of the existence of filmic narratives in these languages, such as Chus Gutiérrez's *Retorno a Hansala* (2008), as well as Mohsen Melliti's *Io, l'altro* (2006), Marco Tullio Giordana's *Quando sei nato non puoi piu nasconderti* (2006), Massimiliano Bulgheroni's *Tornando a casa* (2010), and Emanuele Crialese's *Terraferma* (2011).

18. Maréchaud, "Portrait," *TelQuel 261,* October 15, 2011.

19. The Schengen Area comprises twenty-six member states that have abolished passport and immigration controls internally while increasing external borders and adopting a unique visa policy.

20. Letaïef produced *10 courts, 10 regards* (2006), the 102-minute *El Kotbia* (2002), and the 95-minute *Ghodoua nahrek* (Tomorrow, I'm burning [emigrating]) (2000).

21. The modalities are laid out in detail: 0 mistakes=a three-month visa, 2 to 4 mistakes=a one-month visa, 5 mistakes=a two-week visa, and 6 mistakes and up: visa refused.

22. Some of these items are a caricature of President Jacques Chirac and pictures of French actress Brigitte Bardot and French actor-comedian-singer Coluche. Among other collectables are miniatures of the Eiffel Tower and the Arc de Triomphe in snow globes and the Tati logo—a store brand which at the time had one of its main branches in Barbès (a Parisian neighborhood home to a large Maghrebi immigrant community).

23. The text read by Mr. Dictot is the one that had been read by Mr. Pivot and Catherine Matausch on November 14, 1998, for the regional final competitions.

24. Loshitzky, *Screening Strangers,* 9.

25. Ibid., 4.

26. Programs in these languages have just recently been aired on Radio Tunis. It so happens that the European countries where these languages are spoken represent newer migratory destinations.

27. It is a painstaking challenge in that it awards a happy few who have demonstrated an extremely high level of French knowledge, which the majority of the French themselves cannot attain. It is fair to say that even the most educated French person would consider the dictation nearly impossible to pass.

28. Leila's reference to the *Bescherelle* is to remind the extradiegetic viewer that it is Rachid who is learning the basics of the French language with the help of this manual. The other implication is that nonnational food pronounced the French way needs tea—named in Arabic—in order to digest too much culinary deterritorialization and linguistic denaturalization.

29. Writings in vernacular Arabic are more and more common in the Maghreb, especially in advertisements. However, so far the majority of cultural writings are published in Modern Standard Arabic.

30. A similar effect was experimented with on the cover of the French edition of Youssouf Amine Elalamy's novel *Les Clandestins*. On that cover, letters on the sand are being washed into the sea thus causing that paragraph extracted from the book and shown at the bottom of the picture to dissolve into the water.

31. Thus far the film has only been showed in national and international festivals and is not yet available on the market. It tells the story of Zine and Rayan. One is a musician and the other works in a pizzeria. Both characters dream of a more stable financial life in Europe.

32. In 2005, Spain and Italy regularized over one million undocumented foreigners. See Laacher, *Le Peuple des clandestins*, 44.

33. The generic and neutral word *flouka* is used when the characters have not embarked yet. However, as they get closer to Spain, *flouka* is never uttered again. It is *bote* that replaces it, as if to communicate the idea that the harragas feel the need to internalize Spain through an idiom likely derived from Spanish in order to become successful in their endeavor. Given that in the context of Algerian harga *bote* is preferred to *patera*, I will mostly use *bote* in my analysis of Algerian burning.

34. Laacher, *Le Peuple des clandestins*, 71.

35. "Tout cerveau qui s'exile est un assassinat," *Le Quotidien d'Oran*, January 19, 2009.

36. Though it is not explicit that Hassan killed before, the ship owner warns him that he is responsible if the harragas die on this journey. Out of the ten passengers, four will perish.

37. It should be noted that cargo ships have not always been solely used for merchandise. Just like the ferry, they often served to transport migrants from one continent to another.

38. For this reason, in my analysis I will make the explicit association between a sickly cargo ship resting on Algerian shores and the absent ostentatious ferry.

39. Other films have depicted a chaotic Algeria witnessed through the eyes of either a character who flees France to find refuge in Algeria, such as Samy (Nicolas Cazalé, who plays the role of the son in *Le Grand voyage*, the film I examine in chapter 1), or a character who was expelled to Algeria by the French authorities, such as Issam in the French film *Les Chemins de l'oued* (2002) produced by Gaël Morel.

40. One could see a West/East dichotomy here since the call of the West competes with the call for Muslims to turn their bodies, minds and souls East (in the direction of Mecca) when they perform the act of prayer.

41. Bauman, *Globalization*, 18.

42. A recent film examines cultural alienation from the viewpoint of a female protagonist and demonstrates through the extreme act of deportation how committed *Beurs* are to staying in France. It is interesting to remark that, as in Ameur-Zaïmeche's film, the director of *Paris à tout prix* (translated in the French DVD as "Paris or Perish") plays the main role of the deportee. Reem Kherici's 2013 work is a comedy that tells the story of Maya, a young Moroccan who spent twenty years in Paris. After a routine police check, she is sent to the bled due to her expired work permit. Back in Marrakesh, she tries every possible means at her disposal to get out of a country she refuses to get reacquainted with. Arguing she will never be able to live there and has to return in time to be granted a permanent contract as a stylist in a house of haute couture, she attempts to bribe the French consul in exchange for a visa. She also pays smugglers, who turn out to be her brother's friends playing a trick on her. Eventually, she makes it back to France with falsified documents and later returns to Marrakesh on vacation with friends and her Moroccan boyfriend.

43. Maréchaud, "Portrait," *TelQuel 261*, October 15, 2011.

44. Barlet, "Entretien d'Olivier Barlet avec Yasmine Kassari à propos de *L'enfant endormi*," *Africultures*, February 25, 2005.

45. Orlando, *Francophone Voices of the "New" Morocco in Film and Print*, 52.

46. See Majid's work *Freedom and Orthodoxy*. Also see his *We Are All Moors*, in which immigration and Islam are examined, using 1492 as a central date and point of departure for his analysis.

47. Pisters, "Refusal of Reproduction," 84.

48. Green, *Repenser les migrations*, 112.

49. Orlando, *Francophone Voices of the "New" Morocco in Film and Print*, 143.

50. Pisters, "Refusal of Reproduction," 82.

51. The subtitles of the Dutch DVD show "cupboard," but it is "box" that is being uttered.

6. Heading Home

1. While Gillette and Sayad's study focuses on Algerians, this statement applies to Maghrebis more broadly.

2. The French media provided accounts of the evolution of the request for burial permits. The topic triggered much "confusion," as indicated by the headlines of articles such as "Mohamed Merah: Confusion autour des obsèques" (Mohamed Merah: Funeral Causes Confusion), and "Algérie: Confusion autour des obsèques de Mohamed Merah" (Algeria: Mohamed Merah's Funeral Causes Confusion) published respectively in *Le Nouvel Observateur* and *Le Figaro*.

3. Mehta, "Negotiating Arab-Muslim Identity," 174.

4. Gillette and Sayad, *L'Immigration algérienne en France*, 236.

5. Barte, "Racines et carrés musulmans," 60.

6. Le Bars, "Strasbourg inaugure le premier cimetière public musulman de France," *Le Monde*, February 7, 2012, 12. CRCM stands for Conseil Régional du Culte Musulman (Regional Council of the Muslim Faith).

7. Zohra, "Mourir musulman en France."

8. Mehta, "Negotiating Arab-Muslim Identity," 174.

9. Rouane, *Pieds-blancs*, 218.

10. Ibid., 200.

11. Ibid., 219.

12. Charef, "L'Idée de retour me fait peur," 169.

13. Virolle, *La Chanson raï*, 41.

14. Two spellings of the film title are commonly used (with and without an apostrophe).

15. Alaoui, "Entretien avec Hassan Legzouli, réalisateur du film 'Tenja,'" December 28, 2004.

16. Engelen Loosen, "Hassan Legzouli parle de *Tenja*."

17. Ibid.

18. Alaoui, "Entretien avec Hassan Legzouli, réalisateur du film 'Tenja.'"

19. Lodewijk Crijns's *Hitte/Harara* is another film in which a man is hidden in the back of a van. In this 2008 Dutch film, the body is that of a young clandestine migrant who suffocates to death during the journey to the Netherlands.

20. Engelen Loosen, "Hassan Legzouli parle de *Tenja*."

21. "Diplômés chômeurs: Travailler ou mourir," *Le Soir Echos*, February 3, 2011.

22. Engelen Loosen, "Hassan Legzouli parle de *Tenja.*"
23. See Orlando, *Francophone Voices of the "New" Morocco in Film and Print.*
24. Higbee, "'Et si on allait en Algérie?,'" 63.
25. Ibid.
26. Bernichi, "Legzouli fait les yeux doux aux Français," 42.
27. Engelen Loosen, "Hassan Legzouli parle de *Tenja.*"
28. Higbee, "'Et si on allait en Algérie?,'" 63.
29. Qods Chabâa, "'Tenja' au festival du film à Amiens," *Aujourd'hui le Maroc,* November 9, 2004.
30. Engelen Loosen, "Hassan Legzouli parle de *Tenja.*"
31. Ibid.

Conclusion

1. See Sayad, "El Ghorba."
2. Mehta, *Rituals of Memory in Contemporary Arab Women's Writing,* 3.
3. Ibid., 5.
4. Thomas, "Global Mediterranean," 150.
5. Bauman, *Globalization,* 64.
6. Deszpot, "L'Europe fermée de l'intérieur."
7. Loshitzky, *Screening Strangers,* 4.
8. In Arabic, a proximity exists between Morocco and the Western Sahara, not only on the geographical level but also on the written and phonetic levels. It so happens that in Al-Maghrib and eS-Saḥrā al-gharbiyya, "Morocco" and "Western" contained in "Western Sahara" share the same trilateral roots.
9. Respectively, L'Association Amis et Familles des Victimes de l'Immigration Clandestine, Pateras de la Vida, and Association Marocaine des Droits Humains.
10. Djebar, *Fantasia,* 117, 118, and 146.
11. Many newcomers would secure work in factories and small businesses, for instance.
12. Broadcast on August 26, 2012.

Bibliography

Filmography

14 kilómetros. Directed by Gerardo Olivares. 2007.
Ailleurs et ici. Directed by Hassan Legzouli. 1990.
Bab el Oued city. Directed by Merzak Allouache. 1994.
Beur blanc rouge. Directed by Mahmoud Zemmouri. 2006.
Bezness. Directed by Nouri Bouzid. 1992.
Big City. Directed by Djamel Bensalah. 2007.
Bled number one. Directed by Rabah Ameur-Zaïmeche. 2006.
Bye-Bye. Directed by Karim Dridi. 1995.
Casanegra. Directed by Noureddine Lakhmari. 2008.
C'era una volta il West (Once Upon a Time in the West). Directed by Sergio Leone. 1968.
Chaos. Directed by Coline Serreau. 2001.
Chiens errants. Directed by Yasmine Kassari. 1995.
Chouchou. Directed by Merzak Allouache. 2003.
Chroniques d'un deuil ordinaire. Directed by Hassan Legzouli. 1997.
Coup de gigot. Directed by Hassan Legzouli. 1991.
Dernier maquis. Directed by Rabah Ameur-Zaïmeche. 2008.
Et après. . . . Directed by Mohamed Ismaïl. 2002.
Exils. Directed by Tony Gatlif. 2004.
Gadjo dilo. Directed by Tony Gatlif. 1997.
Garagouz. Directed by Abdenour Zahzah. 2010.
Harraga blues. Directed by Moussa Haddad. 2012.
Harragas. Directed by Merzak Allouache. 2009.
Hitte/Harara. Directed by Lodewijk Crijns. 2008.
Il était une fois dans l'oued. Directed by Djamel Bensalah. 2005.
Inch'Allah dimanche. Directed by Yamina Benguigui. 2001.
Indigènes [Days of Glory]. Directed by Rachid Bouchareb. 2006.
Io, l'altro. Directed by Mohsen Melliti. 2007.
Là-bas si j'y suis. Directed by Hassan Legzouli. 1993.
La Chine est encore loin. Directed by Malek Bensmaïl. 2008.
La Fille de Keltoum/Bent Keltoum [Daughter of Keltoum]. Directed by Mehdi Charef. 2001.
Latcho drom. Directed by Tony Gatlif. 1993.
Le Ciel, les oiseaux et . . . ta mère! Directed by Djamel Bensalah. 1999.
L'Enfant endormi. Directed by Yasmine Kassari. 2004.
L'Ere du soupçon. Directed by Hassan Legzouli. 1994.
L'Exposé. Directed by Ismaël Ferroukhi. 1993.
Le Feutre noir. Directed by Yasmine Kassari. 1994.
Le Grand voyage. Directed by Ismaël Ferroukhi. 2004.

Le Marchand de souvenirs. Directed by Hassan Legzouli. 1992.
Le Raid. Directed by Djamel Bensalah. 2002.
Les Chants de Mandrin [Smugglers' Songs]. Directed by Rabah Ameur-Zaïmeche. 2011.
Les Chemins de l'oued. Directed by Gaël Morel. 2002.
Les Hommes libres [Free Men]. Directed by Ismaël Ferroukhi. 2011.
Le Veau d'or. Directed by Hassan Legzouli. 2011.
Loin. Directed by André Téchiné. 2001.
Lynda et Nadia. Directed by Yasmine Kassari. 2002.
Mare chiuso. Directed by Stephano Liberti and Andrea Segre. 2012.
Mektoub. Directed by Nabil Ayouch. 1997.
Mohamed Dubois. Directed by Ernesto Oña. 2013.
Monsieur Ibrahim et les fleurs du Coran. Directed by François Dupeyron. 2003.
Omar Gatlato. Directed by Merzak Allouache. 1976.
Paris à tout prix. Directed by Reem Kherici. 2013.
Quand les hommes pleurent. . . . Directed by Yasmine Kassari. 2000.
Quand le soleil fait tomber les moineaux. Directed by Hassan Legzouli. 1999.
Quando sei nato non puoi piu nasconderti. Directed by Marco Tullio Giordana. 2006.
Retorno a Hansala. Directed by Chus Gutiérrez. 2008.
Rome plutôt que vous. Directed by Tariq Teguia. 2007.
Tanger, le rêve des brûleurs. Directed by Leïla Kilani. 2002.
Ten'ja [*Testament*]. Directed by Hassan Legzouli. 2004.
Terraferma. Directed by Emanuele Crialese. 2011.
Tornando a casa. Directed by Massimiliano Bulgheroni. 2010.
Transylvania. Directed by Tony Gatlif. 2006.
Une Semaine au Maghreb. Documentary program. France 24, August 26, 2012.
Vengo. Directed by Tony Gatlif. 2000.
Visa. Directed by Ibrahim Letaïef. 2004.
Wesh wesh, qu'est-ce qui se passe? Directed by Rabah Ameur-Zaïmeche. 2002.

Discography

Authentik. Kenza Farah. Up Music, 2007.
Baryton, gracias a la vida. Florent Pagny. AZ, 2012.
Clandestino. Manu Chao. Virgin Records, 1998.
Con otro aire. Chambao. Sony BMG, 2007.
Du Sud au Nord. Cheb Mami. EMI, 2003.
Exils. Soundtrack. Naïve, 2004.
Famille nombreuse. Rim'K du 113. Sony BMG, 2007.
Kount enhawes. Najim. Aladin/WMO/Cheikh Music, 2004.
La Discothèque orientale. Vols. 1 and 2. EMI, 2004.
La Plus grande discothèque orientale. Vols. 3 and 4. EMI, 2006.
Maghreb United. Rim'K du 113. Frenesik Industry/AMD, 2009.
Mariage à l'orientale. DJ Kim. Wagram, 2010.
Patchanka. Mano Negra. Virgin, 1988.
Próxima estación. . . . Manu Chao. Virgin, 2001.

Puta's fever. Mano Negra. Virgin, 1989.

Raï made in bled. Royal Music, 2009.

Raï n'b fever. Kore & Skalp. Sony Music, 2004.

Raï n'b fever 2. Kore & Bellek. Artop Records/Virgin Music, 2006.

Raï n'b fever 3. Kore & Bellek. Artop Records, 2008.

Raï n'b fever 3 L'Issonciel. Columbia, 2009.

Raï n'b fever 3 . . . Même pas fatigué. Kore & Bellek. Artop Records, 2009.

Raï 'n' bled. Wagram, 2013.

Raï rnb night. DJ Malik. MLP, 2006.

Rani m'hayar. Houari Benchenet. n.p., n.d.

Saba. Najim. EMI/Virgin. 2007.

Vrisko to logo na zo. Helena Paparizou. Sony BMG Greece/RCA Records, 2008.

Works Cited

Abderrezak, Hakim. "'Burning the Sea': Clandestine Migration across the Strait of Gibraltar in Francophone Moroccan 'Illiterature.'" *Contemporary French & Francophone Studies: Sites* 13, no. 4 (2009): 461–469.

———. "Entretien avec Boualem Sansal." *Contemporary French & Francophone Studies: Sites* 14, no. 4 (2010): 339–347.

———. "*Halfaouine—l'enfant des terrasses:* L'individu—oiseau face à la communauté." *Expressions maghrébines* 5, no. 1 (2006): 83–96.

———. "L'Intégration sens dessus dessous: Il était une fois dans l'Oued de Djamel Bensalah." In *Les Ecrans de l'intégration: L'immigration maghrébine dans le cinéma français,* edited by Sylvie Durmelat and Vinay Swamy, 93–111. Paris: Presses Universitaires de Vincennes, 2015.

———. "Turning Integration Inside Out: How Johnny the Frenchman Became Abdel Bachir the Arab Grocer in *Il était une fois dans l'oued* (2005)." In *Screening Integration: Recasting Maghrebi Immigration in Contemporary France,* edited by Sylvie Durmelat and Vinay Swamy, 77–92. Lincoln: University of Nebraska Press, 2011.

Aït-Abbas, Jamila. *La Fatiha: Née en France, mariée de force en Algérie.* Paris: Editions Michel Lafon, 2003.

"A Lampedusa, le pape dénonce la 'globalisation de l'indifférence.'" *Libération,* July 8, 2013. Accessed March 5, 2015. http://www.liberation.fr/planete/2013/07/08-a-lampedusa -le-pape-denonce-la-globalization-de-l-indifference_916740.

Alaoui, Khadija. "Entretien avec Hassan Legzouli, réalisateur du film 'Tenja': 'Pour moi, filmer, même en critiquant est une preuve d'amour.'" *Le Matin du Sahara,* December 28, 2004. Accessed June 19, 2012. http://www.maghress.com/fr/lematin/48717.

"Algérie: Confusion autour des obsèques de Mohamed Merah." *Le Figaro,* March 29, 2012. Accessed July 10, 2012. http://www.lefigaro.fr/actualite-france/2012/03/29 /01016-20120329ARTFIG00342-algerie-confusion-autour-des-obseques-de -mohamed-merah.php.

Amghar, Youssef. *Il était parti dans la nuit.* Paris: Editions L'Harmattan, 2004.

Andres-Suárez, Irene, Marco Kunz, and Inés d'Ors, eds. *La Inmigración en la literatura española contemporánea.* Madrid: Verbum, 2002.

Appadurai, Arjun. "Disjuncture and Difference in the Global Economy." In *The Anthropology of Globalization,* edited by Jonathan Xavier Inda and Renato Rosaldo, 47–65. Malden, MA: Blackwell, 2008.

———. "Grassroots Globalization and the Research Imagination." *Public Culture* 12, no. 1 (2000): 1–19.

———, ed. *Globalization.* Durham, NC: Duke University Press, 2003.

Araya, Guillermo. *De Garcilaso a García Lorca: Ocho estudios sobre letras españolas.* Amsterdam: Rodopi, 1983.

Barlet, Olivier. "Entretien d'Olivier Barlet avec Yasmine Kassari à propos de *L'Enfant endormi." Africultures,* February 25, 2005. Accessed October 15, 2011. http://africultures.com/php/index.php?nav=article&no=3702.

Barte, Yann. "Racines et carrés musulmans." *Le Courrier de l'Atlas* 23 (February 2009): 60–63.

Bauman, Zygmunt. *Globalization: The Human Consequences.* New York: Columbia University Press, 1998.

Bekkai Lahbil, Nasser-Eddine. *Le Détroit ou le voyage des vaincus.* Casablanca, Morocco: Imprimerie Attakatoul Al Watani, 1995.

Belghazi, Taieb. "'Economic Martyrs': Two Perspectives on 'Lahrig.'" In *The Cultures of Economic Migration,* edited by Suman Gutpa and Tope Omoniyi, 87–99. Burlington, UK: Ashgate, 2007.

Benaïssa, Aïcha, and Sophie Ponchelet. *Née en France: Histoire d'une jeune beur.* Paris: Editions Payot, 1990.

Bendaoud, Slemnia. *Harraga"s": Ces éternels incompris!* Algiers, Algeria: El Maarifa Editions, 2008.

Ben Jelloun, Tahar. *L'Ange aveugle.* Paris: Editions du Seuil, 1992.

———. *Leaving Tangier.* Translated by Linda Coverdale. New York: Penguin, 2009.

———. "Le Dernier immigré." *Le Monde diplomatique* 629 (August 2006): 24.

———. *Le Labyrinthe des sentiments.* Paris: Editions Stock, 1999.

———. *Les Raisins de la galère.* Paris: Editions Fayard, 1996.

———. *Partir.* Paris: Editions Gallimard, 2006.

Bensaâd, Ali. "La Méditerranée, un mur en devenir?" In *Rencontres d'Averroès #12: De la richesse et de la pauvreté entre Europe et Méditerranée,* edited by Thierry Fabre, 99–112. Paris: Editions Parenthèses, 2006.

Berghahn, Daniela. "Coming of Age in 'the Hood': The Diasporic Youth Film and Questions of Genre." In *European Cinema in Motion: Migrant and Diasporic Film in Contemporary Europe,* edited by Daniela Berghahn and Claudia Sternberg, 235–255. New York: Palgrave Macmillan, 2010.

Berghahn, Daniela, and Claudia Steinberg. "Locating Migrant and Diasporic Cinema in Contemporary Europe." In *European Cinema in Motion: Migrant and Diasporic Film in Contemporary Europe,* edited by Daniela Berghahn and Claudia Sternberg, 12–49. New York: Palgrave Macmillan, 2010.

Bernichi, Loubna. "Legzouli fait les yeux doux aux Français." *Maroc Hebdo International* 693 (April 7–13, 2006): 42.

Bertrand, Morgane, and Céline Rastello. "Mohamed Merah: Confusion autour des obsèques." *Le Nouvel Observateur,* March 29, 2012. Accessed July 10, 2012. http://tempsreel.nouvelobs.com/societe/20120329.OBS5018/mohamed-merah-confusion-autour-des-obseques.html.

Binebine, Mahi. *Cannibales*. Paris: Editions Fayard, 1999.
——. *Welcome to Paradise*. Translated by Lulu Norman. London: Granta, 2004.
Blainey, Goeffrey. *The Tyranny of Distance: How Distance Shaped Australia's History*. Melbourne: Sun Books, 1966.
Boualit, Farida. "La Littérature algérienne des années 90: 'Témoigner d'une tragédie?'" In *Paysages littéraires algériens des années 90: Témoigner d'une tragédie?*, edited by Charles Bonn and Farida Boualit, 25–40. Paris: Editions L'Harmattan, 1999.
Bouchikhi, Ahmed. *Le Cimetière des illusions*. Casablanca, Morocco: SOMAGRAM, 2006.
Brown, William, Dina Iordanova, and Leshu Torchin. *Moving People, Moving Images: Cinema and Trafficking in the New Europe*. St. Andrews, UK: St. Andrews Film Studies with College Gate Press, 2010.
Cadé, Michel. "Hidden Islam: The Role of the Religious in *Beur* and *Banlieue* Cinema." In *Screening Integration: Recasting Maghrebi Immigration in Contemporary France*, edited by Sylvie Durmelat and Vinay Swamy, 41–57. Lincoln: University of Nebraska Press, 2011.
Carling, Jørgen. "Unauthorized Migration from Africa to Spain." *International Migration* 45, no. 4 (2007): 3–36.
Caubet, Dominique. *Les Mots du bled*. Paris: Editions L'Harmattan, 2004.
"Cecilia Malmström Welcomes the European Parliament's Vote on EUROSUR." *European Commission*, October 9, 2013. Accessed October 25, 2013. http://europa.eu/rapid /press-release_MEMO-13-863_en.htm.
Césaire, Aimé. *Discourse on Colonialism*. Translated by Joan Pinkham. New York: Monthly Review Press, 1972.
Chabâa, Qods. "'Tenja' au festival du film à Amiens." *Aujourd'hui le Maroc*, November 9, 2004. Accessed June 19, 2012. http://maghress.com/fr/aujourdhui/22740.
Chaïb, Yassine. "Le Lieu d'enterrement comme repère migratoire." *Awrâq: Estudios sobre el mundo árabe e islámico contemporáneo* 13 (1992): 11–34.
Chambers, Iain. *Mediterranean Crossings: The Politics of an Interrupted Modernity*. Durham, NC: Duke University Press, 2008.
Charef, Mehdi. "L'Idée de retour me fait peur." *CinémAction* 56 (July 1978): 169–171.
Choukri, Mohamed. *Al-khoubz al-Hafi*. Beirut, Lebanon: Dar Al-Saqi, 2006.
——. *For Bread Alone*. Translated by Paul Bowles. London: Peter Owen, 1973.
Dakhlia, Jocelyne. *Lingua franca: Histoire d'une langue métisse en Méditerranée*. Arles, France: Actes Sud, 2009.
Daoud, Zakya. *Gibraltar improbable frontière: De Colomb aux clandestins*. Paris: Editions Séguier, 2002.
Daoudi, Ahmed. *El Diablo de Yudis*. Madrid: Vosa, 1994.
"Débarquements massifs de Tunisiens à Lampedusa: Rome demande l'aide internatio-nale." *Le Courrier de l'Ouest*, February 14, 2011. Accessed March 15, 2011. http:// www.courrierdelouest.fr/actualite/article_-Debarquements-massifs-de-Tunisiens -a-Lampedusa-Rome-demande-l-aide-internationale_18689-34_actualite.htm.
Derakhshani, Mana, and Jennifer A. Zachman. "Melodies and Landscapes: A Journey from *Exils*." In *Coming of Age on Film: Stories of Transformation in World Cinema*, edited by Anne Hardcastle, Roberta Morosini, and Kendall Tarte, 58–67. Newcastle upon Tyne: Cambridge Scholars Publishing, 2009.
Derrida, Jacques. *Monolingualism of the Other: Or, the Prosthesis of Origin*. Translated by Patrick Mensah. Stanford, CA: Stanford University Press, 1998.

——. *The Post Card: From Socrates to Freud and Beyond.* Translated by Alan Bass. Chicago: Chicago University Press, 1987.

Deschamps, Caroline. "Fillon désapprouve les propos de Chantal Brunel." *Public Sénat,* March 9, 2011. Accessed March 17, 2011. http://www.publicsenat.fr/lcp/politique /fillon-d-sapprouve-propos-chantal-brunel82937.

Deszpot, Thomas. "L'Europe fermée de l'intérieur." *Owni,* June 6, 2012. Accessed September 9, 2012. owni.fr/2012/06/06/leurope-fermee-de-linterieur.

"Diplômés chômeurs: Travailler ou mourir." *Le Soir Echos,* February 3, 2011, 10–13.

Djebar, Assia. *Fantasia: An Algerian Cavalcade.* Translated by Dorothy S. Blair. Portsmouth, UK: Heinemann, 1993.

D'Ors, Inés. "Léxico de la emigración." In *La Inmigración en la literatura española contemporánea,* edited by Irene Andres-Suárez, Marco Kunz, and Inés d'Ors, 21–108. Madrid: Verbum, 2002.

Durmelat, Sylvie. *Fictions de l'intégration: Du mot beur à la politique de la mémoire.* Paris: Editions L'Harmattan, 2008.

Durmelat, Sylvie, and Vinay Swamy, eds. *Screening Integration: Recasting Maghrebi Immigration in Contemporary France.* Lincoln: Nebraska University Press, 2012.

Düvell, Franck. "Clandestine Migration in Europe." *Social Science Information* 47, no. 4 (2008): 479–497.

Elalamy, Youssouf Amine. *Les Clandestins.* Vauvert, France: Editions Au Diable Vauvert, 2001.

——. *Sea Drinkers.* Translated by John Liechty. Lanham, MD: Lexington Books, 2008.

El Amrani, Moulay Hachem. *Hmidou el emigrante.* Rabat, Morocco: M.A.F.D.I.S., 2001.

El Driss. *Vivre à l'arrache.* Casablanca, Morocco: EDDIF, 2006.

El Hamri, Rachid. *Le Néant bleu.* Paris: Editions L'Harmattan, 2005.

Engelen Loosen, Aurore. "Hassan Legzouli parle de *Tenja.*" *Africultures,* November 24, 2004. Accessed June 21, 2012. http://www.africultures.com/php/index.php?nav =article&no=3611.

Esposito, Claudia. "Neapolitan Baroque: Tahar Ben Jelloun's Italian Works." CELAAN 4, no. 3 (Spring 2006): 76–88.

Esposito, Roberto. *Communitas.* Paris: Presses Universitaires de France, 2000.

Fadel, Youssef. *Haschich.* Casablanca, Morocco: Le Fennec, 2000.

Faraj, Hocein. *L'Aller et le retour.* Paris: Editions L'Harmattan, 2001.

Fernandez, Marc. "Rencontre avec Manu Chao avant la sortie de son nouvel album *La Radiolina.*" *Le Courrier International,* July 31, 2007. Accessed May 1, 2011. http://www.manuchao.net/new/courrier-international.

Flesler, Daniela. *The Return of the Moor: Spanish Responses to Contemporary Moroccan Immigration.* West Lafayette, IN: Purdue University Press, 2008.

Fox, Tom. *Le Grand voyage. Film Review* 663 (November 2005): 95.

Frontex. "Annual Risk Analysis 2013." Warsaw, Poland: Office des Publications Officielles des Communautés Européennes (April 2013): 1–80.

Gastañaga Ugarte, Mario. *Naúfragos: Pateras en el Estrecho.* Salamanca: Amarú Ediciones, 2001.

Ghosh, Bimal. *Return Migration: Journey of Hope or Despair?* Geneva: International Organization for Migration, 2001.

Gillette, Alain, and Abdelmalek Sayad. *L'Immigration algérienne en France*. Paris: Editions Entente, 1976.

Green, Nancy L. *Repenser les migrations*. Paris: Presses Universitaires de France, 2002.

Guerzoni, Monica. "Fermare la nuova ondata come facemmo per l'Albania." *Corriere della Sera,* February 13, 2011. Accessed October 18, 2011. http://archiviostorico .corriere.it/2011/febbraio/13/Frattini_fermare_nuova_ondata_come_co_9 _110213008.shtml.

Gunatilleke, Godfrey, ed. *Migration to the Arab World: Experience of Returning Migrants*. Tokyo: United Nations University Press, 1991.

Günday, Hakan. *Encore*. Paris: Galaade Editions, 2015.

Hargreaves, Alec. *Immigration and Identity in Beur Fiction: Voices from the North African Community in France*. New York: Berg, 1991.

Harland-Jacobs, Jessica, and Kären Wigen. "Guest Editors' Introduction." *Geographical Review* 89, no. 2 (1999): ii.

Harvey, David. *The Condition of Postmodernity: An Enquiry into the Origins of Cultural Change*. Oxford: Blackwell, 1989.

Harvey, L. P. *Islamic Spain, 1250–1500*. Chicago: University of Chicago Press, 1992.

Higbee, Will. "'Et si on allait en Algérie?' Home, Displacement, and the Myth of Return in Recent Journey Films by Maghrebi-French and North African Émigré Directors." In *Screening Integration: Recasting Maghrebi Immigration in Contemporary France,* edited by Sylvie Durmelat and Swamy Vinay, 58–76. Lincoln: University of Nebraska Press, 2011.

Horden, Peregrine, and Nicholas Purcell. *The Corrupting Sea: A Study of Mediterranean History*. Oxford: Blackwell, 2000.

Iglesias, Eduardo. *Tarifa, la venta del Alemán*. Madrid: El Tercer Nombre, 2004.

"Interview with Marine Le Pen." RTL, March 1, 2012.

"Italy, France to Block Migrants Leaving Tunisia." Al-Arabiya, April 8, 2011. Accessed June 28, 2012. http://www.alarabiya.net/articles/2011/04/08/144703.html.

Jay, Salim. *Tu ne traverseras pas le détroit*. Paris: Editions Mille et une Nuits, 2001.

Jebri, Youssef. *Le Manuscrit d'Hicham, destinées marocaines*. Paris: Editions du Cygne, 2007.

Jerad, Nabiha. "From the Maghreb to the Mediterranean: Immigration and Transnational Locations." In *The Places We Share: Migration, Subjectivity, and Global Mobility,* edited by Susan Ossman, 47–64. Lanham, MD: Lexington Books, 2007.

Kepel, Gilles. *Les Banlieues de l'Islam*. Paris: Editions du Seuil, 1987.

Khadra, Yasmina. "Tout cerveau qui s'exile est un assassinat: Lettre ouverte de Yasmina Khadra à M. Belkhadem." *Le Quotidien d'Oran,* January 19, 2009.

King, Russel. "Generalizations from the History of Return Migration." In *Return Migration: Journey of Hope or Despair?,* edited by Bimal Ghosh, 7–55. Geneva: International Organization for Migration, 2001.

——, ed. *The Mediterranean Passage: Migration and New Cultural Encounters in Southern Europe*. Liverpool: Liverpool University Press, 2001.

Kunz, Marco. "La Inmigración española contemporánea: Un panorama crítico." In *La Inmigración en la literatura española contemporánea,* edited by Irene Andres-Suárez, Marco Kunz, and Inés d'Ors, 109–136. Madrid: Verbum, 2002.

Laacher, Smaïn. *Le Peuple des clandestins*. Paris: Editions Calmann-Lévy, 2007.

Lalami, Laila. *Hope and Other Dangerous Pursuits.* Chapel Hill, NC: Algonquin Books, 2005.

Lang, Robert. *New Tunisian Cinema: Allegories of Resistance.* New York: Columbia University Press, 2014.

Laroui, Fouad. *Méfiez-vous des parachutistes.* Paris: Editions Fayard, 1999.

Lawless, Richard I., Anne Findlay, and Allan M. Findlay. *Return Migration to the Maghreb: People and Policies.* London: Arab Research Centre, 1982.

Le Bars, Stéphanie. "Strasbourg inaugure le premier cimetière public musulman de France." *Le Monde,* February 7, 2012.

Le Bris, Michel, and Jean Rouaud, ed. *Pour une littérature-monde.* Paris: Gallimard, 2007.

Lebrun, Barbara. "Banging on the Wall of Fortress Europe: Music for *Sans-Papiers* in the Republic." *Third Text* 20, no. 6 (November 2006): 711–721.

"Le Pape à Lampedusa: 'Secourir est un devoir juridique et éthique." *Le Monde,* July 8, 2013. Accessed May 10, 2015. http://www.lemonde.fr/societe/article/2013/07/08/le-pape-francois-a-lampedusa-par-solidarite-avec-les-migrants_3443857_3224.html.

López Mozo, Jerónimo. *Ahlán.* Madrid: Ediciones de Cultura Hispanica/AECI, 1997.

Lorcin, Patricia M. E. *Imperial Identities: Stereotyping, Prejudice and Race in Colonial Algeria.* New York: I. B. Tauris, 1995.

Loshitzky, Yosefa. *Screening Strangers: Migration and Diaspora in Contemporary European Cinema.* Bloomington: Indiana University Press, 2010.

Lozano, Antonio. *Harraga.* Granada: Zoela Ediciones, 2002.

Lydie, Virginie. *Traversée interdite! Les harragas face à l'Europe forteresse.* Le Pré Saint-Gervais: Editions le passager clandestin, 2010.

Majid, Anouar. *Freedom and Orthodoxy: Islam and Difference in the Post-Andalusian Age.* Stanford, CA: Stanford University Press, 2004.

——. *We Are All Moors: Ending Centuries of Crusades Against Muslims and Other Minorities.* Minneapolis: Minnesota University Press, 2009.

Maréchaud, Cerise. "Portrait. Yasmine Kassari. Au delà de la fiction." *TelQuel* 261 (October 2011): 46–48.

"Marine Le Pen Says Europe Can't Handle Migrants." *The Telegraph,* March 15, 2011. Accessed February 7, 2012. http://www.telegraph.co.uk/news/worldnews/europe/italy/8382419/Marine-Le-Pen-says-Europe-cant-handle-migrants.html.

"Marine Le Pen Visits Lampedusa." France 24, March 14, 2011. Accessed March 15, 2011. http://www.france24.com/en/20110314-far-right-leader-marine-le-pen-visits-lampedusa-immigration-italy.

Marsaud, Olivia. "Retour d''Exils' en Algérie." Afrik.com, March 24, 2004. Accessed April 19, 2012. http://www.afrik.com/article7578.html.

Martín-Rodríguez, Manuel M. "Aztlán y Al-Andalus: La Idea del retorno en dos literaturas inmigrantes." *La Palabra y el Hombre* 120 (October–December 2001): 29–38.

——. "Mapping the Trans/Hispanic Atlantic: Nuyol, Miami, Tenerife, Tangier." In *Border Transits,* edited by Ana M. Manzanas, 205–224. Amsterdam: Rodopi, 2007.

Mazauric, Catherine. *Mobilités d'Afrique en Europe. Récits et figures de l'aventure.* Paris: Editions Karthala, 2012.

Mbembe, Achille. "At the Edge of the World: Boundaries, Territoriality, and Sovereignty in Africa. " In *Globalization,* edited by Arjun Appadurai, 22–51. Durham, NC: Duke University Press, 2001.

McClintock, Anne. "The Angel of Progress: Pitfalls of the Term 'Postcolonial.'" *Social Text* 31–32 (1992): 84–98.

McMurray, David A. *In and Out of Morocco: Smuggling and Migration in a Frontier Boomtown.* Minneapolis: University of Minnesota Press, 2001.

Mehta, Brinda. "Negotiating Arab-Muslim Identity, Contested Citizenship, and Gender Ideologies in the Parisian Housing Projects: Faïza Guène's *Kiffe kiffe demain.*" *Research in African Literatures* 41, no. 2 (2010): 173–202.

——. *Rituals of Memory in Contemporary Arab Women's Writing.* Syracuse, NY: Syracuse University Press, 2007.

Mellah, Fawzi. *Clandestin en Méditerranée.* Paris: Editions Le Cherche Midi, 2000.

Mrabet Ayla, and Fatym Layachi, "Système hogra." *TelQuel* 449 (27 November–3 December 2010): 37–42.

Muñoz Lorente, Gerardo. *Ramito de hierbabuena.* Barcelona: Plaza y Janés Editores, 2001.

Nancy, Jean-Luc. *L'Intrus.* Translated by Susan Hanson. *The New Centennial Review* 2, no. 3 (2002): 1–14.

Nielsen, Nikolaj. "EU Migrant Mission Will Not Replace Mare Nostrum." *EUobserver,* September 3, 2014. Accessed September 9, 2014. https://euobserver.com/justice /125456.

Nini, Rachid. *Diario de un ilegal.* Madrid: Ediciones del Oriente y del Mediterráneo, 2002.

Nini, Soraya. *Ils disent que je suis une beurette.* Paris: Editions Fixot, 1993.

Noiriel, Gérard. *A quoi sert "l'identité nationale."* Marseille: Editions Agone, 2007.

Orlando, Valérie K. *Francophone Voices of the "New" Morocco in Film and Print: (Re) presenting a Society in Transition.* New York: Palgrave McMillan, 2009.

Ortiz, Lourdes. *Fátima de los naufragios.* Barcelona: Planeta, 1998.

Parati, Graziella, ed. *Mediterranean Crossroads: Migration Literature in Italy.* Madison, NJ: Fairleigh Dickinson University Press, 1999.

Pieprzak, Katarzyna. "Bodies on the Beach: Youssef Elalamy and Moroccan Landscapes of the Clandestine." In *Land and Landscape in Francographic Literature: Remapping Uncertain Territories,* edited by Magali Compan and Katarzyna Pieprzak, 104–122. Newcastle, UK: Cambridge Scholars Publishing, 2007.

Pisters, Patricia. "Refusal of Reproduction: Paradoxes of Becoming-Woman in Transnational Moroccan Filmmaking." In *Transnational Feminism in Film and Media,* edited by Katarzyna Marciniak, Anikó Imre, and Áine O'Healy, 71–92. New York: Palgrave Macmillan, 2007.

"Pour une 'littérature-monde' en français." *Le Monde,* March 16, 2007, 1–3.

Rancière, Jacques. *Dis-agreement: Politics and Philosophy.* Minneapolis: University of Minnesota, 2004.

Rawls, John. *Political Liberalism.* New York: Columbia University Press, 1993.

"Recrudescence de suicides en Algérie." *Le Monde,* February 3, 2012. Accessed March 8, 2012. http://www.lemonde.fr/international/article/2012/02/03/recrudescence-des -suicides-en-algerie_1638753_3210.html.

Redouane, Najib. *Clandestins dans le texte maghrébin de langue française.* Paris: Editions L'Harmattan, 2008.

Reparaz, Gonzalo de. *Política de España en África.* Barcelona: Imprenta barcelonesa, 1907.

Robertson, Roland. *Globalization: Social Theory and Global Culture*. London: Sage
Publications, 1992.

Rosello, Mireille. "The 'Beur Nation': Toward a Theory of 'Departenance.'" *Research in African Literatures* 24, no. 3 (1993): 13–24.

———. *France and the Maghreb: Performative Encounters*. Gainesville: University Press of Florida, 2005.

———. "Ismaël Ferroukhi's Babelized Road Movie." In *Art and Visibility in Migratory Culture: Conflict, Resistance, and Agency*, edited by Mieke Bal and Miguel Á Hernández-Navarro, 257–276. Amsterdam: Rodopi, 2011.

———. *The Reparative in Narratives: Works of Mourning in Progress*. Liverpool: Liverpool University Press, 2010.

Rouane, Houda. *Pieds-blancs*. Paris: Editions Philippe Rey, 2006.

Said, Edward. *Covering Islam: How the Media and the Experts Determine How We See the Rest of the World*. New York: Vintage Books, 1997.

Salhi, Kamal. Editorial. *International Journal of Francophone Studies* 12, no. 2–3 (2009): 165–169.

Sansal, Boualem. *Dis-moi le paradis*. Paris: Editions Gallimard, 2003.

———. *Harraga*. Paris: Editions Gallimard, 2005.

———. "Où est passée ma frontière?," In *Pour une littérature-monde*, edited by Michel Le Bris and Jean Rouaud, 161–174. Paris: Editions Gallimard, 2007.

Santaolalla, Isabel. "Ethnic and Racial Configurations in Contemporary Spanish Culture." In *Constructing Identity in Contemporary Spain: Theoretical Debates and Cultural Practice*, edited by Jo Labanyi, 55–71. Oxford: Oxford University Press, 2002.

Sassen, Saskia. "Migration Policy: From Control to Governance." *Open Democracy*, July 12, 2006. Accessed July 7, 2014. https://www.opendemocracy.net/node/3735/pdf.

Sayad, Abdelmalek. "El Ghorba: From Original Sin to Collective Lie." *Ethnography* 2000, no. 1 (2000), 147–171.

———. *The Suffering of the Immigrant*. Translated by David Macey. Cambridge: Polity Press, 2004.

Sekkouri, Mehdi Alaoui. "Petit Mustapha devenu grand." *TelQuel* 407 (January 16–22, 2010): 60–61.

Sena Rodríguez, Ildefonso. "La Tragedia del Estrecho." In *Literatura y pateras*, edited by Dolores Soler-Espiauba, 17–31. Madrid: Akal, 2004.

Silverman, Maxim. *Deconstructing the Nation: Immigration, Racism and Citizenship in Modern France*. New York: Routledge, 1992.

Silverstein, Paul. *Algeria in France: Transpolitics, Race, and Nation*. Bloomington: Indiana University Press, 2004.

Simon, Daniel. "Toward a 'World-Literature' in French." *World Literature Today* 23, no. 2 (March–April 2009): 54–56.

Skif, Hamid. *La Géographie du danger*. Paris: Editions Naïve, 2006.

Soler-Espiauba, Dolores, ed. *Literatura y pateras*. Madrid: Akal, 2004.

Sorel, Andrés. *Las Voces del Estrecho*. Barcelona: Muchnik, 2000.

Stassen, Jean-Philippe. "Les Visiteurs de Gibraltar." *XXI* no. 1 (January–March 2008): 156–185.

Stora, Benjamin, and Émile Temime, eds. *Immigrances: L'Immigration en France au XXe siècle*. Paris: Editions Hachette Littératures, 2007.

Suárez-Navaz, Liliana. *Rebordering the Mediterranean: Boundaries and Citizenship in Southern Europe.* New York: Berghahn Books, 2004.

Talbayev, Edwige Tamalet. "The Languages of Translocality: What Plurilingualism Means in a Maghrebi Context." *Expressions maghrébines* 11, no. 2 (2012): 9–25.

Tannock, Stuart. "Nostalgia Critique." *Cultural Studies* 9, no. 3 (1995): 453–464.

Tarr, Carrie. *Reframing Difference: Beur and Banlieue Filmmaking in France.* Manchester: Manchester University Press, 2005.

Taylor, Charles. *Multiculturalism and "The Politics of Recognition."* Princeton, NJ: Princeton University Press, 1992.

Teriah, Mohamed. *Les "Harragas" ou les barques de la mort.* Casablanca, Morocco: Afrique Orient, 2002.

Thomas, Dominic. *Africa and France: Postcolonial Cultures, Migration, and Racism.* Bloomington: Indiana University Press, 2012.

——. "The Global Mediterranean: Literature and Migration." *Francophone Sub-Saharan African Literature in Global Contexts: Yale French Studies* 120 (Fall 2011): 140–153.

——. "The 'Marie Ndiaye Affair' or the Coming of a Postcolonial *Evoluée.*" In *Transnational French Studies: Postcolonialism and Littérature-monde,* edited by Alec G. Hargreaves, Charles Forsdick, and David Murphy, 146–163. Liverpool: Liverpool University Press, 2010.

Toler, Michael. "An Interview with Filmmaker Ismaël Ferroukhi." *World Literature Today* 81, no. 1 (2007): 34–37.

"Tunisian Migrants Land in Italy." Al Jazeera, March 2, 2011. Accessed March 15, 2011. http://www.aljazeera.com/news/europe/2011/03/201132135258524383.html.

Urbani, Bernard. "Entre humour et dérision: *Moha le fou, Moha le sage* de Tahar Ben Jelloun." *Expressions maghrébines* 7, no. 2 (2008): 37–49.

Virolle, Marie. *La Chanson raï: De l'Algérie profonde à la scène internationale.* Paris: Editions Karthala, 1995.

Waberi, Abdourahman A. "Écrivains en position d'entraver." In *Pour une littérature-monde,* edited by Michel Le Bris and Jean Rouaud, 67–75. Paris: Editions Gallimard, 2007.

Wihtol de Wenden, Catherine. *Faut-il ouvrir les frontières?* Paris: Presses de Sciences Po, 1999.

Woodhull, Winifred. "Postcolonial Thought and Culture in Francophone North Africa." In *Francophone Postcolonial Studies: A Critical Introduction,* edited by Charles Forsdick and David Murphy, 211–220. London: Arnold, 2003.

Youcef, M. D. *Je rêve d'une autre vie.* Vauvert, France: Editions au Diable Vauvert, 2002.

Zohra, Colin. "Mourir musulman en France." *Saphir News,* November 3, 2003. Accessed May 15, 2012. http://www.saphirnews.com/Mourir-musulman-en-France_a570.html.

Index

HAKIM ABDERREZAK is Associate Professor of French and Francophone Studies at the University of Minnesota.